THE MAN WITH THE GOLDEN TOUCH

THE MAN WITH THE GOLDEN TOUCH

HOW THE BOND FILMS CONQUERED THE WORLD

SINCLAIR McKAY

First published in Great Britain in 2008 by Aurum Press Ltd
7 Greenland Street, London NW1 0ND
www.aurumpress.co.uk

A catalogue record for this book is available from the British Library.

ISBN 978 1 84513 355 9

10 9 8 7 6 5 4 3 2 1
2012 2011 2010 2009 2008

Typeset in Spectrum by SX Composing DTP, Essex.
Printed and bound in Great Britain by
Cromwell Press, Trowbridge, Wiltshire

Mixed Sources
Product group from well-managed
forests and other controlled sources
www.fsc.org Cert no. TT-COC-2082
© 1996 Forest Stewardship Council
FSC

CONTENTS

	INTRODUCTION	vii
ONE	AUTHENTICITY	1
TWO	YOU'VE HAD YOUR SIX	14
THREE	EUROPE BY TRAIN	34
FOUR	THE GLITTERING PRIZE	50
FIVE	RAINCOATS, WALLS AND BETRAYALS	68
SIX	GREAT BALLS OF THUNDER	76
SEVEN	SPIES IN OUR EYES	88
EIGHT	THIS DREAM IS FOR YOU	98
NINE	THE OTHER FELLA	113
TEN	A LITTLE MORE CHEEK	129
ELEVEN	DARK UNCONFIDENT WORLD	145
TWELVE	MAN AT AUSTIN REED	150
THIRTEEN	WILL HE BANG? WE SHALL SEE	165
FOURTEEN	ENGLAND NEEDS ME	180
FIFTEEN	ONCE MORE ROUND THE WORLD	195
SIXTEEN	THE SMACK OF FIRM ESPIONAGE	207

SEVENTEEN	YOU CAN NEVER SAY NEVER TWICE	222
EIGHTEEN	MOST DISARMING	229
NINETEEN	MICROCHIPS WITH EVERYTHING	244
TWENTY	DARLING MONEYPENNY	256
TWENTY-ONE	ONE FOR THE LADIES	262
TWENTY-TWO	NIGHT OF THE IGUANA	276
TWENTY-THREE	BOND IN ABEYANCE	288
TWENTY-FOUR	WE KNEW THE NAME, WE KNEW THE NUMBER	294
TWENTY-FIVE	WE'RE IN A PUDDLE ON THE FLOOR	308
TWENTY-SIX	ART AND CRAFT	319
TWENTY-SEVEN	BIRTHDAY BOY	330
TWENTY-EIGHT	THE AUTOBIOGRAPHY OF DREAMS	344
TWENTY-NINE	YOU CAN NEVER KISS DEATH GOODBYE	361
	NOTES	370
	RELATED READING	375
	INDEX	376

INTRODUCTION

Considering that this image is so very famous, so globally iconic, it is surprisingly difficult to describe.

First, the cinema screen is black. But then, accompanied by a sharp stab of music, it begins. The white circles. The sequence of white circles that move horizontally across the centre of the screen, left to right.

Upon reaching the right, one white circle stabilises, grows, begins moving back. At last we see that it is the view down the barrel of a gun, and it now holds the image of a man, walking casually towards the left.

The man, in a suit and a hat, is held in the lens frame. Suddenly, as we reach mid-screen, he turns and shoots straight at us and the screen, from the top, is slowly filled with the descending scarlet of animated blood.

We have all seen this so often that few of us give it a second thought. It is there merely as a trigger for excitement. But this short sequence is our gateway into a gleefully escapist, gaudy realm, where bizarre acts of violence and absurd insouciance and fingernails-scraping-down-a-blackboard lines of sexual innuendo are offered as a simulacrum of the world.

What can those initial white circles mean, what do they signify? For some years, they always somehow reminded me of codes, of Morse, of secret transmissions, of the pre-computer world of getting the cipher message across to your comrades. Now I am not at all sure. When you look again at them, you realise just what an odd image it is.

And that is the thing about the James Bond films as a whole too. If you allow your mind to brush past them casually, these movies are as familiar as anything can possibly be. Not merely the persona of the leading man, as expressed by different actors – insouciant Sean Connery, dense-but-good-hearted George Lazenby, eyebrow-waggling Roger Moore, dour Timothy Dalton, strutting Pierce Brosnan and nervy new boy Daniel Craig; or the actresses who, across the years, have portrayed vixens with names such as Pussy, Kissy, May Day, Jinx, Octopussy, Plenty and Goodnight. But also the plots, the super-villains, the extravagant sets, the cool gadgets, the count-downs, the impossible car chases, the constant threats to the world, the hollering title songs, the very idea that one man from the English secret service – who has official permission to kill people – can save us all from Armageddon.

But then you look a little closer. You give it just a little more thought. You consider that this formula for what, in the golden era of Hollywood, would be regarded as a shoot-'em-up B movie, has now been running almost continuously since 1962, across twenty-two films. And you find yourself slightly staggered by the whole thing.

It is estimated that half the population of planet Earth has seen a James Bond film. Not the same one, obviously, but still. Few other cultural products have had that sort of reach. The Beatles? The Simpsons? Darth Vader? But then, even the *Star Wars* films ran out of steam towards the end, whereas Bond continually, miraculously, regenerates. It is most assuredly an achievement to give us all a moment's pause.

Eon Productions is the name of the family-run outfit that has been making these films for the last forty-six years. It was started when seasoned movie producers Harry Saltzman and Albert R. Broccoli saw the cinematic potential of Ian Fleming's novels and teamed up after Saltzman acquired the rights to all of Fleming's Bond novels, save one.

Now running the firm is (the late) Broccoli's daughter Barbara, together with his stepson Michael G. Wilson. Jealously they guard the secrets of future productions and also everything that has gone before. And as well they might because, despite endless changes in culture and taste since 1962, staggering numbers of us can still be relied upon to scoot off to the pictures to see the latest Bond.

We will save the bald figures for later; in any case, when we are dealing in multiples of so many million, the whole thing tends to become a little abstract. For the moment, suffice it to say that the Bond films are far and away the most successful franchise (ugly word, almost as bad as 'brand') in cinema history. *Star Wars* is up there at the top, too, clearly; those six intergalactic epics have made intergalactic sums. Oh, and the *Lord of the Rings* trilogy, of course, and the *Harry Potter* sequence too. All have made the box offices resound with record-breaking 'ker-chings' that could be heard from outer space. But for plain reasons of longevity and endurance and quantities of people trooping in to auditoriums, Bond seems to roar ahead every time.

One might broadly say that the series reached its peak of global cultural dominance between the years 1964 and 1966 — starting with the phenomenally successful release of *Goldfinger* and culminating in the even bigger commercial hit *Thunderball*. Thanks to Bond, between those two years, everything, but everything, was about spies. Everything. On every continent. Even the poor Russians, furious about Bond, were forced to invent a Bulgarian version not merely to counter 007, but also to defeat him in a straight battle in 1968.

And when spies went out of fashion, in the early 1970s, Bond still went on. More than went on. It was in this decade that 007 became more famous as a screen character than as a literary creation. To make up for our declining enthusiasm for espionage, the producers instead threw in elements from blaxploitation films, kung-fu films and, notoriously in the wake of 1977's madly successful *Star Wars*, a space station and laser battles in *Moonraker*. Unlike his depression-prone literary equivalent, screen Bond was – and is – a hale and doughty survivor.

There is something about these films that makes fans of us all. Even the novelist Martin Amis, son of famous 007 enthusiast Kingsley, recalls piling into the cinema with mates as an adolescent and getting wildly overexcited about *Dr. No*. On the occasion of their 1981 honeymoon, Prince Charles and Princess Diana sailed off on the royal yacht *Britannia* with a print of *For Your Eyes Only*, which they apparently watched four times.

Elsewhere, during the fraught 1983 TUC conference, where union leaders were squaring up to Prime Minister Margaret Thatcher's implacable determination to dismember the nation's heavy industry, miner's union leader Arthur Scargill, as high-pitched a leftist as one could find, managed to find time to slip out and nip along to the cinema to see *Octopussy*. In wildly different circumstances – but with no less enthusiasm – so did the much-demonised US president Ronald Reagan. There are many more examples of Bond's remarkable capacity to reach across the political and indeed the intellectual spectrum.

These days when we queue up to see the latest Bond, whether in Britain, the USA, Europe or Asia, our expectations remain pleasingly consistent, much as they were when the series began.

None of it is too much to ask for: tuxedos, implausible gadgets, glamorous girls with silly names, slightly naff exotic locations, naffer casinos, weird henchmen, strikingly brassy incidental music and perhaps even – if we are all very good – a monorail system. As we will see, it is the

Bond films that somehow fail to satisfy these modest desires that also tend to do less well at the box office.

Ian Fleming's novels – starting with *Casino Royale* in 1953 – took a while to build up a head of commercial steam. The films, starting with *Dr. No* in 1962, were rather quicker off the mark.

Within any family, any circle of friends, any confederacy of colleagues, there will, to this day, be disputes about who was the best Bond, the best Bond girl and the best/worst Bond film of all. About twenty years ago it was held to be the case that Sean Connery represented the unbeatable peak, and Roger Moore the wisecracking low. As with the works of William Shakespeare versus those of Christopher Marlowe, the issue is no longer so clear-cut.

And something similar happens with the films. For decades, the received wisdom was that George Lazenby's solo outing *On Her Majesty's Secret Service* in 1969 represented the nadir of the series. Now it is instead widely hailed as the zenith, while bitterly slugging it out at the bottom of the barrel are such entries as *Licence to Kill* (1989), *The Man with the Golden Gun* (1974) and *Die Another Day* (2002). They will all be rediscovered in time. Two friends of mine – who have impeccable literary credentials, real Primrose Hill movers-and-shakers – swear that they find *Golden Gun* the most hugely enjoyable of the canon.

Unlike many other fannish preoccupations, the Bond films are an unusually sociable branch of cult enthusiasm. They are not the specialised preserve of intense dweebs. When it comes to Bond, we are all dweebs. We know the gadgets, we recite the worst lines in pubs, we have lively debates involving the mystery of Blofeld's duplicate Persian cats in *Diamonds Are Forever* (1971).

We now also subconsciously use the Bond films as signifiers of social history; for example, Roger Moore's safari-suited tetchiness towards Maud Adams in *The Man with the Golden Gun* must surely be a reflection of the character responding to the increasingly powerful Women's Lib lobby. Likewise the comedy cameo by Faith Brown and John Wells as Margaret and Denis Thatcher in *For Your Eyes Only* (1981) appeared to signal that the films were moving into a more hawkish, right-wing position. (Actually, they weren't.)

Politics, though. Even things that are intended as entirely apolitical cannot help but be political in the end. It seems to have been the producers' intention right from the very start in 1962 to steer the films clear of any obvious form of ideology. Thanks to the villainous – and independent, stateless – organisation SPECTRE, Bond would for the most part find himself facing the private sector of villainy. Never the Russians.

Indeed, back in the late 1950s and after he published *From Russia with Love* (1957), Ian Fleming seemed to take this view too, on the grounds that the Cold War couldn't go on for ever. He and the Bond producers were ultimately proved right, though of course the process took rather longer than anyone would have thought. And in that time, the real Soviets took against Bond very heavily, as we shall see.

When the Bond film series began in 1962, the world appeared poised on the very brink of nuclear apocalypse thanks to the Cuban missile crisis. *Dr. No* was, on the surface, having none of it. But actually, listen closely and you will hear distorted echoes of international tensions. Similarly, today's fresh new Bond Daniel Craig seems thus far to have steered clear of Islamist terrorists. But *Casino Royale* (2006) could not help but reflect a certain unease about the new threats the world faces, and about Britain's place in that world. 'Christ,' exclaims Judi Dench's M at one point, 'I miss the Cold War.'

There are very few, though, who would watch Bond and consciously keep alert for these readings. Whoever would on a Christmas Day, with the film playing on TV, one's fingers scrabbling in the chocolate selection and one's eye fixed on the cat playing with the tree lights? Wherever you happen to be watching it – in a cinema, slobbed out on your sofa with a DVD, in a university common room – a Bond film is your straightforward two hours of faintly absurd entertainment that nevertheless contrives to take itself seriously enough for the illusion to be maintained. Bond may crack the jokes; but you will never catch him laughing at himself. Not even Roger Moore.

In a way, we ask a very great deal of those folk at Eon Productions, because with each successive Bond epic, we want something that is basically the same while being different. How many variations on a car or ski chase or a bomb countdown can you have? A great many, it would seem. But there is real ingenuity at the heart of these films, particularly when one considers that in literary form, Ian Fleming was beginning to run out of puff after *Dr. No* in 1958, confessing to friends that he was finding it harder and harder to invent strong situations to put Bond in.

The films are so much a part of our cultural landscape – these mammoth twenty-two productions loom over all, like the Atlas Mountains – that it is initially a little difficult to unstick them from the works that influenced them, and the times and real events and trends and fashions that, however unconsciously, shaped them.

But as you begin the process of unravelling, you slowly begin to see – with some glee, it must be said – that behind the boisterous façade of these noisy, kinetic, thrilling, sexy, silly films is nothing less than a big-budget Bayeux Tapestry that encapsulates everything from fashion to geopolitics. Who could possibly ask for more?

CHAPTER ONE AUTHENTICITY

As we go back to October 1962, and the world premiere of that first James Bond film, *Dr. No*, in London, let's first, in the manner of Ian Fleming, take a look at how very miserable the capital was in that month. This is a standard gambit in the Bond novels; they will kick off with 007 stuck in London between missions, in his 'dog days'. Fleming usually gives a wonderfully atmospheric description of just how drab the city is, the better to whet our appetites for the colourful adventures to come.

So, autumn 1962, and even though the Clean Air Act was passed in 1956, in order to prevent the toxic 'pea-souper' fogs that had enshrouded the capital, the evenings would still have been murky from all the smoke issuing from the giant industrial chimneys of riverside power stations such as Battersea and Bankside and Deptford. Despite Soho's new, fashionable incarnation as a bohemian quarter of Continental delis, coffee bars, clip joints and boutiques, the colourful neon signs making the evening mist luminous, the rest of the city was dreary, smirched with blackening soot, still pockmarked with muddy bomb-sites. One such lay to the east of Smithfield market, a vast rubble-strewn area, even as late as 1962, with Metropolitan Line underground trains occasionally visible through gaps in the bomb-shattered earth. This area was to be filled with the high-rise flats of the Barbican complex. And all of this was several years before the colourful explosion of Swinging London; this was the rainy, grey prelude. This was the world from which Bond's very first cinema audience would be escaping.

This, indeed, was pretty much the same world from which the British had been seeking refuge in 1953, when the first of Ian Fleming's Bond novels, *Casino Royale*, was published. In the period between 1953 and 1962, the cultural tectonic plates of the West had begun to shift; and Fleming cleverly tapped into a taste for a rather more invigorating, sophisticated form of popular fiction. So before we shuffle through that London Pavilion foyer for the opening of *Dr. No*, we should swiftly survey the circumstances under which this extraordinary cinematic phenomenon came into being.

I am not going to spend pages analysing Fleming himself; this has already been done quite often enough by others. If you really want to know what Fleming was like, simply go back and read his books. There he is, plain as anything. What I will do, though, is point this out from the start: authenticity is key to the Bond phenomenon – films and books – in several different ways.

The first element is to be found in the author himself. Fleming was an Old Etonian (so famous an Old Etonian, in fact, that I jolly well hope the college is paying an annual tribute to his family in return for this ceaseless publicity). He was part of the Fleming banking family, who continue to flourish discreetly in the Square Mile today. Fleming's literary aspirations were manifested at school in the form of a self-published volume of poetry. His seemed always destined to be the unconventional life. Fleming joined Reuters as a young man, becoming a newspaper foreign correspondent; then, as the Second World War broke out, he attained a position in naval intelligence. The position, in fact, that crucially gave him the in-depth knowledge that would allow him to invest his fiction with convincing verisimilitude.

In 1953, among the most popular authors were Mickey Spillane and James Hadley Chase, both of whom had in their own ways upped the sex and violence quotient in the thriller genre. Spillane's Mike Hammer, with his down-at-heel private detective ways and his Manichean world view, was followed especially keenly.

What the 44-year-old Fleming did was take that genre of slightly sleazy, sexy noir thriller and somehow try to wrestle it into a British form. In other words, *Casino Royale* – with its depictions of a sweaty late-night gaming establishment, *unheimlich* villain, sassy heroine and ghastly torture – was in essence the same thing as Spillane, but with the added element of the British Establishment, and most crucially of the Secret Intelligence Service.

Back then, MI6 was very rarely openly discussed in newspapers or on television; everyone knew that it was there but only a chosen few had any kind of access to its mysterious, silent inner workings. Fleming did though, for he had observed it all during the war.

Casino Royale works chiefly because we believe unquestioningly in his account of the paraphernalia of spying; we believe in the way that Bond carefully checks his room for bugs, and in the way that ally René Matthis turns the radio up to foil the eavesdroppers upstairs; we believe in the Bulgarian bombers; we believe in Bond's superior M authorising his agent to spend quite jaw-dropping sums at the chemin de fer table to foil the Soviet patsy Le Chiffre.

If Fleming's moreish prose style has any one outstanding quality, it is that of pinpoint-sharp description. The slightly vulgar, seamy setting of Royale-Les-Eaux, with all its attendant dangers and attractions, was brought to a form of heightened, almost hallucinatory life. This certainty of style constructed an entirely new world; so intensely well-drawn that readers had not the slightest difficulty in believing it. Bond's world had the vital taste of authenticity.

Casino Royale sold about 4000 copies in its first run, not at all bad for a debut novel. It picked up some proper, appreciative reviews as well in highbrow journals. But no matter how good the novel, it is here that we must ask: if it were not for the James Bond *films*, would the Bond novels from *Royale* onwards really have lasted to this day? Indeed, were it not for the films making the character of 007 a globally recognisable figure, would these original thrillers still be in print at all?

Look, for instance, at Fleming's near-contemporary Eric Ambler, arguably the better thriller writer of the two. His finest novels were *The Mask of Dimitrios* and *Journey Into Fear*. When was the last time anyone saw either on bookshop shelves?

How about another distinguished British spy, this one from the late Edwardian period? W. Somerset Maugham's *Ashenden* was popular in its day and was even taken up by Alfred Hitchcock in 1936, adapted as *Secret Agent*, starring John Gielgud. After the war, nary more a squeak was heard from this Ashenden fellow.

In 1954, Fleming published his Bond follow-up *Live and Let Die*, which yanked its eager British readers over to New York and then down to the Caribbean in a lurid story that mixed espionage with voodoo, treasure hunting and scuba diving. The New York passages seemed especially vivid; for the bulk of British readers, it was a city they only knew through film clichés. Fleming's Bond, on the other hand, wandered its streets and brought it to life, giving it a strong flavour of reality.

This was at a time when Britain's younger generation was just starting a long process of cultural cringe, believing that all things American – from movies to fast food to fashion to music – were infinitely superior to anything square old Britain could serve up.

And as word spread through the British reading public of this new, conspicuously consuming hero, there was at last the beginning of film interest. The film mogul Alexander Korda, famous for *The Private Life of Henry VIII* (1933) and *Things to Come* (1936) read *Live and Let Die* with great enjoyment and mentioned to his brilliant directors Carol Reed and David Lean that there might be something in it. Carol Reed is these days best remembered for the noir Graham Greene spy thriller *The Third Man* (1949); one cannot help wondering how dark a Reed-directed Bond film would have been. Elsewhere, Ian Hunter of the Rank Organisation was similarly interested.

Fleming's next novel, *Moonraker*, a very silly story involving a maniac called Hugo Drax, a sinister missile installation on the south coast, and a nuclear warhead pointed at London, was clearly written with half an eye to a screen adaptation.

And when one looks back now, one thinks: of course. What could be a more guaranteed hit than turning these Bond books into spectacular, epic, cinematic thrillers? What idea could be more obvious?

Except at the time, it didn't seem immediately obvious to many film-makers. Perhaps, in the 1950s, the character of Bond himself was widely considered a little too coarse for British big-screen tastes. That was the period of clean-cut Dirk Bogarde and John Mills. British good guys still did the decent thing. They did not go around having sex at the drop of their snap-brim hats, and nor did they refer to their lady friends as 'bitches'. Incidentally, who wouldn't pay good money to see John Mills in a CGI-altered film doing so now?

Amusingly, this might not have been how Fleming intended things to turn out; he once said that he intended his novels to reach an 'ABC1 readership' – in other words, to be enjoyed largely by the smarter social set. The gap between an author's intentions and the response of the public is sometimes comically vast. Fleming did not appear to realise initially that in 1950s Britain, a hero with a licence to use bad language was almost as potent as one with a licence to kill.

Tellingly, Bond's very first screen incarnation was an American effort; it was transmitted in black and white on American TV. In 1954, the CBS television network screened an adaptation of Fleming's first Bond novel *Casino Royale*, as part of its strikingly named thriller slot, *Climax Theatre*. And American actor Barry Nelson was 'Jimmy' Bond. A CIA agent, if you please.

Playing the card-playing villain Le Chiffre – a nice touch of casting, this, which would find a tonal echo in the later films – was Peter Lorre,

Hollywood's bug-eyed doyen of deranged villainy. Given that it is all studio-bound, and in fuzzy black and white, and would have been broken up with endless advertisements for toothpaste, it is an inventive piece of adaptation. The infamous scene in the novel where Bond is tortured with the application of a carpet beater to his testicles is here transmuted into a discreetly shot toenail-pulling sequence. The sensibilities of modern audiences for the 2006 Eon production of the same were not spared. The TV play is a curiosity now, with its own band of ultra-loyal cultist fans.

There was a radio Bond too, in 1956: Bob Holness, later the genial host of teenage TV quiz *Blockbusters*. 'No one realised for years that I was the second Bond,' he told me wistfully, some years ago, round the back of a Midlands TV studio as he was changing his trousers for the second *Blockbusters* recording of the day. He voiced Bond in *Moonraker* for a South African radio station.

Fleming by now was publishing his books on an annual basis – *Diamonds Are Forever, From Russia with Love, Doctor No* . . . and their popularity among the reading public was growing; so why, in the late 1950s, were they still proving so resistant to film adaptation? Part of the reason might very well have been down to notions of Britishness and class. Fleming's creation, though dynamic and rough and sexy, would not, as written, necessarily captivate the American audiences who would be vital for any Bond film to have a hope of succeeding.

Without that American investment, and interest, the very nature of Bond's epic exploits would have proved too expensive for any British film studio simply standing on its own.

Actually, the American CBS television network showed another burst of enthusiasm for Fleming's work in 1958 when its executives entered discussions with the author, asking him to write thirty-two specially tailored episodes of a projected James Bond television series, which later came to naught.

Later in 1958, Fleming had extremely creative discussions with Irish film producer Kevin McClory, that were to end in tears for the writer several years later after he apparently adapted some of these discussions for his novel *Thunderball* and McClory alerted m'learned friends. Meanwhile, there was also a suggestion that Universal MCA was intrigued by the stories and thought that Alfred Hitchcock might be intrigued too.

By 1960, Bond was comfortably ensconced in the British cultural landscape, emphatically a household name, helped enormously by a strip cartoon based on the character which ran in the then extremely popular *Daily Express*. Then, at last, the cinematic interest that Fleming had craved manifested in the shape of two men – based in Britain – whose names now live on immortally in the Bond film credits.

In particular, the name Albert R. Broccoli, even though the man himself passed away in 1996, lives on for modern audiences – still there at the start of each new Bond movie, as 'Albert R. Broccoli's Eon Productions presents...' Harry Saltzman was his co-producer until *The Man with the Golden Gun* (1974). Both film veterans – though not, we note, Hollywood figures – came to the notion of translating Bond for the big screen in not wholly expected ways.

Canadian Saltzman, who had once worked in a circus, was previously better known for producing films at the rougher, more experimental end of the cultural scale. He took John Osborne's original 'Angry Young Man' play *Look Back In Anger* and produced it in 1957 with Richard Burton taking the lead role of Jimmy Porter. It was well received by the critics. But that was about all. 'It didn't do much business anywhere in the world,' said Saltzman. 'I never made a film that got such good reviews and was seen by so few people.'[1]

None the less, Saltzman, having gone into business with Osborne and director Tony Richardson to set up Woodfall Films, turned his attention to another Osborne production, *The Entertainer* (1960), and Laurence Olivier was cast as the seedy comedian Archie Rice. With its references to the recent Suez crisis, its pervasive air of Archie Rice's Britain as a shabby, fading place, one might have expected it to do well. It didn't. Saltzman said: 'After the financial flop of *The Entertainer*, I was as dead as any producer could be.'[2]

Happily, he wasn't any such thing, as his co-producing credit on the seminal *Saturday Night and Sunday Morning* (1960) demonstrates. This grimy black and white work, based on Alan Sillitoe's Nottingham-based novel, cemented the movement known as the British New Wave. Albert Finney was Arthur Seaton, Rachel Roberts was the intense squeeze.

But then Saltzman had an innate sense of showmanship. Film critic Alexander Walker wrote of Saltzman's formative years: 'Moving from the US to France and back again, he had worked in vaudeville, in advertising, in television, in fact in anything that was attractive to his gambler's instinct, his roving curiosity and his genuine fascination with the mystique as well as the machinery of popular culture. He could make money work and things happen.'[3]

After this, Saltzman left Woodfall Films. And in December 1960 bought up the rights to the works of Ian Fleming. By 1961, he had still not exercised his option; the reason was that he needed a business partner.

American Broccoli, familiarly known as 'Cubby' (the affectionate nickname, bestowed by Broccoli's cousin, was a diminution of the surname of the cartoon character Abie Kabibble), had shown a similarly shrewd instinct for what worked during what was actually a rather difficult period for British cinema. He had enjoyed critical success for his production of *The Trials of Oscar Wilde* (1960) with Peter Finch and James Mason. Previous successes included *The Red Beret* (1953) and *Cockleshell Heroes* (1955). Ironically, in the mid-1950s, Broccoli had also shown interest in Fleming's work. In 1961, he was at last introduced to Saltzman.

Together, they went to United Artists to raise the money, and they got it – a budget a little shy of $1 million (or about £300,000, as it was in Britain then – much less favourable exchange rates than now). This was clearly not a great deal. In fact, as a budget for a lavish action adventure, it was on the scanty side. But remember that there would have been some scepticism among the Americans about just how far Bond could succeed in the States.

We return once more to the notion of authenticity. For some people, to this day, actor Sean Connery is the only Bond. All others are but fleeting shadows. Connery was deemed from the start to have that feel of verisimilitude: you could believe that this man could kill as part of his job. But how did Saltzman and Broccoli decide that Connery above all others could carry the weight of portraying on the screen a hero so convincing that they might get another four or five films out of it?

Many other names have been mentioned as having been under consideration. There was young Roger Moore, the star of TV's swash-buckling *Ivanhoe*, although the producers considered him just a little too young at that stage. Also, according to Harry Saltzman, 'he was tied up in a TV show', that TV show being *The Saint*. Trevor Howard was another. Just a little too old. Oh, and Cary Grant, who was, apart from anything else, just a little too expensive for what was actually a rather low-budget film. Patrick McGoohan, who had become well known for his role as secret agent John Drake on ITV's *Danger Man*, was apparently approached. Director Terence Young, it seems, wanted Richard Johnson. On learning that Broccoli had hired Sean Connery, Young exclaimed: 'Oh disaster, disaster, disaster!', though he was later to modify his views.

The name David Niven was invoked. Niven was said to be Fleming's own notion of the perfect Commander Bond. Other than the fact that by 1962, Niven was past his prime, it is interesting how Fleming seemed to plump for the actor who seemed to resemble him most closely in build and to an extent, in facial terms.

But then, in a couple of the Bond novels, 007 himself is described as looking a little like Hoagy Carmichael. This name will mean nothing to anyone under the age of eighty-five. Hoagy Carmichael was an American jazz musician, big in the 1940s – and yes, if you look at pictures of him, you see something of what Fleming was driving at. Sharp-featured, wide mouth, with a comma of dark hair falling over the brow. And not a million miles away from Sean Connery.

One of the oft-repeated – yet nonsensical – stories around *Dr. No* is that Connery himself was an utter unknown, brought up in a shoebox in Edinburgh and only finding fame for winning a 'Mr Universe' competition. It's true that he did come third in some form of 'Mr Universe' contest, after winning Mr Scotland. The photos are there to prove it. Connery would never have realised how those posing briefs would return to haunt him. And he did deliver milk in Edinburgh, and indeed I know someone who had their daily pints placed on their doorstep by his very hand. What's wrong with that?

He also made cabinets, polished coffins, and had a short spell in the Royal Navy. An excellent range of life experience.

In fact, by the mid-1950s, Connery had become a highly spoken of and well-established actor. He had been in a West End production of *South Pacific*. Not actually starring in it, more chorus line – but one woman I know recalls seeing him in that production. She says that Connery stole the show, whipping his top off during a dance number and making some 'tattooed' waves on his chest ripple by virtue of his well-defined muscles. People made their own entertainment in those days.

But it wasn't all beefcake stuff. Connery had been in Chekhov on the BBC. He had performed Shakespeare at the Richmond Theatre. He was profiled in the *News Chronicle* in 1957 and described in the headline as 'The British Brando'. On that occasion, in the face of a tittering lady interviewer, Connery demonstrated the keen self-awareness, seriousness and ambition that were to become his hallmarks: 'Nothing is frustrating if it gets you somewhere,' he said of some unsatisfactory film role. 'I'm not in a selective position yet. I'll do anything I can get my hands on.'

He got his hands on the romantic lead in a Disney film, *Darby O'Gill and the Little People* (1960), in which his nascent 007 fighting skills were honed in a bar-room punch-up scene. We also got to hear him sing, which now looks and sounds extraordinarily odd. He had done caper comedy, playing opposite Alfred Lynch in *On the Fiddle* (1961). He also had a role in Terence Young-directed Cold War drama *Action of the Tiger* (1956).

Producer Harry Saltzman said of these early Connery productions: 'He was dreadful in most of them, we thought. He had suffered a small but fatal miscasting all the way down the line.'[4]

None the less, even before Bond, Connery was very much a rising star, and was certain at some stage to get noticed for something bigger. It was the Disney film that alerted the producers. Broccoli enlisted his wife Dana to give the all-important woman's verdict. She felt that as a potential Bond, Connery was knockout.

Famously, Broccoli said that the attributes they liked about thirty-two-year-old Connery when they met him for audition were that first, despite his build, he had a surprisingly lithe step and second, he looked like 'he had balls'. Oh, and third, this masculinity presented a sharp contrast to many of the other actors – the 'mincing poofs', as Broccoli later termed them – who also applied for the role.

There have been suggestions across the years that posh old Ian Fleming was a little dismayed that his creation was to be played by someone from a lower drawer. 'Not exactly what I envisaged,' he is said to have told one friend. But this, according to Fleming's literary manager, was not really the case.

Indeed, as far back as 1959, when Fleming had been in talks with the Irish producer Kevin McClory about the possibility of filming Bond, there was talk of casting Trevor Howard. Fleming actually thought him too old. He said a little later: 'Well, actually, I'd be happier if the part could be given to a young unknown actor, with established stars playing all the other roles.'[5]

There was another factor in casting. In the wake of *Saturday Night, Sunday Morning* (1960) and even noirish British thrillers such as *Hell Is a City* (1960), it was clear that the notion of the macho British leading man had moved on a little from David Niven and Dirk Bogarde.

Take a look, for instance, at Stanley Baker, now famous for *Zulu* (1963) but earlier best known for kinetic shockers like *Hell Drivers* (1957), which incidentally also starred a young Connery. Baker was brilliant at exuding a quiet, unforced menace and intensity, the sense that he could strike unexpectedly at any moment. He also lacked drawing room manners and a dainty way with a teacup. In 1962, it was clear that Connery – rather like Baker – embodied a very modern form of masculinity, with ragged edges and more sexual sang-froid than the previous generation. Producers Albert R. Broccoli and Harry Saltzman were already aware of the impact that such a leading man could have on the all-important young audiences.

United Artists were apparently disagreeably taken aback by the choice. But Saltzman and Broccoli held firm in their judgement. They had found their real Bond. The next step, as pre-production got under way on *Dr. No*, was to turn this lithe, ballsy Scotsman into a Savile Row-clad Establishment figure.

For this extra dimension of authenticity, Saltzman and Broccoli looked to the seasoned director Terence Young, of whom many have suggested that he was rather like Bond himself. By which they seemed to mean that Young was insanely fastidious about clothes, food and etiquette.

What these producers were looking for was that elusive element of social authenticity: they wanted the urbane, sophisticated Young to convey to Connery how to wear a suit, how to walk into a smart restaurant, how to order wine with confidence, how to adjust one's cufflinks, what sort of tuxedo to sport at the casino. In Britain, such things mattered intensely back then. Notions of deference, of class, and of the bonds of the old school tie were still, in the early 1960s, oppressively prevalent. Yet here with Young, one is somehow reminded of P.G. Wodehouse's immortal Bertie Wooster, and his sole contribution to the world of literature: a piece on 'What the Well-Dressed Man Is Wearing'.

In the Fleming novels, Bond a lot of the time seemed handily to be wearing the same clothes as his author – Sea Island cotton shirts, and the like. Something a trifle more formal was needed for the start of this film. Once Connery had been kitted out in his Savile Row three-piece, Young advised him to sleep in it in order to become utterly comfortable with it. Much has been made of Connery's relatively humble roots and his initial discomfort with this opulent new world; equally, however, am I alone in finding these *Pygmalion*-style tales slightly uncomfortable? The man was an actor, not a nineteenth-century chimney sweep.

In 1961, as Saltzman and Broccoli turned their minds towards pre-production, it had originally been intended that Fleming's most recent novel *Thunderball* would be used as the source material; but even then, it was clear that legal storm clouds were gathering. Out of all the other novels they could have chosen to launch this putative new cinematic hero, it is interesting that Saltzman and Broccoli felt that *Doctor No* would be the most suitable. Because in many ways, it is one of Fleming's more cheerfully old-fashioned and uncomplicated works, featuring an oriental master-villain with a sadistically inventive line in homicide and the technological ability to bring the world to the brink of war . . .

Fleming, as a young man, must have been keenly aware of the Bulldog Drummond novels by 'Sapper', published in the early years of the twentieth century. In the last few decades, these have gained a reputation as books so *horrifically* racist that even to glance at a page would make your eyes fall out. Hugh 'Bulldog' Drummond has for several generations been used as shorthand for a brutishly imperialist outlook, redolent of a certain pre-war anti-semitism. In other words, you will have a job finding these books in university libraries.

Actually, the books are not quite so bad as that. All right, the second in the series has a nasty sequence of anti-semitism, in which two Jewish men who are white slavers are threatened with a flogging by some unidentified men who later turn out to be Drummond's gang. Oh all right, the fourth in the series has an appalling reference to 'the Jews' running Russia.

But by and large Bulldog himself is a startlingly affable figure. He always seems to be facing a multinational villain called Carl Peterson whose aim is − yes − to undermine Western civilisation. In the first book, Peterson − despite his diabolical global ambitions − operates out of a large house near Dorking, in Surrey. No offence to the good people of Dorking, but it is not where you would expect to find Blofeld prototypes.

Bulldog has to face all kinds of ingenious jeopardy, including mechanised crossbows and acid baths, but does so with an endless series of quips and punch-ups that seem to make him a cross between Roger Moore and a hearty prop forward. There is even a Good Girl − who happens to live in the next-door Dorking house − and a Bad Girl, who fancies Drummond and smokes cigarettes.

In the fourth book, Carl Peterson's plan is to float above London in a dirigible and spray the population with a lethal poisonous doomsday liquid that kills all living matter on contact. Obviously it is madly ill-written balderdash, but you can see where a lot of the Bondian cliffhanging japes came from. Fleming in fact nods to this in the novel of *From Russia with Love*, when Bond is trapped by Red Grant at gunpoint in a compartment of the Orient Express and Grant advises against Bond 'trying any of that Bulldog Drummond stuff'.

In the case of *Doctor No*, we also cannot ignore Sax Rohmer's series of Fu Manchu novels, which were required schoolboy reading in the 1910s and 1920s. We know that Fleming was a young fan; his nanny would read them out as bedtime stories.

Their basic scenario was that Dr Fu Manchu was a sinister international mastermind, an insane scientist, whose plan was to soften the West up for an invasion bid from the East. His adversary was Nayland Smith, who would frequently stop to make speeches about 'the Yellow Peril'. Fu Manchu would often base himself among the wharves and opium dens of Limehouse, and use the stinking Thames as a means of disposing of his many victims.

But his real selling point was that he would always devise absurdly ingenious means of murdering people: poison gas in sarcophagi; venomous millipedes; lethal fungi; mechanical devices designed to chop bits off the body one by one (I think that contrivance was called the Gates of the Seven Deaths, or somesuch); and specially trained gorillas, one such known as the Coughing Horror. There was simply no end to the man's fiendishness. What was more, he had a disconcerting pet marmoset that would always startle our heroes by suddenly leaping on to Fu Manchu's shoulder.

It hardly needs to be added that thanks to issues of breathtaking racism, it is quite difficult to get hold of the books these days. More so than Drummond, Rohmer's work is insanely politically incorrect. But it does not take a great leap of imagination to see where this very first cinematic Bond villain might have originally sprung from.

As we shall see, however, Saltzman and Broccoli were both highly creative men in their own right, and it seems they were agreed on the work that had to be done in order for this story to make the successful transition to screen.

And indeed, whether they acknowledged it or not, the template for pretty much every James Bond film had already been set down by director Alfred Hitchcock in 1959. *North by Northwest*, the story of an advertising executive (Cary Grant) who is mistaken for a spy and finds himself sucked into battle against sinister Van Damm (James Mason) while falling for a beautiful agent (Eva Marie-Saint), establishes a sex-and-setpieces sensibility that could not have failed to influence Broccoli and Saltzman.

There is the idea throughout *Northwest* of mad scale: the dizzying overhead shot of the tiny figure of Cary Grant escaping from the United Nations building; the frightening emptiness of the Midwest prairie prior to the crop-duster attack; and of course, the literal monumentalism of the climax set on the faces of Mount Rushmore. This was a cinematic trope that was to become a Bond trademark – Ken Adam's vast, expressionist operatic sets, against which henchmen and good guys alike would be dwarfed.

Northwest also had casual sex, this time on a train and most notably in the film's cheeky final shot; then there is the villain's faintly pervy right-hand man (rather brilliantly portrayed here by Martin Landau); there is the strikingly angled set design of the villain's main hideout (in the shadow of Mount Rushmore); and finally there is the script, which constantly flips and doubles back, as the well-dressed protagonist Grant quips and glugs cocktails throughout the entire thing. It is one of the most perfectly entertaining spy films ever made. And Hitchcock made a great many of the sort, as we shall see.

But we might also see that *Northwest*'s screenwriter, Ernest Lehman, paid a little tribute to Ian Fleming himself. It was in Fleming's 1954 novel *Live and Let Die* that the notion of sex on a train was daringly foregrounded, as Bond and Solitaire travel down to the Florida Everglades.

For Saltzman and Broccoli's first Bond enterprise to work, it had to appeal to a large family audience; was it possible for them to combine that consideration with the perceived sex and sadism of Fleming's novels? In order to see how they pulled it off – and how they captured the imaginations of audiences at a time when the world was facing up to a real and potentially apocalyptic geopolitical crisis – we must take a closer look at the film itself. For as production began on *Dr. No*, it slowly became apparent – through trial and error – that in terms of screenplay and visual flair, the producers really did have that authentic touch.

CHAPTER TWO YOU'VE HAD YOUR SIX

Dr. *No* received its premiere at the London Pavilion in Piccadilly Circus on 5 October 1962. Those who would have trooped in to see it on those chilly autumn evenings (people still got chilblains then; you never hear of them at all now) would have been seduced immediately not only by the pace, but by the sheer warmth that glows off the screen during the frenetic, colourful opening titles and the teaser sequence in Jamaica, awash with sunshine, featuring the 'three blind mice' assassins.

Unlike many of the Bond films that were to follow, the narrative line of *No* is terrifically simple; the murder of a British agent in Jamaica puts Bond on to the trail of a master criminal who, from his secret lair in Crab Key, is deploying a rocket-toppling beam and playing merry hell with the American space programme. During the course of this adventure, Bond gets to sleep with an arch English rose called Sylvia Trench and a pert enemy agent called Miss Taro, fetches up on Crab Key and is aided by fisherman Quarrel and the statuesque shell-collector Honey Ryder. At the end, having destroyed Dr. No and his futuristic HQ, Bond and Honey get to snog. It really couldn't be simpler.

For all this to work, the one vital element was production design: this was a film that had to have terrific visual style. And in the hiring of production designer Ken Adam (now Sir Ken), Saltzman and Broccoli displayed a further level of genius.

Adam was an inventive young pro who had previously worked on such productions as *Around the World in 80 Days* (1956) and various other dramas in period costume. By contrast, *Dr. No* inspired him to think to the future.

Adam was a quite remarkable man. Born Klaus Adam, he and his family had left Germany to come to Britain in the early 1930s. As a young chap, Adam was the only German to fly in the RAF during the war. If any of his missions had resulted in him being brought down over enemy territory, he would, he recalls, have been hanged by the Germans as a traitor.

The immediate influence that he brought to Bond was the Expressionism of Weimar cinema, as most famously manifested in *The Cabinet of Dr Caligari*

(1919). Indeed, from the start, Adam was one of the men most influential in the terrific success of the Bond films; he gave them a stylised panache that countless have tried to imitate, and no one has yet bettered. (It was a flair, incidentally, that he brought unforgettably to Stanley Kubrick's black comedy *Dr Strangelove* (1963) – the War Room set is a work of art in its own right.)

Given that Adam's sets were later to gain a reputation for their dizzying scale and detail, things were a little sparser on this first entry. Adam was initially told that he would only have £14,000 to build all the sets. He successfully petitioned for another £6000. This quibble aside, in the age of the auteur, where director was all, one heard very little about the creative input of film producers. Well, let us be in no doubt that, right from the very start, both Broccoli and Saltzman were very creative men.

Not that *Dr. No* was a masterwork of originality that simply arrived out of nowhere. Far from it. Both the novel and the film are almost deliriously derivative. But the trick, as Ian Fleming once noted of his fiction generally, was to take much-loved ingredients and find the perfect cocktail blend for them. *Dr. No* is a startlingly gaudy cocktail with an umbrella on the top.

We begin, as we must, with those white circles, and Bond in a suit and a hat (not Connery, actually, but his double Bob Simmons) shooting at us – and then a frenetic title sequence involving flashing multicoloured dots, which segues into primary-coloured transparencies of three dancers moving energetically in early 1960s fashion. Thence to the Three Blind Mice – and the film opens properly with the assassination of British stringer agent Strangways at the old colonial club.

Not too long afterwards, we have the rather shocking murder by silenced gun of Strangways' wholly innocent secretary, purely so that the henchmen may steal the secret files on Crab Key and Dr. No; when seeing this again, you realise just how very few innocent women are killed in the course of the Bond movies. It feels very wrong, not a scene suitable for a family entertainment at all.

And so these distasteful events are conveyed to dreary, grey old London. MI6 is conjured in this first adventure as consisting of a dull communications room filled with earnest-looking young people in sensible knitwear listening to massive headsets. What? Missing, you say? But was there no clue of any sort left behind? . . .

Thence to the first of a very long line of naff casinos. The establishment in question is a studio recreation of Les Ambassadeurs in Mayfair, London. This casino's position in film history – and gambling history generally – is so iconic that we tend to overlook the fact that no reasonable person would be seen dead in such a ghastly place, no matter how opulent and exclusive. After a number of fleeting close-up shots of tantalising details of Bond at the gaming table – a hand, a cufflink, a fag in a gob – we have Sylvia Trench's (Eunice Gayson) archly come-hither expression across the card table followed by our first medium shot of Connery, a smouldering cigarette dangling from his lips in a manner that would make lesser eyes water. Sylvia Trench, eyebrow aloft, says: 'I admire your luck, Mr – ?'

Then, of course, he replies: 'Bond. James Bond.'

Try saying that with a lit cigarette in your mouth without looking absurd.

This entrance is rather shrewd. One of the few other iconic cinematic figures to have received such a build-up in terms of montage of detail is Boris Karloff's Frankenstein monster. Terence Young later insisted in interviews that he had intended the whole thing as a subtle joke.

There is a rather lame stab at innuendo-laden backchat with Sylvia (who at one point raises another eyebrow in response to some remark and says: 'It's an idea at that,' a line so dated that it momentarily throws the film back to 1937). After this, though, we settle briskly into a comfortable routine. Bond is summoned from his naff casino by M; peevish Bernard Lee instantly looks completely at home behind that desk in that wood-panelled office (just wood-effect wallpaper at that stage, according to Sir Ken Adam; they couldn't afford the real thing) with its distinctive padded door (not yet real leather).

It's time to say hello to one of the most iconic women in cinematic history. No, not Ursula, she comes later. I am of course talking about darling Moneypenny, as portrayed by Lois Maxwell.

Maxwell had been something of a favourite with 1950s tabloid reporters, who had dubbed the actress 'the girl who walked out on Hollywood', as a result of her refusal to bow to one studio's demands concerning padding out her bust. She asked Terence Young for work and was offered the choice between Moneypenny and Sylvia Trench. Wise Maxwell! For even though she had only a handful of lines, and generally only one scene per film, she none the less stayed with Bond until 1985's *A View to a Kill*.

And in this first entry, the Moneypenny construct is set up so perfectly that it barely wavers for the next twenty-three years. She and Bond flirt and Bond is called in to M's office; following his briefing, they try to flirt a little more but M's voice comes through on the intercom: 'Omit the customary repartee . . .', suggesting that such repartee has been going on for years beforehand.

Before that outbreak of customary repartee, Bond is told by M of rum Jamaican doings, and he and M have the first of their minor comedy tussles, this time involving Bond's choice of gun. There is a Major Boothroyd (Q) present, but he is not avuncular actor Desmond Llewelyn at this stage, he is Peter Burton, so he doesn't count. Bond arrives back home, armed with a plane ticket, to find Sylvia Trench dressed only in his pyjama top, tapping golf balls into a teacup.

What would be a nice little interlude of sauce here is rather spoiled by the overwrought build-up of incidental music – Monty Norman on this first outing, with the enthusiastic encouragement of the film's editor Peter Hunt – that makes it sound as though Bond is facing not a pert piece with nice legs, but an ambush by the Ton Ton Macoutes.

And at last we are in Jamaica, where at Arrivals, Mr Bond fails to notice lurking CIA agent Felix Leiter (as portrayed by Jack Lord). It was not quite fifty years ago but already this Jamaican world seems a very long way away – it is an antique realm featuring white men in suits sitting in wicker chairs drinking from long glasses brought by black servants; above their heads, ceiling fans rotate lazily. It is interesting to see how the classless Connery looks out of place and rather uncomfortable in this milieu, in a way that Bond's creator never did.

The curious thing is that Jamaica gained its independence a matter of weeks before *Dr. No* opened. But the island we see still appears more in sync with Ian Fleming's colonial era, complete with Bond putting calls in to Government House.

In fact, it is redolent of the twilight of the colonial era that Ian Fleming himself had witnessed on the island. We think of Fleming's somewhat ugly house in a beautiful setting, Goldeneye, where he bashed out his Bond novels on a typewriter that, according to some accounts, he had gold-plated. Fleming's wife Ann once gave her friend Evelyn Waugh a poisonously evocative account of their average Jamaican day: 'I love scratching away with my paintbrush,' she wrote to Waugh, 'while Ian hammers out his pornography next door.'[1]

Anyway. The film's cars are from a different era. So are the acting styles. But we are simply setting down the rules here. There is a car chase that, with its creaking use of back-projection, could have come from a Mack Sennett comedy. There is the first of very many horrid hotel rooms. In this one, prior to going out, Bond takes the precautions of putting talcum on the locks of his super-secret briefcase and plucking a heavily Brylcreemed hair from his head and affixing it to the door of the wardrobe, as a means of checking whether it has been disturbed in his absence. What schoolboy didn't instantly follow an identical procedure thereafter? Although we soon found that it never worked unless your head was smothered in oil. Bond also takes his very first vodka martini, obligingly prepared by a room service waiter, 'not stirred'.

Things begin to perk up with a scene involving Anthony Dawson (as obvious bad-hat Professor Dent) being summoned to the industrial-looking villain's HQ, and being shown into a bare room containing nothing but a chair and a small wooden cage.

It is this scene that illustrates the supreme importance of production design in the Bond films, as everyone involved in this production – up to and including the United Artists executives – has acknowledged. What Ken Adam does here – for the first of a great many times – is to take a scenario of almost unbearable B-movie creakiness and lift it right up on to another level.

That set is a marvel! The ceiling with the vast angled circular hole, open to the sky, covered with a lattice grille, the criss-crossing shadows matching the stark, elongated lines of that chair and the sinister vertical slats of the cage, the raised floor and the forced perspective. It is pure Expressionism. And it succeeds in making one feel rather nervous about the not especially large tarantula that we can see in that cage. Other than this, the device of a sweaty second-rank heavy and the booming voice of his unseen master almost pre-dates Fu Manchu. Remarkably, this landmark set, which subsequently featured in art exhibitions across the world as testimony to the creative genius of set design, cost £450 to build.

'The fact was,' Sir Ken Adam said, 'that director Terence Young and I had both forgotten about that scene. So when it came to shoot, we had no money left. I had to get my crews to build the set overnight. When Terence saw it, he asked me to raise the level of it by ten feet, so that the camera could get the whole of the circle in.'

The tarantula is there, of course, to be introduced to Bond's bed in the middle of the night. The resulting episode is still treasured by arachnophobia sufferers the world over. Bearing in mind the modern phrase 'no animals were harmed during the making . . .', it's worth taking a quick look at that tarantula sequence. We all remember it. There Bond is, fast asleep, when he is awoken by some movement under the sheet. There are a few moments of suspense as we simply watch the shape move beneath the bedclothes – and then the spider is disclosed.

There it goes – a-creeping up Connery's hairy chest, on to his arm, on to his shoulder, close to his face . . . Interviewed a great many years later on TV by Dame Edna Everage, Sean Connery was asked if a stuntman was used in the spider scene. Gamely, Connery replied that there was. 'But what I don't understand,' said Dame Edna slowly and wickedly, 'is how the stuntman got into that incy-wincy spider costume.'

It was a nice joke that also drew attention to the fact that on careful examination, the spider wasn't quite so close to Connery's skin as suggested. According to the film's editor Peter Hunt, there was a small, thin pane of glass between them. And in some shots, the creature was filmed on the bare arm of Connery's stunt double Bob Simmons. But, it was argued, these monsters are lethal and so obviously it couldn't have been done in any other way. One other small curiosity, according to Sir Ken Adam, is that for some shots, the bedroom set had to be turned ninety degrees – with the bed actually on the wall, and the wall done up to look like the floor – in order to persuade the spider to walk the right way.

Anyway, having tired of Bond's shoulder, the creature, rather than biting him, simply wanders off on to the pillow. These days – a gentler age – any one of us would have got up, reached for the phone, and perhaps asked a member of staff to collect the arachnid in a box and release it safely outside. Not our hero. Leaping out of bed, he dislodges the poor beast, beats it to death with a boot – with Monty Norman's fretful music adding a note of further hysteria – and runs into the en-suite bathroom to be sick.

At a preview screening, the audience were extremely amused by the neurotic score which in fact had been made extra-dramatic at the insistence of Cubby Broccoli. Terence Young, standing at the back of the cinema, told Broccoli: 'I told you, Cubby. I told you they'd laugh.' Broccoli replied: 'Of course they're laughing. They're laughing with us.'[2] Actually, in a curious way, it's possible that both men were right. And the audience were also laughing at themselves for watching this stuff in the first place.

In Fleming's novel, the creature in the bed was a highly venomous centipede that made its way unerringly towards Bond's groin. Thus the sense of menace was rather heightened. But big spiders are undeniably more cinematic.

As a swift digression, the damage this and other films did to the reputation of the poor old tarantula may be irreparable. Other bad PR for the species came in *Sherlock Holmes and the Spider Woman* (1944), *Tarantula!* (1955), Hammer's *The Hound of the Baskervilles* (1959) where one particular cutie creeps on to Christopher Lee's shoulder, and the opening scene of *Raiders of the Lost Ark* (1981) where Alfred Molina has his back covered with them.

In my London primary schooldays, in the 1970s, people from London Zoo would sometimes come on special visits with a docile Mexican red-kneed tarantula that they had called Belinda. The purpose of their visits was to demonstrate what gentle souls Belinda and her tarantula ilk were. Certainly they could bite, we were told, but only in self-defence, and the bite would be painful but in most cases do little more than make you feel nauseous. Oh, and if they were especially agitated, these spiders would vibrate and eject all their leg hairs, which could irritate and sting. But that was that.

Would any of us volunteer to have Belinda sit on our arms though? Not on your nelly. All of us in that classroom had seen *Dr. No* – it had its British TV premiere in 1975. Did these people from London Zoo take us for fools?

Obviously, after shenanigans of that sort, the dastardly Professor Dent must get his, and so he does, after repeatedly firing a gun into what he imagines is Bond's sleeping form in Miss Taro's bed. 'You've had your six,' is Bond's famous line, disclosing his hiding place behind the bedroom door. He then shoots Dent in the back.

Even now, there are flurries of debate about the ungentlemanliness of Bond's behaviour, and what a shocking break this cold-blooded shooting forms with the more conventional heroism of the 1950s. But there is a symmetry in the narrative that renders it natural; remember, earlier on in the story, we saw the much more shocking murder of Strangways's secretary at the hands of Dr. No's henchmen as she went about her radio business.

And elsewhere, pert Miss Taro is treated with relative lenience, simply being tricked into accompanying the local gendarmerie to help them with their enquiries.

By this stage in the film – certainly when it is viewed now – one is shouting 'Get on with it!' at the screen. Luckily, the narrative obliges, scooting us to ally Quarrel's boat and his trip to Crab Key with Bond. Felix Leiter of the CIA does not go with them. We are entitled to ask exactly what it is that Felix does for a living. Novelist Kingsley Amis later wrote of the character:

> The point of Felix Leiter, such a nonentity as a piece of characterization, is that he, the American, takes orders from Bond, the Britisher, and that Bond is constantly doing better than he, showing himself, not braver or more devoted, but smarter, wilier, tougher, more resourceful, the incarnation of little old England with her quiet ways and shoe-string budget wiping the eye of big global-tentacled multi-billion-dollar-appropriating America.[3]

When the narrative reaches Crab Key the film at last settles into an idiom that is recognisably Bondian. First, there is the colour, sharpness and beauty of the location shoot; and second – it really hardly needs saying, this – there is Ursula Andress rising from the sea. It is all so wholly familiar now that we assume somehow that the scene has been a part of our cultural life since the dawn of cinema. It cannot be stressed enough that nothing like this had ever been seen or shown before. Not even in one of those swimsuity, watery Esther Williams films. Certainly we never saw Esther rising from the waves in a white bikini with a dagger at her hip.

Anyway, here she is, Honey Ryder (Honeychile in the novel). She is here to collect conch shells before selling them on. She is distrustful of Bond, and quite rightly, who wouldn't be? But there is no time for sauce! Dr. No's men are patrolling in boats and Bond and Honey, together with Quarrel, must take cover.

Indeed, it was for this scene that Ian Fleming himself showed up on location. He was there with wife Ann, plus the poet Stephen Spender (it is quite difficult to imagine Spender and Bond in the same part of the Venn diagram) and friend Peter Quennell. This party witnessed Andress rising from the waves, and they were also there for the gun attack on the beach.

Director Terence Young had to scream at Spender and Fleming to 'get down' behind a sand dune for the filming of the bullets hitting the sand, an effect achieved apparently by detonating buried condoms. But it is quite funny to see Fleming's Jamaican paradise being invaded so emphatically by his fictional creation.

Is Quarrel (as played by John Kitzmiller) a shocking example of rolling-eyed racism or actually a rather shrewdly played second-string character? Some commentators have found his relationship with Bond offensively racist, pointing to the way that Bond orders him around. On the other hand, Quarrel is perhaps the only straightforwardly likeable character in the entire film, and that includes Bond.

His function may appear to be one of simple comic relief (and I am willing to bet that the children in the audience both identified with and adored him); but, as in the novel, Quarrel and Honey form a curious partnership – allies of Bond yet somehow both of them making Bond seem parental. Perhaps that is further evidence of both monstrous racism *and* sexism.

So: Bond, Honey and Quarrel are pursued through the lush flora of Crab Key, then face a night-time confrontation with the flame-throwing 'dragon' of local legend – an armoured truck that makes its atmospheric way across the mangrove swamps and shockingly burns poor Quarrel to death. Horrid old imperialist he may be, but Bond's grief is perfectly apparent as he fights off henchmen to take one final mournful look at his comrade's scorched body. It is all part of the rough edges of Connery's performance here. The throwaway insouciance, that post-modernist acknowledgement that this is all pure nonsense, was still a couple of films away.

And thus – hooray! – to the headquarters, and here is where everything steps up a further notch. There was the steamy value in having Honey and Bond undressed to be sent on a conveyor belt through a radioactivity decontamination shower. How ultra-modern this and the Geiger counters must have seemed at the time. After the showers, Bond and Honey are vigorously scrubbed with brooms. There are those who would pay good money for that. Can radiation really be scrubbed off in this manner? If so, what was all that Chernobyl fuss about? Anyway, our heroes progress further inwards into the HQ – nice big copper airlock doors, aesthetically arresting without being too distracting.

One mistake the film makes, upon Bond and Honey reaching the HQ reception area, is that it never explains why Dr. No appears to have built himself his own personal underground Travelodge. We must turn to the novel to find out why. Ingeniously, the place is decked out as a hotel just in case any nosy government officials should ever pay a visit and feel that they want to stay over.

And here we come to the great conversational confrontation between hero and madman villain, a formula to which the series was to remain unfailingly true. Although interestingly this scene acknowledges its own B-movie roots, with Bond accusing No of pursuing 'World domination. The same mad old dream. Our asylums are full of people who think they're Napoleon. Or God.' Dr. No looks suitably unimpressed.

Thence to the climax. Honey's fate is to be tied up near a rapidly filling underground reservoir. This was deemed a more credible peril than Fleming's alternative: that is, having peckish crabs marching all over her and taking bites as they did so. Even Fleming, by the end of the novel, saw the absurdity of such a proposition: Bond asks Honeychile how she escaped with scarcely a nip, and Honey explains simply that *crabs don't eat people*. It was only Dr. No who fondly imagined that they did.

The production team brought in a crate of very big crabs, just to be on the safe side. But these poor creatures ended up getting frozen and when revived, were rather sluggish about clambering over Ursula. They went straight to the cutting room floor.

For us eight-year-old boys, the real nerve-shredding excitement came as Bond escaped his cell and clambered into his first (and I think, only) ventilation duct system, which, as tradition demands, is large enough to accommodate a Nissan hatchback. First he must go through the scorching ordeal as the pipeline heats up; then he must go through the drenching ordeal as water comes whooshing down said pipeline. All to the accompaniment of electronic sound effects that sound like 1950s science fiction. Now Bond must — through the stroke of luck most commonly experienced by those clambering through ventilation ducts — find the grille that leads directly to the villain's command centre.

What a command centre! To see it now is to be instantly hurtled back to a different era — one where modernist architecture, machines with dials, tanks of bubbling luminous radioactive water and people in white plastic suits instantly put one in mind of school trips to the Science Museum to see an exhibition of the Power Station of the Future. It is pure *Look and Learn*. Sir Ken Adam has said that he visited some British nuclear facilities, including Harwell, for inspiration.

Plus there is a countdown! In 1962, countdowns had a certain freshness associated purely with Cape Canaveral and space launches. The phrase 'T minus . . .' was relatively new. And now here was a villain using one. Truly Dr. No must have been a genius.

So it is left to Bond to find a traditionalist solution: punching a henchman, stealing his white plastic suit, and then fiddling with a big dial in sabotage fashion. Dr. No spots this and goes for Bond with his shiny black metal hands. They tussle close to the boiling radioactive water. The countdown approaches zero. Dr. No appears to gain the upper (metal) hand. But Bond feints, No takes a tumble into that glowing water, and we last see his metal hands clawing in vain at the gantry.

Then, setting the marker down for countless reruns and imitators, the following happens: hooting klaxons indicate forthcoming self-destruction of base; Bond desperately looks for girl as panicking henchmen run hither and thither; Bond finds girl and instantly, there they are outside, flames and explosions everywhere, people leaping off platforms into the sea. Bond and girl grab control of boat and the next thing we know, they are out in the open ocean, snogging.

And with this production, the alchemists Broccoli and Saltzman contrived to turn base matter into pure gold. Of course Ian Fleming was a great genius for giving a sheen of sex appeal and sophistication to a daft genre. But these producers gave it that all-important further ingredient that ensured that schoolboys the entire world over would come flocking back: futurism.

In the novel, we hear of 'rocket toppling' but are merely told that it has something to do with a giant gyroscope. Ian Fleming did not want to trouble us with the precise details. Nor indeed did the film-makers in script terms – but Ken Adam gave us a most seductive idea of a scientifically inclined super-villain. This prototype HQ is a thing of beauty that somehow crosses Frank Lloyd Wright with the Smithsonian Institute. Added to this was the mad timeliness of it all. The year previously, the Soviets had succeeded in launching the first man into outer space. Yuri Gagarin was a global hero. The Space Race was at a peak of intensity. Countless young people looked out of their bedroom windows at night, gazed up at the stars, and wondered.

The week the film came out, the number one hit single in the UK was 'Telstar' by the Tornadoes – a suitably futuristic piece of guitar work inspired by the satellite of the same name.

The film's release also came just a week before the Cuban missile crisis, the US/Soviet stand-off that is popularly supposed to have brought the world closer than it has ever been to nuclear war. American president Kennedy and Russian leader Khrushchev squared up to each other over a US blockade preventing Soviet missiles getting to Cuba. The world – as the phrase always goes – held its breath. Both sides eventually backed down but the notion of worldwide nuclear conflict was by then implanted firmly in every mind.

John F. Kennedy – perceived as youthful and glamorous, still wrapped in the mantle of the Camelot image that had been bestowed by journalists – had been elected in 1960. Khrushchev had taken over in 1956, several years after Comrade Stalin's death; many hoped that he would turn out to be a reformer and that the freezing conditions of the Cold War would warm up. The 1956 Soviet invasion of Hungary ensured that that was not to be the case. Then there was the frenetic activity of the Space Race: the multiple launches of satellites and of capsules, occasionally containing dogs.

Super-irritable Khrushchev did not make life easy for anyone. In 1960, British Prime Minister Harold Macmillan went to a great deal of trouble to hold together a superpower conference that had met in Paris. This was impossible after the Soviet capture of Gary Powers, the pilot of a US spy plane which had been deep in Russian territory; it was a deeply embarrassing international incident, made worse by Khrushchev's insistence on a full public apology from the then US president Eisenhower. The conference collapsed.

The election of JFK seemed to hold out the prospect of a new relationship with the Russian bear. The Cuban missile crisis proved that this would not be the case.

And while all this was going on, British audiences were queuing up to see the first of many Bond villains stirring up tension between the two super-blocs. 'East and west – these are just points on the compass,' Dr. No tells Bond, indicating his own airy disdain for geopolitics, and also setting out the template for all the future films in the series. For the first time, while a fictional British secret agent on screen was saving the world, British influence in the real world was starting to wane rather sharply.

But when it came to questions of tensions on either side of the Iron Curtain, curiously, Broccoli and Fleming were in accord, just at the very point when everyone else in the world was assuming that the Third World

War was an inevitability. At the beginning of 1963, Fleming had this to say to the Jamaican newspaper the *Daily Gleaner*: 'They [the superpowers] will finally decide to call the game off and we shall all be able to settle down and not worry about it any more.'[4]

This was important from the commercial point of view as well. Broccoli had sensed from the start that if he wanted these films to have the widest possible international audience, and indeed the longest possible shelf-life in terms of cinematic reissues (this was long before the age of DVD granted all films immortality), then the villains would have to be apolitical and largely from the private sector.

Broccoli was perfectly right. So much so, in fact, that many years later in 1975, he was invited to Moscow; the Soviet authorities were so admiring of his balanced approach that they wondered if he might be agreeable to producing a blockbusting action adventure film in Russia? Nothing ever came of this but the very idea is intriguing and pays tribute to Broccoli's superb commercial and artistic acumen, for there were not many who could be said to have straddled the Iron Curtain in such a way.

The first screenwriter assigned to *Dr. No*, clever Wolf Mankowitz, author of *A Kid For Two Farthings*, was clearly acutely aware of the antique nature of much of Fleming's source material. So he instantly tried to make it a little more post-modern and knowing, with the device of turning Dr. No from a metal-handed psychopath into a monkey. Albert R. Broccoli considered this notion for all of about four seconds before dismissing it sharply.

So Richard Maibaum and Johanna Harwood were hired, the latter acting as a kind of script editor, and the screenplay went back to basics, with the omission of Dr. No's original fate – which was being buried alive under tons of rotting guano at Bond's hand. Also omitted were Bond's climactic crawl through a metal cage full of tarantulas and his subsequent plummet to some sort of rock-pool when he engages in a brief struggle with a giant squid.

The above précis, incidentally, gives a flavour of what happened to Ian Fleming when he started to run short of ideas in any given novel. Such scenarios would not have looked out of place in a black and white Saturday morning serial for children. Combine that with the desperation of the giant crab gambit and you see how – not for the first time – Bond screenwriters actually came to the rescue of their parent author.

Much has been made of the neatness and precision of the directing but here, as with all other examples, being a director on a Bond film is not so much a job for an auteur as a circus ringmaster. Although Terence Young eventually landed the job, the director's chair had originally been offered to Bryan Forbes, who had recently written the brilliantly black-hearted screenplay for *The League of Gentlemen* (1960), and who would go on to direct such classics as *Whistle Down the Wind* (1964) and *The Slipper and the Rose* (1976).

Forbes turned it down, possibly on the grounds that he caught a sniff of B movie. It was then offered to Guy Hamilton, who, it transpires, was otherwise engaged. Hamilton was of course to make a later triumphant Bond debut with *Goldfinger* (1964). So it was to Terence Young – a veteran of not-such-classic films like *Safari* (1956) – that the honour fell.

Young had a budget just short of a million to play with. In the early 1960s, this was not bad money at all, though it wasn't remotely in the super-league. If you want an example of budgetary super-league, look at David Lean's *Lawrence of Arabia* (1962) with its awesome location filming, illimitable desert landscapes and breathtakingly choreographed extras by the thousand.

And Young had his Bond, in the shape of Sean Connery. One of the director's roles now was, as the crew saw it, to be Professor Higgins to Connery's Eliza Dolittle.

It has to be said that in this debut outing, Connery looks distinctly ill-at-ease. He confessed to co-star and friend Eunice Gayson that when he first learned he had got the job, he had thought the idea was mad. Of course, Connery was a perfect professional but for any pro, this would have been quite a tricky role to settle into (look at Roger Moore – he was never completely comfortable with Bond until his third film). In some scenes – most notably in the nightclub where Connery and Leiter are questioning the photographer – Connery's performance is jarringly irritable.

It can't have helped Connery to know that he was being closely observed by Ian Fleming himself. Plus there was the knowledge that Broccoli and Saltzman planned at least five or six Bond films. The success of this enterprise rather rested on Connery's shoulders. He had to ensure that the public would accept him.

This is the reason for the introduction of a note of black humour. Only one note, mind, after Bond has been involved in a car chase with a hearse packed with baddies. The hearse loses control, tumbles over the edge of a cliff, explodes – and Bond explains to another motorist, 'I think they were on their way to a funeral.'

All right, it's not much of a gag, but it was the first inkling of where Connery as much as the producers wanted the films to go. The insouciant quip following the death of a baddie was to become a Connery trademark, while Roger Moore elevated it to something approaching high art. But let us not jump ahead. Connery was swift to see that without this saving grace, the character of Bond could quite easily become repulsive.

In later interviews, Terence Young suggested – on the face of it, erroneously – that the vital addition of humour was down to him. Every single gruelling grinding minute of his later Bond effort *Thunderball* (1965) puts that assertion straight back in its box.

The casting of the first – and most iconic – Bond girl had been rather less exhausting than that of Bond himself. What happened very simply was this: Broccoli was sent a photograph of Ursula Andress, taken by her husband John Derek. She was depicted in a drenched T-shirt. About fifteen seconds later, Andress had the job. Her Swiss voice was not right and she didn't at that time have fluent English. Indeed, Broccoli repeated the comment of his casting director, that Andress sounded like 'a Dutch comedian'. So she was dubbed throughout the film by Monica van der Zyl. Who would ever know?

Equally important was Bond's first adversary. Noël Coward, Fleming's Jamaican neighbour (he had the house next door to Goldeneye), was apparently offered the job. His famous response came in the form of a telegram: 'Dr. No. No, no, no.' There is a sweet photograph of him posing with Sean Connery in Jamaica, on location for that very film. Nope. You can't see Coward with those epicanthic false eyelids. He did right to pass it up.

Next up was well-respected New York actor Joseph Wiseman who, with a few qualms (he made comments about not wanting to become known for a 'Charlie Chan murder mystery'), donned the eyelids and the black metal hands. Now, of course, Wiseman is remembered for nothing other than this Charlie Chan murder mystery.

In the novel, Julius No is an uncanny creature. Other than his metal hands – pincers in the novel – he has a high-domed forehead and some-thing of his shape and gait remind Fleming of the venomous centipede introduced into Bond's bed a few chapters earlier. Born of a German father and Chinese mother, No swiftly became a criminal mastermind, diddling the Tong out of a million dollars and being forced to go on the run before ending up working for SPECTRE.

In the film, Wiseman makes No a slightly less layered creation. Indeed, in his first confrontation with Bond (in the lounge area of his lair, complete with jumbo aquarium, antique furniture and recently acquired stolen Goya), the conventions are openly mocked in post-modernist fashion. But, in cinematic terms, there hadn't been too many villains who had been so ambitious. There had been Ming the Merciless from the *Flash Gordon* serials, of course. The great Fu Manchu himself had been personated on the screen by Boris Karloff in 1932. Perhaps more interestingly, Fritz Lang's Dr Mabuse was a rather more serious super-criminal from the 1920s Expressionist film series of the same name; but even Dr Mabuse had his limits.

None the less, Wiseman is there as a template that would be followed with remarkable fidelity over the next four decades. Even the recent incarnation of Le Chiffre, as played by Mads Mikkelsen in *Casino Royale* (2006), with his tendency to weep tears of blood, can trace his noble heritage back to Wiseman's remarkably restrained performance.

In *No*, despite the dazzling entrance of Ursula Andress, sex is rather on the back burner, certainly compared to subsequent films. The swift bout of tonsil tennis with Sylvia Trench and a scene in bed with naughty Miss Taro aside, the film is surprisingly chaste. But then, so too is the novel. Indeed, in Fleming's original, there is a curious innocence about the relationship between Bond and Honeychile.

She is seen as a child of the wild, though one who has been horribly abused by men on previous occasions; now, Honeychile openly wonders why Bond is not making moves on her and if his reluctance might have some physical cause. In the film, Bond and Honey are chaperoned for the first part of their partnership by Quarrel. And in any case, they are being hunted down by Dr. No's guards and when you are sitting underwater at the bottom of a river, breathing through a hollowed-out bamboo shoot, there is precious little opportunity for sizzling sauce.

Later, there looks like there might be a quick opportunity in Dr. No's subterranean hotel as Bond and Honey are decked out in their new orientalist costumes; but the Doctor thwarts them with spiked coffee. It is only in the final scene that Bond and Honey get to clinch; in other words, nothing here that could cause a backlash of outrage.

For if there was one thing that Broccoli and Saltzman knew about their new formula, it was this: the film had to get past the censors and it had to be family-friendly. Now in those days, the British film censors, headed by John

Trevelyan, were a twitchy lot. They had already been through the grief caused by the advent of Hammer horror, and by the British New Wave, with such epics as *Leather Boys* (1963) and *A Taste of Honey* (1962). It has been argued that if Broccoli and Saltzman had tried to produce Bond in the 1950s, they would never have got past the BBFC. But actually they went into fairly detailed discussions with Trevelyan before production in 1962 to map out what would be acceptable and what wouldn't.

The critical response was enthusiastic (with the exception of the *Monthly Film Bulletin* which described Connery as 'wooden and boorish'). For instance, Dilys Powell of the *Sunday Times* had these admiring words to say: 'The jokes . . . are tossed away with exactly the right carelessness. The excitements have a . . . skin-crawling effect, but they aren't overemphasised; the hair's breadth escape from the ambush is handled with the nonchalance proper to agent 007; all in the day's work, now for the next, please.' Margaret Hinxman in the *Daily Mail* had this to say: 'While deploring its sadism, its ethics and its amorality, I admit I enjoyed every depraved and dazzling moment of it.'

Incidentally, Hugh Gaitskell – then leader of the Labour Party and also lover of Ian Fleming's wife Ann – was all for the film himself. He wrote, with a nice touch of irony, to Fleming: 'The combination of sex, violence, alcohol and – at intervals – good food and nice clothes is, to one who lives such a circumscribed life as I do, irresistible.'[5]

We all know of Paul Johnson's immortal 1958 description of the novels – intended as a denouncement rather than an endorsement – that they were little more than 'sex, snobbery and sadism'. The films anaesthetised the snobbery and pulled back a fraction on the sex and sadism; but they still gingered up what was becoming a slightly jaded genre.

One of the reasons the British public, as well as the critics, were so keen – we will get on to the Americans later, when they become keen – was that British thrillers in recent years had tended either towards gangsters or war. Either you had Jack Hawkins, or John Mills, or Dirk Bogarde in uniform, re-fighting the battles of just a few years previously on sea, on land, in the air; or you had Stanley Baker, William Hartnell and Diana Dors firing very smoky guns in very smoggy streets, with people in loud suits running protection rackets. In terms of family cinema, the idea of colourful adventure did not run much beyond this. Heroism chiefly meant military operations of great daring and endeavour, and in large teams. In other words, it was all a little backward-looking. With that dash of science fiction – and the element that this agent was in effect a lone freewheeler – Bond pointed towards a space-age future.

So the boys, the critics and the wider general public loved Bond's screen debut. And what of Bond's creator? Various accounts across the years have suggested that Ian Fleming was not tremendously thrilled by Connery's interpretation of his baby. But Fleming's literary agent Peter Janson-Smith – who later went on to manage Glidrose, the company that oversaw Fleming's literary estate – recalls somewhat differently.

'Initially, I think his eyebrows went up on hearing the news – but actually, very quickly, Ian was all for Sean,' Janson-Smith says. 'In fact, he was all for him ever since they had met out in Jamaica during the filming of *Dr. No*. From my own point of view, I was simply pleased that a movie was at last up and running. And Cubby Broccoli was a very clever man, clever and nice.'

The other point to make here about Fleming's reaction to Connery is that Fleming was a literary snob. He considered that he knew what fine writing was. He protested that the Bond books were mere 'cosh-boy' thrillers, suggesting that it was just something that he did out of amusement. The great success of his creation would have brought him financial relief, but possibly also a certain amount of secret embarrassment, particularly in his smart social circle. The advent of the films would have amplified this embarrassment.

Think of what the social agony must have been like to be Fleming at a special preview of the film, described in a letter from his wife Ann to Evelyn Waugh. She told the great author how the producers hired a private cinema at the smart Travellers' Club; how among the guests were the Duke and Duchess of Bedford, and Lord and Lady Bessborough; and how everyone in this small audience 'roared with laughter' at the tarantula scene in particular.[6] Fleming must simply have been writhing.

In fact it is all too easy to see Ann, and Peter Quennell and Evelyn Waugh and all the rest of the gang, pointing and laughing and generally mocking Bond – another of their literary friends, Cyril Connolly, wrote a spoof entitled *Bond Strikes Camp* – and it is equally easy to imagine Fleming feigning a certain self-deprecation about it all and confiding to his friends that he thought Connery a little below the salt. Indeed, some years later, Connery remarked of Fleming that he was 'a terrific snob but very good company'.[7]

But of course for the final proof of what Fleming really thought, we only have to turn to the Bond novels that he wrote after Connery took the role; Bond is belatedly given a (dead) Scottish father in his 1963 novel *On Her Majesty's Secret Service*. Prior to this, we had heard nothing of Bond's childhood. Indeed, Fleming admitted that he continued writing the books with Connery in mind.

On his first outing, Connery was aware of the rougher edges of his performance, but in an interview in New York some twenty years later, he insisted that Ian Fleming himself had to take some of the responsibility for that. 'I had to start playing Bond from scratch,' said the actor. 'Not even Ian Fleming knew much about Bond at this time. He has no mother. He has no father. He doesn't come from anywhere and he hadn't been anywhere when he became 007. He was born – ker-plump! – 33 years old.'[8]

Some critics were less forgiving, including Ian Cameron of *The Spectator* magazine who said that the film was 'too inept to be as pernicious as it might have been'. Elsewhere, there were interesting comparisons with the works of Alfred Hitchcock, suggesting that Terence Young's direction wasn't up to that mark, but that the thrills conveyed were none the less Hitchcockian in nature.

So, naturally, *Dr. No*'s large and enthusiastic UK audience was welcome news for Broccoli and Saltzman and United Artists, who had stumped up the money and who quickly saw a handsome return. The film was not released in the US until the following year. It fared middlingly well there – nothing spectacular in terms of receipts, but it did good word-of-mouth business with the drive-in theatres. But Bond had to wait until 1964, and the phenomenon of *Goldfinger*, before the American audience – vital to the success of any film if the producers wanted to turn a proper, decent profit – became properly enthusiastic.

There is simply not enough sex in *Dr. No* to make the claim that the film was instrumental in opening the 1960s free-love floodgates. But its release in 1962 does now seem extraordinarily timely. The Beatles released their debut single 'Love Me Do'; the satire boom as exemplified by the BBC's *That Was the Week That Was* threw aside any old-school notions of deference and the Establishment; on television, new series such as *Z-Cars* were bringing a startling grittiness to popular drama while ABC's home-grown espionage thriller *The Avengers* had introduced a radical new heroine – Mrs Cathy Gale – who was a leather-sporting, man-throwing judo expert. Overall, for the younger generation, there was a thrilling sense of transgression in the air. And against all this, Old Etonian Harold Macmillan was Prime Minister, but his Conservative administration was starting to struggle.

Into such a febrile atmosphere strode this fundamentally classless secret agent. How really could Sean Connery have failed?

Y ou cannot go far wrong with a film if it involves a sequence in which the screen is filled with a map, an animated red line showing the route through the map, and a mixed shot somewhere of train wheels revolving furiously. It is the classic cinematic method of conveying a long journey. Steven Spielberg even paid tribute to it in *Raiders of the Lost Ark*, this time using the map and the red line to depict the route of a U-boat.

Even by 1963 – the dawn of the age of mass air travel, all those silvery gleaming Pan-Am and BOAC planes – that image of the map, and the animated red line, was looking a little foxed. That didn't stop director Terence Young though.

After the glittering futurism of *Dr. No*, there is much of this surprising olde worlde feel running through the sequel, *From Russia with Love* (1963). The opening teaser sequence is set in the night-time ornamental gardens of a large country house (this was apparently a tribute to Alain Resnais's *Last Year at Marienbad* (1961), a profoundly enigmatic and elegant art-houser that might not have seemed quite so lengthy if it had featured psychopathic lesbians and garotting wires concealed in wristwatches); among these beautiful topiary structures, a Bond lookalike is stalked to the death in a training exercise by Red Grant (Robert Shaw).

And from this point on, all the flashing lights and countdown stuff was jettisoned in favour of a story that harked back to an older form of espionage thriller, the type that one would have found in Eric Ambler, or in Graham Greene's 'entertainments'.

Ian Fleming's novel of 1957 is one of his tightest and best. In it, the Soviet counter-espionage organisation SMERSH constructs a complex plan to destroy agent 007 – not merely to kill him, but also to humiliate him and bring shame down upon the entire British secret service. The plan involves a honey-trap in the shape of beautiful cipher operative Tatiana Romanova, a code-breaking machine called the SPEKTOR and a lethal ambush on board the Orient Express from Istanbul to Paris.

The novel was unusual in that Bond was absent for the first hundred pages or so. Instead, we are drawn into the chilly, oppressive world of Soviet politics and the KGB, and are pulled into their manoeuvres and plots. Slowly we are introduced not only to young, vulnerable Tatiana but also her SMERSH spy chief Rosa Klebb, one of Fleming's most exuberantly horrible creations. This toad-like predatory lesbian brings a reluctant Tatiana under her wing, failing to disclose the full nature of her mission to entrap Bond. And thus, the wheels are in place for a genuinely electrifying thriller.

Bond is lured to Istanbul with the twin promise of the girl and the SPEKTOR, while knowing that some form of trap must be waiting for him. In this city, where East and West commingle, Bond deals with the charismatic Kerim Bey, who introduces him to the vast Byzantine subterranean halls from where he can spy on the Russian embassy. There is a gypsy fight, Tatiana insinuates herself into Bond's bed, they are filmed through a two-way mirror while 'forming passionate arabesques', then it's off to catch that train, with girl and code-breaking device, and also to meet the Irish psychopath Red Grant, now a fully trained SMERSH killer and the man sent to end Bond's life in ignominy.

The tone of this novel is quite different to more rumbustious fare like 1959's *Goldfinger* and *Live and Let Die*; this is the first time that Fleming has allowed us to become so intimate with the villains of the piece. And the old-fashioned exoticism of the settings — Istanbul, the Golden Horn, Saint Sophia, the Orient Express — pulls one back a few years to earlier espionage dramas. In particular, one might see that Ian Fleming was doffing his hat to his great thriller-writing contemporary Eric Ambler.

In *The Mask of Dimitrios* (1938), Ambler's novel-writing academic protagonist is drawn into a murky pool of intrigue and espionage that drags him all over Europe, from Greece to Paris, on the trail of a double-dealing agent who might not be as dead as people believe him to be. The protagonist encounters a variety of spectacularly untrustworthy figures, while the continent itself is presented as a shifting, blurring backdrop almost specifically designed to confuse a fish-out-of-water Englishman.

Ambler and Fleming eventually came to share an agent — Peter Janson-Smith. They also struck up a friendship and enjoyed the occasional lunch together. This must be why Ambler gets the supremely post-modernist double-take name-check in *From Russia* as 007, on board a plane to Istanbul, settles down to read *The Mask of Dimitrios*!

The two other great Orient Express thrillers that possibly influenced Fleming were *Stamboul Train* (1932) by Graham Greene and *Murder on the Orient Express* (1934) by Agatha Christie. The latter, although an ingenious whodunnit, none the less manages to use the train in the same manner as Greene's twisty thriller: that is, as a setting, the train seems to encourage transgressive behaviour. When everyone is in transit, speeding through the valleys of all those different countries of Europe, national laws – and indeed more basic moral laws – somehow no longer apply.

In fact *Stamboul Train*, Greene's first bestseller, gives us much of the train suspense paraphernalia that would come to be reused in *From Russia* – from the claustrophobia of enclosed apartments (and the corresponding erotic frisson of such places), to people ducking their heads in crowded corridors to avoid detection, to bribable conductors, so useful when seeking out the identities of fellow passengers, to the immense difficulty of even finding a hiding place on a train.

Ian Fleming would no doubt also have been familiar with the 1938 Alfred Hitchcock entertainment *The Lady Vanishes*, once more set on some sort of trans-Europe express. This is a brilliant slab of pre-war spy suspense. The 'lady' in question, a sweet and elderly party called Miss Froy (played by Dame May Whitty), very simply goes missing as the train rattles along. Trying to solve the mystery are Margaret Lockwood and an initially sceptical Michael Redgrave. There are moments of revelation in the dining car and a fight in the guard's van, and passengers in different compartments behave suspiciously when their compartment doors are opened.

Beastly foreign nationals are behind the whole thing; for Miss Froy is in fact a spy who is carrying a secret message back to England, coded in the form of a whistled tune. The enemy have tried to kidnap and substitute her but they are no match for the indefatigable Brits. It ends with an amusing shoot-out between uniformed bad guys and stiff-upper-lipped Basil Radford and Naunton Wayne. Ian Fleming had some highly distinguished footsteps to follow in.

The choice of *From Russia* as the second Bond movie was made relatively simple for Broccoli and Saltzman: the novel had received an unbelievably good dollop of publicity from young President Kennedy, who disclosed that it was among the ten books he was currently reading. It was not possible to have a more glamorous endorsement than one directly from Camelot and Fleming's sales went into orbit accordingly. (By some dark symmetry, it later emerged that another of *From Russia*'s great fans was Lee Harvey Oswald.)

But the producers also realised that one crucial modification would have to be made to the story: instead of the Russians trying to bring Bond down, it should instead be the apolitical forces of SPECTRE. SPECTRE had a neat motive too: the organisation would be seeking revenge for the destruction of Dr. No's rocket-toppling shenanigans.

In script terms, however, this would prove to be a headache, for they could not lose Rosa Klebb or Red Grant. It was explained that Klebb and the strategist Kronsteen were in fact secretly working for SPECTRE without actually having defected. According to screenwriter Richard Maibaum, best-selling author Len Deighton – he of *The Ipcress File*, of which we will hear more later – was in on early drafts and then ducked out.[1] The difficulty comes in accepting that these very senior KGB people are in fact working for someone else on a mission with transnational significance that somehow won't be traced back to them.

But . . . oh well, it actually doesn't matter a very great deal. This sort of confused narrative contortion was something that would happen to later Bond films too, with no apparently harmful side effects. Look at *The Living Daylights* (1987), which involves a plot so complex that entire teams of decoders at Bletchley Park would have found themselves stumped. What matters, as we knew even by the second Bond movie, was the ride.

The ride, to begin with, is a rather stately one. After a cracking opening title sequence – the colourful credits projected on to the gyrating body of a belly dancer to the accompaniment of Lionel Bart's jaunty faux-Russian main title song melody, instrumentally arranged by John Barry – we have a rather grand chess match and then our first meeting with Lotte Lenya's unforgettable Rosa Klebb and Robert Shaw's creepily implacable Red Grant.

What a world of perversity is there in that shot of the bare-chested Shaw, in the SPECTRE garden, being physically appraised by Rosa Klebb, who quietly puts on a knuckle-duster and then punches him with maximum force in the stomach.

What a nice contrast, then, to have a subsequent shot of Bond with our old friend Sylvia Trench (Eunice Gayson), by an English river, picnicking and snogging. Actually, the contrast isn't so very great. It actually looks as though Connery and Gayson were filmed literally around the corner of the same hydrangea bush from the Klebb scene. And indeed, they were, more or less. Never mind! Sylvia's plan for further snogs goes awry when Bond is comically summoned back to HQ by a clumping communications device. And for the first time, we see that it is not ideal for the character of Bond to be seen in shorts. They lack a certain dignity.

Sylvia Trench, incidentally, is the only squeeze to have been permitted to return, presumably to give some kind of hint to the censors that while Bond is uproariously promiscuous as he travels the world, when he gets home he is strictly a one-woman man. If so, it is a hint that they were wise to drop. You could not have competition for darling Moneypenny.

What immediately strikes one now is how very European the whole thing feels in contrast to the previous film, and in much sharper contrast to the more transatlantic feel of the films that were to follow. Lotte Lenya was the widow of the brilliant composer Kurt Weill and was well known for her early 1930s German film career. Here, she represented an extraordinary collision of high art and big budget; possibly the most perfect casting ever seen in a Bond film. The scene in which Tatiana – possibly the most beautiful of the Bond girls, as played by Italian actress Daniela Bianchi – meets her for the first time still carries a punch.

Klebb, wearing insanely bottle-lensed spectacles, begins a lesbianic appraisal of her lovely new recruit. The only pity is that we are spared Fleming's original coda to this scene, in which Klebb briefly leaves the room, and then returns wearing grotesquely overapplied make-up and a transparent nightie, beneath which can be seen 'a brassiere consisting of two large pink satin roses' and 'old-fashioned knickers of pink satin with elastic above the knees', and then asks Tatiana to 'come and sit beside me. We must get to know each other better.' Tatiana runs out of the room, literally screaming.

The Istanbul setting gives the film a certain texture that future entries would somehow lack, no matter how exotic the location. Possibly this is because of the age of the cars on the road, or the quality of that Bosporus light. The scene inside St Sophia, which makes very little narrative sense, is none the less rich and beautiful.

The production team made a return to leafy Pinewood in Buckinghamshire for the scenes involving the gypsy encampment, where head of Turkish section Kerim Bey (a brilliant Pedro Armendáriz, who was sadly terminally ill throughout the shoot) takes Bond as some form of a treat. Dinner among these folk comes with extra entertainment thrown in: a bitch-fight between statuesque Martine Beswick and another sparsely clad gypsy lady. While the Bond films could not portray full-on sex in any sense, the sublimated sexy spectacle was clearly permissible. The sequence has not dated especially well, it has to be said; but then it is relatively rare to see on the big screen these days fights between young women that involve scratching, pulling hair and rolling back and forth on straw.

All this nonsense comes prior to an attack on the camp by some Bulgars that in narrative terms is rather difficult to understand. Somewhere in the background, Red Grant saves Bond from a bullet, because he wants the eventual kill to be his. It is all mildly exciting. But what about the main business of cipher-snatching, sex and betrayal?

Hooray! For we are back at Bond's hotel – medium nasty on the scale of such things – and who should that be chastely glimpsed behind some gauzy net curtains, nipping into Bond's bed wearing nothing but a black velvet ribbon around her throat? Good evening Tatiana! But behind a two-way mirror behind the bed, a 16mm camera is whirring away.

Interestingly, it was in 1963 that notions of spying and sexual scandal reached a fevered height in Britain. First, and most famously, they were intertwined in the Profumo affair. As has been well rehearsed across the years, defence minister Jack Profumo had an affair with a call-girl named Christine Keeler who had also been seeing a naval attaché to the Soviet embassy – in other words, a spy – named Yevgeny Ivanov.

Now, after all this time, can we judge whether the public was not so much shocked and outraged as actually secretly rather thrilled by the notion of this *ménage à trois*? After all, there was no suggestion, even in Profumo's subsequent deceit before the House of Commons and his consequent fall from grace, that secrets of any kind had been passed. It was nothing more than a coincidence that the two men had been seeing the same woman; this was really no more than the rather sorry story of a government minister who lied. Nevertheless, the thrill of it was clearly tangible.

Elsewhere, there was real-life blackmail in the Vassall affair. William Vassall was in the 1950s an attaché to the British embassy in Moscow. He was homosexual and in 1955, the KGB entrapped him at a party, first spiking his drink, then photographing him in compromising positions with several men.

Back then in Britain, homosexuality was illegal, and punished with custodial sentences. The KGB began to exert pressure on Vassall; over several years, he passed on information concerning British radar, submarine tracking technology and torpedoes to his Soviet contacts. By 1962, he had been discovered and was put on trial and imprisoned for eighteen years. Once more, the tang of illicit sex made the story utterly compelling for newspapers and general public alike.

It is perhaps unsurprising that by the end of 1963, cloaks and daggers were everywhere to be seen, real or otherwise. For years, there have been rumours that Hugh Gaitskell, leader of the Labour Party (and lover of Ian Fleming's wife Ann), died not of lupus, but of poisoning deliberately carried out when he visited the Soviet embassy in London. And what exactly would have been the purpose of such an assassination? The rumours at this point grew wilder. The theory was that the Soviets might see their favoured man, Harold Wilson, rise to the leadership, and thence into Number 10 Downing Street.

Well, if that really was the master plan of the Supreme Soviet Praesidium, then it is difficult to see how it did them any good in the end. Unless they were plotting to put Britain through an embarrassing devaluation crisis.

There was one other insane rumour around at the time too: that in order to ensure his compliance, the Russians had 16mm film of Harold Wilson taken while he was at the Board of Trade in the 1950s, engaging in unusual activity in a Moscow hotel bedroom. God, but doesn't such stuff make you nostalgic for the Cold War? When was the last time anyone heard such an amusing rumour about a serving Prime Minister?

Slightly more seriously, 1963 also happened to be a rather sensitive year for the real-life MI6. Some seven years previously, it – and the nation – had been stunned by the defection to Russia of two Foreign Office men, Guy Burgess and Donald Maclean. The treachery of these men, it seemed, had stretched back through the war, right back to the starry idealism of 1930s Cambridge, when even Stalin's purges and reign of terror against the kulaks could not cloud youthful enthusiasm for the intellectual ideal of communism.

Now, it was time for Maclean and Burgess's old accomplice, 'the Third Man', to cross to the other side of the Iron Curtain: Kim Philby. In fact, on the occasion of the original defections, Philby had been asked to leave the service. But he was subsequently deemed not to be a risk and reinstated. His days of dealings with the Russians were not over, though, and, after questioning by an MI6 officer in Beirut, Philby defected to the Soviet Union via 'tramp steamer'.

Once again, there was almost preternatural timing on the part of Saltzman and Broccoli. Although at the time the general public knew nothing of this, there was also great internal disquiet at MI6 at the prospect of a 'fourth man', not to mention rumours of a 'fifth' at the very top of the security service itself.

Incidentally, the Soviets might just have had a sneaking admiration for *From Russia*: for five years later, in 1968, the British ambassador to Moscow, Sir Geoffrey Harrison, had a 'moment of madness' assignation with a woman called 'Galya', which was dutifully filmed from behind a two-way mirror. But the Soviets gained little from the exercise: Sir Geoffrey instantly confessed all to the Foreign Office.

So much for the sleazy world of real-life spies. For Bond, the compromising reels may be rolling but he is back on more familiar territory when next, he has to steal the LEKTOR decoding device, a plan which involves heading underground and blowing up the Russians' Istanbul base from below. Such is Connery's ease now in the role that he makes this section of the film – quietly putting on a gas mask as Soviet officials run hither and thither in panic – look comically simple. His insouciance was already to the fore.

And so, with the girl and ally Kerim Bey and the MacGuffin, it's off to the railway station to catch that Orient Express. Just a few days trailing through the Balkans, and thence into Venice, and all will be well. But here is where the film reaches its suspenseful peak as Robert Shaw's psychotic Red Grant boards the train at Zagreb in the guise of an English agent come to aid Bond.

In the novel, there is certainly a great deal of snobbery in this sequence, though not of a sort that actually helps Bond. 007 notices the slightly wandering accent, the Windsor-knotted tie (to Bond, an indicator of vanity) and 'agent Nash's' infuriating use of the endearment 'old man'. But still nothing actually clicks until Grant has pulled the gun.

In the film, Bond is famously on to Grant's case very much faster in the dining car as the hapless assassin, so ignorant of the vital do's and don'ts, orders red wine to accompany fish.

Ironically, in this day and age, there's simply nothing wrong with that. Why the hell shouldn't you order red wine with fish? Yum. Go ahead, Liberty Hall. Although the red should be chilled and not matched with anchovies. Anyway, as a consequence, anyone under the age of thirty might find that part of the film a little baffling now.

But even in the context of the time, this part of the story fails to ring true on another level. And that is that we are expected to believe that Connery's Bond belongs to a much more rarefied social class than Shaw's Grant. The thing is, of course, that there is nothing public school about Connery's Bond at all – nothing that hints of etiquette or debutante balls or Eton or not holding a knife like a pen or flinching at the word 'toilet'. He is classless. As is Grant.

Anyway, Grant slips a knockout pill in Tatiana's drink (and hooray for that – it might be a thriller device that has its origins somewhere in the early eleventh century but it is always cheering to see it) and it's back to Bond's compartment for one of the most famous fights in cinematic history.

In fairness to director Terence Young, despite the uninspired stolidity of much of his Bond work, this is a sequence that builds in suspense as effectively as any Hitchcock – Bond forced to kneel before Grant, hands in his pockets, as Grant stands over him, gloating, and aiming the gun at Bond's groin with the promise that 'the first bullet won't kill – nor the second, nor the third . . .' It is a moment where the audience can really see no way out of this for Bond.

And then the fight itself. It's the implacable violet of the compartment night-light that somehow sticks in the mind, the only point of stability in a breathtaking blur of fists, punches, swings, kicks, all choreographed in this claustrophobically small space. Praise has justly gone to the film's editor, Peter Hunt; with his lightning-fast cuts, not all of them matching perfectly (some left-handers become right-handers), he rewrote the grammar of screen action. It is a violent, pacy impressionist blur as opposed to the more traditional medium shot of two actors taking fake swings at one another.

What happens afterwards is a fault that became increasingly common in Bond movies, a structural flaw all the more baffling for its constant repetition. Having served up the truly exciting scene, the producers should then have moved us swiftly to the final poisoned-stiletto-in-shoe showdown between Bond and Rosa Klebb. Instead, what we have is a rather tiring extended chase, as Bond and Tatiana with the LEKTOR machine make a bolt from the train and end up being pursued on some Balkan hillside and across a lake by motorboat. (It is supposed to be the Balkans but in fact it is Scotland, on the edge of the Cairngorms, and there are a very great many people who, upon seeing this sequence, jump up and down shouting 'I've been there!')

Tatiana is still unconscious, but now hidden at the back of a flower truck. Elsewhere, Bond is being harried up and down by a helicopter with mounted machine gun. It sounds exciting but it isn't. Perhaps it is something to do with helicopters, which never carry any charge of real menace. Anyway, with the 'copter shot out of the sky, it's on to the motor boat and another chase. That's another thing that Bond producers never really learn: boat chases are intrinsically dull. What can the boats do other than swerve a little? So the bad guys are all blown up by a floating petrol barrel ruse that they would have had to be blind not to have seen coming. Then, finally, to Venice, and to the perfect Lotte Lenya deadly shoe sequence.

But all the puff has been taken out of the end. You want to slip off to the pub. And just as a side note, the producers do this again and again as the films go on. The reasonably rousing duel between Christopher Lee and Roger Moore at the end of *The Man with the Golden Gun* (1974) is followed by a tiresome epilogue involving a solar energy device, an unconvincing exploding HQ and a dwarf in a suitcase. Similarly, the electrifyingly exciting climax of *Octopussy* (1983) – where Bond's only chance of defusing a ticking nuclear bomb in a circus in a US army base is by dressing up as a clown – is followed by some silliness with Bond clinging on to the roof of a plane in flight.

Broccoli and Saltzman would have responded by citing the nature of cinematic spectacle; that Fleming's novels, though brilliant, had to be opened up for the big wide screen. And that helicopters were new and sophisticated and expensive. Indeed, in various other respects, the producers' instincts in making alterations to the novels for the screenplays quite often saved Fleming from himself. We have seen how they quietly dispensed with the risible giant squid fight at the end of *Dr. No*. We will also see how they took *Goldfinger* and wrought a rather more convincing climax out of it than Fleming's.

From Russia with Love is a film that would have played to all the audience's preconceptions about spies and spying. Thanks to the Cold War climate, and also to the rise of rivals to Fleming such as Len Deighton and John le Carré, people were starting to pick up on the lingo, and on the tricks. And whereas Fleming is humorously conscious of the antiquity of devices such as code-greetings, in this film these are all taken with perfect seriousness. As are the gadgets, introduced properly this time by the Q that we all came to know and love, Desmond Llewelyn.

There is the briefcase with the explosive, the secret guineas, the concealed knife . . . again, in the novel, Bond himself maintains an amused incredulity at the latest inventions of the boffins. Here we are invited to marvel unquestioningly at their cleverness.

And despite its occasional longueurs (I know it is heresy to say so, and that some enthusiasts regard *From Russia* as the perfect Holy Grail of Bond, but – let's be searingly honest – some of it is crashingly dull), this is the film that set in place the 'Bond family', both on screen and off, that was to endure in the coming years. M and Miss Moneypenny are now firmly there as vital fixtures – Bond's flirting with a mature but not yet past-it Moneypenny is rather sweet in these first entries. Peevish fusspot Q – Desmond Llewelyn's finest hour – is established. And behind the camera, as well as regular producers Saltzman and Broccoli, were editor Peter Hunt and composer John Barry.

Indeed, it is a cracking showcase for Barry, a young man previously best known for heading up the jazzy combo the John Barry Seven and for hits such as 'Walk Don't Run'. He had previously scored lower-budget British films *Beat Girl* and Bryan Forbes's *The L-Shaped Room* (both 1961) and he was clearly felt by the Eon production team to be the man to appeal to the ears of the nation's youth.

What is quite startling about his first Bond score, however, is that young Barry largely sidestepped any temptation to make the music hip or jazzy; instead he composed lush orchestral cues (especially striking is the music for the St Sophia scene, with its doomy, tolling bell) and a high-spirited, playful action theme for the boat climax that he would reuse in *You Only Live Twice* (1967), *Diamonds Are Forever* (1971) and *Moonraker* (1979).

Indeed, Barry would go on to score a further ten Bond films, only ending his association with the series in 1987. As we shall see, his wildly creative contribution, together with that of production designer Ken Adam, was to give the films an extra dimension of style that no competitor could convincingly imitate. (Adam was absent for *From Russia*, but was due to return in triumph for the next film.)

In some ways, the family feel of the production team was essential. Unlike many other films, Bonds were intensive productions that would be shot over many months, and the cast and crew's familiarity with each other would have eased this process.

This sense of togetherness also helped in the face of what, by 1963, was already ceaseless press attention on the shoots. A good example was that final boat chase sequence of *From Russia*, filmed in the north-west of Scotland, doubling as the Balkans. For some of the footage, director Terence Young wanted to film from a helicopter. But as he and the pilot were up aloft, a problem developed and the helicopter, frighteningly, was forced to ditch into the icy waters. Miraculously, both director and pilot got out alive – Young sustained a broken leg but heroically carried on filming. The press was in a frenzy. Daniela Bianchi helped them out with some glamorous quotes.

Part of the obvious appeal of the novel, and thereby the film, was the notion of sex as an espionage bargaining tool; the idea that part of being a spy was that one literally had to engage in sex as part of the job. These days, as a quasi-fantasy notion, it seems a little quaint; but back in 1963, the timing could not have been more perfect. For the men in the audience, at last here was a hero who could indulge in guilt-free, commitment-free extra-marital sex. For the women, here was the idea of a woman who had to give herself, only a little unwillingly, to beautiful hunk Sean Connery. Thus did the dreams and desires of that original audience merge.

The year 1963 also saw the introduction of the pill; and while it is broadly assumed now that this led to an instant outbreak of wild sexual abandon, the truth was perhaps a little closer to Lindsay Anderson's *This Sporting Life* (1963) than *From Russia*; here we see Richard Harris's brooding, inarticulate rugby player Frank Machin in an unbearably tense and raw relationship with Rachel Roberts's grieving widower Margaret, conducted in black and white in a very dank-looking house, with a dour view through the window.

From Russia, by contrast, offers colour and soft focus; even the seaminess of Bond and Tatania being secretly filmed in bed is turned round in the final frames as Bond produces the offending cine film and drops it into the waters of Venice.

That same year saw the Beatles rise to their position of pre-eminence. In America, Elvis was still King. Sex was clearly much on the minds of the newly confident and aspirational younger generation. And it is always supposed that the synchronous rise of the Bond movie was somehow tied in with that sense of youthful energy and anarchy. This is not quite the case, however.

Bond – even as portrayed by Connery – is by no means a hipster. His Jermyn Street tailoring and seeming disdain for any aspect of pop culture (particularly in the following year's *Goldfinger*, where he asserts that one can only listen to the Beatles with ear muffs) would be jarring on the TV music shows, or when placed in juxtaposition with a Soho coffee bar or Mary Quant boutique. Indeed, there is evidence to show that while the Bond films have always appealed to the young, they have – crucially – also appealed to the old.

Certainly, it appears that 007 appealed to the old-at-heart, for following the release of *From Russia with Love*, Ian Fleming received a fan letter from Metroland-loving poet John Betjeman. 'The Bond world is as real and full of fear and mystery as Conan Doyle's Norwood and Surrey and Baker Street,' wrote Betjeman enthusiastically. 'I think the only other person to have invented a world in our time is [P.G.] Wodehouse. This is real art. I look up to you, old boy, rather as I look up to Uncle Tom Eliot and Wodehouse and Henry Moore and I suppose Evelyn Waugh.'[2] Even if he was being wickedly sarcastic, Betjeman none the less has a very good point about the completeness of Fleming's fictional world.

James Bond as a character was more ruthless than boyish old Bulldog Drummond, certainly a great deal more ruthless than any of the protagonists of 1950s wartime dramas starring John Mills; none the less, there was something in him that perhaps appealed to a genuine wartime spirit, as opposed to the Rank film artifice. A tang of sourness that might have pulled people back to the vinegary 1930s thrillers of Dornford Yates. While Connery was perfectly contemporary in every way, some aspects of *From Russia* were antiquated, even in sexual terms.

The character of Tatiana Romanova is one. In the novel, Fleming draws her as a keen Soviet citizen, dreading being drawn into this entrapment plot; in the film, she is instantly relocated to Istanbul, where she is recruited by Klebb. The actress Daniela Bianchi is given very little to do after this point, other than look beautiful in hotel and train bedrooms. There seems to be absolutely nothing to the character of Tatiana at all. She is one of the least progressive of what would later be termed the Bond girls. And that is saying something, because she faces stiff competition from Jane Seymour and Britt Ekland.

In the sexual scheme of the film, she is the bargaining counter, used both by Klebb and by Bond. While it is true that Bond's affection for her seems to grow throughout the course of the narrative, Tatiana is still in the position of the arranged wife. Her sexual passivity curiously reminds us of the hissing, spitting, scratching gypsy ladies in the fight scene earlier on; while these women are apparently quite happy to fight sexily to the death over a man, the payoff of their struggle is that it is the spectator Bond who ultimately gets to choose which of them should win. And as these two women are now presented to his tent, both entirely supplicant, we are left in no doubt about the method he will employ to make his choice.

Similarly, Bond's first view of Tatiana is through a spy periscope installed in the Russian embassy in Istanbul, and the angle he sees from below is that of her legs. From the start, Tatiana is, as the old 1980s wimmin's groups would have said, 'objectified'. This is made explicit as, after blowing up that embassy, Bond escapes with the code-breaking machine and the code-breaking girl. The two are prizes of equal value. It seems fitting that she has to spend much of the film's climax in a drugged condition. It somehow reflects her entire role throughout.

To be fair to Daniela Bianchi, this was all in the script, and there was not a great deal she could do about that. On a happier note – and one that would also have enraged wimmin everywhere – she is still one of the most beautiful heroines to have featured in the series. Some argue that only Carole Bouquet, Roger Moore's co-star in *For Your Eyes Only*, could match her.

By way of contrast, *From Russia*'s only genuinely liberated woman is Rosa Klebb. In the novel, as we have seen, Ian Fleming hit some seam of hideous exultation in her lesbianism, flourishing it as evidence of a fundamentally warped soul. This aspect of the character is toned down a little in *From Russia* – wouldn't want to frighten the family audience – but it is still unmistakably there. Incidentally, it was quite a year for unsympathetic cinematic portraits of lesbianism. In Robert Wise's fraught adaptation of *The Haunting*, Claire Bloom portrays a psychic who is arch, calculating, bitchy and intensely allergic to the overtures of Russ Tamblyn. That somehow seems fair enough.

Fleming ventured elsewhere into this field of sexuality in his novel *Goldfinger*, where Bond is struck by Pussy Galore and the 'unhappy' kink in her nature (a kink that only he can 'cure'). Once again, as we shall see, in the film this was toned down to a mildly reluctant Pussy in an improbable hay-loft.

But Klebb also set a further template for the Bond villains to come. Dr. No had merely been a psychotic half-Chinese/half-German with metal hands; Klebb was a far more distorted figure, and one who could insinuate herself anywhere. Thus the scene is set for Bond's final battle, this time in Venice's Hotel Splendide, as the frowsy cleaning lady reveals her true poisoned-shoe colours. It still remains a wonderful image, that of Bond trapping Klebb against the wall with the legs of a chair, as she furiously kicks out at his shins with her lethal stilettos. It seems a bit of a letdown to have her shot by Tatiana.

Even before shooting began on *From Russia*, Saltzman, Broccoli and United Artists – who were paying for it – knew they were on to a sure thing. The budget for the film was duly double that of *Dr. No*, going up to almost $2 million. This was epic stuff but still not in the top drawer. Once again, it's interesting to compare this to the budget of around $13 million given, the year previously, to David Lean's sumptuous British production of *Lawrence of Arabia*. And that memorable 1963 disaster *Cleopatra*, starring Elizabeth Taylor and Richard Burton, cost somewhere in the region of $44 million.

In fact, in *From Russia*, a couple of lavish locations aside, it is rather difficult to see now what the money would have been spent on. Certainly the Pinewood gypsy encampment and the studio-built Orient Express compartments can't have cost much. Even the grand hall in which Kronsteen plays his chess match is mostly a glass painting of a fancy ceiling.

Word of Bond had already spread around the world. By the time the crew came to Istanbul for the location work, they found themselves having to deal with hordes of eager fans in the street scenes. The native success of 007 was being matched across Europe; he swiftly picked up a vast fanbase even in Japan. In America, things had yet to take off to quite that degree.

And Saltzman and Broccoli were also setting up in *From Russia* what would now be described as a 'story arc', with our first oblique glimpse of a certain diabolical criminal mastermind. There he is, on board a luxury yacht, admonishing a sweating Klebb and Kronsteen, while feeding some exotic fighting fish in a tank and stroking a white Persian cat . . . Though it would be a while before we saw this fiend fully disclosed, Saltzman and Broccoli had their game-plan set up for the next few films.

For certain highbrow critics, *From Russia* was the source of some distress. 'It's terribly lowering,' wrote Isabel Quigley in *The Spectator*, 'to sit unamused while everyone around you is yelping with glee. Unless you have an outsize bump of self-confidence, it makes you feel there's something wrong somewhere – with you, them or it; preferably it but probably you.'

In *The Observer*, critic Penelope Gilliatt regretfully conceded the cleverness of Eon. 'The Bond films are brilliantly skilful,' she wrote. 'Among other things, they seem to have cottoned on to a kind of brutal flippancy that is a voice of the age, the voice of sick jokes about the Bomb and gruesomes [sic] about Belsen.'

Meanwhile, from the smouldering brazier of the far left came this shout of rage from *The Daily Worker*'s Nina Hibbin. 'Do you find this amusing?' she demanded of her readers. 'Fun? That only makes it worse! What sort of people are we becoming if we can accept such perversion as a giggle?' It's the sort of review that would make one sprint through the cinema foyer in eagerness. Nearly fifty years on, I am struggling to work out what perversion she meant.

To look back now, you can see that *From Russia* was actually the last Bond movie of its type. It was the last to play a gadget-filled briefcase absolutely straight. It was the last to make Bond the centre of an essentially small-scale spy-versus-spy melodrama. It was the last (for a while) in which Bond's attentions would be focused on just one woman. It was the last in which the exotic locations were treated as a genuinely integral part of the story's character, as opposed to a mouth-watering backdrop for Bond to be pursued through. And even though this time the film is graced with that evocative and suspenseful John Barry score, with accompanying Lionel Bart song – no more fretfulness from Monty Norman – this was also the last entry where even the music would be played straight.

And just as 007 was poised to make his next evolutionary step – the truly defining one – the world was becoming aware of the amazing cultural repercussions of the character. Television executives began to wake up to espionage. Eight-year-old boys began playing 'spies'. Authors other than Ian Fleming – among whom were Len Deighton and former SIS man David Cornwell, aka John le Carré – began contributing their own particular narrative approaches to the entire notion of spookdom. Indeed, from this point onwards, the entire world went secret agent mad.

CHAPTER FOUR THE GLITTERING PRIZE

Before we knuckle down to the gloriously vulgar gold-burnished phenomenon that sealed James Bond's screen immortality, it is worth asking exactly how it is that a spy — very often a figure of some moral ambiguity both in fiction and in real life — came to be regarded by half the planet as a pure unalloyed 100 per cent hero.

Let's go back a few centuries — no, really, it'll be worth it and it won't take long — to the alleged origin of Bond's serial number. One story, never completely confirmed, is that Ian Fleming owed this number to Queen Elizabeth I's astrologer Dr John Dee. Dr Dee, considered at the time to be the most learned man in England as well as one with a direct line to the world of spirits, apparently used to sign himself with a symbol that was formulated thus: '007'. The meaning of that 007 may be debated — and various mystic numerologists have — but it is certainly the case that Dr Dee, when not scrying angels and summoning forth visions, was occasionally in communication with Elizabeth's feared spymaster, Sir Francis Walsingham.

Dr Dee introduced Walsingham to the use of new and complex cipher systems, for instance when he acquired a copy of *Stenographia* by Trithemius, the Abbot of Sponheim. From his base in Prague, Dee sent Walsingham a couple of cryptic letters, one of which stated briefly: 'That which England suspected was also here.'[1]

But this was a murky era when spying was not a heroic or noble activity at all. Quite the reverse. And even to be suspected of being a spy could lead to catastrophe. Such a thing happened to Dr Dee; he and his family and colleague Edward Kelley were banished from Prague by the emperor Rudolf, and given just six days to leave.

English espionage in the late sixteenth century was chiefly concerned with one thing: suspected papist plots against the Protestant Queen. Sir Francis Walsingham used young recruits, many from the universities, as agents and counter-agents, running missions throughout Catholic Europe to gather intelligence on any plans that ran contrary to the interests of the state. But Walsingham was a chillier figure than M could ever have been.

The perceived threat was so grave, the apparent stakes so high, that Walsingham and his Star Chamber were utterly, frighteningly ruthless.

For an especially good account of the terror that his prototype police state could inspire among Catholic recusants, it is worth looking at Antonia Fraser's magnificent *The Gunpowder Plot* (1997) which places Guy Fawkes and his fellow conspirators in a sweatily understandable new context. Walsingham was a powerful man with no compunction about the use of torture that would maim and disfigure for life.

It is believed by many that playwright Christopher Marlowe, a contemporary of Shakespeare, was also a spy, who had been drawn into Walsingham's web when he was a scholar at Cambridge. There is also speculation that Marlowe was a double agent; and that his violent death – he was stabbed through the eye in an inn in Deptford – was connected with these muddy and sinister activities. As a career, it seems more le Carré than Fleming.

And that is the point about the dawning of the era of espionage. A spy was, by necessity, a shadowy, untrustworthy figure, dislocated from society, operating in the dark.

Much later, as Britain's imperial grip over the world tightened, in competition with other European states, the late nineteenth and early twentieth century saw the beginning of the modern fictional spy in the fantastically popular works of William Le Queux. His works included *Spies of the Kaiser* and *Terror in the Air* and were, in their own way, remarkably prescient. Le Queux's fictional secret agent Duckworth Drew – I know, but it might have sounded sexy back then – is called upon time and again to defend the interests of the British Empire against the beastly Hun and beastly Boers and beastly pretty much everyone. Including, especially, double-agent saboteurs already lurking within England.

This was still espionage as a defensive countermeasure; it would not have been at all seemly for one of Le Queux's gentlemanly heroes to be seen rifling through the wall-safe of a foreign ambassador under cover of darkness, for instance. That was the sort of thing those untrustworthy foreigners did to the British.

The Edwardian age brought the real-life development of the Secret Intelligence Service, later to become MI6. The pioneer 'M' figure was Sir Mansfield Cumming; he signed all documents with the initial C, in a special green ink. Added to this, owing to a leg injury, he often made his way around HQ on a child's scooter.

The British Empire was under constant threat: from Russians, from Islamic fundamentalists, from pretty much everyone. Real-life gentleman spies, sometimes posing as clerical tourists making studies of local wildlife, would undertake missions of intelligence gathering – and, indeed, sabotage – in places such as Istanbul, Baku and the Northwest Frontier. This was, in all conceivable senses, the Great Game.

Back in the realm of gaudy fiction, author William Le Queux was also a pioneer of the spy genre's tradition of the outlandish and bizarre; he was not only there to introduce us to the very first car chases, at the dawn of the automobile era, but also to lethal exploding cigars (how much later the CIA was to catch up with an alleged plot to sabotage Castro's tobacco thus) and prototype death rays.

Curiously enough, the plot of his 1899 bestseller *England's Peril* foreshadows Fleming's *Casino Royale*, though minus the sex and gambling; it involves an unhappily compromised female spy (called Irma) and a roguish head of the French secret service called Gaston Le Touche. In those days, France was perceived as the secret enemy. And whereas now we have the wonders of electronic transmission of information, double agent Irma had to record the positioning of defence positions with tracing paper.

Fiction soon began to catch up with Sir Mansfield Cumming's real agents. That Indian summer of empire brought forth an array of square-jawed protagonists – inspirations to a generation of schoolboys – who were there to protect the nation and its colonies, especially at a time when the nation was fighting its most bloody, desolating war.

Erskine Childers gave us the hero Carruthers, in *The Riddle of the Sands* (1915); then of course a fellow called Richard Hannay stepped forward to solve the mystery of *The Thirty-Nine Steps* (1915), courtesy of author John Buchan; even more pressingly, he was called upon to face down the prospect of jihad and Islamic revolt in *Greenmantle* (1916).

W. Somerset Maugham was a little later to introduce the world to his *Ashenden* stories, which were inspired by his own real-life experiences working for the fledgling Secret Intelligence Service. These caused uproar among the intelligence hierarchy because it was felt Maugham was simply giving too much away about real operations.[2] The other interesting point about these stories was that, among all the trotting back and forth across Europe, these narratives introduced a note of regret and melancholia that was later to find its fullest expression in the works of John le Carré.

So while we might see that Bond — and the literary form within which he operated — did not spring wholly from the imagination of Ian Fleming, we also see, especially by *Goldfinger*, that Fleming had brought one vital ingredient to the mix that had perhaps evaded all his predecessors. That was that the whole game of espionage was highly amusing, and also guaranteed vast amounts of sex. Oh all right, perhaps that might also have been the case for bisexual Christopher Marlowe as he spied and slept around Catholic Europe. But *Goldfinger* — and in particular, Guy Hamilton's film of the same name — was the production that would have made everyone want to join MI6.

And no matter what Terence Young may have said in interviews about having introduced an element of humour into the stories, it was Hamilton who gave the films a genuine belly-laugh quality.

The pre-credits teaser sequence alone marked a sharp swerve in style; in terms of tone, it might well be one of the most influential sequences of that decade. We are in some South American country, by an industrial harbour, and a seabird is bobbing along in the night-time waters. It is not a seabird at all, of course. It is a decoy model sitting atop Sean Connery's head, a fact disclosed when he emerges from the water in a wetsuit.

But the serious laugh comes when Bond unzips that wetsuit to reveal an immaculate white tuxedo with a scarlet carnation in the lapel. This one shot placed Bond on a higher rung of meta-secret-agenting, far above the po-faced cloak and dagger stuff of *From Russia*. Camp does not climb higher; and it might be debated whether such an approach did the integrity of the character any good. But this was the film that hit the worldwide nerve and turned Bond into something a great deal more than a parochial character from some books and films.

The tone of the thing is one of unblushing glitz. From the cheesy poolside in Miami, where Bond thwarts Goldfinger's card game, and where Goldfinger exacts his macabrely vulgar revenge on Jill Masterson, to the ingot of Nazi gold used as bait in the English golf match, from the laser beam of pure gold that threatens Bond's crotch to Ken Adam's hilariously glitzy realisation of Fort Knox, this was a film that exulted in its own excess. After the absurd insouciance of the pre-credits teaser — Bond blows up refinery while also electrocuting assailant by throwing heater into a bath — we are into the title sequence that set the standard for all Bond movies to follow.

It is so well known that it takes an effort to put yourself into the minds of the original audiences, who would have been rather taken aback both by

Robert Brownjohn's cheeky visuals – scenes from the film projected on to the gold-painted body of a model – and by Shirley Bassey's hollering rendition of one of the oddest songs ever written. All together now: 'For a golden girl knows when he's kissed her/It's the kiss of death from Mr Goldfinger'.

This was the first time that song and opening credits were married. In the previous film, Matt Munro's deep, crooning account of 'From Russia with Love' was sung over the closing titles. Shirley Bassey has said that she was nonplussed by the lyrics to 'Goldfinger' when first presented with them, but was advised by John Barry to think of the old hit 'Mack the Knife' with its equally violent lyrics.

Robert Brownjohn had also designed the title sequence for *From Russia*, and the motif that he brought to both productions was the 'objectification' of the female form. What he does is to divide it into sections – abdomen, breasts, legs – and use the body as a screen. In *Goldfinger*, the features of Gert Fröbe and Sean Connery are projected on to the model.

But there is startling and faintly macabre imagery here too: the revolving number plates on Bond's Aston Martin are here projected on to the golden model's mouth, giving for one second a strange impression of a tooth X-ray and the skull beneath the skin. Then there is the laugh-out-loud shot, that of the projected golf ball heading straight for the model's cleavage.

Bond title sequences are such distinctive things that they have become a renowned part of film history on their own account. Steven Spielberg is said to be a huge fan of the titles of *Diamonds Are Forever*, in which a white Persian cat wearing a diamond collar saunters past – and through – the thighs of various ladies.

And despite Robert Brownjohn's proud efforts, the name we still associate most strongly with this curious little aesthetic side-alley is Maurice Binder. From *Thunderball* in 1965 onward, Binder was firmly in charge of the titles, right up until *Licence to Kill* in 1989. In the 1990s, Daniel Kleinman took over. To this day, his work has always paid homage to the style that Binder perfected.

The main leitmotif that we think of with Bond titles is the dancing silhouettes: naked ladies performing cartwheels, or using giant guns as gymnastic props. In the 1960s, Binder suffused the whole screen with eye-scorching colour. In the 1970s, his style became a little more chiaroscuro, though the hints of nakedness went up. In the 1980s, the titles became a shade more bonkers – one thinks immediately of the naked skiers painted in fiery make-up for *A View to a Kill*, or the nude blonde sitting in a gigantic champagne glass for *The Living Daylights*.

In those days, the titles were always the last thing to be filmed, and sometimes they were completed only a day or two before the picture was due in the cinemas. When he was on form, Binder was blindingly brilliant. The Japanese-themed visuals for *You Only Live Twice*, with all those expanding fans and rivers of lava, are the perfect complement to John Barry's haunting, romantic theme.

Similarly, the energy of the titles for *Live and Let Die* (1973) – skulls, blue flames, beautiful women with very big eyes – keys one up so far that the film's following scene, introducing Roger Moore as Bond, has a touch of suburban bathos. For *The Spy Who Loved Me* (1977), Binder did détente, Bond facing a marching line of naked women in Russian army caps and boots, and casually pushing them over.

Occasionally it looked as though Binder had run out of ideas – the titles for *Octopussy*, featuring a sort of laser projection, are disappointingly low-key; and those for *Licence to Kill*, featuring some grotesquely blatant product placement for Olympus in the form of a screen-filling camera, are also pretty flat.

How influential that Binder style was though. Not merely was it copied slavishly by spy imitators (rare was the British or US TV spy series that didn't feature silhouettes, moving gun target sights, revolvers, etc. in its opening credits), but it bled into a wider pop-cultural arena. The most recent homage was there to be seen in the 2007 advertising campaign for the notoriously kitsch Ferrero Rocher chocolates: the screen is filled with female silhouettes and gold-painted women in gold bikinis. In the 1970s, the body-stockinged woman who danced, à la Binder, against images of spinning roulette wheels for the title sequence of ITV's *Tales of the Unexpected* became a much-fêted tabloid figure.

One rather sweet note about changing times: Daniel Kleinman's titles for *Casino Royale* (2006) are sharp, colourful, fast and incredibly detailed – but feature no women. Except for a brief glimpse of the face of actress Eva Green, seen in a playing card, we have instead an animation of Bond and foes as silhouettes who are slugging it out, hand to hand, against the elaborate patterns of card backs. You sense that Binder, while approving, would have wondered where the ladies had got to. His was a working life filled with women wearing body-stockings throwing themselves into various unlikely poses for his camera. Someone had to do it.

Back at *Goldfinger*, as Shirley Bassey shrieks the final bars of that mad song, we dissolve to an aerial view of a hotel in Miami, with suitably brassy music from John Barry. The aerial shot is the only bit of location we get here; almost instantly, we are in the studio with Connery wearing an astounding powder-blue shorty towelling jumpsuit. Nothing of its ilk had been seen before or indeed has been seen since. Forget what the character was thinking – what on God's good Earth were Connery and the entire crew thinking?

But never mind, for here we are with Shirley Eaton as Jill Masterson; a small but extraordinarily iconic role – no more than five minutes of screen time – that would hang over the rest of her career, as the actress has acknowledged good-humouredly many times. Jill is employed by Goldfinger to spy on his card-game opponent's hands with binoculars and a miniature radio; Bond seduces her and makes Goldfinger lose his game. What seems lightly comical, however, swiftly turns to a scene that is by turns chilling and shockingly sexy. Bond is knocked out by an as yet unseen heavy; and when he comes to, he finds the naked girl stretched out on the bed, quite dead, painted head to toe with gold.

Again, the image is so familiar that you forget just what an extraordinary and darkly ingenious notion this is. Any run-of-the-mill villain would simply strangle the girl; to asphyxiate her with gold leaf is utterly baroque.

Incidentally, this wasn't the first time that such a death was seen on screen. In Val Lewton's 1946 production of *Bedlam* for RKO, one of the male unfortunates in that eighteenth-century lunatic asylum is forced to dress up as a cod Greek god, painted gold. He too collapses and dies. Doesn't quite pack the same punch as Shirley Eaton, though. Those three or four seconds of screen time as Connery stares with disbelief at Eaton are possibly the most memorable of the entire series. Certainly, future Bond Pierce Brosnan counted it as the moment when his fifteen-year-old eyes were opened to the power of cinema.

Shirley Eaton formed the spearhead of the film's US opening, touring all over that country, her gold-painted image appearing on the cover of *Life* magazine. 'Harry Saltzman had seen my work,' she said later, explaining how she became this extraordinary 1960s icon. 'And he just wanted to know if I would agree to be painted gold in the nude and I said, "yes, as long as it's done tastefully".'[3] And what could have been more tasteful?

And so the game is afoot. M has an inkling that Goldfinger is involved in a smuggling scheme and Bond is sent to lure him into a trap with a bar of Nazi gold. The two men play a round of golf for it. Goldfinger cheats, Bond cheats better, Bond wins — then Goldfinger's Korean henchman Oddjob takes off his bowler hat, throws it at a statue and decapitates it. The hat is razor-edged. As if things could not have become any camper.

Overall, the golf match is a wonderful sequence that you couldn't get away with in an action film now; it is a montage of leisurely dissolves and gentle golfing comedy that puts one in mind of an earlier era of Charters and Caldicott. Goldfinger's plus-fours and cap help the humorous feel. As a matter of interest, neither Connery nor Gert Fröbe could play golf when they began the shoot. It was on this film that Connery first learned and then swiftly developed his love for the game.

And the scene also gives us a clever means by which hero and villain encounter one another without either side having to make tiresome rhetorical speeches concerning power or liberty. We see what an inspired choice for the role Fröbe was. A popular and well-known actor in Germany, his English was extremely limited, which probably goes some way towards explaining the character's constant facial expression of belligerent confusion. Fröbe simply didn't understand a word of the script. As a result, he cuts a wonderfully mad figure, impossible to envisage anywhere other than within the confines of the film.

There was an untrue story claiming that Fröbe had been a member of the Nazi party, and that this had led to the film being boycotted in Israel. In fact there had been no truth in the rumour and the film did spectacularly well in Israel.

The other splendid thing about Fröbe is that you believe his Goldfinger to be capable of anything. Here was a man simply too bonkers to be reasoned with in any kind of way.

And foxy old M is quite right; the man is indeed smuggling, even ingeniously using the bodywork of his Rolls-Royce to carry gold across borders. Bond follows him to Switzerland, but not without first visiting Q. Again, this scene would lay down the law for all the Bond films to follow. And Desmond Llewelyn's prissy tetchiness finds its highest expression when he is taking Bond through the specifications of his Aston Martin DB5, with its revolving number plates, spikes that emerge from the wheel caps, primitive sat-nav (an illuminated dashboard map with a green dot on it) and ejector seat. 'You're joking!' exclaims Bond when Q solemnly explains the workings of that seat. Director Hamilton shrewdly heads the audience laughter off by making the joke before they can.

This good-humoured knowingness would also become part of the essential formula. This is also the point where the gadgets became a focal point, completely fetishistic in fact. But detractors who say that these gizmos rob the films of their humanity are killjoys. The gadgets are funny, and the children in the audience – not to mention their fathers – are fascinated.

The car went on to tour the world, publicising both the film and Aston Martin. The Queen looked on with polite interest as its smokescreen was deployed in a Midlands factory. Sean Connery drove it around the Arc de Triomphe. It was shipped to America, and eventually sold and bought at auction. It fetched £250,000 in the 1980s. It remains the most famous car in cinema history. The toy version of it – complete with working ejector seat – was a Christmas best-seller for several years running.

Back in the film, the spikes in the wheel hubs are deployed on a Swiss mountain road against Tilly Masterson, who isn't to know that the one way for a woman to *really* get Bond revved up is to overtake him at speed. (Take a look at Fleming's 1963 novel *On Her Majesty's Secret Service*, in which Tracy does that very thing, and sets the story in motion.) None the less, it is quite a coincidence that Bond and Tilly should meet, for it turns out that Tilly is the sister of gold-leafed Jill, and plans to avenge her by assassinating Goldfinger.

We somehow sense that that's not going to end happily; and indeed it doesn't, as Tilly, fleeing from Oddjob in a night-time wood, is felled by his lethal razor-lined bowler. Bond's regret – and indeed ours – is short-lived as the agent manages to get into a brisk car chase in which he deploys oil, a bullet-proof shield and of course, that ejector seat (the effect is not quite so spectacular as we had been led to believe). And then a crash! Unconsciousness! And awakening to find . . .

. . . possibly the most famous Bond scene of all, and surely the most famous line. Bond is strapped spreadeagled to a table. As a smoking-jacketed Goldfinger looks on, a heavy machine above Bond emits a golden laser, which slowly burns up the table in between Bond's legs. The most famous line ever is worth repeating. Bond exclaims: 'Do you expect me to talk?' 'No, Mr Bond,' replies Goldfinger, his voice rising maniacally, 'I expect you to die.'

Three things make this scene work brilliantly even now: Connery's sweaty portrayal of fear as the laser beam creeps towards his crotch; the deployment of the laser itself, a ground-breaking notion in 1964, even though it was descended from innumerable lo-tech 'death rays' as seen in the 1930s *Flash Gordon* serials; and finally, once again, Gert Fröbe, whose performance is so very unreadable that he leaves you convinced – for the first time ever – that the villain in this hackneyed scenario actually means it. Thus we get a few moments of proper, genuine, squirmy suspense, with no idea of how Bond will escape. Futurism, gold and castration anxiety, all there in the space of about ninety seconds. Imagine how disastrous it all would have been if the screenwriters and Guy Hamilton had stuck to Fleming's original version, involving a large circular saw.

And, of course, this leads us directly to possibly the second most famous scene of all. Bond, once again knocked unconscious, having convinced Goldfinger that he knows enough to be kept alive, recovers to find himself looking into the eyes of Honor Blackman, who introduces herself as 'Pussy Galore'. 'I must be dreaming,' mutters Bond.

Is it possible that the name seems more outrageous now than it was then? It is simply inconceivable that the lead female character in any kind of production now, save the most puerile porn, would be called anything like this. It caused flutters of disquiet at the time among the American censors and the money men at United Artists. They requested that 'Pussy' should become 'Kitty'. Kitty? Get out of here! But production was already under way, and Saltzman and Broccoli responded by telling them that the name had already been aired in front of His Royal Highness Prince Philip when he had visited the set and met Honor Blackman. On top of this, the character's name had been mentioned in a report on this visit by the *Sunday Express*, a newspaper edited by the famously fierce John Junor, who was not at home to filth of any sort.

Actress Honor Blackman, upon being introduced to the press as filming began, was ingeniously calm about the whole thing. 'I think it's a lovely name, don't you?' she lied to the *Daily Mail*'s reporter. 'It will be different anyway.'

But where could Fleming have hit upon the notion of such a name in the first place? In the 1930s, at the fashionable Kit Kat Club in the Haymarket, London, there was a singer called Harry Ray who had something of an underground hit with his song 'My Girlfriend's Pussy'.[4] Well, it's possible at any rate that Fleming might have come across it. In any case, the possibilities for double entendre went on long after *Goldfinger*, especially in the case of Mrs Slocombe's notorious pet from the smutty 1970s BBC sitcom *Are You Being Served?*

Following Honey Rider and Tatiana, Pussy is a more mature sort of Bond girl, and very much none the worse for that. Honor Blackman was in her mid-thirties when she took the role, directly after leaving the long-running British TV thriller series *The Avengers* in which she played a leather-wearing anthropologist. Clearly the perceived toughness of Cathy Gale was something she was expected to bring to *Goldfinger*.

The actress has said often that before Cathy, heroines in British dramas were expected to be English roses — Cathy was the first woman who could not only out-think the male lead, but out-fight him too. This led to the actress receiving a great deal of eyebrow-raising fan mail, involving leather and whips. On the one side was a perception of female emancipation; on the other was the role playing up to a pretty vintage male fantasy. So Blackman's Pussy is a shrewd challenge to lay before Connery's Bond.

Pussy Galore is Goldfinger's personal aircraft pilot and when she is not running errands for him, she is in charge of a team of aeronautical blondes styled Pussy Galore's Flying Circus. In the novel, Pussy and her team were a straightforwardly lesbian gang of criminals calling themselves 'The Cement Mixers'. In either case, once again, what would the chances be now, eh? Anyway, touchdown in Kentucky, where Goldfinger appears to have a ranch. And brilliantly, here is Gert Fröbe again, in a loud waistcoat, with a quizzical expression on his face that suggests he is no closer to understanding any of this than he was at the beginning of the shoot.

His dubbed voiceover — actor Michael Collins — explains the loopy plot to Bond: explode a nuclear device within Fort Knox, irradiate the gold reserves therein, and instantly increase the value of Goldfinger's own stash of ingots. But, but . . . oh, we'll come back to all that in a minute. Pussy's role in all of this is to fly, with her fellow blonde pilots, over the area, spraying deadly gas, in order to immobilise all the guards around the fort.

Bond and Pussy end up in a barn where, à la *The Avengers*, she gets to rebuff his advance by throwing him over her shoulder into the hay. 'It was much better than *The Avengers*,' explained Blackman. 'In that, I always had to land on concrete studio floors. In this, there was all that lovely hay.'[5] Unlike *The Avengers*, however, Bond gets to win the fight, as the reluctant (and lesbian, according to the novel, remember) Pussy struggles, then relents. It's mildly amusing and somehow faintly chilling at the same time.

And unlike her predecessors, it is clear that Pussy is not going to be a conventional squeeze. In the first place, it is not merely a matter of her orientation, but also a matter of her employer: Bond must convert Pussy to the side of the angels. As it happens, that unlikely haybarn roll plays a pivotal part in this. For if Pussy could be persuaded to switch the flypast plan to involve sleeping gas instead of lethal vapours . . .

No, it's still not making a whole heap of sense. Although screenwriters Richard Maibaum and Paul Dehn definitely rescued Fleming from his even more absurd novel, in which Goldfinger's plan simply involved removing all the gold from Fort Knox – an operation which, in terms of weight issues alone, would actually require a workforce equivalent to that of the State of Tennessee. The nuclear bomb idea makes a little more initial sense, although *surely* it wouldn't change the Fort's status as a reserve? After all, given a few years, the radioactivity would have died down and the gold would be safely retrieved, if needed at all. In fact, wouldn't the radiation simply make it all the safer?

One more thing, on top of that: in the very old days, up to the Second World War, economies used to be underpinned by something called the gold standard; that is, a nation would own the equivalent of all its currency in the form of gold, which was held as a surety. But this was a model really for the nineteenth century. Come the twentieth, with the twin pressures of super-industrialisation and war, it became increasingly difficult to cling on to it.

By the time of 1944 and the Bretton Woods agreement, where the Allies tried to make economic plans for a shattered post-war world, the gold standard had pretty much disappeared as a sustainable idea. There was simply more printed money than there was gold. So instead, after D-Day and the later surrender of Japan, the dominant economic unit would become the US dollar: a unit of currency that could earn interest and generate more money, unlike gold.

Therefore, while obviously gold remained in itself the most valuable commodity, its symbolic value in economic terms had dropped a little. So – deep breath – would an attack on the Fort Knox reserves have made any real difference either to Goldfinger's bank balance or the world's economies as a whole?

Ah! But in fact it is not just Goldfinger, for lurking in the background is actor Burt Kwouk playing a sinister Communist official, Captain Ling, from the People's Republic of China. So it's their fault! A plan perhaps to destablise the economies of the West? Such things, I suppose, have been known ...

Whenever the Bond films are in doubt about the villain being able to carry the whole gibbering plot by himself, they tend to reach for Red China. There is a suggestion of it behind Blofeld's astronaut-kidnapping antics in *You Only Live Twice*. It also gets a fleeting – and almost wholly unnecessary – mention in *The Man with the Golden Gun*. In fact, not really until *Tomorrow Never Dies* (1997) is China regarded as a superpower that Bond can do business with, in the shape of agent Wai Lin (Michelle Yeoh). In the case of *Goldfinger*, Saltzman and Broccoli were once more spot on with their timing; for in real life, 1964 was the year in which Red China exploded its first test nuclear weapon.

Back to the world of fiction. Goldfinger invites some hoods to his ranch to give them a chance of buying into Operation Grand Slam, as his loopy and illogical plot is called. The hoods aren't sure – and to be frank, who can blame them? – so Goldfinger kills them with some of the gas intended for the Fort Knox troops. Booo! Meanwhile, back *outside* the ranch is the ever-hapless Felix Leiter, attempting to keep an eye on Bond's movements. A further layer of confusion: if Goldfinger is on American soil, and planning some form of spectacular criminal act on American soil, then surely it's time for Leiter and his CIA chums to move in, as opposed to leaving it all to Bond?

Look, there are few thrillers ever made that could survive any detailed examination, and that goes just as much for Raymond Chandler – a big favourite of Ian Fleming – as anyone else. Chandler, in an essay entitled 'The Simple Art of Murder', was critical of ill-thought-out thrillers. Pussy Galore and her Flying Circus could fly through the holes of this one. But it doesn't matter because soon we are at the wonderfully iconoclastic climax.

Pussy's planes fly overhead and hundreds of Fort Knox infantrymen keel over. Next, Goldfinger takes his laser beam to the very door of the fort. Then Bond is handcuffed to a nuclear device that looks like an old fridge-freezer, and taken deep inside the fort, this glittering cathedral piled high with towers of gold. There to keep an eye on him is Oddjob. The countdown – hooray! – is ticking away very fast indeed. How in the name of all that is absurd can Bond possibly get out of this one and save the day?

What follows is one of the most wonderful sequences ever seen in a comedy-thriller, proving that in very rare cases, it is possible to have knuckle-biting tension and hearty laughter at the same time. While Oddjob and his hat are otherwise distracted by a disturbance on a higher level, Bond, handcuffed, has to drag the nuclear device on its trolley round to where a dead guard lies, so that Bond can get the man's keys to undo the cuffs. Those off, he tries to get into the bomb's casing itself, the countdown now running dizzyingly fast. But Oddjob is having none of it; and the two men grapple against the backdrop of all that gold, the Korean throwing Bond around mercilessly, and Bond increasingly desperate about that nuclear countdown.

Bond of course gets the better of Oddjob in a final *coup de grâce* involving an electrical cable and Oddjob's metal-lined hat. But how the deuce does one switch off a nuclear bomb? Happily, by this point, the American troops who were only pretending to be unconscious show up, and some chap switches the darn thing off, just as the count reaches 007 . . . Then it's time for one final showdown with Goldfinger in his private jet. A gun is fired, the cabin depressurises and Goldfinger is unforgettably sucked out through a porthole. And at last, Bond and Pussy get their clinch.

Splendid stuff, obviously, but how did it come to set the world on fire? This, after all, was the first Bond movie to really hit it big in the US. The American setting was obviously a slight help in this regard – and 007 was to return shamelessly to the States many times throughout his career – but that still doesn't quite cover it.

That year, 1964, also saw another British cultural invader storming through US customs in the form of the Beatles. The Scouse moptops took their first giant step to world domination when they performed 'I Want To Hold Your Hand' on the hugely popular and influential *Ed Sullivan Show*. They, and Bond, were projecting a hitherto unsuspected side of fusty, tweedy old Britain – a sexy, irreverent modernity. London – which we all knew to be sooty and wet and cold and largely shut by 10.30 p.m. – was somehow gaining a reputation as the coolest city on Earth.

Previously, in 1961, we had given the Americans the eloquent impudence of *Beyond the Fringe* – Peter Cook, Dudley Moore, Alan Bennett and Jonathan Miller performing their skits on the British Establishment on Broadway. Bond, in the form of Sean Connery, was in some curious way the logical extension of that. Here was a new kind of British hero – Savile Row-suited but classless – who ostensibly answered to the Establishment, in the form of M, but in fact overturned all those previously admired British traits such as restraint and understatement. His appetites were mighty, and, for the British, remarkably uncouth.

The production values – given that the budget was still not enormous, at around $5 million – were exceptional this time around. From the very opening, where an industrial gasometer is shown to contain an expressionistically angled Ken Adam operations centre – director Guy Hamilton described Adam's work as 'ritzy-titsy' – to the absurdity of the Flying Circus/Fort Knox finale, the thing looks drenched in gloss. And the sex element would have been a great deal stronger than the Americans were used to in a family film.

More than this was the truly brilliant score provided by John Barry, who was now perfectly into his Bond stride. The music of *Goldfinger* links Bond at last with the beat of the modern world. The title song is one thing, but the recurrence of that wah-wah brass throughout is both exhilarating and amusing – the best theme ever composed for a villain, in fact. The swing/jazz feel continues through to the climax, where it is winningly blended with a military drumbeat, giving an unexpected nail-biting exuberance to the nuclear device countdown (and as we shall see later, no one did countdown music better than John Barry).

To this day, it remains the most entertaining and, in feel, the most cynical of all Bond scores. At the time, the soundtrack was a best-selling record in the UK.

In general, the film's impact was huge. *Goldfinger* hysteria spread to Paris, where cinema queues were half a mile long, and Japan – just about everywhere really, except of course behind the Iron Curtain, where the Soviet authorities had already taken note of this appalling figure.

Actually, in Paris, the mania caught the eye of serious cultural commentators, for the French had never previously been famous for their welcoming attitude towards foreign films. It was noted, to the bemusement of *The Observer*'s Paris correspondent, that 'a James Bond cult is sweeping France . . . at Galeries Lafayette, a special James Bond boutique is selling trench-coats, gold-bordered handkerchiefs, 007 cuff-links and cool English James Bond shirts . . . it may be symptomatic of a changing France'.

In the *Daily Worker* over here, Nina Hibbin was still very much not amused. 'Bondists are expected to shriek with laughter even before the first victim is kicked in the guts or battered against the wall,' she wrote. Expected? We couldn't help ourselves. 'They must gurgle with relish whenever their nonchalant hero . . . rolls a girl he's hardly met and certainly hates into the nearest bed.' Hold on, hate? Tish and fie, Miss Hibbin, Bond's an old softy at heart. But to continue: 'Above all, they [the fans] must be ready (as soon as they are given the magical wisecrack signal) to roll in the aisles as a man is electrocuted and disintegrates in a flame-coloured flash . . . the racialism, the cold-war implications of the plot – they are not in the film for a joke. All this is the underlying menace of the film which gives laughter a dangerous and sinister ring.'

Bravo! This was a view very much shared by the Soviet newspaper *Pravda*. For in public, the Soviets were comically sniffy about the idea of spying, having climbed atop a very high horse indeed in 1960 when an American U2 spy plane was forced down in Soviet territory. Amusingly, this snootiness about cloak-and-dagger operations continued, as though the very idea of spying were merely an extension of Western decadence. You had to admire their nerve.

For Connery, the whole thing had already become a matter for another form of snootiness, the artistic variety. Earlier in 1964, he had taken the lead in the unusual Hitchcock psychodrama *Marnie*, starring opposite a memorably nervy Tippi Hedren as the eponymous kleptomaniac, sexually dysfunctional heroine. Here Connery was a rich Philadelphia businessman, Mark Rutland, who falls for the woman who has stolen from his safe but who is also determined to fathom the reasons for her hysteria. And it is this almost forensic interest that gives his character some disquieting shading. Though of course, this being Hitchcock, the entire thing is edgy.

In the film's most controversial scene – halfway into their honeymoon – Rutland takes his new wife by force, which leads to her attempting suicide. For many years, this was one of the least-regarded Hitchcocks but now it seems to have come into its own; Connery's performance is intriguing and layered, giving hints of the depth that he would find in later years. Anyway, to have moved from the profoundly unsettling climax of *Marnie* – where finally Rutland witnesses his wife in a traumatic trance, remembering the night when, as a child, she accidentally killed the sailor who was sleeping with her prostitute mother – to *Goldfinger* must have seemed like moving from third gear back into first.

Not that Connery would ever let it show, of course, and his performance in *Goldfinger* is his best as Bond; light, laconic, amused, though also thrillingly believable in moments in crisis. And after the rather straighter directorial stance of Terence Young, Guy Hamilton steps up to inject what would become known as the trademark Bondian sense of humour.

It is not merely a matter of glib, callous throwaway lines, as Nina Hibbin would have had us believe; rather, it is there in the very weave and texture of the film. Much as Gert Fröbe is a darkly comical triumph as Auric Goldfinger, who in the world other than the Hawaiian Harold Sakata could have played the implacable henchman Oddjob? It is a wonderful performance, a blend of genuine physical menace and brilliant comic timing. Given that he doesn't have a single line (because of the character's muteness), Sakata none the less has given cinema one of its most distinctive and memorable figures. He never quite threw off the role; a few years later, he reprised it in a series of cough mixture ads on US television.[6]

Nor did Honor Blackman ever quite throw off the immortal Pussy Galore, but neither has she given any indication of wanting to. Given the way that some subsequent Bond heroines were to go – yes, Jill St John and Britt Ekland, you might well blush – Pussy is quite a character. Not in terms of depth – we barely know a single thing about her; but in what she represents. With her stylish suede trouser suits and easy, apparently non-sexual relationship with the film's villain, Pussy is something of an enigma for Bond. While the novel's lesbianism has been largely erased, her initial distaste for 007's advances has not. For anyone who argues that the Bond stories are misogynist fantasies, Pussy at least partly answers the case for the films; she and Bond do not get a bed scene, and nor is Pussy required to perform in either bikini or simply in a bra. She is a strong character in her own right.

A slightly more difficult case to answer is that she wasn't as strong a character as the gadgets. It was in *Goldfinger* that we saw the first of 007's visits to the laboratory of querulous Q. The relationship between the two men was a nice touch apparently invented by Guy Hamilton, who told actor Desmond Llewelyn that the whole thing would work better if Q considered that 007 showed an utter lack of respect to all the equipment provided.

In fact, thanks to the absurd hardware, *Goldfinger* inspired an onrush of merchandise: Bond soap, Bond pyjamas, Bond action figures, toy Walther PPKs. It was the *Spider-Man* of its day. Several years previously, Ian Fleming had registered a touch of discomfort that his Bond novels were being read so closely by countless adolescents; they were, he insisted, really aimed at adults. The same was not true of the films. While they had sophistication and gloss and sex, all those on the production team knew that, really, they were aiming squarely at lads, young and young at heart. Women in the audience were expected to fancy Connery; the boys and men were expected to fall for every single aspect of Bond's life.

In March 1964, while the film was midway through production, Ian Fleming visited the set of *Goldfinger* at Pinewood, and had conversations with Sean Connery and Shirley Eaton. He was conspicuously not a well man and his health was deteriorating fast. In August, Fleming died, at the sadly young age of fifty-six. One month later, *Goldfinger* opened, and instantaneously began breaking records. And with this success came a concomitant surge in the popularity of Fleming's novels, all over the world. Fleming's cultural legacy is incalculable. To this day, the producers of the Bond films try to follow the spirit of his original works as closely as others follow religious texts.

Crucially, in 1964, *Goldfinger* hit the jackpot in the US. So from now, the pressure was very much on Saltzman and Broccoli to produce a follow-up that was even more epic and outrageous. But while they made a deal with producer Kevin McClory, who had the film rights to *Thunderball* (of which more later), others were beginning to contribute very different approaches to the notion of fictional espionage. The mad jet-set consumerism of Bond was to be countered by rather more realistic accounts of secret service life; and these, together with Bond, somehow meant that for a few years in the 1960s, espionage was the dominant metaphor for life.

CHAPTER FIVE RAINCOATS, WALLS AND BETRAYALS

We have already seen how, in some ways, the very form of the James Bond film was initiated by Alfred Hitchcock in 1959's *North by Northwest*. This was the film that gave spying a glossy cocktail feel as well as high aesthetic sense. In fact, Hitchcock had been dealing with espionage for quite a long time. In the 1930s, when he was still in Britain, he made *Sabotage* (1936), an adaptation of the 1907 Joseph Conrad novel *The Secret Agent*, the bitter tale of a shabby pornographer/spy called Verloc and his shadowy associates, among whom is a bomber. Hitch made Verloc a cinema owner. As we have seen, in 1936 there was also (a little confusingly) *Secret Agent* starring John Gielgud, itself an adaptation of W. Somerset Maugham's *Ashenden*; the narrative here involved cloak-and-dagger shenanigans in Switzerland.

Hitchcock contrived to make a dark joke of espionage in *The Man Who Knew Too Much* (1935) with Peter Lorre as the villain in the story of a spy ring and a child kidnap, and which he would later remake, with less humour, with James Stewart and Doris Day. One final British spy drama was *Foreign Correspondent* (1940), in which American Joel McCrea comes to London and gets caught up in a variety of striking spy set-pieces, including pursuit through a forest of raised umbrellas, and, in Holland, a landscape of windmills turning – one of them in the wrong direction.

The climax of *Foreign Correspondent* is set aboard an aeroplane diving out of control, hurtling downwards. How often Bond would return to such a thing – in *Octopussy*, *The Living Daylights* and *Die Another Day* to name but three.

Once Hitchcock arrived in Hollywood, he just could not let the espionage drama go, for the simple reason that such a narrative would afford him the opportunity of returning time and again to a favoured theme, that of an innocent man on the run from both good and bad guys. This is the case in *Saboteur* (1942) when Joel McCrea is wrongly accused of causing a fire at a munitions factory and is forced to flee in order to track down the real villains, who are trying to undermine America's war effort. The climax famously involves a fight to the death at the top of the Statue of Liberty; thank you for that symbolism, Mr Hitchcock, I think we got it.

Then in 1946, Hitchcock used espionage in a much darker way, and to much more electrifying effect, in a way that Ian Fleming would occasionally try. *Notorious* remains one of the Master of Suspense's most brilliantly nerve-jangling efforts. Alicia (Ingrid Bergman) is the daughter of a convicted Nazi war criminal, and she is trying to lose herself in a constant drunken debauch. Devlin (Cary Grant) is the CIA man who recruits her into a secret mission: to travel to South America and bewitch Alex Sebastian (Claude Rains), a Nazi friend of her father's who has plans concerning a quantity of enriched uranium.

Alex falls head over heels for Alicia; Alicia in turn has fallen head over heels for her controller Devlin. An ugly love triangle is made all the worse by Devlin's manipulations, on one side, and by the weird and terrible jealousy of Alex's mother on the other. The climax involves a large house party, during which Devlin has to gain access to the strictly locked cellar without betraying Alicia to the Nazis. Even now, it is almost too fraught to watch. But we can see that Cary Grant's Devlin is a clear forerunner to James Bond: dark, ruthless, seemingly impervious to emotional appeal yet underneath it all, clearly in love with Alicia himself. It may have been this performance, rather than his larkier role in *North by Northwest*, that led to Cary Grant being considered for the role of Bond.

As mentioned, 1956 brought Hitch's Hollywood remake of *The Man Who Knew Too Much*, which placed much emphasis, as many later spy dramas were to do, on the incongruous: the dark make-up that runs off a murdered man's face; James Stewart's fight in a north London taxidermy workshop, surrounded by stuffed crocodiles; a dowdy Methodist chapel in Camden Town revealed as the sinister spies' headquarters; the grand climax in the Royal Albert Hall.

This leitmotif of the forces of evil and chaos lurking beneath the everyday came to dominate the entire genre, especially in Britain, where in the 1960s an agent could scarcely walk into a red telephone box without it turning out to be a secret lift into some underground HQ. Interestingly, come 1961, just as Broccoli and Saltzman had gone into partnership, executives at Universal made enquiries into the Bond rights, feeling that Hitchcock would be the most natural director to bring them to the screen. The mind slightly boggles at a rewrought *Dr. No*, with all its perversity brought to the fore.

It was not to be. But Hitchcock returned to espionage in 1966, at the point where Bond had comprehensively conquered the world. *Torn Curtain*, with a screenplay by Brian Moore, was an emphatically chilly Cold War thriller, widely disliked at the time, and regarded as a misfire from an increasingly elderly director. All tremendously unfair; with hindsight, we have a better view of what the old Leytonstone boy was up to. And it really is worth a look now, particularly when placed alongside the gaudy excess of Bond.

Paul Newman is *Torn Curtain*'s lead, playing nuclear scientist Michael Armstrong with Julie Andrews as his fiancée. After a cruise to Oslo – the icy conditions on board the malfunctioning ship perfectly prefiguring the story to come – he starts behaving strangely and catches a flight to East Berlin. Doughty Julie just manages to slip on to the same plane – to his evident horror – and then has to watch as, at a press conference, her fiancé defects to the Eastern bloc. Of course it is not so simple – we soon discover that Armstrong has crossed the Iron Curtain in order to trick nuclear secrets out of a top scientist. But if Julie Andrews finds out, then they will be in double jeopardy.

The tension is racked up slowly, as first the authorities begin to suspect Newman and then start putting the pressure on Andrews. And the escape in the fake bus – the real one gaining inexorably along that country road – is one of Hitchcock's finest suspense sequences. On top of this, aesthetically, we can now see that this film is perfectly satisfying. The new Communist world in which Julie Andrews finds herself is filled with drab greys and browns, the landcapes flat, city scenes of bombed-out desolation and chilly new concrete. The clear implication is that all the colour has been drained away by oppression.

We have a burst of rich and welcome blue sky in the studio-bound hillside scene where Armstrong finally, whisperingly, tells his fiancée what he is up to, as the couple are watched from a distance; but generally the depressive murk is intended to feel suffocating.

And curiously, this sense of gloom and oppression and the down-at-heel came to be quite prevalent as the 1960s marched on, in British espionage sagas at any rate. *Torn Curtain* now fits neatly into a subcategory of the genre, in which America's various dimwitted answers to Bond – from Derek Flint to Matt Helm – play no part. We will deal with them in a later chapter. For now, it's worth looking at how authors and film-makers reacted against the Bond phenomenon, as opposed to trying to compete with it.

In 1963, as Ian Fleming was publishing the baroque *On Her Majesty's Secret Service*, Len Deighton was elsewhere launching *The Ipcress File*. The spy hero of this yarn – unnamed in the novel – was a direct counterpoint to the suave, posh Bond. Here, in the book, the agent moves through a realistically depicted down-at-heel London; and even though the grindingly complicated plot also takes him out to some island in the Pacific and bullet-dodging to-ing and fro-ing in Morocco, it is still low-key and concerned not with diabolical masterminds, but – to use that most heart-sinking of phrases – a traitor in the organisation.

Certainly Ian Fleming was not impressed by this new agent on the block. He read *The Ipcress File* while in hospital and said that he could not 'be bothered with all [Deighton's] kitchen sink writing and all this Nescafé'.[1]

None the less, it was critically well received, and shrewd old Harry Saltzman jumped in and acquired the film rights. After all, the colour and whizz of Bond might go out of fashion; in which case, there would be no harm in having quite a different form of spy out there on the big screen.

The Ipcress File is one of those films that improves on the book enormously – rather like Hitchcock's version of *The Thirty-Nine Steps*. Now the agent has a name – Harry Palmer – and is played by an actor who, like Sean Connery, came from a gritty background. To watch Michael Caine in the film now is to shake one's head at what contemporary audiences – expecting a shoot-'em-up, car-chase-filled epic – thought of his supremely laid-back performance, to say nothing of the film itself, in which almost precisely nothing happens.

There is still a traitor in the organisation; but no trips to the Bikini Atoll for our Harry. No sir. Instead, he stays firmly in a rather wonderfully filmed London. We see him in a drab supermarket, in his drab flat, in the drab HQ of the service, at a drab bandstand, in a drab undergound garage. Despite his apparent gourmet credentials, he cooks sultry Sue Lloyd a drab omelette. It couldn't be more anti-Bond if it tried. And they clearly tried quite hard.

The only stage when it begins to take off into something a little more fantastical is when Palmer is loaded into a brainwash box – cue traditional 1960s lighting effects – and led to believe that he is being held behind the Iron Curtain, when in fact he is in a warehouse in Wapping. The climax, against a bare brick wall of that warehouse, is a classic of its kind, so I shan't spoil it by saying who actually *was* the traitor in the organisation. Fairly obvious though.

The restraint was admirable – even a fist-fight scene between Palmer and a thug outside the Albert Hall is deliberately realistic and consequently lame. And they held on to this restraint with the sequel, *Funeral in Berlin* (1966), in which the almost impossible to follow cloak-and-dagger operations (involving fake deaths, fake defections and a traitor in the organisation) are enacted against the atmospheric backdrop of this still shattered city. But clearly the temptation to break out and place Michael Caine first in some picturesque locations – snowy Finland – and then in the middle of a Big Set with flashing lights, dials and a diabolical mastermind got too much, and we had *Billion Dollar Brain* (1967), directed by the ebullient Ken Russell.

One film that maintained a tone of near constant bleakness and heartbreaking cynicism was *The Spy Who Came in from the Cold* (1965). This was based on a 1963 novel by John le Carré, whose real name is David Cornwell. Cornwell had seen some time in MI6, and his conjurings of George Smiley and of the operations of 'the Circus' grip like a vice from the start. His books would later go on to be adapted to great acclaim for BBC Television – *Tinker Tailor Soldier Spy* and *Smiley's People*. *The Spy Who Came in from the Cold*, filmed in crisp black and white, kicks everything off.

Richard Burton is Alec Leamas, the agent of the title: alcoholic, alone, broken after a series of failed missions, kicking around at a labour exchange. Getting a job in a private London library, he strikes up a stuttering relationship with devoted and beautiful Communist Liz Gold, played by Claire Bloom. But then, when asking his greengrocer for credit, which is refused, he responds with violence and is sent to jail. This is only the start of Leamas's terrible, almost existential tribulations, at first fabricated but then real, which involve him apparently going over to the other side.

His secret mission is revenge on East German spymaster Mundt – but Leamas comes to realise that his own spymaster, icy Control (Cyril Cusack), has landed him in an appalling double-cross. Poor Liz is unwittingly sucked into this maelstrom of deceit, hauled before an East German kangaroo court, and the whole thing becomes suffocatingly depressing and bleak. This was spying for grown-ups; the book was beautifully written, the film crisply produced and ultimately heartbreaking.

To work for intelligence is to succumb to a form of insanity, wearing so many masks that you can forget which one is the real face. And unlike gruff but loveable M, sending Bond out on his missions, Cyril Cusack's Control is a frightening manipulator, ultimately without pity for his human chess pieces.

Incidentally, John le Carré has been consistently rude about Ian Fleming's work across the years, describing James Bond on one occasion as a 'sort of licensed criminal who, in the name of false patriotism, approves of nasty crimes' and on another as the ultimate 'prostitute'.[2]

And it might be argued that there is plenty of cinematic room for them both: recent le Carré adaptations include *The Tailor of Panama* (2001) starring Pierce Brosnan and *The Constant Gardener* (2005) with Ralph Fiennes.

Unlike Fleming, who was in naval intelligence but never actually a spy out in the field, Le Carré with his MI6 experience was the real deal. While many have assumed that Fleming's Bond was a work of projection – the author making his creation do all the things that he had most wanted to do – Le Carré's world was grim, downtrodden, the circular, existential games of spying seeming to reflect a wider futility. Le Carré's Circus, however noble its original aspirations, could never have saved the world from Blofeld.

It is also fascinating now to look at the ideological questions raised not only by Le Carré but elsewhere. In *The Spy Who Came in from the Cold*, the character Liz Gold's seemingly wide-eyed membership of the Communist Party – she says she believes in history – curiously echoes Peter Sellers's satirical portrayal of the union leader Fred Kite in *I'm All Right Jack* (1959), in which Kite dreams of visiting the Soviet Union. 'All them cornfields and ballet in the evening,' he sighs.

But actually throughout the 1950s, 60s and 70s, the Iron Curtain did have the odd tiny chink, in the sense that in Britain, to be a Communist was a respectable if faintly socially regrettable political stance. We are not just speaking of spies such as Burgess, Philby and Maclean, whose political views were shaped in 1930s Cambridge; we are talking of real-life union leaders, of writers, journalists, actors, politicians who, if not signed-up members of the Party, were sufficiently left-wing to view the Soviet Union as no greater a menace than the United States.

This was not strictly treachery, for we were not strictly at war. The Cold War was something that went on out of sight, an invisible conflict between ghostly armies, or sometimes a war fought by proxy in other poorer Third World countries. However, although it now seems improbably naïve, given that we all now know about the nature of life in the USSR from Stalin through to Brezhnev, it was then neither a mad nor a bad thing to see the Soviet system as something pure to be aspired to, like the kibbutz system in Israel wrought on a grand scale.

Throughout the stagflationary 1970s, as the West staggered under the economic repercussions of the OPEC oil crisis, people with such views were regarded by certain members of the security services as the enemy within. One has only to read the works of veteran spy specialist Chapman Pincher, written at the end of that decade, to get a flavour of the hatred and contempt held in certain right-wing quarters for perceived traitors and 'useful idiots'.

But then it was only during the 1980s – and the advent of President Reagan and Prime Minister Margaret Thatcher – that strong left-wing views were either loudly ridiculed or demonised; witness, as a small example, the mockery and scorn of the right-wing British press when in 1981, a group of women established a camp at Greenham Common in Berkshire to protest against the US nuclear weapons that would be based there.

Although a James Bond film would never be so impolite as to mock or scorn anyone, the 1983 production of *Octopussy* was the only film in the series to use, head-on, the danger of latent Soviet sympathies as the keystone of the mad villain's plot, as we shall see. By setting the climax in an American base in West Germany, the screenwriters came as close as Bond ever did to acknowledging a real world of nuclear anxiety and rising Cold War animus. Though they also managed to do so without making the Russians the bad guys – instead, the force of evil here is a rogue general acting without the knowledge of the Soviet praesidium. Genius!

Back in 1963, what le Carré did with *The Spy Who Came in from the Cold* was extraordinarily prescient and humane; while acknowledging the Soviet Union as a powerful and dangerous enemy, it also skilfully established a degree of moral equivalency, one that is pondered over disingenuously by the frosty Control. Near the start of the book, and indeed the film, Control tells the wary Alec Leamas: 'The ethic of our work, as I understand it, is based on a single assumption. That is, we are never going to be aggressors. Do you think that's fair?'

But it is Leamas himself who, towards the climax of the story, turns angrily on Liz and tells her about the nature of espionage: 'What do you think spies are: priests, saints and martyrs? They're a squalid procession of vain fools, traitors too, yes; pansies, sadists and drunkards, people who play cowboys and Indians to brighten their rotten lives. Do you think they sit like monks in London balancing the rights and wrongs?'[3]

As the 1960s wore on, the Bondian version of spying – that is, the colourful whirl of sex and conspicuous consumption – came to dominate the genre and the idea of spy story as bleak philosophical enquiry retreated. Except, that is, for one unusual 1968 production directed by Anthony Mann entitled *A Dandy in Aspic*. In this (unfortunately Mann died part way through filming), Laurence Harvey plays a rather snooty British agent called Eberlin. But he has a secret: he is a double agent and his Russian identity is an assassin called Krasnevin. Gradually the British become aware of the threat of Krasnevin and order Eberlin to eliminate him. In other words, his role is to wipe himself out. Mia Farrow is the doe-eyed love interest in this espionage psychodrama that clearly could not end happily.

Come the 1970s and the spy cycle inevitably waned; even Bond, in the deftly comic persona of Roger Moore, was carefully repositioned into the role of slightly more straightforward adventurer as opposed to shadowy operative. But the more serious 1960s spy films now look like a fascinating reflection of a very strange period of history. In terms of fiction, we had moved, through two world wars, from a position where Richard Hannay and Bulldog Drummond were in no doubts about the superiority of the British Empire, via the gung-ho British war movies of the 1950s, dramatising our Second World War triumphs, to this sudden depression in the 1960s where Empire was being swept away like sand and suddenly the mother country was left to defend what little it had left, with a marked increase in self-loathing.

After *Goldfinger* and the Beatles, and the emergence of the Rolling Stones; after the breathless American headlines about Swinging London, the Mersey Beat, kookiness, kinkiness and the mini-skirt, Britain was at least established as the world's centre of excitable sexy ephemera. For the Bond producers, the success of their latest film had ratcheted the pressure up, for how could one top the attempted conquest of Fort Knox? Clearly, they needed something with a little more global reach.

CHAPTER SIX **GREAT BALLS OF THUNDER**

There is a song that one very rarely gets to hear, the Bond song that got away. Among the rather brilliant lyrics are the lines: 'He's tall and he's dark/And like a shark, he looks for trouble/That's why the zeroes double'. It was called 'Mr Kiss Kiss Bang Bang', it was sung by Dionne Warwick and it was originally intended for the opening titles of *Thunderball*. John Barry's composition has a sort of seductive jazzy cheek about it, and echoes of this unused song can be heard throughout the film's incidental score; the title itself apparently derived from the term that Japanese fans had for their secret agent hero. However, Saltzman and Broccoli did not care for it, and so Barry instead composed *Thunderball* for Tom Jones. It is a shame because the first song might have given a small lift to what is a quite spectacularly boring film.

On paper, this shouldn't be the case at all. You have Bond's arch-nemesis, Ernst Stavro Blofeld, and a plan to hold Britain and America to ransom by kidnapping two nuclear warheads; you have a villain with an eyepatch called Emilio Largo who has a huge yacht with hidden subterranean doors (something the Russians were supposed to have had ten years previously at the time of the Buster Crabb frogman controversy, when said British agent went missing while spying underwater on a Russian vessel docked at Southampton); you have a location in the Bahamas, a good girl called Domino, a bad girl called Fiona Volpe, and people being killed by sharks in a swimming pool. In other words, it all sounds extremely promising. What went wrong?

The legal battle over the rights to *Thunderball* has been covered in print almost as exhaustively as Princess Diana's final night in Paris. We still hear the echoes even now. Certainly the damn thing was to hover over Broccoli and Saltzman until 1983, when it resulted in the production of the first serious rival Bond movie – *Never Say Never Again*.

Here is the dispute in a nutshell. Just when literary Bond was beginning to take off, and before the film rights to the books had been sold, Ian Fleming got together with film producer Kevin McClory and associate Jack

Whittingham and the three of them discussed a story and a script that could bring Bond to the screen. This was not the first time Fleming had tried scripting; he also wrote a putative film version of his novel *Moonraker*. On this occasion, though, the *Thunderball* script was a collaborative process. And it got nowhere.

A couple of years later, Fleming took the story of *Thunderball* and turned it into a novel, apparently without reference to McClory or Whittingham. 'It's difficult,' says Fleming's literary agent Peter Janson-Smith, 'for when three people are sitting together one evening discussing a thing like this into the small hours . . . well, who can really say who came up with what?'

Duly, in 1963, it came to court. Obviously Fleming had absolute rights over the character of Bond himself. Under question though was the paraphernalia of hijacked missiles and health farms and sinister yachts. But by 1963, Fleming was not a well man, and the court case, it is popularly believed, took a further toll on his health. Certainly, he did not allow it to proceed to its conclusion – he settled out of court.

And when it came to production of the film in 1965 (a year after Fleming's death) there was an unusual stipulation that arose from the court action. Saltzman and Broccoli would be billed as 'executive producers' on the picture; but the role of 'producer' would, for this one occasion, be credited to Kevin McClory.

On the face of it, this made little difference as once more, the Bond family was swinging back into action. Terence Young returned to helm the proceedings (though he later said that he had rather regretted doing so). Ken Adam was once more designing the sets. Peter Hunt was there editing, John Barry was scoring. Lois Maxwell's Moneypenny got a shade more involvement this time around, as did Bernard Lee's M. And now looking utterly at home with the role was a slightly fuller-figured Sean Connery, his dubious hairline becoming apparent for the first time.

The French-set pre-credits sequence – involving a SPECTRE operative dressed as a grieving widow, and Bond (or his stunt double) eventually making his escape via a real-life jet-pack – had a certain sort of charm, at least for the eight-year-olds in the audience. Oh, and for *Observer* writer Ronald Bryden, who noted: 'The Bond of *Thunderball*, leaping into the sky . . . has more in common with Superman and Flash Gordon than with the puzzled grey hirelings of Greene and Ambler.'

And the title sequence – with Maurice Binder back at the helm – became the Ur-text for this kind of thing, featuring naked ladies in silhouette swimming about in bright primary colours underwater while being shot at with harpoon guns. After this, however, everything subtly begins to go wrong.

We are in Paris, where a dowdy institute for displaced refugees is revealed to be a SPECTRE conference centre. Emilio Largo (Adolfo Celi) joins the other hoods in the Ken Adam-designed chamber as, behind some opaque plastic, Blofeld sits stroking his Persian cat, telling someone off for embezzling funds and then electrocuting said chap in his chair.

The set is striking. 'I wanted to get away from f****** boardroom tables,' laughs Sir Ken. And indeed, tribute to his vision was paid in 1997 in the form of the set for Dr Evil's conference chamber in the first *Austin Powers* film.

But in terms of sophistication, this original scene barely rises above the absurdity of Bulldog Drummond. Since when would top-secret criminals gather together to discuss their rather banal blackmail and extortion schemes? And why? Don't they have telephones? And surely, when Largo comes to discuss his own plans for the hijack of two NATO nuclear missiles, he would prefer not to be overheard by all these other Toms, Dicks and Harrys?

The second thing that goes wrong is the very next part of the film. It's set in an English health farm where, by wild coincidence, Bond happens to be staying just as the Largo masterplan – involving duplicating an RAF commander at that very health farm – is under way. Despite one moment of inventiveness – in which Bond is strapped to a mechanical back-stretching traction machine turned into a rack – this section of the film seems to go on for a fortnight. Rooms are crept about in; saucy backchat is had with the nurse; duplicate patients are swapped; more rooms are crept about in. It is lethal.

Curiously, better use of a health farm as a backdrop for sinister activities came in a 1978 episode of the TV thriller series *The New Avengers*, when such a place was covertly used to turn senior government officials into human lab rats, brainwashing them and trapping them in a frightening human-size rat's maze with the reward of water at the centre. But then, the adventures of the bowler-hatted secret agent John Steed often carried curious parallels with Bond, as we shall be finding a little later on.

So, right then. Back to this bomb hijack plot. Someone made to look like an RAF commander is now on board a nuclear-missile-carrying Vulcan, which he contrives to take over and land in the sea near Nassau in the Bahamas. Then Largo's scuba divers throw a camouflage net over the plane and kill the pilot, cruelly. SPECTRE has the missiles! And its blackmail demands are relayed to London.

So, about forty-five minutes into the film, we at last have Bond on the mission and it's off to sunny Nassau. There he immediately meets Domino (Claudine Auger), who describes herself successively as Largo's niece, then his mistress, though quite what is wrong with the term girlfriend I don't know. Bond plays an inexplicable card game at a naff casino with Largo, and then more to-ing and fro-ing sets in. For a while, Bond is trailed by someone who looks like a young Sir Les Patterson, but who is revealed to be Felix Leiter (played by Rick Van Nutter) again. Then – oh God! – we head out for some underwater spying.

Let's get this in some sort of historical perspective. These days, scuba diving is commonplace. In 1965, it was terribly exotic. As indeed was the spectacle of shoals of tropical fish. Why else would every Chinese restaurant the length and breadth of Britain throughout the 1960s and 70s feature large garish aquariums as centrepieces? None the less, watery sequences are the enemy of any James Bond film. And here is why.

First, everything is just so damned slow. And obscure, as we see when Bond tries to get submarine pictures of Largo's boat. In order to show up for the camera, Connery is required to wear a bright orange shorty wetsuit. Is bright orange really the ideal colour for an undercover spy? On top of this, only three things can happen underwater: first, someone cuts your air pipe with a knife; second, someone pulls your face mask off and threatens you with a harpoon gun; third, you swim through the wreckage of a ship and get a fright when a shark suddenly swims through a hatchway. That's it, the long and short of it. *Thunderball* is not alone; other Bond films that slow up quite horribly beneath the waves are *For Your Eyes Only* and *Tomorrow Never Dies*.

It's not that such scenes are done badly. The coordinator here was one Ricou Browning, who some twelve years previously had portrayed one of Hollywood's most iconic monsters, the Creature from the Black Lagoon. That film also featured a great deal of underwater action, but rendered palatable on that occasion by the attractions of 3D – making all the floating plant-life poke out of the screen – and crisp black and white photography, making the underwater lighting very much easier on the eye.

In *Thunderball*, they tried speeding up the action a little by undercranking the camera, but with the speeded-up bubbles that resulted, the effect was simply absurd. So they were stuck with frogmen in real time.

Out of the water, there seems — unless this is imagination — to be an unconscious move towards making Bond a team player as opposed to a lone wolf. In his secret harbour HQ, Bond is accompanied by local agents Paula and Pinder, plus Felix Leiter and tetchy old Q in comedy shorts. Why the crowd? Bond doesn't need any of these bloody people — even Q might simply have posted his devices in a diplomatic bag. The effect is to erase any remaining feeling of suspense that there might have been.

Making matters worse are a curiously unmotivated villain and two dull henchmen (the actor Philip Latham is wasted in the role of Vargos — such a part should have been camped to the hilt but he is clearly under instruction to rein it in). The only bright spark among all of these elements is the female villain, Fiona Volpe (as played by Luciana Paluzzi). Whether firing missiles from her motorbike, or taking Bond on a hair-raisingly fast night-time drive, Fiona is the classic Bond Bad Girl.

She and Bond get to make love. But afterwards, Fiona mocks the notion that such an act would convert her to his side, noting that unlike other paragons of goodness Bond has slept with, she can hear no choirs of angels singing. Hooray for the Bad Girl telling it like it is! Then some more to-ing and fro-ing, this time a chase through a Nassau night-time carnival that ends, most unsatisfactorily, with Fiona Volpe being accidentally shot by one of Largo's henchmen.

Throughout all of this, Connery is remarkably good-humoured, especially given the unusually clunky nature of the script, with convoluted entendres that are almost triple, rather than merely double. In fact, through much of it, Connery has to use wry facial gestures to indicate not only to other characters but also to us that he can see just how ker-plunking this all is. How strange that it should have come from the same production team that gave us the comic genius of *Goldfinger*.

Actually, no matter how good-humoured he looks in the film, Connery by 1965 was starting to chafe. Rather sweetly, he and his wife Diane Cilento and two young children lived in a large house in the otherwise dowdy west London suburb of Acton. Bond, naturally, was bringing an unprecedented amount of attention, and people would very often simply stare in through Connery's front windows. It is all too easy to imagine just how infuriating this must have been.

But it wasn't just the constant attention; Connery had clearly clocked that the script of *Thunderball* was not Pirandello. In February 1965, just before shooting began, he told the *Sunday Express*: 'I'd like to see someone else tackle Bond, I must say, though they'd be crazy to do it . . . There was talk of Richard Burton doing one.'[1]

Connery, meanwhile, was impatient to get to work on chewier cinematic material. He found some in the tough 1965 Sidney Lumet melodrama *The Hill*, set in a British army prison in Libya during the Second World War. The Hill of the title is an artificial construction, there to punish the convicted soldiers of the camp, who must run up and down it repeatedly under the scorching Libyan sun. In a cast that included Harry Andrews and Michael Redgrave, Connery's character was the most sympathetic of the piece. The reviews at the time were mixed.

On top of artistic satisfaction, there was another issue that — to put it delicately — was beginning to throb like an angry boil: money. The previous year, Connery had told Barry Norman that Bond had given him 'security'; but as time went on, the actor increasingly compared the amount that he was getting — estimated by Norman in 1964 to be in the region of £100,000 — with the sums that were perceived to be filling the pockets of Messrs Broccoli and Saltzman.

In short, over the next few years, Connery became increasingly convinced that he ought to be on a rather better cut. And, since he was (and is) an exceptionally self-possessed man, he was not shy about letting his producers know this.

But enough intermission, and back to the main feature — and now we are all looking at our watches repeatedly. How is it possible for a drama involving nuclear blackmail to drag on so? I will tell you how: no countdown. Lethal mistake. Never feature a nuclear missile unless said missile is equipped with ticking clock. To be fair, Saltzman and Broccoli were mindful of this with every subsequent Bond, but on this occasion, hell! Bond is now among the bad guys — an array of wetsuits in twilight — prior to the cavalry showing up, in the form of American soldiers in (handily) different coloured wetsuits.

As we have seen, the rather narrow gamut of things that can happen underwater is now run through: masks are pulled off faces; air pipes are cut with knives; harpoon guns are shot. At very great length. This climactic battle beneath the waves must be up there in the Ten Most Boring

Cinematic Scenes Ever (others in this category – you will have your own – include the moon scenes in *2001 – A Space Odyssey* (1968) and practically the whole of *Blow Up* (1966)).

One last effort to create a stir of excitement: a fight on board Largo's yacht, the *Disco Volante*, in which the boat suddenly speeds up and heads towards some rocks, all rendered in flashes of action by Peter Hunt's unique editing. But too late! As the closing credits flash up, one is left feeling as bloated and listless as though one had just eaten an entire box of cheap chocolates in one sitting.

And no disrespect to either Kevin McClory or Jack Whittingham, but it is very obvious that the script is the trouble. You can tell that it is not pure Fleming, even though Fleming attempted to run off with the plot; the structure is just too floppy and self-indulgent and ill thought out and weirdly lacking in either jeopardy or the sort of near fairy-tale villainy that Fleming usually excels in.

Just compare this to another of Fleming's straighter Bond adventures – *On Her Majesty's Secret Service* – and you will see the difference. Even in the latter – as straight a thriller as Fleming ever wrote – there are still wonderfully vivid and unforgettable details, such as Blofeld's demonic emerald-green contact lenses, designed, he claims, to shield his eyes from the bright sunlight reflected off the snow.

Along with *Thunderball*'s lumbering storyline is some excruciating dialogue. Now let's be honest, those naff sexual one-liners were never Bond's subtlest point, but here, when he is trying it on with the health farm nurse, it is as if he is clubbing her over the head with a wet cabbage. One ends up cringing with Connery, rather than laughing with the character. One might argue that in cultural terms, the mid-1960s were one long string of awful sexual innuendo, but that is still no excuse. The double entendres that featured in *Carry on Spying* were Wildean compared to this eyewash.

A thought here for poor old Claudine Auger as Domino Durval; one might have thought that after Pussy Galore, the Bond girl would have become a rather more colourful figure in her own right. Domino is unquestionably very beautiful but in terms of characterisation, she is as grey as London drizzle. How odd to think that the supremely un-grey Julie Christie was mooted for this role. How doubly odd to consider the rumour that Christie didn't get it because her breasts were deemed insufficiently enormous.

How trebly odd to think that other names in the hat were Raquel Welch and Faye Dunaway. Why, why, why would you throw such a script at actresses like this? Incidentally, a few years later, Cubby Broccoli declared: 'It is not necessary to use established actresses in these films. It's entertainment, after all, not *Macbeth*.'[2] Which puts Shakespeare firmly in his place.

The same year as *Thunderball*'s release, Julie Christie starred in a rather larger epic: David Lean's extraordinary adaptation of *Doctor Zhivago*. Imagine just for one moment if Christie had chosen *Thunderball* above that; or that her breasts had in fact been deemed by Saltzman and Broccoli to be sufficiently huge. We might never have heard of her again. Without wishing to be unkind, we certainly did not hear many subsequent peeps from Claudine Auger.

At the time, Auger made this claim: 'The Bond women are women of the nuclear age: they are free and they make love when they want to without worrying about it afterwards.'[3] This despite the fact that her character was a chattel – more like a woman of the Middle Age.

Aside from Connery, Adolfo Celi does at least give his thinly drawn villain a little welly; he is convincingly hands-on in his perfidy. Whether torturing Domino with a combination of ice cubes and burning cigar (to be honest, I still don't quite understand this – surely the cigar burns would be awful enough? What do the ice cubes add? Or am I being naïve here?), or having hapless henchmen hurled into his shark-filled swimming pool, Largo lacks the insanity of Goldfinger but at least convinces as one who is thoroughly horrid. Celi was a big star in South America; he later turned up again on British screens in the BBC's lurid and widely ridiculed serial *The Borgias* in the early 1980s. Sadly minus the Largo eyepatch.

In Britain, the lustre had worn off among many of the critics. 'Thunderballs, really,' said Robert Robinson in the *Sunday Telegraph*, adding that the script was composed of nods and winks but that 'it is a contemptuous wink'.

Elsewhere, the magisterial critical voice of Kenneth Tynan boomed down from on high in *The Observer*: 'It's like a prodigious toyshop cum travel agency,' he wrote. 'Sean Connery strolls through the gimmick-laden decor like an immortal shop-walker . . . instead of Websterian monsters like Oddjob and Rosa Klebb, we get nothing more eccentric than a silver-haired Italian thug with an eye patch . . . Bond's world has been conquered by the dreaded cohorts of gadgetry.'

Similar sad head-shaking went on at the *Guardian*: 'It's difficult to say who killed James Bond – but one thing does seem clear. He is certainly dead. My guess is that market research did it.'

And no comfort from that usual cheerleader of all things Bond, the *Sun*: 'He very nearly bored me this time around,' wrote its critic of our hero. 'No one, not even James Bond, can work well without a good script.'

Well, if Albert R. Broccoli and Harry Saltzman wept bitter tears at these judgements, their eyes would soon have been dried by the resounding echoes of the cinema cash registers. The thing, it seemed, was critic-proof. The film cleaned up, especially in the States.

Perhaps boredom thresholds were lower in those days. Certainly the audiences trooping in would have been largely lured by fond memories of *Goldfinger*. Strangely, though, we see the start here of something that would remain largely true of Bond throughout the decades: that by and large, the critics' verdicts were utterly superfluous. Even if these wiseacres tried to tell us that the film was a stinker, we simply brushed them aside.

It works the other way around too. On its opening in 2006, *Casino Royale* attracted arguably the best critical response ever received for any Bond film, with performances, script and direction being praised to the high heavens. The film did extraordinarily well, but *not* because of the critics. Who cared what they thought? We would have gone to see it no matter what. It was one of those occasions that demonstrated that the Bond phenomenon represents something more than a cinematic experience.

Of course *Thunderball* has its good points. Ken Adam's quite wonderful set design for British intelligence HQ is one such example. This towering space – clearly supposed to be somewhere within the environs of Whitehall – blends grandiose nineteenth-century architecture with very twentieth-century technology, in the form of the vast oil paintings that become screens and maps, and it dwarfs M and the Home Secretary. It is a wry visual suggestion that Britain is not only still a formidable imperial power, but also one that is very much in the forefront of new technology and a swaggering player upon the world stage. By 1965, this was very much not the case.

The 'winds of change' that Harold Macmillan had referred to several years previously had swept across the entirety of Britain's empire; there was very little left and the little that was, was troublesome. Macmillan's Labour successor, Harold Wilson, was tested sorely by the racist recalcitrance of white Rhodesia and its leader, Ian Smith, who refused any form of interracial power-sharing. When *Thunderball* was released, the Americans had just sent their first marines to Vietnam, and president Lyndon B. Johnson was putting pressure on Wilson to provide British support.

There was a suggestion that Britain's economic dependence on the States – particularly rescuing the UK from a devaluation of the pound – would come at a diplomatic price. To Johnson's fury, however, Wilson refused any military help. The conceit of 1960s James Bond is that in matters of espionage and heroism, America absolutely relies on Britain, and that ultimately it is British pluck and intelligence that saves the day. How LBJ must have laughed at that.

But the confidence implied by the Whitehall intelligence set design does reflect the fact that in pop-cultural terms, Britain was now very much leading the world. London was still one year away from being declared the grooviest place on the planet by *Time* magazine but our entertainment exports, and our fashion, were deemed by the US to be cool and sexy.

Of course, Bond was there in the vanguard, with the ever more popular Beatles, but amusingly, *Thunderball* is determinedly unhip in every way. Carnaby Street modes had no place in Bond, and the reasoning was not aesthetic; rather, Saltzman and Broccoli knew that if the films were to have any shelf-life beyond initial release, then they had to transcend the fleeting fads of the day so as not to look too badly dated five or ten years hence.

Shelf-life was a terrifically important issue at that point; a few years previously, it had looked as though the relatively new medium of television might, in terms of competition, destroy film. But by the mid-1960s, film producers could see that actually, television offered up a potentially lucrative new market, in terms of selling screening rights. This was fine for most low- or mid-budget films, but at the higher end of the scale, every last penny first had to be wrung from cinema admissions.

Saltzman and Broccoli were brilliantly cunning about this. They withheld TV screening rights for Bond until well into the mid-1970s. The reason was that the films could regularly be reissued at cinemas as double bills. The first instance of this was the American pairing of *Dr. No* and *From Russia with Love* in 1963, which did storming business. The same tactic was employed in the UK. Indeed, one of my own earliest memories of cinema is being taken in 1974 to a double bill of *Thunderball* and *You Only Live Twice*. These reissues continued in the UK until 1980, when *The Spy Who Loved Me* was shown in a double bill with *Moonraker*.

Another high point of *Thunderball* is the silky musical score from John Barry, which – after we rub our ears following Tom Jones's rendition of the title track like a tuneful bull bellowing in a field – is alternately seductive and invigorating. Indeed, it saves the film – and its audience – from complete narcolepsy. While not as brassy as the *Goldfinger* score – there is more use here of subtler instruments like the piano – it infuses slightly ropy spectacles like the fight in the chateau and the final underwater battle with melodic interest at least. These days, it is more enjoyable to listen to the soundtrack in isolation than it is to watch the film. Here, Barry hit his super-confident stride; as with the fashionable factors mentioned above, his music was too properly composed to date. Compare it with most of its contemporaries, and their cheap Hammond organ stings.

Indeed, it was around this time that Barry's formidable talent was being properly recognised. He won an Oscar for the title song of *Born Free* (1966) and another in 1968 for his evocative score to *The Lion in Winter*. The wonderful thing is that there is never any sense that he is slumming it in a Bond. For instance, his lush, richly textured score for *You Only Live Twice* – especially in the 'Mountains and Sunsets' track – creates the illusion that there is something genuinely resonant and emotional going on in the film. There isn't. Occasionally, one wonders just how far Bond would have got had it not been for the combined genius of Barry and Ken Adam.

Thunderball rode a triumphant wave with British cinema generally at this period. The monochrome soot-and-rain-and-knitting-needle phase of the New Wave in the early 1960s had given way to something a little more frenetic and certainly more glamorous. We think of 1965's *Darling* starring Julie Christie (again), a splendidly horrible cautionary tale about beauty and materialism, which threw a bucket of sick over such trendy pursuits as photography, hairdressing and casual sex. A couple of years earlier, the costume drama had been sexed up for a full-colour adaptation of Fielding's *Tom Jones* starring Albert Finney – all winks and nods to camera, and speeded-up sequences, and sauce.

There were the (now irksome) Beatles films, with their post-modernist slapstick. What's more, all the big Hollywood studios had offices in London, and the British studios – Pinewood, Borehamwood, Shepperton, Elstree – were all in constant use. One actor recalls how it would be possible during this period to walk through the Pinewood canteen and bump into Ingrid Bergman.

Curiously, though, no one ever quite associates the Bond movies with the British film industry, despite the fact that all bar two (*Moonraker* and *Licence to Kill*) were made on British soil. It can't simply be because they have always been funded by American studios – from United Artists to MGM; after all, ninety per cent of all British films made during this period relied on such investments. Nor can it be because they used their own facilities – Bond was a Pinewood mainstay for the best part of two decades, and indeed bequeathed it the '007 stage'.

Possibly it is something to do with the determinedly internationalist outlook of the films. Look at the European cast of *Thunderball* – a French leading lady, an Italian villain. Bond seemed to have little time either for Britain's new swinging status, or indeed for the trendiness of its new generation of leading actors. Never would you see the likes of Terence Stamp or Michael Caine gracing a Bond. Not even a Rita Tushingham or a Lynn Redgrave. Though the production crew might have found their busts insufficiently awesome anyway.

This was Terence Young's final foray as Bond director; the next time around, veteran Lewis Gilbert, who had such a roaring success with *Alfie* (1966), would reintroduce the baroque comedy that made such a success of *Goldfinger*. In the meantime, though, Bond now had to face serious competition, both direct and indirect.

CHAPTER SEVEN SPIES IN OUR EYES

If one was not a fan of the spy genre, the period from 1965 to 1967 must have been exceptionally trying. Even if one managed to avoid Bond – and that meant not just at the cinema, but also at the shops, where Bond merchandise from watches to model cars filled the shelves – there was suddenly a milling throng of fictional agents. There was Michael Caine's Harry Palmer, as discussed. But then the Americans decided to throw their two dollars' worth in as well.

There was James Coburn as agent Derek Flint, whose first spoof outing was *In Like Flint* (1966) and who got another bash in *Our Man Flint* (1967). Some have described these films as amusing and entertaining, but I can't help feeling there has been some sort of mistake here, for the Flint I have seen is not only galumphingly unfunny but also so penny-pinching that even the camp appeal is diminished.

Perhaps acknowledging that they could not quite keep pace with the budgets of Saltzman and Broccoli – certainly, the model work seems to have an apologetic jokiness about it – the Flint team, like many who claim to be making jokes while actually being rather serious, none the less is obviously angling to set their man up as the USA's answer to 007. We meet Derek Flint (a name almost as unsexy as Duckworth Drew) in his perfectly hideous yellow and brown bachelor pad, surrounded by a gaggle of silly dollies. There, you see, the producers seem to be saying: Bond only ever had one bird at a time! Look at this man with his harem!

A cabal of scientific super-villains is holding the world to ransom with some form of dam-busting, weather-changing death ray. The authorities beg Flint to help. This he does, via a series of judo moves and improbable escapes from assassination attempts in ghastly restaurants. As the Bond films raised the aesthetic bar for escapist production design, so Flint conversely boasts a series of the most horrid sets in cinema history.

Are there any saving graces? Well, Flint's long-suffering boss has a communications device that makes a maddeningly familiar noise. The reason for its familiarity is that it subsequently featured in the wonderful 1990s

Austin Powers films, with which we will deal in a later chapter, since they caused so much grief to Eon Productions. Anything else? Well, when watching now, there is some satisfaction in watching an unsuccessful American attempt to shamelessly rip off Bond with big sets and girls in tinselly mini-skirts. The excuse is that the film is played for laughs; yet the Bond films are of themselves sufficiently amusing.

Derek Flint, as portrayed by James Coburn, is one of the most singularly charmless creations ever to make it to celluloid; and the script works on the assumption that the entire audience is moronic. But the thing is that this was not uncommon in the cinema of the mid-1960s. I refer you back to the Beatles films.

Indeed, the 'spoof' comedy is one of the curses of that age. Let us turn to a more continental effort from 1966 – *Modesty Blaise*, starring Monica Vitti and Terence Stamp and directed by the eminent Joseph Losey. *Modesty* was based on a character in a long-running newspaper strip cartoon by Peter O'Donnell. The film does not trouble itself with any further dimensions.

Modesty is a sort of quasi-spy; the idea is that in a neat role reversal, Terence Stamp, as Willie, is her dolly sidekick. The villain, a chap called Gabriel, is played by Dirk Bogarde, in a fashion very far removed from that of his persona in the 1950s *Doctor* films. Like *Thunderball*'s Emilio Largo, he has a luxury yacht.

Other than this, the narrative involves very many speeded-up sequences, scenes of parasexual activity, eye-popping op-art set design and a baffling climax involving Bedouins. Like *Flint*, it is only the dated period details of the thing that make it remotely endurable. Monica Vitti and Terence Stamp have all the sexual chemistry of two dead haddock on a slab. The comedy – like so much comedy of that period – has a desperate, frenetic, bulldozer quality.

Only the truly committed will now make it to the end. One word of praise though, and that's to jazz musician Johnny Dankworth's score – catchy, jaunty, and rather amusing. As with *Thunderball*, there is now more pleasure in listening to the music in isolation from the film.

Those Americans wouldn't give up: they tried Dean Martin in a series of films featuring agent Matt Helm, starting with *The Silencers* (1966) which again focused heavily on the dolly-bird element. But on the whole, it was difficult for film-makers to even try to emulate the Bond style, for the budgets required for proper espionage were quite enormous. For excruciating proof of this, try watching, through tightly screwed eyes, the horror that is the British production of *The Second Best Secret Agent in the World* (1965) and its sequel *Where the Bullets Fly* (1966), starring Tom Adams as secret agent Charles Vine. Possibly these unloved films have simply disintegrated in some vault, so you can't see them, ever again, not ever. If so, don't shed too many tears.

But whereas Bond's competitors on the big screen suffered, the spies that emerged on the small screen did a very great deal better. Before the Bond movies started, for instance, new channel ITV had an early hit with Patrick McGoohan in *Danger Man*, which began in 1960. At the start, this was a series of monochrome half-hour episodes – espionage as brisk short story. As the show took off, and became more successful, the stories were expanded to an hour, and then made in colour.

The dour intensity that McGoohan brought to the role of John Drake brought him briefly to the attention of Saltzman and Broccoli when they were first casting Bond. Would he have been any good? Judging from these outings, the vital element of humour might have been a little lacking. *Danger Man* was one of those shows that cheerfully pretended, on a weekly basis, to be set in countries all over the world. This simple conjuring trick was achieved by buying in stock footage of exotic locations, playing a few frames of same with a caption superimposed, and then cutting straight back to the Elstree studio floor. *Danger Man* was not alone in its prolific use of this trope; *The Saint* also played a similar weekly trick on its easily pleased viewers.

After some years, it all became a little one-dimensional and repetitive for the serious McGoohan, so he conceived what became one of the most famous television shows of all time. *The Prisoner* (1967) takes 1960s spying and turns it into a Lewis Carroll nightmare: McGoohan is the unnamed protagonist who, upon his attempt to resign from the secret service, next awakes to find himself in The Village, surrounded by a nightmarishly compliant population, told that he is 'Number Six', answerable to a constantly changing Number Two, and periodically chased by white balloons that can suffocate a man to death. Escape from this (aesthetically pleasing Italianate) village appears impossible. This is a man without a name whose daily struggle is now simply to retain his individuality in the face of ruthless onslaughts upon his sanity.

Even to this day, the industry surrounding attempts to decipher the multiple meanings of this series is enormous. Books, conventions, academic essays, university courses are all devoted to the travails of Number Six, and what the whole thing can signify. Was it all about the horrors of conformist Communism? Was it a sly satire on the impregnability of the British Establishment? Or did it have even greater metaphysical resonance? Was The Village in fact the very world itself, and Number Six Everyman? The debate will continue as long as there are DVD players and internet chat rooms. None the less, how very remarkable it now seems that this could have been screened on ITV in primetime on Sunday evenings in 1967. Admittedly, it was pulled after seventeen episodes, but still. You wouldn't catch the schedulers letting anything like this into the peak slots now.

If McGoohan brought a creepy existentialism to spy sagas, an ITV stablemate brought an exquisitely witty British sensibility that ended up conquering America in much the same fashion as James Bond. When it started in 1961, *The Avengers* was a gritty affair made in the studio on fuzzy black and white videotape. The set-up was that of a crime-busting partnership between earnest humanitarian Dr David Keel (Ian Hendry) and a rather shadowy, aristocratic figure called John Steed (Patrick Macnee).

This drama was set among the clip joints and coffee bars of fashionable Soho, and featured call-girls and razor gangs, but as the series wore on, it became apparent that Steed was in some way connected with the intelligence community. Hendry decided to leave after the first series; and the stroke of utter genius was that the producers replaced him with a woman. Mrs Cathy Gale (Honor Blackman) was a young widow with a degree in anthropology, an aptitude for martial arts and a penchant for leather catsuits.

Steed became rather more stylised; he now regularly sported a bowler hat, an umbrella, and a carnation in his lapel. The stories accordingly became more bizarre. On a weekly basis, Steed and Cathy would face infiltrators, saboteurs and assassins, all operating under the most incongruous covers, such as a conference of clergymen in 'The Little Wonders' (1964) or undertakers in 'Mandrake' (1964), and a New Year's fancy dress party in 'Dressed To Kill' (1963).

Because of studio and budget restrictions, Steed and Cathy could clearly never compete with Bond in any direct sense; but in terms of sensibility, style, fashion and narrative ingenuity, the series could. Steed's absurd insouciance, there right from the start, was one very obvious influence on the movie 007. His teasing partnership with Cathy Gale was something that

Broccoli and Saltzman couldn't match — too way out for a more conservative international audience. But Honor Blackman made too great an impact for them not to hire her for Pussy.

And when Blackman went off to do that, *The Avengers'* producers replaced her with Diana Rigg as Mrs Emma Peel, arguably the finest of all the series' women. Warmer, funnier and sexier, the partnership of Steed and Mrs Peel proved an even greater hit. And at this point, the series made the transfer to film, which made it easier to sell to American television. The production values rose accordingly; not only were the new stories intriguing and witty, they were quite beautifully shot too, first in crisp black and white, then in full gaudy 1960s colour.

The situations became more outlandish: the tiny population of a remote Suffolk village replaced by an invading spearhead taskforce, poised to take over the country; a nuclear bomb hidden within the electricals section of a London department store; a plot to blow up a diplomatic conference under the cover of a reincarnation of the eighteenth-century Hellfire Club . . .

It was elegant, amusing, beautifully scored by composer Laurie Johnson, sold all over the world — the only British series to make it to primetime American network TV — and Diana Rigg was noted by Broccoli and Saltzman as future Bond girl material.

Elsewhere, perhaps the KGB were also fans of *The Avengers*, for there does seem to be a quite remarkable parallel between Steed's ubiquitous umbrella — which conceals a swordstick and a radio — and the real-life lethal umbrella used to stab poison into the ankle of Bulgarian dissident Georgi Markov in London in 1978.

In the mid-1960s, the authorities behind the Iron Curtain were consistently shrill in their disapproval of the decadent capitalist Bond. State newspaper *Pravda* sternly noted: 'Fleming invented a world where the laws are written with a pistol barrel and rapes and outrages on the female honour are considered gallantry.' Steady on, there, comrades, lighten up!

But clearly some Bond was being smuggled through that Curtain in some form — probably the books — because the authorities then felt that they ought to respond with a super secret agent of their own, notwithstanding the fact that the official line on espionage was that it was a low-life activity only good for the fascists. And so the Bulgarian thriller writer Andrei Gulyashki was called upon to invent the heroic spy Avakoum Zahov. Indeed, in one of Zahov's adventures, he got to take on none other than James Bond himself. And in this battle, Bond was soundly defeated by the superior intelligence and strength of his Soviet counterpart.

It was only when a British publishing house took an interest in getting the book translated and put out in the UK that Fleming's agent Peter Janson-Smith called a halt, even though he was amused by the notion. Having someone else hijack the character of Bond was one thing. To have the character of 007 then ignominiously defeated was a shade too far. Thus the Bulgarian effort never saw publication over here.

In any case, it may not have been as rapturously received in Eastern Europe as the authorities cared to believe, for somehow, the Lord knows how, news of the Bond adventures was still managing to seep through those borders. Janson-Smith tells me how in the 1970s he visited Poland and was eagerly asked by friends about the nature of Bond's latest challenges.

Back in the US, 1964 saw the debut of a wildly popular networked spy caper called *The Man from U.N.C.L.E.* starring Robert Vaughn as hatchet-chinned hero Napoleon Solo and David McCallum as his enigmatic blond Russian chum Illya Kuryakin. Here again we had popular culture flying in the face of the Cold War; while Lyndon B. Johnson and Nikita Khrushchev (soon to be replaced by the chillier Leonid Brezhnev) continued their geopolitical struggles, escapist television, like Bond, summoned a world threatened not by the unbridled forces of either Communism or capitalism, but rather by a sort of privatised villainy.

Leo G. Carroll was the U.N.C.L.E. boss, Alexander Waverley, and each week saw Solo and Kuryakin involved in bizarre and lightly comic adventures, involving very old-fashioned cliffhangers and some rather wonderful music from Jerry Goldsmith. Indeed, so popular was the series both in the US and in Britain that a few of the two-part stories got stitched together to make full-length films for the cinema, including *The Karate Killers* and *One of Our Spies Is Missing* (both 1966). The series ran until 1968 and even begat a spin-off starring Stefanie Powers entitled *The Girl from U.N.C.L.E.*, clearly intended to jump on the emancipated bandwagon started by the Avenger women.

Then there was the fancy teamwork version of espionage, as practised weekly by the *Mission: Impossible* team from 1967 onwards. Led by Peter Graves, and featuring Barbara Bain and Martin Landau, this was a show that focused on the technological and strategic skill of the spies concerned – getting into impregnable buildings, pulling off absurdly complex microdot heists.

Unlike *The Avengers*, it was all done with a preternaturally straight face. We will see later what sort of impact Tom Cruise's transformation of the show into a big-screen hit was to have on the Bond films of the 1990s.

There were, of course, many less satisfactory spy shows around during the mid-1960s; in the US, there was the not especially amusing *I-Spy*, and *Get Smart*; in Britain, we had the less than scintillating adventures enjoyed by *Department S*, although this series, featuring an absurd character called Jason King played by Peter Wyngarde, spawned a culty spin-off, with crushed-velvet poodlefaker King inexplicably held to be the epitome of all things male and lady-killing.

Meanwhile, throughout the 1960s, Simon Templar – otherwise known as 'The Saint' and personated by young Roger Moore – had made the journey from straightforward crime-busting dilettante to quasi-spy. In one episode, 'The House At Dragon's Rock' (1966), Templar even encountered a scientifically engineered nest of giant ants in the Welsh valleys. That famous Moore eyebrow was almost worn out by the ensuing proceedings. It was the mid-1960s and things were clearly getting out of hand.

This was precisely the reason why, a couple of years earlier, Harry Saltzman had sniffed the air and set out to make Michael Caine a star. Critic Alexander Walker said:

> Caine had been put under contract and into *The Ipcress File* at the end of 1964 by Harry Saltzman, both because he felt he recognised material that could be groomed to stardom and because he wanted a hedge against the innumerable imitations which the James Bond films were now spawning worldwide and which, he feared, might make the public weary of the original. Although Cubby Broccoli asked 'why compete with ourselves?', Saltzman believed that the time was ripe for an anti-hero of the espionage world.[1]

Saltzman also might have been able to foresee the worst nightmare for the Bond production crew: that of a rival Bond production so insanely and terribly bad that the real thing would simply be buried for ever. And that rival Bond production was gearing up in 1966 under the auspices of producer Charles Feldman. It was the first film production of *Casino Royale*.

For various reasons that go back to the 1950s, rights to this first Bond novel had always been out of the hands of Broccoli and Saltzman. By 1966,

Feldman clearly felt that it was time to make good on his golden egg. The only explanation for what followed is that everyone at that time felt that excess in itself was a good thing. And that surrealist slapstick was automatically side-splitting.

It's pointless to give a blow-by-blow account of the plot; basically the thing involved Sir James Bond (played by David Niven) – a refined and retired man of taste – appalled by the antics of the agents who subsequently inherited the name Bond. But when the head of the secret service is blown up, Sir James is summoned out of retirement to call on the services of Jimmy Bond (Woody Allen), his daughter Mata Bond (Joanna Pettet), the agent Vesper Lynd (Ursula Andress, this time sporting her very own Swiss accent) and a card-sharp called Evelyn Tremble, played by Peter Sellers.

Le Chiffre was played by Orson Welles. Deborah Kerr was in near the beginning, playing some form of Scotland-based superspy. In between, there was a slew of cameos from George Raft and Jean-Paul Belmondo, and even some startlingly familiar domestic faces like Anna Quayle and Ronnie Corbett.

Eventually it turns out that little Jimmy Bond is in fact the villainous Doctor Noah, who aims to destroy all men taller than himself, leaving him with a planet full of women. There is a UFO; there are spinning custard pies; there are deadly mechanised flying ducks; there are faux Ken Adam sets, though so vulgarly rendered as to make the homage insulting; there is a quasi-Indian dance number; and Peter Sellers and Ursula Andress get to snog to Burt Bacharach's 'The Look of Love'. The song is the only thing that emerges from this film with any credit.

The problem wasn't just the exhausting, undisciplined screenplay; there were also multiple directors, from Joe McGrath to John Huston. Peter Sellers behaved in a particularly vile fashion throughout production – eccentrically insisting, at one point, that he would not share any shots with Orson Welles, thus necessitating their scenes being filmed on different days. It is impossible not to suspect, watching Sellers's strange performance, that he believed he really could be a proper, straight James Bond. In any case, his antics held production up, costing poor Charles Feldman a very great deal of money. And what was the end result of all the confusion and the angst?

Well, these days, it is a film that gets relegated to TV's mid-afternoon slot, and those who happen across it accidentally are almost hypnotised by the colossal badness of it (although we all secretly quite like the segment set in a jokily expressionistic East Berlin with Anna Quayle). At the time of its release, though, in early 1967, it actually did rather well. Not perhaps as well as the real thing – and many of the reviews stank – but still enough to help recoup its insane production costs. As Harry Saltzman had dreaded, the public flocked into the cinemas. Why so?

There must have been a point, in 1966–7, where it became axiomatic that to simply point a film camera at a famous person, and to have something zany happening in the background, was the very acme of cinematic achievement.

Look at *Casino*'s cannonball-throwing scene. Not only is there slapstick, but there is dignified old David Niven in the middle of said slapstick, with Deborah Kerr looking on. Similarly, when Le Chiffre inflicts mind torture on the Peter Sellers Bond, there is a scene of Sellers being harried by a mass pipe band, against a bare white backdrop. For some reason that no one in this day and age would ever be able to explain, this was deemed sufficient to make the film's audience faint with laughter.

And canny old Harry Saltzman was right. This sort of life-sapping wackiness had clearly become associated in the wider public mind with the name of James Bond. One phrase more heart-sinking than 'there's a traitor in the organisation' is the promise that 'anything can happen – and probably will'. Never mind the prospect of suspense, or thrills – this was Bond as dry-skulled imbecilic spectacle, nothing more.

This sort of camp extravaganza was rather wonderfully sent up in the satirical magazine *Private Eye*, which would run spoof news items on such a film spectacular currently in production, entitled *2001 Poofs on the Moon*, in which the director would promise girls, glamour and glitter and various veteran British actors would give shame-faced interviews about why they had taken roles ('Well you see, I got this tastefully worded letter from my bank manager . . .').

In America, the entire burgeoning phenomenon of camp – itself possibly a by-product of the TV age, making everyone aware of the trash aesthetics of bygone entertainments such as the 1930s *Flash Gordon* serials – was explored by literary and cultural critic Susan Sontag. 'The whole point of Camp,' she wrote, 'is to dethrone the serious. Camp is playful, anti-serious. More precisely, Camp involves a new, more complex relation to "the serious." One can be serious about the frivolous, frivolous about the serious.'[2]

In the 1960s, when consciousness of camp was becoming a mainstream thing, it at least had a certain novelty value. Time, however, has not been kind to such self-indulgence. Which is why, even as the Bond films, in plot terms, took a step closer to the amphitheatre of camp, the producers strived all the harder to ensure that 007 himself remained as serious a hero as possible.

CHAPTER EIGHT THIS DREAM IS FOR YOU

As ever, the *Daily Mail* reporter, this time at the royal premiere of *You Only Live Twice* in 1967, was in no mood to hold back. His breathless account of the line-up went thus: 'He said it to the producers and he said it to the Press. And last night Sean Connery said it to the Queen: "I'm not making any more James Bond films."'

Was it tiredness? Creative exhaustion? Fury that Saltzman and Broccoli were not sending adequate financial rewards his way? Almost without question the latter.

The subject of money always brought out the spikiest side of Connery. In 1966, he told David Lewin: 'I still can't get over the fact that when some producer signs a dinner bill for six people for £80, he is spending in one go more than my father had to live on and bring up our family for longer than a month. I'm not stingy with money — just careful.'[1]

Indeed so. But profligate film producers: who could he have had in mind?

In fairness, the artistic restrictions of Bond were now also making Connery tense. 'What am I supposed to do about it?' he said. 'Go around wearing a sign that I have played the classics on stage and read books including the whole of Ibsen and Pirandello and Shakespeare and some Proust which went on forever because 12 volumes of the stuff was too much. I think this question of changing an image is much easier to arrange in Russia. In Russia — and perhaps in America — you can have someone who looks like a plumber and is really a physicist. We still expect our poets to have long hair and suffer from malnutrition.'[2]

The call of the stage, that's what it was. The desire to take on rather chewier roles, as well as to shake off an increasingly oppressive alter ego. Towards the end, Bond's creator Ian Fleming tried hard to shake 007 off as well.

And curiously, the novel of *You Only Live Twice* also has an air of finality hanging over it.

Indeed, when you read Fleming's penultimate work, published in 1964, you sense very strongly that you are reading a book written by a dying man.

Not that it is sloppy; quite the reverse. Fleming's eye for weird detail – on this occasion, the tics of Japanese social customs – is as alert as ever. But the thing seems suffused with melancholy and self-loathing, especially as it reaches a quite bizarre climax. 'You only live twice,' goes Fleming's haiku on the title page. 'Once when you are born and once when you look death in the face.' In the lyrics of the opening title song, this is amended to the slightly more romantic 'One life for yourself/And one for your dreams'.

As the novel opens, Bond is still traumatised by the murder of his wife Tracy at the hands of Blofeld and Irma Bunt (at the end of *On Her Majesty's Secret Service*). He is not a great deal of use to M in this condition, and he is sent out to Japan to make some deal with the Japanese secret service concerning a cipher-breaker called MAGIC 44. But while there, in the company of Tiger Tanaka, Bond is made aware of the activities of a reclusive expat Swiss called Dr Guntram Shatterhand, operating out of an old samurai castle on the coast.

In the estate of Dr Shatterhand is an area known as the Garden of Death, seething with molten mud pools, lethal insects and venomous plant-life, and the Garden is proving a powerful draw for suicides. In one passage, one man calmly walks into such a lethal pool and sinks until only his hat remains.

The idea by itself is macabre, but then Bond sees a snatched photograph of Shatterhand and realises that it is in fact Blofeld. It is clear that Bond must assassinate him and avenge Tracy, and in order to do so, must turn himself into the semblance of a Japanese fisherman, with the aid of one Kissy Suzuki. Finally, he infiltrates Shatterhand's castle. A fight to the death ensues, Bond is threatened with a molten mud enema and then, as Shatterhand is caught in a boiling mud explosion, Bond escapes in a hot air balloon. But his mind has slipped its moorings.

First he stays with Kissy, his amnesia so complete that he cannot remember his name. London loses sight of him completely and Bond is presumed dead. M writes his obituary for *The Times*. But, one morning many months later, a fragment of memory comes back to the agent – and he sets off for Russia, the region that has rung bells, convinced that he has some business there . . .

In other words, it is all as grippingly readable as usual, even though the climax is weird and off-puttingly detached, almost as though Fleming didn't quite believe it himself any more. But the other point is that it was fundamentally unfilmable. The first half of the novel consists of Bond and Tiger Tanaka having lengthy and witty conversations about the nature of Japanese culture. The second shows our hero apparently losing his mind. From Eon's point of view, this was obviously not on. 'They had to lose everything from the novel,' recalls Sir Ken Adam. 'All those gardens full of poison.'

There was one other slight hurdle. After *Thunderball* in 1965, it had been decided to follow the sequence of the novels and have *On Her Majesty's Secret Service* as the next film. But the logistics on that occasion were against the extensive Alpine ski location work that would have to be carried out. *Service* would have to be postponed. *Twice* was brought forward.

As Broccoli and Saltzman had bought the rights to the books, there was no reason why they should not make changes for the purposes of a workable screenplay. Also, since Fleming had died in 1964, he would not be there to object (and it is highly unlikely that he would have objected anyway). But the changes they made to *Twice* were rather more than cosmetic. The screenplay bore almost absolutely no relation to the novel bar the retention of a couple of character names.

The novelist and short story writer Roald Dahl was brought in to write the screenplay – his first, in fact, demonstrating a certain level of trust from the producers. Dahl's sardonic short stories were famed for their sudden unpredictable twists; and right from the first scene, *Twice* follows a similar labyrinthine pattern, beginning with the apparent murder of Bond in a Hong Kong foldaway bed.

But this was also the advent of a bigger kind of Bond than before. More than that, this was the film that settled on the mix of outrageous action, lurid, highly coloured visuals and humour that would become the benchmark.

This time, the threat was not merely global, but also galactic, and immediate. I first saw this film when I was ten years old and it seemed to me almost impossibly exciting for the following reasons: space capsules; volcanos; countdowns; and MONORAILS! Indeed, watching it now, that pleasure never entirely goes away. For those who were that age at the height of the Space Race in the late 1960s, it must have been mind-blowingly exciting.

Here is the deal: Bond of course hasn't been murdered – but we do none the less see him buried at sea. His shroud-wound corpse is retrieved by divers and taken to a submarine, where it is revealed that 007 within has been wearing breathing apparatus. The point of the exercise was to give super-villains the idea that he was out of the picture. The effectiveness of such a strategy, by the way, can be measured by the number of bars Bond walks into worldwide where he is greeted personally and loudly by the maître d'. No matter. He is shot out of a torpedo tube and straight into the heart of the mystery.

An American space capsule has been attacked while in orbit – the umbilical line of one of the spacewalking astronauts horribly cut, leaving the fellow to float off into space – and the Americans presume that the aggressor craft is Russian. So America and Russia – as represented by delegates sitting in an Alaskan geodesic dome – are at each other's throats. But who is this delegate in the middle, his table bearing a little Union flag? Yes, it is veteran British actor Robin Bailey, once again giving the profoundly erroneous impression that the only country that both America and Russia will listen to is good old Blighty.

But the Soviets are about to launch their own capsule into space, with warnings of woe should anything befall it, and only M and Bond seem to realise that sinister third-party galactic sabotage is at work, centring on the Sea of Japan.

So off Bond goes, on to the streets of Tokyo, and into the underground HQ of Japanese secret service chief Tiger Tanaka and Tanaka's own private tube train. In order to go effectively undercover, Bond must first train to become a ninja warrior, and then have some false eyelids fitted in order to take on the guise of a Japanese fisherman. Why? Oh hush now, no matter. Also, for further verisimilitude, Bond must marry a pearl-diving Japanese girl called Kissy. This he does.

As a honeymoon treat, Bond and new wife Kissy explore an extinct volcano, Kissy attired in bikini and high heels. And before long, the wondrous truth is revealed: the volcano is hollow and contains the quite stupendous HQ of Blofeld. From here, he is launching his aggressive rockets, which capture the orbiting space capsules and bring them back down to earth, the aim being to create tension and ultimately war between America and Russia. In Blofeld's tastefully appointed volcano-conversion apartment, complete with Radox-green piranha pool, we glimpse two gentlemen who would appear to be from the Chinese military. Once again, no guesses as to who is bankrolling this one.

As to Bond: well, all those false eyelids and ninja lessons seem a little wasted as, first, he pretends to be an astronaut, being loaded into the rocket that will shoot into orbit and steal another American capsule. Blofeld rumbles him, however, so Bond misses out on going into space. His job, instead, is to escape Blofeld's clutches and stop the countdown as World War Three looms just seconds away . . .

Given the campery of all the espionage activity of the preceding two years, *Twice*, while not exactly playing it straight, gave Bond a surprisingly rich aesthetic sense, even a feeling of luxuriance, that no competitor could match, and which lifted the film far above the level of tongue-in-cheek spoof.

First, the stars of the film are without question the sets of Ken Adam and the evocative score by John Barry. Adam's Japan is a land of jutting interior angles and deceptive shining surfaces. A passageway in a disused Tokyo underground station conceals a false floor through which 007 plunges, down a gleaming chrome helter-skelter, into the hyper-modern concrete bunker of Japanese secret service chief Tiger Tanaka, with its televisions in copper bowls. The office of sinister industrialist Mr Osata is a blend of antique artefacts and sharp triangular corners, with drinks cabinets and safes once more concealed behind polished metallic surfaces.

This is of course without mentioning the most imposing star − the volcano set itself. Some 150 feet in height, a vast oval structure in depth, this was a construction that the films would not match until some ten years later with Adam's equally breathtaking work on *The Spy Who Loved Me*. The features of this volcano included a vast roof that would slide back, admitting both helicopters and returning space rockets, a fully working gantry lift with many levels, and most mouthwateringly of all, a fully functioning monorail, scooting around the circumference of the set.

Leading off was a tunnel that went to the astronauts' holding pens, while set halfway up in the volcano wall was Blofeld's control room, a super-futuristic thing of computer banks, shiny metal and strip lighting. And leading down from this (without wishing to sound too much like *Through The Keyhole*) was a staircase leading to Blofeld's private apartment, hewn out of the volcanic rock, furnished with tasteful antiques, and framed with a piranha pool spanned by a rather treacherous footbridge.

In other words, the attention to detail was so insanely meticulous that no other celluloid megalomaniac could hope to match it. Wherever did such an inspired notion come from?

In the early stages of production, producers Broccoli and Saltzman flew with Ken Adam and director Lewis Gilbert to Japan on a location recce; the original plan had been to try and find a medieval castle on the coast to match the one in Fleming's novel. But according to Ken Adam, such a thing could not be found – the Japanese simply did not build such structures on the coast.

But it was while they were out flying high above the landscape in specially chartered helicopters – 'we covered two thirds of Japan in the space of three weeks', recalls Adam – that the eyes of Broccoli and the designer were caught by a number of extinct volcanoes, wonderfully dramatic natural structures.

The thought took a hold. Could such a structure be a lair? And how much would such an epic piece of set design cost? Adam didn't know. 'Could you do it for a million dollars?' Broccoli asked him. 'Sure, I'll have a go,' said Adam.

And so in 1967, this vast cone rose and loomed over Pinewood, an unexpected eyesore for those residents who lived close by. The technicalities were daunting; would it be possible to fly a real helicopter into it? Adam, himself a former Second World War fighter pilot, was particularly concerned about any destabilising updraughts that might occur. He did it though, and that real helicopter jolly well does land, missing its mark by only a couple of feet. The set would also have to withstand an attack from a hundred abseiling ninjas jumping from the roof, plus guns and explosions, not to mention the very smoky retro rockets of a landing 'spacecraft'.

To Adam's great annoyance, Saltzman and Broccoli, while showing a tour of European distributors around this awesome construction, deliberately exaggerated the cost of it all, from $1 million to $4 million. Thus it was that word spread, falsely, throughout the industry that Adam was a wildly profligate designer. None the less, the scale was pretty extravagant.

The construction of this set proved to be an immensely complex and hazardous business in itself, with teams of plasterers and scaffolders working around the clock to get it done. The monorail was real – it actually worked, and Adam recalls how it not only added to the spectacle, but was also a splendid place to position the camera as Lewis Gilbert's direction showed us the vast scale of the place. 'Someone said to me, "Why don't you just build a model of the set?"' Adam said. 'But then how would you see all those hundreds of ninjas abseiling?'

The sets received almost as much space in the press reviews as the film itself. In the *Sunday Times*, Dilys Powell wrote: 'In the design of the production, Ken Adam has outdone himself . . . everyone concerned with the creation of the huge sets has done wonderfully . . . technically, *Twice* is overpowering, so overpowering in fact that it threatens to extinguish the players.' In any other film, this would be regarded as a grave setback. Not necessarily here.

But Powell also has this to say: 'Odd that among Fleming's novels, one of those with the fewest fights, tortures and escapes, should provide the basis for the most violent James Bond film.' One of those scenes of violence was the moment at which naughty redhead Helga Brandt (Karin Dor) is pitched into the piranha pool and the green water begins to seethe and Helga is pulled under by the killer fish. In the novel, a suicidal man may have walked into a molten pool. But no glamorous redhead was eaten alive by piranhas. Often, the zest with which each film's Bad Girl is disposed of is a little eyebrow-raising.

Incidentally, the character of Helga is emblematic of the film's element of glamour with concomitant loss of logic. She is the statuesque personal assistant to Mr Osata. She gets to menace Bond when he is pretending to be an 'industrial spy' called Mr Fisher and is tied up on the vessel *Ning Po*. Attired in strappy cocktail dress, she waves a scalpel and threatens him with amateur plastic surgery. But within seconds she has apparently succumbed to his charms and unties him, leaving him to cut the straps of her dress with the scalpel.

The next thing we know, they are both in a tiny two-seater plane; suddenly she detonates a small flash and bails out with a parachute, leaving Bond in the free-falling plane. I mean, it is all exciting and amusing but it does not make a very great deal of sense. If Helga knows fine well, as she says, that he is actually Bond, then why not just kill him? What is all this nonsense about parachutes that, by the by, affords Bond a reasonable fighting chance to escape?

Still, Helga pays for these lapses of narrative logic by being plunged into Blofeld's piranha pool. Especially unfair since we consider all of this to be more the fault of the snivelling Mr Osata.

Through the figure of Osata, as portrayed by Teru Shimada, we are offered what perhaps is not the most flattering portrait of Japanese commerce. Although he operates from within a fantastically stylish office suite, he is marked by a tendency to say things such as 'Ah so' and utter gnomic faux-oriental sentiments, while making deals to do with monosodium glutamate.

And in a wider sense, here we bump into the difficult issue of racism. One tries, one really tries, to take the film in the spirit in which it was intended, but one only has to look at Bond's treatment of Tiger Tanaka to get a sense of where the production team stood. The character of Tanaka is, of course, Japan's answer to M. So why then does Bond treat him like an under-butler? 'Get this letter analysed, will you?' 007 commands at one point. 'Get this picture analysed,' is the even more peremptory command a few minutes later.

Things relax a little when we are aboard Tanaka's rather wonderful private tube train, with sake being served at the correct temperature of 98.4 degrees. But even though Bond is complimentary, he is simply not giving the man an ounce of the respect that he shows before Bernard Lee's grumpy old M.

Is this oversensitivity? One might argue that Tanaka is there largely for the purposes of exposition, and that Bond is treating him no differently to any other character who performs such a role. And after all, Bond clearly suffers no cultural misunderstandings with female agent and squeeze Aki. But in the case of Tanaka, it doesn't look like that.

Similarly, the wedding scene in the Japanese fishing village, though quite beautifully filmed and scored, makes one shift a little with discomfort. Possibly because of the quite insane spectacle of the stocky six-foot-three Connery with false eyelids and a Three Stooges wig pretending to be Japanese.

Still, I must be mistaken, for here is our old lefty friend Nina Hibbin of the *Daily Worker*, who seems to have had a little bit of a Bond epiphany. 'It's way ahead of all previous Bond films – there's no racialism,' she wrote, which rather puts me in my place. 'A very suspect formula has been transformed into a bit of all right.' Really? Then I take it all back.

Oddly less wince-making is the scene in which Bond's progress through the streets of Tokyo is tracked by geisha girls in kimonos. And at least Japan is portrayed as a land of formidable technological innovation.

All this, remember, came just twenty-two years after the war; a conflict in which the cruelty of the Japanese soldiers still inspires horrifying books today – but equally, a conflict in which the atomic bombings of Hiroshima and Nagasaki sent shockwaves that were to echo around the world for decades to come. The film *Bridge Over the River Kwai* (1957) had been released only ten years previously. Now Bond was firmly allied with the old enemy, in a fight to prevent – without wishing to sound tasteless about it – nuclear Armageddon.

Japan of 1967 was famed as the inventive home of the transistor, of electronics miracles, of miniaturisation. In *Twice*, it is not merely enough to show a telephone inside Aki's car. There is a tiny television in her dashboard too. A Sony television, we can't help noting. We will be returning to the subject of product placement elsewhere. But there it is. What is depicted is the idea of the prosperity that such futurism brings, allied to the centuries-old traditions of ninja training and bare-handed fishing in white bikinis.

The fishing village segment of the film is notable not merely for its unintended low-level racism, but also for a level of lyricism and indeed romanticism hitherto unseen in a Bond movie; and it is this element that really gave the entire series the extra oomph it needed to rise far beyond its competitors.

The cameraman brought in by Lewis Gilbert was Freddie Young, a brilliant Oscar-winning veteran who had recently photographed *Doctor Zhivago*. In that film, the landscapes were as integral to the story as the main characters themselves: the vast, sun-scorched steppes; the bitter snowy wastes of the north through which Zhivago has to trudge with icicles on his eyebrows. Similarly breathtaking vistas – illimitable shimmering desert views – were captured by Young in his other David Lean collaboration, *Lawrence of Arabia*. *Twice* does not give Young quite the same opportunities, one might say – but what he does bring are beautiful sweeping shots of mountains and sunsets, the rich blue and white of a sparkling ocean, and more than this, a sense of visual depth not often captured in a Bond. We see this especially in the wedding ceremony scene – despite the fact that it is an utterly hollow narrative construction, it looks strange, beautiful and rather haunting.

Add to this the swooping lushness of John Barry's score – a very far cry from the saucy big band hooting of *Goldfinger* – and you have a Bond movie with an extra layer of texture. One measure of Barry's success here is the number of times his *Twice* themes have been sampled by twenty-first-century pop acts, such as Robbie Williams and the Stereophonics. Even the spacewalk scenes were scored with a silky, malevolent elegance; space had never sounded quite so menacing or doomy.

Indeed, an utterly crucial element in the film's success was the space factor. Between 1965 and 1967, the United States was flying the Gemini missions as means of preparation for the ultimate goal of landing upon the moon. This was the era of the frantic 'space race' in which the US and the Soviet Union vied for dominance. Back in the late 1950s and early 1960s, the Soviets had established an impressive lead, first with the launch of the satellite Sputnik and then, several years later, with the successful mission of Yuri Gagarin, the first astronaut to float in orbit above the Earth.

The object of the Gemini missions was to perfect such manoeuvres as docking: that two spacecraft might meet and astronauts might pass from one to the other. One can see exactly the effect such a notion had upon the producers of *Twice*. Imagine then the effect that all those geostationary orbit scenes had upon the rocket-crazy boys in the audience. For them, the not too distant prospect of the first landing on the moon was impossibly exciting, the subject of ceaseless daydreaming, and NASA's team of intensely trained astronauts were, even before Neil Armstrong and Buzz Aldrin, celebrated as national heroes.

This might perhaps be why the normally cold-blooded Blofeld elects to spare the lives of so many bloody astronauts. There the kidnapped men are, being held in those stylised Ken Adam-designed cells; it is most unusual for Blofeld to be so considerate. Surely these men would logically be dumped in the ocean, along with the unfortunate tourist who, earlier on in the film, has foolishly taken a photograph of the *Ning-Po*?

But you couldn't kill these particular heroes, Americans and Soviets all; to do so would have been viewed as sacrilege by both the US audience and indeed any potential audience in the Eastern bloc that Broccoli might still have been hoping for. It was considered sufficiently shocking for the lifeline of the US astronaut in the teaser to be cut by the kidnapping craft.

And as to Blofeld's notion of setting off World War Three: it may sound amusingly hyperbolic now but it may not quite have caused the same amount of laughter in 1967. This was the year of the Arab–Israeli Six-Day War, which a good many people feared might prove the trigger for a nuclear conflict between America and Russia, with America backing Israel and the Soviets allied with the Arab states. It is difficult to recall now just how jumpy the nuclear arms race made the world back in the 1960s. 'This is the big one,' says M gravely when he is debriefing Bond. To many watching the film, the shadow of 'the big one' had been looming ever since the Cuban missile crisis of 1962. It was certainly a narrative threat that put the film into a different league from the waterlogged *Thunderball*.

Happily – and once again, this is due to the instincts of director Lewis Gilbert – the casting of Blofeld would have diluted the anxiety a little. Donald Pleasence's glowering boiled-egg characterisation at last brought to the screen the grotesque fairy-tale quality of Ian Fleming's villain and equalled the standard set by Auric Goldfinger. Saltzman, who seemed to have a weakness for these Euro-folk, had originally assigned the part to a genial bearded Czech called Jan Werich. But the actor had to be dismissed as shooting began because director Gilbert felt that he 'looked like a benevolent Santa Claus'.

Pleasence stepped in at the very last minute, and what serendipity that he did. The Chairman Mao suit, the dreamy camp malevolence of his boggling eyes, not to mention the splendid make-up scar that bisects the right-hand side of his face, gave audiences the very archetype of a super-villain that would find fresh life in the 1990s thanks to the Canadian comedian Mike Myers and his *Austin Powers* films.

Even though we have heard his voice throughout – and seen his rather naff shoe push the pedal that operates the piranha bridge – Blofeld is only fully disclosed at the film's climax, in the control room, as his spacecraft is approaching the American ship. 'You can watch it all on TV,' he tells Bond absently. Thanks to a trick exploding cigarette – a device that would not have looked at all out of place in Bulldog Drummond – Bond scuppers the countdown, all hell breaks loose in the control room and Blofeld makes for his monorail.

A word here for the heroic qualities displayed by the white Persian cat that portrays Blofeld's pet. Earlier films such as *From Russia* and *Thunderball* gave small glimpses of cinema's most iconic feline. But the creature comes into its full blaze of Garbo-esque stardom in *You Only Live Twice*. In the quieter parts of the climactic scene, the cat sits on Blofeld's lap, seemingly not entirely happy to be there but being held firmly by Pleasence none the less. Come the first explosion, though, and the cat understandably is having absolutely none of it.

Watch as its head twists this way and that in its desperation to get out of Pleasence's hands. Also, if you look extra closely at Pleasence's Mao suit, you can see cat-scratch bobbles all over it. These days, they assure us that no animals were harmed, etc. I cannot help wondering about Blofeld's cat, and the ordeals that it had to go through, and whether it received counselling or extra fish afterwards.

The cat had a slightly quieter life in *On Her Majesty's Secret Service* – just a little lap scene there, and no loud bangs. But it took its proudest starring role in *Diamonds Are Forever*. First, it is there throughout the naughty title sequence, scampering past the legs of naked ladies, and wearing a twinkling diamond collar of Liberace-level vulgarity. Then, in the film itself, the cat gets the run of an entire luxurious penthouse suite, before being peremptorily kicked across the room by Bond and then uncannily running into a Persian cat doppelgänger.

In the pre-credits sequence of *For Your Eyes Only*, the cat makes a triumphant final bow on location in the decaying docklands of east London, with his wheelchair-bound master on top of an East End warehouse. Once more, in time-honoured fashion, the cat is required to hiss in close-up as Bond turns the tables on his master.

Cats do not always lead such happy lives in Fleming's world. In the novel *Goldfinger*, the villain has a fat ginger moggy. When Bond is investigating Goldfinger's house, he opens a cupboard containing hidden film equipment, the celluloid spooling into a basket. After exposing the film, Bond places the purring moggy in the basket to make it look as if the cat – rather than Bond – caused the disturbance. On Goldfinger's return, the cat is discovered thus and its master is not amused. The last we see of the mog is when it is in Goldfinger's arms. 'Here, have this for dinner,' he tells his Korean manservant Oddjob. For years, this was cited as evidence of Fleming's racism. It is nothing of the sort; rather, it is an irresistibly good joke about how thoroughly bad and heartless Goldfinger is.

The main point is that back in the late 1960s, creatures such as Persian cats were regarded – rather like their Siamese counterparts – as tremendously sophisticated animals to own. But tastes change and by the mid-1970s, they were as naff as Terry's All Gold. The other point is that in *Twice*, the rococo camp of such details helped to inject levity.

Speaking of camp, it is here that the Bond series says a fruity 'hellooo' to actor Charles Gray playing English expat Henderson, complete with silken Japanese dressing gown and a voice that purrs with debauchery. He offers Bond some vodka, telling him that 'I get it from the doorman at the Russian embassy – amongst other things . . .' It was in 1967 that homosexual acts between men were finally legalised in England, some ten years after the

Wolfenden Report had recommended that the law be changed. But on screen, homosexuality was portrayed in this particular feline, transgressive way for many years afterwards. Indeed, as we shall see, the character of Henderson was merely a dry run for Gray's stratospherically over-the-top interpretation of Blofeld in *Diamonds Are Forever*, a film that simply couldn't be gayer if it tried.

For any women in the audience of *Twice*, though, the film was spectacularly regressive, making *In Like Flint* look like a Germaine Greer monograph. When we look at *Twice* now, we see, with a certain amazement, that the role of every single woman on screen is utterly submissive. Even that of bad girl Helga, who doesn't get a moment of independent thought or action. Then there is secret agent Aki, who coquettishly lures Bond into Tanaka's lair, nearly gets involved in a brawl at Kobe docks but is ordered by Bond to run away, and ends up giving 007 a massage. Is that what she was taught in secret agent school?

Aki meets a horrible end in her sleep, with poison rather ingeniously dripped down a wire, and clearly intended to land on 007's lips. There was a touch of Jacobean revenge tragedy about this means of dispatch, one of the most inventive in the Bond oeuvre.

Then there is Kissy (Mie Hama), who is the most thinly drawn Bond woman ever. And bear in mind that there is some hot competition out there. Here is how it goes: she and Bond marry in that rather nicely filmed local ceremony. Then they go up the mountain; Kissy, as mentioned before, is attired simply in white bikini and high heels. The only dialogue that she and Bond share is to do with him demanding his 'honeymoon' conjugals and her protesting reluctance. There are more resonant relationships formed on the darkened back streets of King's Cross than this.

Then as Bond descends into the volcano, Kissy goes back to the village to fetch Tanaka, and has to evade helicopter fire while front-crawling through the sea. In the final scene, she and Bond snog in an inflatable boat. That's it. It seems to be a feature of many films of the 1960s that the lead female character would simply be known as 'The Girl' and this is most assuredly the case here. How strange to think now that the auditions for the roles of Aki and Kissy caused two unsuccessful Japanese candidates to threaten suicide, much to the horror of the producers. A sign of how far the Bond phenomenon had come.

In the 1980s, the feminist movement routinely denounced the Bond films as 'misogynist', a line gleefully picked up by the new generation of producers in *GoldenEye* (1995), but *You Only Live Twice* stops to make you think twice. 'In Japan, the man always comes first,' pronounces Tiger Tanaka as he and Bond are stripped naked, preparatory to being soaped down by a bevy of bikinied lovelies. 'I might just retire here,' says Bond. As ever, the test for these things is to ask whether they could get away with such a scene now, even ironically. Surely not? What's more, the film did tremendous business in Japan, which does lead one to wonder what sort of injured state, in 1967, the national psyche was still in.

In fact, thanks to Japanese adulation, the filming itself was an irksome business for Sean Connery. Upon arrival in Tokyo, he was set upon by screaming mobs (well, that Japanese mop-top wig does make him look a little like a Beatle). He and then wife Diane Cilento could not even dine in peace. There is some wonderful black and white footage of Harry Saltzman berating members of the Tokyo press, complaining that 'Mr Connery hasn't even been able to have his lunch yet.'[3]

That was the least of Mr Connery's problems. When he went off for a pee, he found the conveniences were full of photographers. (By the by, the latest Bond, Daniel Craig, has said in an interview that incredibly, he is still getting the same thing in public loos, but this time from amateur mobile phone photographers.) So if Mr Connery had any doubts at all about his decision to stop playing Bond, these incidents – and a subsequent review in *Time* magazine stating that Connery's Bond looked 'uncomfortable and fatigued' – must have reassured him that he was doing the right thing.

Perhaps it was the discomfort and fatigue that caused Connery to be so rude about Saltzman and Broccoli in an interview given that year: 'I won't put up with bores any longer, or have people living off my back,' he declared. 'And having made the jump from employee to employer, I now intend to help a few mates.' He continued in this vinegary fashion: 'If the whole thing had been handled a little more generously, it could have gone on for ever. But it wasn't. There was a lot of greed around, you know. Everyone has made enough money to live for ever and bury themselves and their families.

'I don't know what they'll do about replacing me. Though I imagine the next film will be made on a relatively small budget.'[4]

Certainly, Broccoli absorbed this peevish broadside and was to cite it many years later as an example of what he considered to be Connery's epic ingratitude. But at the time, Broccoli and Saltzman simply pushed on.

To be fair, *Twice* was Connery's fifth Bond and it was perfectly reasonable that he should now want to give the part up. He was one of the most famous actors in the world and now would have had the weight and the influence to take on any project he pleased; a time to nourish his artistic side after all this cartoon stuff. There was press speculation that Connery's departure would mark the end of the Bond series. But Saltzman and Broccoli were rather cannier creatures than that.

CHAPTER NINE THE OTHER FELLA

I have been to Ernst Stavro Blofeld's Alpine lair.

It was some years ago. I recall the plane touching down in Geneva, and being met by my old university chum, who was now a shipbroker, though puzzlingly a shipbroker operating out of a landlocked country. I remember finding his business dealings a little opaque, like those of Blofeld's solicitor Gumbold. And I remember some of the drive through the Swiss countryside, up to those mountains.

Then into that great gondola to be swooped up the mountain on cables. In the distance, my first glimpse of that mountaintop structure, like some form of corrugated hat. I recall the entrance fee to the mountain and ski runs being something in the region of £80, which came as an extremely disagreeable surprise.

And then further, further up until finally, I was into Blofeld's lair itself. The first thing that confronted me and my shipbroking chum was a gigantic wall-mounted photograph of George Lazenby. Then, up that curving staircase and into the lounge and restaurant where – yes! – a be-kilted Bond had once met a bevy of international beauties, among them Joanna Lumley, and where, at dinner, racy Angela Scoular got her hand up Lazenby's kilt and wrote her room number with lipstick on his inner thigh.

Such golden Alpine memories! Such a tribute to the majesty and grandeur of the landscape all around. Actually, it was a distinctly odd experience, for one never expects to find oneself standing in the same physical space that one of Bond's adventures took place in.

It is not exactly that the illusion is shattered; otherwise visitors to the Pyramids, the Eiffel Tower, New Orleans and the Rock of Gibraltar, among many other locations, would be left feeling rather disappointed. No, it was the business of standing in what was supposed to be the villain's purpose-built headquarters. Good old Ian Fleming, when writing *On Her Majesty's Secret Service* in 1963, had simply seen this construction and swiped it for his novel, much as he swiped the names of friends and enemies for his heroes and villains. A novel is one thing, though, and a big-screen film is another. I suppose one of the strangest things about the place was that when I had seen it on screen, it looked so naff that I automatically assumed that it must be a studio set, with Alpine scenes simply projected on to screens behind the 'windows'. How peculiar that someone had built such a lair for real.

Piz Gloria, the place is called, and when my friend and I visited, it was doing brisk business with skiers and non-skiers alike, and that bevy-of-beauties lounge was now a revolving restaurant. Through the windows it was possible to see where Bernard Horsfall had been shot by Blofeld's guards and then hung upside down by his mountaineer's bootstraps. It was possible to see where Lazenby made his moonlit dash for it on skis down the mountain, closely pursued. It was possible to see the exact spot from which, as dawn rose over the distant peaks, Diana Rigg recited some poetry (Browning? Tennyson? Actually, no, James Elroy Flecker, according to the film's surprise screen co-writer Simon Raven) to an unimpressed Telly Savalas.

All sounds rather good, doesn't it? Yet for years and years, *On Her Majesty's Secret Service* was routinely described as the turkey of the Bond films. Mostly the reason for this is the man whose name has become synonymous with one-off failures: George Lazenby. And can I just say, right now, that his was no failure at all. Nothing like it. Emphatically not.

Indeed, after the shock of the first few minutes – a simple matter of readjustment, the same thing happens every time the BBC changes the lead actor in *Doctor Who* – you find as the film goes on that Lazenby grows more and more into the role. By the end, he has given the character a weight of pathos (thanks in part to his co-star, the classical actress and former Avenger Diana Rigg) that no other Bond save Daniel Craig could have carried off.

Before we get into how Saltzman and Broccoli came to select this twenty-eight-year-old Australian male model with absolutely no acting experience whatsoever to be the successor to the world's most famous film star, it is worth having a quick look at other occasions upon which, in a film series, the lead actor has left and has simply been replaced with another one. In B movies, it was a fact of life. The detective Charlie Chan was portrayed in the 1930s by Warner Oland, then Sidney Toler. Tarzan was Johnny Weissmuller; but then he was also Lex Barker. The asphalt spreader's boots worn by Universal's Frankenstein monster, an unbelievably distinctive creation summoned by Boris Karloff, were passed on to Lon Chaney Jr, then Bela Lugosi, then Glenn Strange.

Naturally, the Bond industry, which by 1969 was worth many many millions, was perhaps in a slightly different league and the risk attached to the changeover of leading man very much greater. The risk was: after the stratospheric success of Connery, could anyone follow him with the same sort of momentum?

But this is precisely why the choice of Lazenby was so shrewd, as I will explain shortly; and there is another factor here too. It is possible – just possible – that after Connery's latest outing as Bond, this time with the wig and the eyebrows and the slight paunch and the thickening face, the public might just have been looking forward to seeing how a younger man would reinterpret the part. After all, when one goes to the theatre to see *Macbeth*, one does not expect to see it with the same actor time and again. The element that revitalises any drama is the fresh approach to a role, and the con-comitant fresh thinking about the entire enterprise that has to go with it.

So, to take stock: *Twice*, in 1967, had been a roaring success, making £111 million, though not quite so much of a success as *Thunderball*. More and more critics had started to complain that the 007 films were becoming dominated by hardware and empty spectacle and comedy gadgets and guns and explosions, and that an element of Fleming's original stories was getting lost in the process.

Thus, if Saltzman and Broccoli were to introduce the public to a completely new Bond, what better approach than to strip away the gizmos and return to the very letter of Fleming's novel? And this is exactly what they did in 1969 with *On Her Majesty's Secret Service*.

Unlike *Twice*, the novel of *OHMSS* is tight, taut, crammed with believable jeopardy and features, at its heart, the most serious and moving of Bond's relationships. It can now hardly count as a spoiler to say that the romance of Bond and the Comtessa Theresa (Tracy) Di Vincenzo is doomed. But unusually for Fleming, there is a forward echo of this in the novel's very first chapter, as the self-destructive Tracy leaves the casino, goes down to the beach and walks out into the sea. It is Bond who saves her. Tracy's father, Draco, is the head of a Mafia-like crime syndicate. He wants Bond to marry his daughter – as a means of rather pre-Freudian sexual therapy – and is prepared to pay a very serious dowry of £1 million. But Bond is after Blofeld. It is not long before SPECTRE's finest is tracked to his mountaintop eyrie, running – apparently in all innocence – an allergy clinic for pretty ladies and attempting to validate his claims on an old aristocratic title.

Posing as a representative of the College of Arms, Bond ventures to Piz Gloria and it isn't long before he is caught in a vortex of ski chases and close escapes, and indeed an unexpected and timely rendezvous with Tracy. Meanwhile: Bad Blofeld! That's no allergy clinic! Instead, the pretty ladies are being hypnotised into carrying crop killers back into their respective countries. If Blofeld doesn't get his title and a full pardon for his crimes, then the world's harvests will fail!

In other words, pretty much perfect 007, in that the story only very slightly tips into the absurd and it blends, to perfection, breathtaking excitement with healthy slabs of snobbery (the College of Arms detailing is inspired beyond words) and sex (the bevy of beauties is Bond's most amusing soft-porn scenario, and the character of Morecambe Bay belle Ruby Bartlett is perhaps the most charming characterisation to be found anywhere within the novels, in spite of the fact that one suspects that Fleming had never actually met anyone from the North before and had copied her off the television).

And also, for screenplay purposes, it made pretty much the perfect big-screen romantic action adventure; the only occasion, bar the first Daniel Craig outing, where the characters of both Bond and the girl are seen to develop and change as the film progresses.

And so to return to the point I started making: one of the best ways to refresh a long-running series is to fizz the audience up with a new approach and a new leading man. And Lazenby could not have been further from Connery if he had turned up in a ginger fright wig.

The story of how he came to be chosen by the hard-headed, commercially minded Saltzman and Broccoli has been rehearsed by all parties, to an extent where one wonders if it could really have been the case.

They all seem to agree on one unlikely-sounding detail: that at the point when it became known that they were looking for a new 007, Lazenby deliberately took himself to the tailor in Jermyn Street where the Bond suits were made, and acquired an unused Connery cast-off; thus attired, he made his way to the barber's in the Dorchester Hotel that he knew to be frequented by Connery and also Cubby Broccoli. And Lazenby somehow ensured that Broccoli noticed him. Broccoli apparently remarked that he looked like a 'very successful young businessman'.

There was another story: that as casting was in progress, Lazenby showed up to the Eon offices at Audley Street and used his wiles to slip past the receptionist directly to the inner sanctum of Saltzman and Broccoli, which was said to have impressed the men.

Here is a third story: that as part of a screen test, Lazenby was required to demonstrate his fist-fighting techniques with a stuntman who posed as a Russian heavy. As the legend goes, Lazenby was so manly that he accidentally broke the stuntman's nose.

There is no reason to doubt any of this, but it still leaves the larger question – why go with an inexperienced unknown rather than a tried and tested pro? – up in the air.

It is not as if more established actors were not approached to audition. Among them were Michael Jayston, Michael Billington (the handsome Roger Moore lookalike actor, not the *Guardian* theatre critic), the gangling news-pundit-to-be Peter Snow, and future Bond Timothy Dalton, fresh from the Plantagenet costumer *The Lion in Winter* (1968) but a shade too callow for Bond then at only twenty-two years old.

At one stage, it seems that Roger Moore's name was once more in the frame. The actor himself recalls that the production office were considering a scenario set in Cambodia. But Moore at that time was still The Saint and that series had another full season to run.

Anyway, according to the production office, hundreds of actors were tested. So why was the former car salesman Lazenby deemed a much more attractive option than any one of them?

There are three possible answers (on top of the obvious one, that the handsome Lazenby very much looked the part). The first is that Lazenby would have been *very* cheap. As we have heard, by the end of his run, Connery had twigged just how much was sloshing into the Eon accounts and had become increasingly vocal in his belief that a larger proportion of these monies should by rights by re-routed in his direction.

Indeed, a news story published in the *Daily Mirror* in October 1968, just after the announcement of Lazenby's casting, appeared to confirm this financial suspicion. 'Actress Diana Rigg will be paid £50,000 for her role as Mrs James Bond,' declared the report indiscreetly. 'This is more than twice the salary that former male model George Lazenby will get for taking over as the new 007. Bond producer Broccoli explained: "Diana has more experience and of course, she is a bigger name."'

The second reason for his casting could have been that in dramatic terms, it would help to have a wholly unfamiliar face playing the lead, for that actor would not carry the inevitable aura of indestructibility attached to Connery by that stage. And the third is, quite simply, that the day-to-day experience of a five-month shoot would prove a running acting tutorial for Lazenby, and that his rough edges would be smoothed out by it.

Director Peter Hunt (stepping up to the plate after his innovative period as editor) certainly believed so, and in later years has voiced his conviction that had Lazenby done another Bond, he would have been regarded as a 'very creditable' incarnation of the role. Certainly, to Hunt's mind, Lazenby was unquestionably the man for the job from the start. Indeed, it seems that Hunt was the one who had first spotted Lazenby in a cheesy but widely seen television commercial for Fry's chocolate, messing around in a boat and being pursued by Sixties dollies.

Broccoli and Saltzman seemed equally convinced, especially after having seen the test fight and the test bedroom scene. But even several weeks before shooting began towards the end of 1968, the whole thing was still apparently up in the air. According to the *Daily Mail*'s showbiz correspondent, 'They [the producers] will try to persuade 38 year old Sean Connery to change his mind about giving up the role. If he refuses, George Lazenby, the Big Fry man in the TV commercials, is strongly tipped to take over . . .'

(Indeed, after shooting had begun, Connery appeared to confirm this last-minute plea to the *Sunday Express*: 'Yes, I said I'd do it for a million pounds, tax free,' he said. 'But I didn't want to know, really.')

Days before the news was confirmed, the indefatigable Victor Davis of the *Daily Express* had this to report: 'The selection of George will be the signal for mass suicide among the 400 professional actors who sought to slip on Bond's shoulder holster . . . the Bond producers are buying up the advertising material intended for future publication for which George has modelled. They don't want 007 promoting deodorant. They've also had him medically examined . . .'

Poor George! As well as 'big name' and apparently big earner Diana Rigg, further acting backup came with the casting of the new Blofeld; after the ping-pong-eyed insanity of Donald Pleasence's interpretation, the character was reined right back in with Telly Savalas's quietly menacing and intimidatingly intelligent performance.

Also vital for Mr Lazenby were the familiar faces of the Bond family; a noticeably warmer outing for his superior M and Miss Moneypenny. At the start, M removes Bond from the hunt for Blofeld; in a huff, Bond dictates his resignation and has Moneypenny deliver it to M. There is a nice scene of continuity as new Bond goes through his office desk, and finds souvenirs such as conch shells from his five previous adventures – a very deliberate link to the past. Indeed, similar links are made in the Maurice Binder title sequence, which features Bond in silhouette running as scenes from previous films flow through an hourglass.

New Bond is clearly hurt when M apparently accepts his resignation; but of course darling Moneypenny has simply turned this request into one for two weeks' leave. Bond exits, pleased and mollified; then M comes on the intercom to thank Moneypenny for her fast thinking. No other Bond since has seen the new boy getting such a wholehearted endorsement from the Boss.

In the pre-credits sequence, we saw Lazenby rescue the troubled Rigg from her walk into the waves, and then get into a blistering fight with two heavies ('This never happened to the other fella,' is Lazenby's cheeky payoff); now Bond returns to Portugal, ostensibly on a golfing holiday, in an amazingly hideous orange zip-up leisure suit. Come evening, and it is off to the hotel casino, the most eye-poppingly horrible in the series' long history.

No, no, this isn't Sir Ken Adam having an off day; he was absent from *OHMSS* and boy does it show. Syd Cain was the chap in charge of production design this time around. Admittedly the late 1960s was not a great time for subdued tones. But the chief decor theme behind this particular casino is purple flock wallpaper, of the sort most commonly associated with East End strip pubs.

In fact, the garishness goes on throughout the film – even Blofeld's laboratory contrives to look like a 1960s self-service snacketeria in a provincial bus station. Peter Hunt has said that he wanted the film to look as though the sets were real-life locations. If that is what his world looked like, then our sympathies to Mrs Hunt. Even the modernist sculptures featured in the lift hallway of Piz Gloria would struggle to reach £4 on *Bargain Hunt*.

Anyway, back to the horrid casino in the vile hotel. To further establish Lazenby's credentials, he is there at the table with a gaggle of plug-ugly Euro-folk, as tradition demands, playing a card game that no one in the audience could ever hope to understand, involving turning cards over with a giant spatula. And into frame loom the bosoms of Diana Rigg, recklessly betting all on this weird game and then losing. Bond rescues her again; this time, Tracy insists that she pay Bond back in bed. This despite Bond wearing a ruffled shirt.

How did Diana Rigg justify all of this to herself? 'I had never been in an epic before,' she explained carefully. 'And I just wanted to know how it would feel to be in one.'[1] If memory serves, she featured in no subsequent action adventure epics, so this one must really have told her all that she needed to know.

Dame Diana's assistant, by the way, very politely explained to me that 'she has no wish' to talk about Bond these days. In a sense, I can understand why.

Anyway, after a lickety-split fight with a heavy, Bond and Tracy get their first love scene. It is very clear that she is a sophisticated woman of the world whereas he used to sell minty chocolates, and the thing is that it actually works rather beautifully. This is a Bond who, while trying to pass himself off as an international playboy, is in fact more of a wide-eyed, good-hearted lad. Thanks to his acting inexperience, there is a disarming innocence about Lazenby's 007. Even his post-fight line about good caviar sounds as though the character acquired this information from *Look and Learn*.

Time to meet Tracy's father. Here, as he takes on Draco's thuggish employees, we see the other appealing facet of Lazenby – his ability to fight convincingly, helped enormously by Hunt's lightning-pace cuts and weird sci-fi sound effects. His reaction to Draco's proposal that he marry Tracy – the poor girl has gone off the rails and 'joined the international fast set', if you please – is to turn it down with something like real compassion.

Equally, when Tracy attends the bullfight at her father's birthday, Bond finds himself sitting between father and daughter; when the daughter turns up the emotional heat on her father, we are left in no doubt that it is the character of Bond, as well as perhaps the actor, who is out of his depth. It is a hugely refreshing change of pace. Here at last is a hero who, while obviously manly, is also rather vulnerable.

The other brilliant gear-change is in the action sequences. In fairness, these had always been fast in Bond movies, but here they are slicker and better put together yet. Part of this can be attributed to the *mise en scène*; Blofeld's Alpine fastness is a wonderfully believable location to make one's escape from. But the shooting of the ski chases is sheer poetry, the camera smooth, finding unexpected angles. On the first occasion, it is Bond escaping at night, the snow a deep shade of twilight blue. In this chase, Bond is forced to descend the slopes on one ski and has a nail-biting, literally cliffhanging fight on a precipice overlooking a Swiss village.

Fleming would have loved all of this; in his novel, he goes into intense detail about the sort of skis Bond had to wear, and the sort of manoeuvres that were possible in them. Fleming himself had spent an apparently golden period of his youth living against this Alpine backdrop after leaving Eton.[2] In the 1920s and 30s, there was quite a vogue for this sort of scenery among the wealthier British; the mountains and the snow were deemed to have a wholesomeness and purity that made them perfect for recreation. It was the genius of Fleming to turn this wholesomeness round into black-hearted jeopardy.

In the film, the second ski chase involves Bond and Tracy and an awesome avalanche so superbly shot that belief wavers not for a second. The verve, the pace and the sheer rhythmic pleasure of seeing the slopes from the skier's point of view, as well as via some amazing overhead shots, is breathtaking. Contrast this, curiously, with a very similar scene from the 1999 Pierce Brosnan outing *The World Is Not Enough*. The later film's version looks utterly anaemic by contrast.

But then Peter Hunt had a mustard-keen second unit, led by John Glen who was himself later to direct Roger Moore Bonds. The challenges were immense; as well as innumerable skiing stunts, Glen also had to film a bobsleigh chase, Bond's perilous escape along the cables of a fast-approaching cable car, and indeed an icy stock car rally, in which Tracy and Bond seek to elude their pursuers. It was terrific, non-stop stuff, and aesthetically, wonderfully easy on the eye.

In charge of devising all the skiing excitement was Olympic veteran Willie Bognor, who could ski at tremendous speeds while pointing a bulky film camera, going not only forwards but backwards. It was his work that gave the film so much of its memorably kinetic quality, as the stuntmen swooped and glided down those mountains in strange, almost geometric formations. Incidentally, according to stuntman Vic Armstrong, George Lazenby was always at his happiest 'when he was being one of the boys'. On the way up to the location, Broccoli spotted him travelling alongside the stuntmen and had a word with production associates. 'I want you to start treating him like the star.'

Similarly, for insurance purposes, Lazenby was forbidden to ski unsupervised; but when he wasn't required on set, he went out on to the slopes in defiance of his producers anyway. This sort of wilful behaviour was noted, and vehemently disapproved of.

The young Lazenby also found Telly Savalas quite a hypnotic influence. Savalas liked to play card games deep into the night; crew members recalled how he would turn up for morning calls 'looking a little pink-eyed' but always behaving with the utmost professionalism.

Press coverage of production was as intense as one might expect; journalists from all over the world demanded interviews and set visits practically every day that the film was in production. And it was halfway through the Alpine location shoot that the biggest tabloid story of the film suddenly developed a pair of legs: that Diana Rigg could not stand George Lazenby.

Here is what appeared to have happened, according to Lazenby himself. 'There was a press lunch and Diana was sitting at another table,' he recalled in an interview. 'She called over and said "George, I'm having garlic for lunch so I hope you are too."' This was before they were due to film Bond and Tracy's great romantic scene in the Swiss barn. According to the press, the eating of garlic before such a tender scene was, in effect, a declaration of war. Lazenby subsequently said in interviews that this really wasn't so, while at the same time giving the impression that although he and Rigg were 'allies' at the very start of filming, the relationship was perhaps a little more complicated later.

One can see how the scenario might have been a little trying for the brilliant Rigg. According to Lazenby, at the beginning, she offered to help the inexperienced actor in whatever way she could. But it's asking a bit much of an actress to star in her first 'epic' and simultaneously coach the leading man.

Whatever happened, though, and whatever tensions there may have been on set, they don't show on screen. And the love scene in the Swiss barn was the one that all Bond fans would have been both dreading and looking forward to.

It is the one in which, having temporarily evaded their relentless pursuers, Bond and Tracy snuggle down for warmth in the straw, lit by the red lights of Tracy's car, and Bond proposes marriage. The eternal bachelor, wedded! Yet who could disagree when Bond told Tracy that he would 'never find another girl like you'? She was the only one in the series thus far to have actually come to the rescue of 007, rather than the other way around.

And now, it is time to bring in that parlour game of trying to imagine Sean, Roger, Tim or Pierce doing the same scene. We discount Daniel, because he has already shown that he can do it. Sean might have done but it wouldn't have felt right – we would have been on the lookout for a cynical undertow. Roger, ditto, and without being unkind, you would wonder what was going through Tracy's mind when she said yes. Dour Tim would probably get off-puttingly moist-eyed; Pierce would perhaps deliver the lines in a naff, soupy fashion, while crinkling his forehead up to indicate manly sensitivity. George, on the other hand, is young and seems not hugely intelligent and so he plays it dead down the line and it completely works. Whether you think it is actually Bond or not is quite another question.

But dramatically, the emotional stakes are raised very much higher than they are in any other Bond movie save 2006's *Casino Royale*. Because once the engaged couple are chased out of the barn by the bad guys, we know that Blofeld will do everything in his power to ruin things for them. This he first tries to do by means of summoning a mighty avalanche down on to their heads. Then he hauls an insensible Tracy from the snow and holds her prisoner in his mountain base. The stage is set for a bendy, twisty climax.

One of the curiosities of the Bonds is that the more spectacular and explosive the final showdown, the more ho-hum it is to watch. For instance, the fighting ninjas of *Twice* went on about five minutes too long. The storming of Piz Gloria is a similar watch-glancer. Helicopter rotors blow snow; machine guns are fired; explosive charges are set and placed. And all the while, you are thinking 'Oh come on, just get on with it.' But on this occasion, Diana Rigg puts up an extremely spirited, rather dirty fight with a heavy, which serves to remind us of her days as Mrs Peel, and out of which she finally emerges triumphant, having skewered said thug on a piece of modern sculpture.

The base is blown up; Bond pursues Blofeld down a bobsleigh run, a brilliant sequence of audacious stunt work helped with lightning inter-cuts. And thence to *that* ending: the wedding.

As we must surely all know, tragedy strikes: Mr and Mrs Bond are driving away along the Portuguese coast after their nuptials, enjoying some rather deft and amusing dialogue, when suddenly Blofeld and Frau Bunt (Ilse Steppat), Blofeld's portly right-hand woman, drive past, firing a machine gun. Bond is unscathed. Not so Mrs Bond. As a motorcycle cop pulls up, Bond, cradling dead Tracy, looks up distractedly and explains that 'It's all right – she's just resting.' We have a final shot of the bullet hole in the windscreen, over which the closing titles roll. It is impossible not to get moist-eyed.

Of course this was all in the novel; indeed, Bond is so traumatised that in his subsequent literary adventures *You Only Live Twice* and *The Man with the Golden Gun*, we see him suffering a form of mental breakdown. But it has been asked – was such an ending right for the essentially frothier films?

Recently, Peter Hunt mused that he could have done it another way; as Bond and Tracy drive away from her father's estate, the camera swoops up over a sea of flowers decorating the place, 'and we could have stopped it there,' said Hunt, 'starting the next film with the shooting'. Hunt and others have wondered whether *OHMSS*'s comparatively slow performance in cinemas – bear in mind it opened close to Christmas – was down to the tragic ending. It is not that the film bombed – very far from it, the box office receipts were fine, if not up to the levels of *Thunderball* – but it was noted that it took rather longer than usual to make its money back. There seemed to be a little reluctance on the part of the audience to stampede in there. Was it the fault of the end, or the leading man?

Certainly, the leading man had no finer moment than in that final scene. Lazenby played it beautifully. The actor has said in interviews that he did one take 'and there were tears rolling down my cheeks', but this was vetoed by the producers on the grounds that 'Bond doesn't cry.' In any event, they went for the right version – Lazenby's puppyish 007 reduced to a whispering trance of horror.

No, the leading man wasn't the problem. Nor indeed was the rest of the film. It is not for nothing that many fans now consider it to be the very finest of the lot. It has suspense, comedy, sauce, pathos, character development and unusually slick dialogue, largely free of ker-plonking double entendre. Even Blofeld's dastardly plot gives a little more flesh to the character; his yearning for social advancement is very much stronger than his taste for holding the entire world to ransom.

The tabloid newspapers were nevertheless keen to expand on what they saw as a juicy theme: the first Bond to tank. After endless negative reporting,

Cubby Broccoli was almost levitating with indignation. 'I don't agree with the press,' he told the press. 'They should have given [Lazenby] A for effort.'

Any blush of pride that George might have felt would have subsided quickly afterwards though. 'It's true he's not Olivier,' Broccoli added. 'But Olivier could not play Bond in any circumstances. I've given private viewings to people from Annabel's to Aspinall's, to the people who are opinion makers, and some of them say this is the best of the Bond films. John Aspinall's mother Lady Osborne told me that she thought George was the best James Bond.'[3]

Did she indeed? Well, it would have seemed that Lady Osborne was very much a voice crying in the wilderness.

Rude jibes at Lazenby's performance aside, the reviews for the film itself were largely positive and warm. 'It's quite a jolly frolic in the familiar money-spinning fashion,' wrote Derek Malcolm in the *Guardian*. 'The general level of everything is quite as good as ever it was, except for Mr Lazenby, who looks like a Willerby Brothers clothes peg and acts as though he's just come out of Burton's short of credit.'

Similarly, Ian Christie's suspicion of the new leading man didn't seem to spoil his enjoyment. 'I don't believe for a moment that this chap George Lazenby is James Bond,' he wrote in the *Daily Express*. 'I know, and you know, that 007 is Sean Connery . . .' But he went on to add: 'Diana Rigg looks delicious, Telly Savalas is convincingly nasty and the entire work is thoroughly entertaining.'

The *Evening Standard*'s über-critic Alexander Walker was much more positive than this. 'Forget the rumours. The ones obviously put about by SMERSH,' he wrote. 'The truth is that George Lazenby is almost as good a James Bond as the man this film calls "the other fella". Next time,' he added, 'he'll have eased himself even more comfortably into the tailored shoulder holster.'

Next time. Ah.

So, if we presume that the film didn't sink under the weight of negative publicity, what then *did* do for it? Now, after all these years, it might be possible to consider that there was another reason for the film's relative failure: and that is that the general public were sick to the back teeth of spies.

In cultural terms, by 1969, things were moving on a little and a new, younger generation was starting to push through. The year 1967 had famously seen the Summer of Love, though we should always remember that these apparent landmarks were fully participated in only by hundreds, or at most thousands of people. The rest of the population, by contrast, got up early, went to work, and went to the pub and the flicks at the weekend, much as now.

The news was dominated by the war in Vietnam; even though Harold Wilson had refused Washington's request to help out with British troops, the conflict still managed to spark furious scenes in the UK, most notable of which was the riot outside the American embassy in Grosvenor Square in 1968. In the US, traditional feelings of patriotic support for the troops were now mingling with the sour sense that those troops should never have been sent into such a a conflict. To the younger generation, the perceived threat of the spread of Communism throughout South-East Asia was simply not worth this grim and filthy war.

Having been elected in 1968, President Nixon viewed this younger generation with distrust and distaste. With Nixon came the coining of the phrase 'the silent majority', meaning the overwhelmingly conservative, middle-aged middle classes who hated all these outbreaks of youth culture. Nixon in turn was an object of deep suspicion to many.

The frothy feel of the mid-1960s, this colourful world in which, for the young, a whole new raft of possibilities had opened, was dissolving by 1969. Just a few years previously, jobs had been plentiful, and inflation never so great as to cause concern. But in Britain, Harold Wilson's government had been scrambling to get out of an entire series of financial cliffhangers. The moment in 1967 when Chancellor James Callaghan was finally forced to devalue the pound was the point from which it could not recover. By 1969, the country was riven with wildcat industrial disputes and rising unemployment figures.

Another point for Bond was that the escapism of the films was, in part, consumerist, as reflected in the expensive cars, clothes, and extensive foreign travel. But the mood of pop culture was turning away from such vulgar glitz. The era of the spiritual backpacker in an old van was upon us. In various interviews across the years, George Lazenby insisted that the reason his friend and adviser Ronan O'Rahilly (founder of Radio Caroline) persuaded him to give up the role of Bond is that the 'short back and sides Establishment figure' of Bond looked increasingly out of place in the *Easy Rider* generation. Obviously Lazenby's adviser could not have been more howlingly wrong if he had tried, but it was none the less an interesting judgement to make.

In his autobiography, Albert R. Broccoli threw a slightly different light on Lazenby's withdrawal from the role. 'In my opinion, George ruled himself out of the reckoning by behaving like the superstar he wasn't,' he wrote. 'Lazenby didn't get on too well with the director nor, apparently, his co-star . . . we put limousines at his disposal and he quarrelled with the chauffeurs. I was astounded. Here was a guy taken out of the modelling business . . . yet here he was, sawing off the branch he was sitting on.'[4]

And Lazenby himself seemed a little rueful about some aspects of his brief time as 007. 'The trouble was I lived Bond out of the studios as well as in,' he said. 'I had to have a Rolls Royce to go round in, and women just threw themselves at me. I couldn't count the parade that passed through my bedroom.'[5]

Quite so. But was the era of the randy undercover man drawing to a close? On television, spy sagas such as *The Man from U.N.C.L.E.* and *The Avengers* had, by 1969, run their course. In the case of *The Avengers*, this was partly because these inventive spy sagas were so damned expensive to make. But in the perceived age of the hippy, and of Woodstock, and of the dawn of prog rock and the genesis of the new age Glastonbury Festival, there was actually a case to be made that 'For Queen and country' sounded, well, a little square.

All of which makes *OHMSS* utterly fascinating to watch today. It is that aesthetic collision between purple-lit high street boutique tat and a sincere, rather moving script, and Alpine scenes of almost breathtaking beauty. No other Bond film looks or feels remotely like it. Even the absence of an opening title song – instead, we have John Barry's magnificently driving, sombre, electronic theme – gives the film an altogether different footing.

And on this one occasion, when a young, naïve Bond is literally and metaphorically saved by a strong, sophisticated woman, the story somehow chimed with the heavily disguised yet deeply felt romantic yearnings that were present throughout Fleming's original novels. What everyone tends to forget now is that the literary Bond was not some form of callous automaton; very far from it. In the opening chapter of *OHMSS*, Bond even has a flashback to childhood seaside holidays. This is the Bond that we see in nascent form in George Lazenby – a man who can outfight anyone, but whose heart is bigger and more open than anyone might think.

So the silly man turned down a reported 'seven-year' deal with Eon, and denied us all the chance to see how his Bond would have grown. These days, he is married to former US tennis star Pam Shriver. Lazenby more or less retired from film in the 1970s, and instead branched out into property and other business ventures. Give him his due: he has always looked a cheery soul.

While *OHMSS* certainly made its money back, it took significantly longer to do so than any previous effort, and Broccoli and Saltzman were faced with a nightmare prospect as they went into a new decade: either recasting the role of 007 again or luring back – presumably between vast mouthfuls of sickly humble pie – their original world-beating leading man.

CHAPTER TEN A LITTLE MORE CHEEK

How hearts must have sunk in Eon headquarters, Mayfair, when Saltzman and Broccoli came to reread the novel of *Diamonds Are Forever*. It really is not Fleming's finest hour. Trailing from the diamond mines of Sierra Leone over to America, where we meet a gang of cardboard heavies calling themselves the Spangled Mob, and then into the Nevada desert, where there is an extraordinarily old-fashioned semi-denouement involving a western ghost town and a steam train, it was as though the genius of Fleming had somehow been deflated.

There was little in the way of jeopardy, and there was a tiresomely extended Las Vegas episode involving Bond diddling the villainous Spang brothers for little apparent reason. Indeed, the overall threat was weakened by making the villains brothers, thus splitting the dramatic focus. Surprisingly, it was only the fourth book into the run; in some senses, Fleming was clearly still finding his feet and did not know quite yet how much wilder and more exuberant his fictions could be.

But once again, we see that this happened to be rather serendipitous for the Bond producers. As previously mentioned, the spy genre by 1970 was regarded as utterly clapped out. No number of gadgets and widgets could change that. The essential plot of *Diamonds*, though, conveniently took Bond out of conventional cloak-and-dagger activity and placed him more in the mould of private detective/sophisticated adventurer, on a much more picaresque quest than usual. In fact, it is not entirely clear either in the novel or the film why Bond gets put on to this case in the first place.

One recurring thing we tend to see with Saltzman and Broccoli is that if they were at all concerned about the series financially, then they tended to head back for American settings with American actors, in the hope that they would at least pull those vast US audiences in. When it came to *Diamonds*, they were apparently on the brink of taking this pro-Americanism one dramatic stage further.

As we have seen, Mr Lazenby declined to do a second Bond movie. The producers were left without a leading man. And it has been suggested that the financial backers, United Artists, started a campaign of gentle persuasion. Would perhaps Burt Reynolds be suitable as the new 007? Nobody thought so. 'Wouldn't have worked,' was the later sage view of Roger Moore. Ah, but what about this chap – young, good-looking, but a bit more experience, name of John Gavin? Broccoli and Saltzman were interested.

Gavin is perhaps best known now for his role as Marion Crane's lover Sam Loomis in Hitchcock's *Psycho*. If we recall the opening scene of that film – Gavin and co-star Janet Leigh half naked in that sweltering Phoenix hotel bedroom – then we can see that actually, yes, it would be possible to imagine this chap in the role.

What we do know is that he was hired by Saltzman and Broccoli. Properly hired, that is, not just tentatively approached, or used in one test scene. There was one point in 1970 when to all intents and purposes, John Gavin was James Bond, at least on paper, as far as the film's pre-production processes.

What we don't know is: would Gavin have played it with an American or a British accent? It seems inconceivable that the producers would suck up to the US so far as to transform 007 into a Yankee. What would this doodle-dandy Bond say to M? What on Earth would M say back? And how could 007 behave in that amazingly patronising way towards the CIA's Felix Leiter?

One day, via the ever-evolving miracles of CGI, someone will devise a means whereby previous film images of John Gavin will be somehow super-imposed over images of Connery, and Gavin's voice will be manipulated accordingly, and then perhaps we shall see. Until then, all we can do is speculate wildly.

Anyway, it never happened, for in the mean time, David Picker, a senior executive at United Artists, approached Sean Connery with a view to luring him in once more. And finally Connery agreed to come back – to the apparent mixed feelings of Broccoli – for just one film.[1] His terms, however, made cinema history.

Connery asked for – and got – the then jaw-dropping fee of $1.25 million, plus a small percentage of the profits, having calculated that his pulling power as Bond had generated quantities of cash very many times this for Eon Productions. But Connery wasn't doing this out of greed; the fee concerned was used to set up a Scottish educational charity. So it wasn't the money. Part of it must have been the pride, though.

Incidentally, the actor also got a most unusual agreement that UA would back two further films of his choice. The first, released in 1972, was a highly controversial left-field piece called *The Offence*, in which Connery portrayed a policeman being questioned about the killing of a rapist (Ian Bannen) who was in his custody. As the film goes on, it slowly becomes apparent that Connery's policeman is rather darker and more degenerate than anyone would have suspected. Although critically praised, the film did not do roaring box office. And the second proposed UA film, a version of *Macbeth*, was scuppered when Roman Polanski got in there first with his Jon Finch-led production.

Prior to *Diamonds Are Forever*, Connery had certainly nipped along to the flicks to catch the Lazenby film, and indeed took a keen interest in the behind-the-scenes politics. This much became apparent in an interview he gave to the *Guardian* in December 1971, in which he explained his own approach to the part:

Because of my word-stress, I was able to get away from the original Bond character and take the sting out of the bad taste jokes that crop up in the films . . . Poor Lazenby couldn't do that because he just didn't have the experience, though the director Peter Hunt was quoted as saying he had taught Lazenby all I knew.

And in three months, Lazenby couldn't do a good job because you have to have technique to get a character right. I know he behaved like a prize shit, alienating people, from what they tell me – but it wasn't all his fault.[2]

How immensely gracious! But upon returning, Connery was also keen to let it be known what he thought of that character. Although he generously remarked of the *Diamonds* screenplay that it was 'better than usual', he went on to say: 'I've only read two Bond books; I found Ian Fleming himself much more interesting than his writing.'

Director Guy Hamilton, who had delivered the triumph of *Goldfinger*, was prevailed upon to return, and scriptwriter Richard Maibaum was teamed up with the young Tom Mankiewicz, a twenty-eight-year-old American with a distinctly light and jokey touch. In these terms, Saltzman and Broccoli might have thought, with a sigh of relief, that they had a banker.

The only problem was the story. It was not going to be possible to follow

Fleming's original, even though the diamond-smuggling element could be retained. So what would be the big plot, and who would be the villain?

It is at points like this – I don't know about anyone else – when I really admire the producers of those films. You might think, at first glance, that there could be nothing easier in the world than thinking up a plot for a Bond film. Well, try it for yourself. Go on, even the most basic, simple Bond premise. Give yourself an hour or so and see if you can do it. I bet you can't.

One of the difficulties is that you want to stick to tried and trusted elements while not battering the audience with repetition. You have to find a villain sufficiently outlandish and ingenious for Bond, along with henchmen who are sufficiently amusing, and who use amazingly diverting means of murdering those who stand in their way. You have to invent truly novel scenes of jeopardy – as we have seen, anything involving large circular saws simply will not do. You have to have a Bond girl who is alluring yet sufficiently left-field to be properly memorable; and on top of all this, you need action, chases, spectacle, and a grand climax that has never been done before.

As I say, it's not an easy proposition. And by the time of *Diamonds* pre-production, it was clear that just a little tiredness was beginning to creep in. When it came to the vexed question of the villain, one suggestion was that they should get Gert Fröbe back to play Goldfinger's twin brother. That is a terrible idea and thank the Lord they never did it.

Happily, by his own account, Cubby Broccoli had an intense dream one night about an old friend. That friend was the famously eccentric billionaire recluse Howard Hughes. In the dream, Hughes somehow ended up getting replaced with an imposter, and when Broccoli awoke – if only all our dreams were so creatively productive – he knew that he had his new Bond scenario.

Hughes became Las Vegas hotelier Willard Whyte, whose identity is stolen – honestly, these Eastern European criminals! – by Blofeld. Because Whyte is a recluse, the only person aware of this sinister personality takeover is Whyte's treacherous right-hand man Bert Saxby. So while Whyte is imprisoned in his desert house, an amazing glass and concrete bunker construction, Blofeld gets on with his latest insane plot . . .

Actually, in narrative terms, all of this comes very much later in the film. For the beginning, the producers gave at least a token nod to the Fleming original. In the pre-credits sequence, as a means of reintroducing the presence of Connery, we zoom from Tokyo to Cairo to South America as he hunts down Blofeld. Finally, he finds his prey in a curious cavern laboratory (hooray, Ken Adam is back!) where Blofeld — now played by the feline Charles Gray — is attempting to have himself facially duplicated.

After a short and intense struggle, Blofeld is consigned to the sort of molten mud pool that Fleming had in mind when he wrote *You Only Live Twice* (and which plays a rather more gruesome role in the novel *Diamonds*, as a hapless jockey is scorched with boiling mud). Connery is back and the titles begin.

But what then follows is yet another curious change of pace for the series, and one that must have been deliberate, given the waning public enthusiasm for all things spy. Bond is summoned by a rather wan-looking M ('liver trouble', we are told, and given Bernard Lee's real-life aptitude for grog, we wonder if that was actually in the script) to meet with a diamonds expert. Then, in a series of nifty cross-cuts, Bond is told of a diamond smuggling operation that has these experts baffled.

Bond and diamonds? Surely this is more a matter for The Saint, or any number of amateur gentleman British adventurers snuggled deeply in the bosom of the Establishment? Luckily, primarily because this is a Bond film, we in the audience know that rather greater perfidy than mere smuggling is afoot. That is the great advantage of a long-running series of films. One can play on the already high expectations of one's audience, and tease them with a low-key opening. Except in *For Your Eyes Only*, where the director tricked us with an epic introduction, and then made the story progressively more and more low-key, so much so that at one point, the greatest jeopardy is posed by a giant roll of paper that might squash someone.

Anyway, back to *Diamonds*: The exposition-speeding cross-cutting sequence features a short sequence filmed in Nevada but set in apartheid-era South Africa — a region, wisely, that the narrative spent no more than a few minutes in. How extraordinary it now seems that, amid faint, pipsqueak international condemnation, British firms in the early 1970s were heavy investors in white-ruled South Africa; to many old-fashioned conservatives with a pre-war colonial mindset, there was nothing especially wrong about the apartheid system. It is as well that the film moved us swiftly on from the diamond mines (with their 'superb facilities', according to Bond's establishment informer Sir Donald Munger) to the first appearance of the gay assassins Mr Wint (Putter Smith) and Mr Kidd (Bruce Glover).

There they are, in the middle of a desert landscape, prodding a black scorpion and awaiting the arrival of a corrupt dentist who is the courier from the diamond mines. By means of a simple trick, Mr Kidd drops the scorpion down the back of the dentist's shirt. The assassins rendezvous with the next pick-up, a helicopter, and blow it up. Then they walk off into the desert sunset, holding hands.

For many years, the relationship between Mr Wint and Mr Kidd was cited as evidence of homophobia among the production team, an extension of Ian Fleming's own anti-homosexual stance. Neither claim is as straightforward as it looks. True, in the novel of *Diamonds Are Forever*, Felix Leiter is not backward about coming forward with his view that 'some of these homos make the worst killers', although that is not necessarily as homophobic as it first sounds.

There are other instances. In the novel *From Russia with Love*, one character in MI6 refers with distaste to the service attracting intellectuals – or 'pansies drenched in scent'. But Bond's own view on this is that 'not all intellectuals' are homosexual and in any case, the service needs 'all sorts' in order to be able to effect successful infiltrations.

Oh, all right, it's not exactly pro-gay either, and one is also drawn back to Fleming's view of Pussy Galore's lesbianism – how Bond felt 'sorry' for such people 'but had no time for them either'. As for Fleming himself: well, he once gave an account of a visit to Tangier in 1957: 'There's nothing but pansies and I have been fresh meat for them. They do absolutely nothing all day long but complain about each other and arrange flowers.'[3]

It's bigotry; but actually, it sounds like secretly intrigued bigotry. Why did Fleming consider himself 'fresh meat'? All that can be said was that it was a different age. Male homosexual practices were not to be decriminalised until 1967. But homosexuality as a dramatic – and indeed comic – subject was becoming more widespread in the years before that.

The most famous dramatic example was Basil Dearden's film of *Victim* (1961), starring a career-challenging Dirk Bogarde as a gay barrister who is defending an ex-lover threatened with blackmail. There had also been prominent gay characters in *A Taste of Honey* (1961) and *The Leather Boys* (1963). In terms of wide appeal, however, it was the camp characters in the *Carry On* comedies who found the most appreciative audience. Kenneth Williams and Charles Hawtrey were there at the centre of the majority of the long-running broad-humoured series of films, though neither publicly acknowledged their real homosexuality.

Meanwhile, on BBC radio, Williams and Hugh Paddick portrayed the gay characters Julian and Sandy in *Round the Horne*. If there might still have been an element of ambiguity in the *Carry On* films, here it was brilliantly and – for its time – daringly swept aside, as on a weekly basis, Julian ('and this is my friend Sandy') would engage Kenneth Horne in exchanges of entendre-loaded polari.

Again, to balance any accusations of stereotyping and homophobia, the fact was that Julian and Sandy were not only a rather happy couple, but were also apparently untroubled by their position in society, and how they might be perceived by others. Comic creations they may have been, but they also seemed perfectly integrated into what one might have assumed was a largely hostile world. We can see now, however, that the whole show was years ahead of its time. By the late 1960s, there was still widespread hostility to the very idea of homosexuality, among the young just as much as the older generation. It was apparently fine when presented in comedy, but not when it actually walked down the street.

We have to take into account not merely the countless instances of 'queer bashing' seen on streets throughout Britain, but also landmark events such as the US Stonewall riot of 1969. The Stonewall Bar in Greenwich Village, New York City, was much favoured by Latino gay men and lesbians, with a good sprinkling of cross-dressers. One night, the police raided the place on the grounds that it was hosting indecent acts, and the officers concerned were violent. As a result, the clientele fought back. This in turn led to the first 'Gay Pride' marches in New York and in other cities across the United States. There were also protests calling for 'gay lib' and 'gay-in' events were held. These were not always serious in tone; quite the reverse, there was also a measure of flamboyant comedy. But this is the background against which we must place Mr Wint and Mr Kidd.

Unlike most other Bond henchmen, they have no unusually gimmicky means of killing. Most of the time, we don't even see *how* their victims are killed – in the case of the old lady schoolteacher, and the ghastly comedian Shady Tree, the crimes are committed off-screen. Not for this pair the gizmos of razor-edged hats or metal teeth. No, the measure of their scary perversity was in their very homosexuality itself. To balance this, however, their indefatigable propensity for one-liners and their apparently ceaseless good humour when going about their murderous duties makes them far and away the most engaging characters in the film. And yes, that includes Bond himself.

'Audiences loved those villainous gays,' mused Albert R. Broccoli later. 'By then, 1971, it was an acceptable theme in the cinemas.' What, homicidal homosexuality? 'A few years earlier,' Broccoli added, 'and I might have objected.'[4]

007 joins the diamond-smuggling daisy chain in Amsterdam under the guise of Peter Franks. Bond travels to Holland via what was then regarded as a madly futuristic mode of transport: hovercraft. Every time I see that shot now, of the deafeningly loud hovercraft leaving Dover harbour, I am reminded of a mid-1970s primary-school day trip to Calais on such a thing, where a combination of the juddering, the lack of fresh air, and the insensitive bright yellow of the hovercraft's interior walls caused half my class to fill their sickbags.

In Amsterdam, Bond is let into the apartment of one Tiffany Case (Jill St John), a wig enthusiast who is blonde one moment, brunette the next, then red. She asks Bond if he is bothered by this. He shrugs. 'As long as collars and cuffs match . . .' he says. Just one horrid line out of a great many horrid lines in this film, but director Guy Hamilton was completely unrepentant when interviewed, claiming that dialogue such as this was fine for a family audience because 'If any ten year old understood it, then he was a dirty little bugger and there was nothing anyone could have done anyway'.[5]

Tiffany is an all-American, smart-talking, quick-witted, tough dame – for all of one scene. However, following Bond's fight with the real Peter Franks in an enclosed antique elevator – a brilliant meld of careful set design, inventive stunt work and neurotic music, by the way – Tiffany instantly transforms into one of the dopiest women ever to grace the cinema screen.

Let's not point fingers at gorgeous Jill St John – she didn't write the script. And she was very pleased to be in it. 'Cubby Broccoli asked me and I was thrilled,' she said.[6] But just a year after Germaine Greer's *The Female Eunuch* had become a transatlantic publishing phenomenon and not long before Erica Jong caused a sensation with *Fear of Flying*, and with the Women's Lib movement starting to pick up a great deal of steam, were the Bond producers projecting this daft image of womanhood on purpose or did they simply not realise? We will return to Tiffany a little later.

In the meantime, it's off to Las Vegas with the diamonds concealed within

Franks's corpse ('Alimentary, my dear Leiter' explains Bond in another of the film's horrid lines). This is where we are lifted firmly out of the spy genre altogether by a scenario that seems more a throwback to the gangster movies of the 1930s and 40s. Bond and his diamond consignment are met by a bunch of hoods with a hearse; he is taken to a tasteless crematorium run by one Morton Slumber (a nice nod here to Evelyn Waugh's *The Loved One*) and, in a speedy chain of confusing events, gets knocked out and frighteningly shut into a coffin, shunted along on a conveyor belt through to the flames of that crematorium.

It is a brilliant cliffhanger; Bond in that silk-lined coffin regaining consciousness just as it glides into the horrible brick-lined cremation chamber, and then struggling to escape as the flames start to burn the coffin away − all against a background of hair-raising gothic choral music from John Barry. I remember first seeing this as a lad, and being open-mouthed with suspense and fear. How in the name of God could Bond possibly get out of this one? The thing now is that one tends to remember the crisis rather than its frankly improbable resolution, involving the coffin having been drawn back into the chapel, and the angry hood/comedian called Shady Tree demanding to know what 'the goddamn limey' has done with the real diamonds.

And here we are in the casino, and for once, this one is *supposed* to be horrible. For some years, Bond enthusiasts have complained that aesthetically, *Diamonds* is a rather lowering entry − they have been depressed by the tawdry Las Vegas settings, and the equally tawdry scenes and dialogue that unfolded therewith. But these enthusiasts have missed the point: it is purposely ghastly. You don't set a story in Las Vegas and expect viewers to take it for Siena. Like the set design of prime-time ITV light entertainment programmes − 'shiny black floor shows', these are termed − it is deliberately revolting. For Bond is moving through a tacky, gaudily lit world of profound amorality. Apologies, by the way, if you have recently taken your holidays in Las Vegas. I didn't mean you.

For once, Bond is on the craps table, though we still are none the wiser about the rules, and he is joined by Lana Wood, playing Plenty O'Toole. Madame Bovary she is not. Cue a horrid line about the character being named after her father and literally seconds later, they are upstairs in the horrible hotel. Before anything can happen, however, the lights are switched on by those 1930s hoods and Plenty is thrown out of the window, happily landing in a swimming pool below. Who is behind all these shenanigans? Why, hello again Miss Case!

This is the stage of the film where, having slept with Bond, it is now up to the girl to switch her allegiance to the side of the angels. Tiffany, spotting the chance of a pardon for her previous diamond-smuggling exploits, throws herself into it, even making friends with crabby Q, who has invented a ring that can defraud fruit machines. We think back momentarily to the sharp, cynical woman who featured in that first scene, and then we shake our heads and get on with it.

Bond, meanwhile, rather stylishly rides up to Willard Whyte's penthouse apartment on the top of an outdoor lift. After using suction pitons fired from a gun — well, you know, it's a Bond film, so why not, reasoned screenwriter Tom Mankiewicz — he breaks in to the apartment via a skylight, and promptly lands on a lavatory. What *is* going on with the vulgarity levels in this film? Ken Adam, though, was rather tickled by the idea of designing that particular set, revelling in the grotesque detail. And according to Sir Ken, Howard Hughes did indeed like to brief subordinates from the comfort of his loo seat. Anyway, Bond is greeted by the voice of Willard Whyte and wanders through to the living room — as it happens, one of Ken Adam's most memorable and influential designs.

It's really the floor that does it; that is, a vast, oval perspex floor beneath which can be seen a map of America, dotted with various scale-model rockets, and bases, and oil rigs, and other tokens of industry, representing the numerous interests and great wealth of the reclusive Whyte. The rest of the apartment — a blend of brushed steel, spindly lamps, white walls and deluxe sofas — is also rather stylish, and very faint impersonations of it can now be seen in yuppie blocks all over London's Docklands. But it is not Willard Whyte in residence. It is instead a *very* camp man with grey hair and a cigarette holder; in other words, Charles Gray as Blofeld.

To Bond's confusion, there are not just one, but two Blofelds, the other mincing down some stairs as the first sits at a desk. So! Those duplication experiments seen in the pre-credits must finally have worked! But wait: there are also not one but two *Persian cats*. That, surely, is going a shade too far, even for Blofeld? As the dual super-villains purr gloatingly to Bond, the agent somehow sees a chance to work out which Blofeld is the real one — by kicking one cat at the second Blofeld, now sitting on the sofa. This Bond does, rather cruelly, and as the sofa Blofeld grabs the moggy, Bond shoots him.

Then the cat runs off and collides with its doppelgänger. If someone could help me out here, I would be obliged, because I have never understood this stratagem, and I don't think I ever will.

Incidentally, the film's continuity director, Elaine Scheyreck (who went on to work on all the 1970s and early 1980s Bonds, as well as a great number of other epics), recalls the fun and the beauty of the Ken Adam set but also the 'absolute nightmare' of making sure everything in that rather complicated scene fitted together.

In any case, it appears Bond has buggered it up: the *real* Blofeld was the one sitting behind the desk. 'Right idea – wrong pussy,' says Blofeld, notching up yet one more horrid line.

Let's dwell for a moment on this double-entendre-strewn script: surely Connery – that aficionado of Pirandello and Ibsen – found it all a little crude and unsubtle? Well, perhaps not. For a couple of years later, when being interviewed on quite a different subject, Connery suddenly made the most startling admission. 'The only films I never miss are the "Carry On" farces,' he said. 'To tell the truth, I find they have less boring bits in them than most of the message films.'[7] Well, that much I suppose is true. And Connery's antennae for boredom were clearly very finely tuned – in 1966, he had turned down an offer to star in Antonioni's *Blow Up*.

Back to the matter in hand: a further attempt on Bond's life, this time by means of trapping him first in a gas-filled lift and then in a stretch of pipeline buried beneath the Nevada desert, the latest in a series of lame-brained assassination attempts by Mr Wint and Mr Kidd. A mildly disconcerting encounter with an automatic welding machine follows, and then a fantastically easy escape through a hatchway.

This was not the only easy ride. Once more, Bond enthusiasts have claimed that set-pieces such as the moon-buggy chase through the desert and the car chase through the night-time streets of Vegas are simply not proper 007; the former too childish, the latter too ugly. But both sequences are extremely memorable – the bizarre limbs of the experimental moon buggy flailing as Bond attempts to navigate across dunes, and then whole crowds of Vegas passers-by almost being mown down as speeding cars mount the pavements in front of lurid casinos. Certainly there is great pleasure to be drawn here, though in terms of sophistication it does seem to be a couple of notches down from *Goldfinger*.

But there was another cultural consideration at this time, and that was the apparent slow demise of the family film. In the early 1970s, the onward march of colour television had almost conquered all, certainly for this sector of cinema audiences. In Britain, it is estimated that in the early 1970s, sixty per cent of all films were classified as 'adult only' X-certificate. Even seemingly guaranteed family pleasers like Disney films were sputtering a little by this time; the studio was becoming better known among younger audiences for the television anthology series *The Wonderful World of Disney*.

To give an idea of the cinematic landscape in Britain into which *Diamonds* was released in 1971, here were some other key films of that year: the ultra-violent rural thriller *Straw Dogs*; the ultra-violent urban thriller *Get Carter*, starring Michael Caine as the man out for revenge in the bleak North-East; not forgetting the official 'ultra-violence' of Stanley Kubrick's *A Clockwork Orange*, adapted from Anthony Burgess's grimly dystopian novel. And as a final flourish, how about the ultra-unfunniness of the year's biggest comedy hit, *On the Buses*? Even though that was classified as a family film, you would have had to dislike your family very much to have taken them.

One of the reasons for the increased general level of screen violence — other than a perception that this was reflecting an increasingly violent society — was that changes to cinema classification had given film-makers the opportunity to explore darker, more 'adult' areas that television would never have been allowed to do, and that by doing this, an audience could still be counted upon.

This is not to say that any of the films mentioned above are bad, either aesthetically or morally — in some ways, one might argue that the more realistic depictions of harrowing violence, and the consequences that followed, were much more honest than the deodorised shoot-outs and punch-ups that had featured in previous years.

Perhaps *A Clockwork Orange* doesn't stand up quite so well now; possibly its artistic reputation grew as a result of Kubrick banning it for so many years in Britain following apparent copycat 'droog' attacks. The film these days seems too mannered and self-conscious to pack the punch that it was supposed to have. Conversely, *Get Carter* has belatedly gained a reputation as a screen classic, an unflinching revenge tragedy with an unforgettably bleak final scene on a dark grey beach littered with coal that was intended by the director to represent a form of hell.

The point is this: much of British cinema — and indeed, the new American cinema personified by the rising star Jack Nicholson — was leaning towards a new, and markedly uglier realism. Bond was among the very few films left to which one could take children and grandparents. And possibly to reassure the censors that all was proceeding as normal, this new cartoonish element – as typified by the slapstick moon buggy – was intended to compensate for any other violence or unpleasantness that might take place. Whatever happened, it was vital that children, as well as grown-ups, could see the films. For instance, in 1989, the classification for the much more violent *Licence to Kill* was 15 – and that seriously hurt the film's box office.

Interestingly, though, the film did spark some irritable correspondence in the letters page of *The Times*, as parents wrote in complaining that *Diamonds* was utterly unsuitable for children. This provoked a backlash from other readers begging to disagree, and insisting that children and parents alike had had an absolute ball; and that on top of this, there were so few other family films out there to enjoy. A similar debate began in the wake of 2006's *Casino Royale*, which had a 12A certificate; many parents took that to mean that it was on roughly the same level as *Pirates of the Caribbean* and then were horrified by the torture scene where a naked Bond has his genitals beaten.

In the case of *Diamonds* and its cartoonish elements, one also has such capers in order to make up for the lack of espionage activity. By the end of *Diamonds*, Bond is that fully fledged gentleman adventurer, albeit a slightly heavy one. We are pleased to make the acquaintance, quite late on, of another couple of villainous gays – this time the athletic lesbians Bambi and Thumper, who attack Bond against the striking concrete and glass backdrop of Whyte's country retreat.

A note on sexual politics: for the majority of this scene, it does appear that women have, in the crudest terms, got on top of Bond. Bambi and Thumper twirl and cartwheel gymnastically, in between kicking and punching poor Bond nearly senseless. But after they hurl Bond into Willard Whyte's infinity pool, and then dive in after him, Bond gets the upper hand – as he always must – by ducking their heads beneath the water as though they were medieval witches. Any point at which Dr Germaine Greer might have risen from her seat and cheered is swiftly extinguished by this cheerfully sexist denouement.

In this day and age – an era in which things appear to have evened up between the sexes sufficiently for both to relax a little – the scene just looks like plain fun. Back in the 1970s, this and other examples of blatant patriarchy drove the sisters mad, as we shall be seeing a little later. By the way, I am only supposing that Bambi and Thumper were lesbian; there was nothing in the script that pointed one way or t'other. It just seems to fit, and everyone else has made the same assumption.

As if the producers hadn't had enough fun with deviant villains, it is time for Blofeld to take his leave of Vegas – and this he does, in full drag and make-up and wig, disguised as a middle-aged woman, who is only spotted by Tiffany Case because of his giveaway pussy (forgive me, but I wanted to write a horrid line of my own).

So, gay assassins, gay bodyguard women (we think) and a cross-dressing gay super-villain – what do we suppose director Guy Hamilton was telling us here? Bond himself takes all of this very much in his stride. But one tries to imagine the Bond of Fleming's novels confronted with such a colourful array of non-conformists, and sending his martini down the wrong way.

It seems to be a general repositioning of Bond into broader entertainment, with a new accent on comedy. This in part would have been a reaction to what had been regarded as the excessive doominess of its predecessor *On Her Majesty's Secret Service*. But there is an aesthetic repositioning too. Ken Adam is leaving behind the gaudiness of the 1960s.

The look of the film is a very long way from Syd Cain's purple-hued Biba emporia; Ken Adam has instead fully embraced the stark concrete textures of modernism. 'I loved to contrast the futuristic with the antique,' he told me. 'Like the old refectory table seen in Willard Whyte's penthouse suite.' What one always tends to forget, in an age of computer-generated effects, was the amount of work that went on before the actual shooting began. Ken Adam flew out to Vegas at the behest of Cubby Broccoli – the wily veteran producer had used his friendship with the notoriously unwell Howard Hughes to gain entry to places that otherwise would have been closed off.

'On the side of one building,' remembers Adam, 'I saw a then revolutionary outside elevator, and I took my 16mm camera and went up in it but some men from the building confronted me and were very unfriendly. I had a word with Cubby and Cubby had a word with Howard and I was told to return within ten minutes. When I did so, they had put out the red carpet.'

As production designer, Adam was not only responsible for the awesome sets: he also designed crucial elements such as Blofeld's 'bathysphere' – the miniature submarine in which he tries to escape at the end of the film – and the logo of the Willard Whyte empire. On top of this, he was responsible for the howlingly camp diamond-encrusted death laser that Blofeld attempts to manipulate from space. The sheer range of invention was one of the things that kept Adam returning to the films. Indeed, as we shall see, in 1976, work on *The Spy Who Loved Me* provided him with a great deal of psychological satisfaction after a difficult period working with director Stanley Kubrick.

Clearly, for Blofeld, it all has to end in tears, and it does so by means of an unusually farcical climax set on board an oil rig off the coast of California. For some curious reason, the computer codes for the diamond laser are encoded upon a cassette tape labelled 'Great Marching Bands'. Bond gets on board the rig, to find Blofeld outside, smoking, and a bikinied Tiffany sunbathing. You wouldn't get that in the North Sea. 007 contrives to switch tapes – his cassette a *genuine* marching band compilation – but cat-eyed Blofeld thinks he has spotted Bond's attempted sabotage. Craftily, Bond secretes the laser-code tape down the back of Tiffany's bikini bottoms, producing the sort of facial reaction that was soon to become familiar in *The Benny Hill Show*.

Well, of course, Bond is locked up in the brig, or somesuch, and it is up to feather-brain Tiffany to save the day, but unfortunately Blofeld's gaze alights upon her bottom – 'We seem to be showing a little more cheek than usual,' he says – and the laser-code tape is put back into the clunky reel-to-reel computer. My dear, it is simply all too exhausting. There is however one nice gag beforehand, as Blofeld demonstrates his laser beam to Bond, claiming that he could target Kansas, but no one would ever notice.

He also wonders why Bond is especially bothered, 'since your pitiful little country isn't even being threatened'. Good question, actually. But in the world of Bond, he jolly well has to bother, for only the British appear qualified to take on diabolical masterminds. You can't rely on Felix Leiter – you might as well rely on the cat.

Anyway, here come some helicopters containing good guys. Bond escapes from the brig, Blofeld makes for his sub, Tiffany literally falls off the side of the rig – *very* Camille Paglia – and Bond contrives to use Blofeld's sub as a battering ram, bringing the whole rig crashing down.

The final scene acted as a sort of coda that would become compulsory throughout the 1970s – that is, the final attempt on Bond's life by the villain's henchmen. 007 and Tiffany are in a suite on some luxury cruising ship. Mr Wint and Mr Kidd – whom Bond has not thus far actually set eyes upon – come in, pretending to be waiters there to serve up dinner. But Bond recognises Mr Wint's overpowering scent. Mr Kidd attempts to skewer Bond with two flaming kebabs, Mr Wint tries to stab him with a corkscrew, Mr Kidd goes up in flames and overboard, Mr Wint gets a bomb tied between his legs and is also thrown into the sea. One is irresistibly reminded of an old Julian and Sandy gag, coming after they have also been involved in some maritime disaster involving falling overboard. 'Did you manage to drag yourselves up on deck?' asks Kenneth Horne. 'Oh no, just ordinary evening suits,' says Julian. Please yourselves.

In his review of *Diamonds* for *The Observer*, musician and critic George Melly spotted where the films were going. 'A formidable pair of rather endearingly lethal homosexuals bitch our hero's footsteps,' he wrote, 'and Ken Adam's great baroque sets are an important contributory factor to the success of this monument to low camp.'

The high-minded *Sunday Telegraph* went a little further with this shriek of glee from Margaret Hinxman. '*Diamonds*, I think, comes close to being the ideal Bond film,' she wrote. 'As fast, exciting, and ingenious as a live cartoon.'

The cartoon ends with Tiffany wondering how on Earth the authorities are going to get all of those stolen diamonds down from space; Bond looks up at the sky with a gentle, amused smile. It was the smile of an actor who thought he knew that he was shaking off a role that had become a burden. Look closely, and you might see a little relief in Connery's eyes. James Bond would return, as the end credits insisted; but as Connery put it, 'Who would play me?'

CHAPTER ELEVEN DARK UNCONFIDENT WORLD

Before we raise the curtain on the new – and to some, most controversial – era of the Bond films, it is worth quickly setting it in a historical context, and especially against the backdrop of 1973, a pivotal year in political and cultural terms worldwide.

Both in the US and throughout Europe, this was the dawn of the age of stagflation; all the effervesence of the 1960s was seemingly forgotten in a morass of clumpily conducted industrial relations and nit-witted economic mismanagement. The theories of John Maynard Keynes were held as self-evident truths; that it was the role of government to regulate supply and demand through the means of public spending. The underlying philosophy – a noble one that went back to the hardships of the 1930s – was that unemployment had to be kept low, even if this came at the cost of stoked inflation. The aim was to keep the two in balance. This was, however, a balancing act beyond the powers of most governments.

In Britain, the Conservatives under Edward Heath had been in power since June 1970 and by 1973, the government's repeated tussles with the big industrial unions had brought the country to an extraordinary state of crisis. In particular, the miners' strike of 1972 had resulted in power cuts; in some cases all power was cut off at 10.30 p.m. Britain at that stage was dependent on electricity from coal-fired power stations. It was dizzyingly simple for the miners to disrupt supplies.

But the miners were not acting out of malice, no matter what a later Conservative government was to think; rather, they wanted pay deals that would match the underlying inflationary trend. And nor were they alone in wanting such pay deals. The result was a vicious circle, for the more money was awarded, the more inflation was stoked. This was the era before credit cards, when the measure of money supply – literally, the amount of cash sloshing around in the economy – was all-important. As prices rose in shops, so demands for higher wages were further fuelled, and Britain – then very much a nation of heavy industry – saw stoppages take place all over. In 1973 came the three-day week – a government-enforced curb on production caused by fuel shortages. It was desperation on the part of Heath but no one had yet formed an intellectual way out of this impasse. Save, that is, for an American economist called Milton Friedman who at that stage had only a few disciples.

Then in the summer of 1973 came a blow that hit the whole world, sparked by the Yom Kippur War, in which Israel turned the tables on the invading Egyptians. This led to the Arabic oil-producing nations, through their cartel OPEC, suddenly cutting back on production, massively inflating the price per barrel. The knock-on effect throughout the Western world was volcanic inflationary pressure as the cost of production rose inexorably. And this in turn made all sorts of goods and activities, such as cars and driving, much more expensive. The US, at that stage clumsily pulling out of the Vietnam War, got a taste of recession.

But the US was also suffering its own trauma, in the form of the unfolding Watergate scandal, in which a night-time break-in at Democratic headquarters in Washington, carried out in order to plant surveillance equipment, was gradually traced all the way back to Republican President Nixon. Non-Americans often tend to forget just how important the President is to the American people, whatever that President's political background may be; and back in 1973, the idea that the President might have been caught out in wrong-doing of any kind was shattering. Nixon had never been a great favourite of what the musical *Hair* described as 'the youth of America', but none the less this was unprecedented. It is perhaps little wonder that a film as openly nostalgic as the 1950s-set *American Graffiti* (1973) proved such a huge hit that year.

Indeed, it's interesting to see how, in the 1970s, nostalgia in terms of both entertainment and style took a grip. On television, Americans became hooked to a 1920s-set family saga called *The Waltons*, the location of which was a large farmhouse in the Blue Ridge Mountains of Virginia. On British TV, top-rated dramas included the Edwardian soap *Upstairs Downstairs* and the BBC's Victorian shipping saga *The Onedin Line*. In musical terms, Roxy Music, with their lead singer Bryan Ferry, deliberately adopted a sleek, cool, smart look that directly harked back to the 1940s. In fashion, the leading style retailer Biba was redecorated in elaborate Art Deco fashion, and some of the dresses it sold harked back to a similarly elegant mode. Elsewhere, such items as grandad shirts and farmhand dungarees became prevalent for a while.

The tendency to reach back into the past happens when society as a whole finds the present just too uncomfortable to take. For an older generation, nostalgia would provide a comforting anchor at a point when the present day was so unstable and unpredictable and depressing. As a movement in Britain, it perhaps reached its apogee in 1977 with the event of the Queen's Silver Jubilee, a celebration purposely resurrecting such old standbys as street parties and indeed the Union flag. (We will hear a little more of this later, for it coincided with a terrific and shrewdly calculated high point for Bond.)

Author Howard Souness has recently made the convincing claim that a lot of the pop culture of the early 1970s was every bit as vibrant and sparky as any in the preceding years and it is certainly true that in musical terms, acts such as Bowie, Marc Bolan and Queen were strikingly good.[1] Also, interestingly, after all those years of 1960s sexual frankness, androgyny became the order of the day, with the advent of 'glam rock'; when David and Angie Bowie announced in an interview that they were an essentially bisexual married couple, they didn't appear to cause that much of a stir. Even the hideous and utterly heterosexual Brummies who comprised the band Slade were coated in glitter and eyeliner.

In terms of film, the economic shocks of 1973 had a deleterious effect on an industry that was already suffering in an almighty way. Cinema attendances both in the US and Britain were right down. In Britain, this resulted in the closure of many cinemas; in America, such difficulties proved a tremendous spur to creativity, with a whole new generation of directors, from Coppola to Spielberg to Lucas to Scorsese, starting to push through. After the ceaseless froth of the 1960s, their vision of cinema was marked with a greater sense of realism.

And when it came to film that the entire family could enjoy – well, by 1973, there was very little of that indeed. There would be occasional treats, such as Richard Lester's handsomely mounted The Three Musketeers (1973) and its several sequels, but otherwise, it was left to a struggling Disney to fill the family-shaped gap. Escapist adventure had given way to hard-bitten bleakness, as exemplified by the television series and spin-off film Callan (1973), starring Edward Woodward as a cynical, low-key intelligence operative.

Walk down a British high street in 1973, and you would have been wading through litter and staring at the dark-grey-stained concrete of NCP car parks and what were then termed 'shopping precincts', wind-blown

wildernesses with benches that no one wanted to sit on. The shops —
Woolworth's, Timothy Whites, the Co-op — were drab and primitive.
Orange and brown were the predominant colours. Whenever the BBC
wanted to make a drama set in Moscow, they tended to shoot the location
stuff in the middle of Dundee.

On the other hand, life went on much as before for the well-off, and into
this bracket I naturally slide Bond producers Harry Saltzman and Cubby
Broccoli (who at that time owned, as one hack noted, 'a gold-plated digital
watch'[2]). For Britain's wealthy, there was still a world of country estates — as
any Rolling Stone or former Beatle could have attested — and fine cuisine
enjoyed at Mirabelle's and sophisticated 'nitespots' such as Tramp and
Regine.

One had to be canny only when it came to travel, for at that period (and
this now seems eye-rubbingly incredible) one was not allowed to take more
than £50 out of the country at any one time. This was still several years
before the super-taxes imposed by the Labour government which caused so
many rich people to flee and go into tax exile. But the conditions for super-
rich disgruntlement were brewing.

Like every other industry, film was patrolled carefully by trades unions,
from electricians to designers. This was an era when 'demarcation' — that is,
the necessity to stick absolutely to one's own job and under no
circumstances carry out labour allocated to another man — was supreme.
Therefore life in TV and film studios tended throughout this period to be a
little jumpy, with producers having to ensure that lines were not crossed on
either side.

When one looks at Saltzman and Broccoli, one does not immediately
sense that they would have a great deal of time for unions. But is this really
fair? The Bond films had always had a reputation as being great fun for cast
and crew alike, and were noted for their unhierarchical set-up. At
Pinewood, meals were taken together like some vast family (although
according to Peter Janson-Smith, alcohol with lunch was banned in the
early 1980s after two second-string actors turned up for the afternoon
scenes worse for wear); and the most obscure set dressers were there
mingling with the big stars at on-set parties. In an era of general industrial
unrest, it is telling that no such anecdotes of stoppages ever seem to
emanate from the sets of Bond films.

By 1973, James Bond was the only real hero on screen. As we shall see, while thrillers and action films were in plentiful supply, there was only one sort that grandmothers enjoyed especially. Kung fu and blaxploitation – both popular subgenres that by 1973 were edging into the mainstream – tended to end up with X certificates, putting them beyond the range of the under-18s, and they were not to the taste of the over-65s. Happily, the Bond producers ensured that those particular audience members were not left out of these new enthusiasms. But what was this period to hold for Broccoli and Saltzman? How could they sustain audiences for a character who was now reaching his eighth film – itself quite a feat? As we shall see, while Albert Broccoli kept the faith, Harry Saltzman found the going tougher and tougher.

CHAPTER TWELVE MAN AT AUSTIN REED

You can say what you like about Sir Roger Moore – people often do – but over the very many centuries that he has been in show business, he has been consistently good-humoured. And there was a point in the 1970s when he was pretty much the acting equivalent of Hugh Grant. The light quips, the very slightly spikey edge, performances based upon a sort of feckless English charm that women found surprisingly appealing . . . in 1973, when Moore at last took on the role of 007, it was as though M, Moneypenny and indeed the entire audience had been waiting for him.

We have already seen how he was there on the shortlist back in 1962 for the role, but had then been deemed a little too young; how he got a mention in 1968 but Eon went with the car salesman instead. His name came up again in 1970 prior to Connery's return, but by that stage, Moore was committed to an ITC television series with Tony Curtis called *The Persuaders!*. The public on both sides of the Atlantic, and across much of Europe, were most familiar with Moore as the Saint; he played Simon Templar from 1962 to 1969 across what seemed like millions of episodes, all apparently identical save for the mad one with the giant ants. Each story would begin with a short teaser culminating in a halo appearing above Simon Templar's head. The key elements would be a character-actor bad guy and a starlet guest girl.

Among those guest girls were Lois Maxwell of Miss Moneypenny fame and Angela Scoular of *OHMSS* fame; the idea was that Templar would come to their rescue week by week. The Saint was not as ruthless as Bond, but he did have a way with a throwaway line. Moore, incidentally, has revealed that Leslie Charteris, author of the *Saint* books of the 1930s, loathed Ian Fleming, for he considered that Bond was in essence a rip-off of the Simon Templar adventures.

In *The Persuaders!*, Moore played Lord Brett Sinclair, something of a long-haired bachelor roué, forever sparring with Tony Curtis's Danny Wilde; in this role, Moore seemed a trifle more sophisticated, a man who looked quite accustomed to arriving at Nice airport of a weekend and knowing of a fine little place in the hills that did a marvellous bouillabaisse. Naff as a pair of purple knickers, in other words, but so indeed were about ninety-eight per cent of his audience, so it didn't matter. For the avid readers of women's weeklies, Moore was, as people used to say then, 'dishy'. In women's puzzle magazines, where the crossword required you to also find the name of the celebrity, it was Moore's photo that was always used as the clue.

Moore is the south London-born son of a policeman (in fact, according to the actor, his father was based at Bow Street in Covent Garden and his job was to draw the scenes of accidents and crimes); certainly, his father was encouraging when it came to young Roger's ambition to break into film. Perhaps following the drawing theme, Moore pursued an early interest in animation. Following his National Service, however, he steered towards acting.

The actor's lower-middle-class south London background has been mentioned many times as an illustration of how one does not have to go to Eton to play Bond – he is compared in this respect to the working-class-born Connery. This says more about journalists' attitude to class across the last few decades than it does about Moore's acting abilities, which have always been greater than either he or his critics have claimed.

In some respects, cinematic Bond as opposed to the literary version is a blank slate; an action-packed cipher waiting to be coloured in by whichever actor happens to take the role. Some quips here, some sex there, and a fight and a climactic showdown over there. There are not a great many occasions when the audience is permitted a look into Bond's soul. In fairness, there are not a great many occasions when an audience would want such a thing. None the less, the minute Moore steps into Bond's naff crocodile moccasins, you can feel that the entire tenor of the films has changed.

Before he signed up for the role, several other actors were checked out by Eon. 'Until last week, it looked like a photo finish between the dashing odds-on favourite Jeremy Brett and a dark horse outrider, Michael Billington, who impressed TV viewers with his suave appearances in the BBC's *The Onedin Line*,' reported the *Daily Mail* in June 1972. 'Now I hear the two leaders have been challenged by Julian Glover, a seasoned sprinter in many notable classics.'

'I was one of several people tested,' confirms Mr Glover. 'But it was revealed that Roger Moore was going to see the producers the next day and I knew really from that point that he had it.'

Glover went on to be a Bond villain in *For Your Eyes Only* and is still one of

Britain's most sought-after actors; his *King Lear* won him an award and he has recently toured in the part of Mikhail Gorbachev. Occasionally – just occasionally – he allows himself to wonder what it would have been like had he and not Roger been hired to fill the 007 shoes.

'I'm not sure my heart would have been fully in it,' Glover says carefully. 'But I have a good presence and I think what I would have done would be to show the steel behind the smile.'

The opening of *Live and Let Die* made Roger Moore what would then have been termed 'an international sex symbol'. Here is an entry from a diary that he wrote of that time: 'Thursday's mail brought an offer from *Cosmopolitan* to be their centre page pin-up for the June issue to coincide with the opening of *Live and Let Die*,' Moore mused. 'Fame at last! Me to be the bunny for liberated ladies!'[1]

A sweet sentiment; as for the film, though, there were precious few 'liberated ladies' to be found within this narrative. For *Live and Let Die*, Saltzman and Broccoli went back to Fleming's pre-civil rights 1954 novel and retained a surprising amount of it. The villain was still the black Mr Big, with his chain of 'Fillet Of Soul' restaurants, and his strategic use of voodoo and Tarot both to control his empire and to frighten his enemies. The main difference was that in the novel, Mr Big was smuggling treasure trove gold coins whereas in the film, he was aiming to flood the US with cheap drugs in order to become the main supplier. Like the novel, though, all the villains in this new Bond were to be black.

Now, if that seems as eye-poppingly racist as Fu Manchu, throw in a scene involving Roger Moore in Harlem, change the lead girl from being black into pale Jane Seymour, and surely you would have something that could never now see the light of day. But it isn't quite like that, and somehow it wasn't in Ian Fleming's much more inflammatory-sounding original.

Like many of his generation, Ian Fleming had a view of race that would now rightly be regarded by most as distasteful; but it can't, I think, be strictly put in the same bracket as the xenophobia of today's BNP, for very often, his views were not exactly pejorative. Fleming was born in 1908, when the British Empire was at its height, and he, along with everyone else of that age, would have been brought up with a certain view of the world, and a conviction that different peoples shared different and distinct 'characteristics'. In other words, it is racism as condescension, based on a belief in the inherent superiority of the Anglo-Saxon strain.

In the novel of *Die*, while there are uncomfortable scenes of Bond visiting black jazz clubs and the like, there isn't a sense that 007 feels superior to the people around him; there is a cultural gap but one that Bond apparently finds interesting, rather than repellent. In conversation with Leiter, Bond expresses the view that 'the blacks' are producing great intellectuals and businessmen so it is about time that they also produced 'a great criminal mastermind' like Mr Big. Yes, of course it is howlingly bigoted; but it is a different sort of prejudice than that which is still found within the ranks of the loony far right. It is a racism based on horrible assumptions, but Bond does not see people of colour as being in any way lesser than he (well, not in this novel anyway – get Fleming started on the Germans or the 'Chigroes' and it is quite a different matter). Much racism today is based on insularity; both Bond and his creator were, by contrast, better acquainted with the wider world than so many of today's generation.

Later in the novel, Bond embarks upon a relationship with the Creole Tarot reader Solitaire. One might say that the voodoo stuff is racist but again, there is no denying that such traditions have indeed been strong in places such as Haiti, where in the 1960s leader 'Papa Doc' Duvalier practically made it part of the constitution, shrewdly using it as a means of exercising control the icons of voodoo and a machete-wielding police force known as the Tontons Macoutes (a name which translates as 'bogeymen').

And the other, really crucial, point is that Mr Big is an excellent opponent for Bond: clever, devious and strong. This also comes across very strongly in the film, through Yaphet Kotto's muscular portrayal.

It would not have occurred to Saltzman and Broccoli that what they were doing could have been construed negatively; their motives were doubtless utterly pure when they looked at the growing popularity of 'blaxploitation' films such as *Shaft* (1971), *Superfly* (1972) and *Cleopatra Jones* (1973). For any film to succeed, Bond included, young audiences had to be lured into the cinemas, and the producers would have seen the fashion for 'blaxploitation' as exactly the sort of trendy subgenre they could profitably appropriate.

Nor were they wholly insensitive throughout production; according to the diaries kept by Roger Moore, questions were raised about making every single one of the bad guys black. The team ploughed on, however, convinced that the light-hearted tone of proceedings would keep the thing hovering above controversy.

However, others saw it differently, and when the film opened, there was a bit of a critical row in America at what was seen as the shocking stereotyping. Did the critics have a point? Let's look very quickly at the real-life background that the producers appeared not to be acknowledging. For all of the growing impact and influence of Afro-Caribbeans in the realms of music and fashion and film, racial tensions still ran boilingly high in the industrial heartlands and big city centres of America. The Civil Rights movement may have made profound changes but the tide of everyday bigotry showed little sign of receding. Mixed marriages, for instance, were still extremely rare. The Deep South remained, it seemed, utterly intractable and unrepentant on the issue, and even after the infamous Mississippi murders, branches of the Ku Klux Klan still operated. There were no black faces to be seen in the higher reaches of business, or in politics. In some senses, the view of Fleming's Bond in 1954 that black people were at last beginning to break through seemed premature by many decades.

In Britain, it had only recently been made illegal for boarding houses and landlords to put up signs saying 'No coloureds'. One of the most popular programmes on television was the sitcom *Love Thy Neighbour*, based on the premise of the social earthquake caused when a black couple move in next door to a white couple. There were still pungent memories of Enoch Powell's infamous 1968 'rivers of blood' speech; then there was the recently passed Race Relations Act, which specifically forbade workplace discrimination, clearly the sort of law that would take a while to really permeate through society.

In other words, race never ceased to be a fantastically sensitive issue and *Live and Let Die* appeared to some critics and journalists to promulgate all the bigoted myths concerning the urban black population – steeped in crime, drugs and occult practices. Throw in with this the incendiary implication of miscegenation with Solitaire and Mr Big – the white woman at the mercy of the powerful black man – and no, it doesn't look terrifically good.

Similar accusations of racism were raised after *You Only Live Twice* in 1967 and the depiction of India to be found in 1983's *Octopussy*. And just to state that there were no racist intentions does not let the producers off the hook. Offence is offence. But there is another factor here: that Bond is always an elaborate fantasy, and as such, the normal rules are suspended to a certain extent in a way that they are not in other films.

After all, could one argue that the mechanical-clawed henchman Tee

Hee is some form of black stereotype? No, of course not; he is an amusing
Bond henchman. Likewise, Dr Kananga is not representative of anything –
he is simply a formidable Bond villain. One finds when one is watching that
one does not wince, for all the characters take their correct positions in the
Bond universe, where all are ultimately equal, in some weird way.

With the introduction of any new Bond, one always wonders if the
producers are going to employ some trick to make the new actor's opening
scene that much more dramatic. Not here. The film's teaser doesn't involve
Bond at all. A diplomat is killed at the UN; a spy is stabbed at a New Orleans
funeral; an agent is sacrificed by means of snake bite in a creepy voodoo
ritual on the island of San Monique. Thence to the opening titles, and Paul
McCartney's rather wonderful song – a highly unusual Bond song, as Harry
Saltzman admitted when he first heard it, but a knockout all the same.

Then Moore's debut scene, and what a lulu it is! It encapsulates absolutely
everything that one either loves or loathes about this era. It is a scene that
simply could not have happened with any other Bond. It is quintessential
Roger.

So here is our man, at home in bed with cheeky Madeline Smith (playing
Agent Caruso), and checking the time on the sort of red LED digital watch
that only worked when you pushed the button. How impossibly sophisticated this must have seemed in 1973; and how savagely it had dated by 1976.
There is someone at his front door, and Bond gets up to answer it. It is M.
The various wrongnesses start piling up like a motorway collision in the
fog. Judging by the brick and trellis backdrop seen outside the front door,
Bond lives in a basement flat, but it must be the biggest basement flat in the
world. The living room leads directly, without any doors, to the bedroom,
which itself puzzlingly leads to the kitchen and thence back to the living
room.

So anyway, here is M, making an early morning house call, rather than
simply telephoning Bond. Saucy Madeline Smith has to run and hide
wrapped in a bedsheet, like a Ray Cooney farce starring Brian Rix. Bond
invites M in, and this gives us all an opportunity to absorb the impact of
Bond's lemon-yellow dressing gown, which is monogrammed with the
initials 'JB'.

M makes a beeline for Bond's bedroom – what's got into him? – and Bond
gently re-routes his boss to the kitchen. The exuberant tiling in Bond's
kitchen immediately puts one in mind of *The Galloping Gourmet*. Bond has a

cappuccino machine, with which he insists upon making M a very noisy cup of comedy coffee, despite M trying to get through some complicated exposition. Meanwhile, Miss Moneypenny walks in through Bond's front door – no, don't bother knocking, just stroll in, liberty hall – and spots Madeline Smith making a dash for the wardrobe. We are entitled to ask why Bond has chosen to place his wardrobe not in the bedroom, but right by the front door.

Tiring of Bond's kitchen, M goes back to the living room and makes for that wardrobe to get his coat, but Moneypenny saves the day by getting it for him. All this precisely so that M could tell Bond to catch a flight for New York. M and Moneypenny leave, and Bond uses his magnetic watch to lower the zip of Madeline Smith's dress, when he could simply have used his fingers like a normal human being.

So there we have it: smarm, sauce, and the aesthetic sensibility of a gay chihuahua. Personally, I love it. However, whenever I speak warmly of scenes such as this, there are plenty I know who howl me down. We shall all just have to agree to differ on this one. But Roger certainly started as he meant to go on.

And as filming began in 1972, Moore was on hand to give his thoughts on his fresh interpretation of the role. 'Gielgud has played Hamlet but that doesn't stop a lot of people having a crack at the role,' he said, with a mix of self-deprecation and unintentional absurdity. 'They bring their own individuality to it. Hopefully, I'll do the same. It is inevitable that comparisons will be drawn with Connery but it is better to go into a vehicle that's successful than one that is not.'[2]

Quite so. And off he goes, into the adventure. In a rather neat scene, we see young Jane Seymour as Solitaire reading the Tarot cards, and predicting a man who brings 'violence and destruction', beneath which we see the image of Bond's jumbo jet heading for the States. This was the first – and only – Bond film to suggest the power of the supernatural. From here, Roger is hurtled into his first cliffhanger. The driver of his car is shot by one of Mr Big's men; with Bond in the back, that car weaves at top speed in and out of New York traffic before 007 manages to regain control.

Here comes yet another Felix Leiter, this time played by David Hedison, who had the goodness to return in 1989's *Licence to Kill*. Once again, it might be pointed out that for an American agent working in American territory, Leiter seems remarkably un-proactive. It is left to Bond to visit a voodoo shop (nicely called 'Oh, Cult!'), spot Mr Big's henchmen wearing vast platform shoes, and follow them into the heart of Harlem and then into a tricksy booth in the 'Fillet Of Soul' restaurant. I rather treasure the sequence in which Mr Big instructs his heavies to 'waste' Bond in the middle of a bleak Harlem wasteland, a striking vista of grey urban gloom, most unusual for a Bond film; Roger himself strikes a pleasingly incongruous English figure in a dark Jermyn Street overcoat.

By day, Mr Big is in fact Dr Kananga, PM of San Monique. As well as consorting with the sinister Baron Samedi (Geoffrey Holder), Kananga seems rather reliant upon the clairvoyant skills of Solitaire. As Bond arrives at San Monique's premiere hotel – not quite so horrid as on previous occasions – the serious voodoo begins. First, a snake is introduced to the bathroom as Bond is shaving – however, no one bargains on Bond smoking a cigar at the same time as performing his ablutions, and using this together with some deodorant as a flame thrower. Then, as Bond meets inept CIA agent Rosie Carver (Gloria Hendry), someone leaves a powerful voodoo warning symbol on his hotel bed pillow – a filthy top hat dappled with bloody white feathers, as opposed to the customary chocolate.

For any children in the audience – and yes, I first saw this film in 1976 when I was nine – all of this was brilliantly frightening. Even more terrifying were the voodoo scarecrows dotted around the countryside of San Monique; as well as delivering a minor jolt in themselves, these mechanised marionettes also monitored with camera eyes and killed by means of bullets shot from their mouths. As a kid, I remember them being among the most original threats ever. I still rather love them, actually.

Incidentally, Rosie would appear to be a further witness for the defence of the producers against the charge of racism; she is Bond's first black squeeze. As is frequently the case, despite her CIA training, Rosie is also the world's worst secret agent. So, while we pronounce innocence to the accusation of racism, a resounding guilty verdict comes in over the issue of sexism. And poor Rosie doesn't last long, for she is a double agent also in the pay of Kananga; as she runs away from Bond, she is shot by one of Kananga's terrifying scarecrows. So how does one defeat such a creepy foe?

Well, by hang-gliding in to meet with Solitaire, is the unobvious answer. The hang-glider was a new craze seized upon by director Guy Hamilton, who was always keen to get the latest fads and gimmicks up on the screen. Bond sidles into Solitaire's green and red-lit Tarot-reading grotto. We can only presume that designer Ken Adam is absent again, and we are right. It's welcome back to our old friend Syd Cain, of purple flock wallpaper fame, who this time has opted for a provincial hairdressing parlour feel. After predicting Solitaire's future by stacking the Tarot cards in a preposterous fashion – every card in his hand shows 'The Lovers' – Bond sleeps with her, taking both her virginity and – uh-oh – her supernatural powers.

Oddly enough, this scene is one where you end up actually hating Bond. This poor naïve girl, tricked into bed by a safari-suited smarmster, is incredibly forgiving about the fact that he has robbed her of her magical talent of foresight. If I was her, I would have killed him. What makes things worse is Bond's insistence on teaching Solitaire 'lover's lessons' – and her coy little request to be taught 'lover's lesson number three', to which Bond assents, stating that 'There's no point going off half-cocked.' Ugh!

But by 1973's standards, that was Molière. In Britain, cinema screens were still jammed with the bawdy *Carry On* films, presumably much to the delight of Sean Connery. For some curious reason, the Bond production team felt that agent 007 too should trade in double entendre. To this day, when people talk of 'Bond's famous one-liners', I always feel like quoting back the Roger Moore oeuvre.

Anyway, robbed of her powers, Solitaire is no longer of any use to Kananga, and she must go on the run with Bond. This is a rather good sequence, involving a creepy Baron Samedi playing the flute in a cemetery, Bond's discovery of Kananga's drug crop, more of those frightening bullet-firing voodoo scarecrows, and finally, a terrific chase in which Bond is forced to drive a delapidated double-decker bus at a low bridge, memorably severing the bus's top deck.

This sort of thing is where director Guy Hamilton excelled; he recalled seeing an old London Transport training film in which a double-decker driver had to negotiate a skid-pan without knocking over any dummy bus stops. It was a beautiful touch to apply this principle to the potholed roads of San Monique, and so much more amusing and exciting than any straight car chase. According to excited red-top tabloids at the time, Roger learned his bus driving skills in the Chiswick depot, west London. One of the drivers there stated that if Moore should ever tire of Bond, there was a double-decker waiting for him back at home. 'He'd make a good bus driver if he's ever short of a job,' declared Maurice Patchett.[3] And the bus scene has made everything all right again: we no longer hate Bond.

But it's a form of extended chase and things slow up a little as Bond and Solitaire reach the bayous of Louisiana; Kananga's heavies simply capture Solitaire and Bond is forced on the run again, this time by jet-powered speed boat.

Speedboat chases must always look terribly exciting on paper and on the storyboard, for the Bond producers always seem drawn back to them. Other such pursuits can be found in *The Man with the Golden Gun*, *Moonraker* and *The World Is Not Enough*. But you would have thought they had learned that lesson after the climax of *From Russia with Love*: no matter what you do, or how fast the boats go, a boat chase is always curiously dull. This particular example looks rather elegant — boats powering through wedding receptions, boats filmed from above roaring through bayous leaving beautiful white trails, boats performing stunt jumps over roads. But it is no good. It just feels like it has gone on for about three and a half hours. Guy Hamilton has described what a difficult technical feat it all was — with the angles of stunt boats having to be calibrated just so, and no one paying attention to the difference that rising tides would make. But really, he would have been better off sticking to the double-decker bus.

Time here for actor Clifton James to take a bow, as redneck Sheriff J.W. Pepper. He is there purely as a comedy character, to react to the boat chase. And it is a tribute to the actor that he struck some kind of chord with audiences and critics alike. The figure of a belligerent know-nothing sheriff was echoed throughout the decade in American productions such as *Smokey and the Bandit* (1977) and the TV series *The Dukes of Hazzard*, and James has said that he has been mistaken for each and every sheriff concerned. Certainly, with his molasses-thick accent and voice high-pitched with continual outrage, he provided welcome distraction from the longueurs in the bayous, and deserved his cameo rematch in the following film.

J.W. Pepper also laterally reminds us that, as in *Diamonds Are Forever*, Bond no longer seems to be a spy; more of a gentleman adventurer, an Allan Quatermain in chocolate-brown flares. Drugs? Since when was that the business of MI6? For the purposes of the story, it is the murder of a diplomat that seems to pull Bond in; but the resultant capers are to do with something quite different.

Britain had by 1973 more or less completely lost its empire, save for the odd outpost like Gibraltar and Hong Kong; but it had, in its place, gained a Commonwealth. The fictional island of San Monique is portrayed as the personal fiefdom of Dr Kananga, though with scenery and indeed buses remarkably reminiscent of Jamaica. And Bond by now has become some sort of world policeman, thinking nothing of national borders or national laws as he pursues the criminals. In this, he operates with the tacit approval of the CIA who indeed come in at the end to plant the explosives that will destroy Kananga's poppy fields; but all the hard work has been done by Bond.

It is an arresting idea that the producers have unwittingly floated: that by 1973, the world ceaselessly trembles on the brink of crime-fuelled anarchy and that only the assured Establishment Englishness of Bond can hold such horrors at bay. For this is another point; whereas Connery, with his Scottish accent, always managed to exude a sense of being anti-Establishment, Moore, with his bass Received Pronunciation, is very much the Mayfair boulevardier, and loyal servant to the government and the Crown. Events on occasion comically undermine his authority – such as the scene in the following film where Bond is aggressively squeezed by a sumo wrestler – but Roger's confidence never slips, to the point where the character of Bond allows himself some self-deprecation.

The film also swerves past some of the more paranoid American theories that small Caribbean states would be seduced, like Cuba, into the thrall of the Soviet Union. There was much propaganda in the early 1970s directed against the 'Black Panther' group based on its alleged Marxist leanings. Fleming himself mentions the possibility of links between Black Power and Communism in the 1954 novel. Luckily, the producers and directors were having none of this. As ever, Bond strove as far as possible to avoid anything remotely close to a geopolitical stance.

In an era starved of old-fashioned escapism, director Guy Hamilton was keen in this era to ramp up what he termed 'the snakepit situations', and one such was a poser that he put to screenwriter Tom Mankiewicz: having seen a crocodile farm while out on a recce, Hamilton wanted a scene where Bond would be trapped on a tiny islet, surrounded by approaching snapping reptiles. The question was: how would Bond get out of such a fix?

By using his magnetic watch to tug on the rowlocks of a nearby rowing boat? Too easy! The boat would be tied up. So how, then? I recall the eventual solution as being a fantastic playground talking point at school. As the beasts snap at his ankles, Bond sees four crocodiles roughly lined up in the water, and hastily uses them as stepping stones in order to get back to dry land unscathed.

It's preposterous but utterly wonderful and made all the more so by the fact that the stunt was filmed for real, the legs of the farm's owner standing in for Roger Moore's heavily insured pins. The crocodiles he treads on look astonished by his impertinence. And again, this was less the cliffhanging peril normally encountered by spies, and more a throwback to children's Saturday morning serials.

This was the major change from the novel, in which Bond and Leiter were put through darker and more gruelling ordeals. In the novel, Leiter is lowered into a shark tank; incredibly he survives, but is maimed for life. Then, at the climax of the novel, Bond is tied up and hauled through seawater across razor-sharp coral reefs, the idea being that the blood from his torn wounds will bring the sharks in for the kill. Interestingly, this scenario was deemed suitable eight years later in *For Your Eyes Only*. And the gruesome Felix Leiter scene was used in *Licence to Kill*, and was instrumental in that film being given a 15 certificate.

The early days of Roger Moore were a little lighter going, thank the Lord. Talking of whom, who is to save poor Solitaire? Kananga feels terribly betrayed, as well he might, for no one wants to be cuckolded by a man who wears a reversible safari suit, so Solitaire has been sent back to San Monique to become the centrepiece of a macabre voodoo ceremony involving a lot of frenzied dancing, flickering torches, and a coffin full of writhing snakes. The supernatural stuff is a wonderful change of pace for Bond — who needs a countdown when you have pulsating drums and the bound heroine being threatened with a puff adder?

Still, all good things, and it's time for the denouement in Kananga's underground lair, which looks very small in comparison to Ken Adam's wondrously operatic sets. Clearly, even for Bond, the world recession was starting to bite. This time Kananga's getaway monorail is clearly a prop that doesn't work. A final exchange of unpleasantries and clunking quips follows between hero and villain, then a quick tussle in a shark pool before Kananga swallows a bullet that inflates its victims, and blows up like a balloon. Interviewed recently, prolific actor Yaphet Kotto had only the warmest memories of the role — except the undignified final shot. 'Kananga was the equal of Bond and I wanted him to be better dressed, drink better champagne than Bond . . . to compete with him properly.' He also recalled how well he was treated by Eon Productions, and how, after this whirl of chauffeurs and hotel suites and champagne, for a while afterwards he had to carry on living like that — 'living like Bond'.[4] But without the reversible safari suit, we trust.

In many ways, it is a remarkable debut for Roger Moore, who looks assured from the off. There were, according to Moore, a few tussles off the set. For instance, Harry Saltzman for some reason fired Moore's hairdresser; this threw Moore into a bait, as he confessed in his diary of filming: 'I finished my work-out in a furious mood,' he wrote, 'and flung my breakfast toast across the room in a rage.'[5] We will put to one side the unforgettable bathos of that image and instead concentrate on happier memories. 'I was so nervous of doing a love scene with Roger,' said Gloria Hendry in a TV interview, 'because Roger's wife Luisa was there on location watching him. But I was told I had to get on and do it because it was my job.'

Indeed, as his time in the role went on, Roger's then wife Luisa was consistently there scrutinising the snog scenes. No matter where he went in the world on location, she was there, looking on beadily. Actually, Broccoli encouraged spouses and families to spend as much time as possible with the crew. He was genuinely big on the idea of a family atmosphere.

Moore was a man in early middle age and the five-month shoot was quite a serious proposition, both physically and in terms of keeping the focus on the character consistently tight. He said: 'I didn't realise just how hard it would be. Twenty-two weeks of non-stop action. On the first day of shooting, Guy Hamilton said: "On the last day, you're going to see a very drunk director." And I did. He also saw a very drunk actor. We both got paralytic.'[6]

The other striking aspect of the film now is that it was scored not by regular John Barry, but by Beatles producer George Martin. In contrast to Barry's magnificently ironic military marches and lush romantic themes, Martin's score is determinedly more youthful, faster, with more guitar. Like any good score, it does not intrude or draw attention to itself, but none the less we are keenly aware of it, for it is an attempt to get across to us just how much of a new era Moore's Bond is going to be. Also, thanks to Martin's old protégé Paul McCartney turning around the title song so far in advance, Martin was able to incorporate its melodies into every part of the film, from the glissando-plagued love theme to the more raucous voodoo scenes towards the end.

The mere fact that McCartney was so keen in the first place was quite telling. By this stage, the Bond song had clearly been marked out as the smart thing to be heard singing. In the years to follow, artists such as Alice Cooper and Blondie would be invited to submit compositions that sadly weren't used. Occasionally one gets to hear Cooper's version of *The Man with the Golden Gun* – a little monotone, but certainly less hysterical than the tune that Lulu sang. Just a few years ago, top Britpop band Pulp decided to compose a theme song for the 007 film in production called, at that stage, *Tomorrow Never Lies*. It is fascinating to listen to now, Jarvis Cocker's rich, dark Sheffield voice blending with John Barry-style strings as the singer performs lyrics such as 'the night-time blazes with all your nightmares come to life . . .' As in the previous examples, the song was not used. Instead, *Tomorrow*'s composer David Arnold wrote a loungecore tune – 'Surrender' – for kd lang – and that got vetoed in favour of a brassier Arnold tune, 'Tomorrow Never Dies', for Sheryl Crow. The kd lang composition instead featured at the end of the film. Competitive business, Bond songs.

The occasions on which John Barry was absent and had to be replaced did not always work out quite so satisfactorily; but *For Your Eyes Only* is a little way off yet.

Our Roger received slightly mixed press when the film opened. Whereas chirpy tabloid the *Sun* was happy to proclaim that 'Roger is the best Bond of all!', others were not quite so sure. 'Mr Moore as Bond is exactly like the Mr Moore who played The Saint, who in his turn is the nearest approximation to the Mr Moore who plays anything,' wrote the *Guardian*'s Derek Malcolm unkindly, adding a back-handed compliment to the series: 'He is the perfect cypher through which the glamorous hardware of the Bond movies can express themselves.'

Indeed, other critics were now responding to Bond as a cultural phenomenon, as opposed to a family-friendly adventure film. 'As long as they keep making James Bond films,' declared *The Times*, 'the 1960s will never die.' The high-minded journal *The Spectator* took a dimmer view. '[This Bond] is a lethal comedian let loose in a world of thuggish buffoons,' it declared. I wouldn't necessarily regard that as being a bad thing myself, but there it is. Despite the muted response, the audiences were still bundling into those grubby high-street Odeons, and Moore's immediate future was looking secure.

Incidentally, the terms 'Roger Moore' and 'fashion plate' are not often placed together in the same sentence; and indeed his era of Bond is renowned for its sartorial awfulness. Not just because of the early world-infamous white safari suits with flared trousers a-flapping, but also in the later films, that curious avuncular form of Moore leisure wear that seemed to put the focus on grey suede zip-up blousons and slacks that came up to his nipples.

But we would do well to remind ourselves that back in the early 1970s, as Roger was enjoying the success of *The Persuaders!*, he was not only designing his own costumes for that series but was also approached by men's clothing chain Austin Reed over the possibility of launching a 'Roger at Austin Reed' line.

Imagine if he had – and imagine just how very expensive those clothes would be on stalls in Camden Market now. It is not enough for us to look at Roger in hindsight, for all we will tend to see is the smirk, the mole, and the crocodile-skin slip-ons. To audiences of 1973, Roger was quite a different proposition; women fancied him. A lady of a certain age told me recently that she was always drawn in by Roger's 'piercing blue eyes'. He also did the business in box-office terms. *Live and Let Die* was a galloping success and got reasonably good reviews. The new 007 was all set to dominate the decade.

CHAPTER THIRTEEN WILL HE BANG? WE SHALL SEE

'**O**ut of the two, Harry Saltzman was the volatile one,' Sir Ken Adam says. 'Always blowing up, shouting and swearing, and all you would do was smile through it. Cubby Broccoli was the easy one, more charming. But they were both equally tough – very tough men.'

By 1974, Broccoli and Saltzman had been in partnership for twelve years. They had, according to some, developed a pattern whereby they would take it in turns to handle the bulk of the production on the Bond movies. For instance, when Saltzman was out in Switzerland overseeing *On Her Majesty's Secret Service*, Broccoli would be back in London attending to other operations.

In addition, when they weren't producing Bond, they would be producing other films; Saltzman went off to do the insanely star-studded *Battle of Britain* while Broccoli was doing *Chitty Chitty Bang Bang* (both 1968). Busy men, in other words – and according to some, men who were often barely on speakers. Sean Connery was especially interested in what he perceived as the mutual frustrations these two men would feel about one another.

One can see how a juggernaut like Bond would produce creative friction. Glidrose chairman Peter Janson-Smith, who sat in on some occasions when production of the films was fully under way, remembers the large office in Mayfair, with lots of people sitting round a big table with telephones everywhere, including on chairs beside them, as assistant directors and assistant producers rang in with logistical problems – a prop lost on location, a difficulty in booking a specific flight, permission needed to film on a particular cable car . . .

'As I looked around at all this, with the cigarette smoke thick in the air like fog,' recalls Janson-Smith with a laugh, 'a phone on a chair started ringing and Harry Saltzman looked up from his own phone and barked at me to answer it.'

'Harry was extremely creative though,' says Sir Ken Adam. 'You know, he would come up with twenty ideas – nineteen of them would be terrible but one would be really good.'

In short, Saltzman was described as the kind of man who would have a telephone receiver at each ear at the same time.

For those of us who have difficulty organising a Christmas shopping list, the sheer pernickety nightmare of pulling a Bond film together does not bear thinking about. Think first of finding a suitably exotic set of locations; then think of getting permission to film in those locations; think next of shipping not only actors, but also expensive cars and gadgets over to said locations; think then of organising all the explosions, the stunts and the car chases, ensuring that none of the locals get caught up in all this. Think merely of the culinary arrangements: a crew of hundreds to feed and water every day, often far from the nearest hotel. Remember that the role of producing is one not merely of ultimate creative control, in the case of the Bonds, but also of the grind of setting that creativity off. It would have been a miracle if Saltzman and Broccoli hadn't had their off days.

And by the early 1970s, there appeared to be more off days than before. It has been written by some that Saltzman had investments in many other parts of the film business, including the company Technicolor. But the early 1970s was not a propitious time for film investment. Hollywood was suffering from the continued and growing success of television, combined with an apparent failure to regularly draw in the young audiences it needed.

Things were worse in Britain, where – aside from the trusty Hammer horrors and the Carry On films – production was thinning out to the extent that studios such as Shepperton were facing closure. The upshot is that this apparently proved a difficult financial period for Saltzman, with a Swiss bank threatening to foreclose on him; in order to protect the interests of Eon Productions, Broccoli was going to have to buy him out. And so it was that *The Man with the Golden Gun* was Harry Saltzman's last Bond epic.

It was based on Ian Fleming's final Bond novel – and based extremely loosely at that, for the novel didn't cut the mustard at all, owing to the fact that poor Fleming had died before he had the chance to revise it. The story – a thin affair – features a brainwashed Bond returning from Russia and attempting to assassinate M with a cyanide bullet. A well-timed descending plate of bulletproof glass saves M from that particular fate. Bond is thus turned over to the department's psychiatrists. After a while, when he appears to have come round, M sends him on a simple undercover mission as a means of recuperation; he is to get close to and eliminate paid assassin and Cuban sympathiser 'Pistols' Scaramanga in Jamaica.

But Scaramanga, unaware of Bond's true identity, rather warms to this fellow. There is the suggestion of a homosexual flavour to his fancy. But Bond's cover gets blown and it all turns nasty, first on an old-fashioned steam train and then in a foul-smelling mangrove swamp, where Bond and Scaramanga duel to the death.

Recently, British newspapers latched excitedly on to the fact that Scaramanga was named after a boy at Eton for whom Fleming did not care. But this was hardly news. After all, Blofeld was named after Tom Blofeld, a Norfolk farmer, chairman of the Country Gentleman's Association and fellow member of Fleming's club Boodles; Goldfinger was named after modernist architect Erno Goldfinger (the brutalist Trellick Tower in North Kensington is one of his most abiding works), who considered suing Fleming for turning him into a homicidal gold-coveting criminal. Everyone in Fleming is named after someone he knew. Pussy Galore was probably his cleaning lady.

But the more melancholy fact was that there wasn't enough in *Golden Gun*'s original scenario to work for a film. So once again, director Guy Hamilton and screenwriter Tom Mankiewicz put their heads together with the producers to work out the story of the ninth Bond film.

One main idea might have come from 1973's smash hit *The Day of the Jackal*, starring Edward Fox as the eponymous assassin aiming the crosshairs at General de Gaulle, and Michael Lonsdale as the cop charged with stopping him. Frederick Forsyth's novel turned conventional thriller assumptions on their head by the fact that its millions of readers knew fine well that the General *wasn't* assassinated. None the less, suspense was ratcheted up by the chilly efficiency of the Jackal. It was obviously a terrifically good suspense scenario for Bond, turned around so that the target would be the secret agent himself, a golden bullet bearing his number sent to M.

The next question was how to bolt that together with another villainous plan, for an attempt on Bond's life would clearly not last for two hours of screen time. The OPEC crisis of 1973 appeared to provide secondary inspiration; with oil now such an unstable commodity, the hunt was on for other sources of energy, and so the Bond producers had their MacGuffin — the Solex Agitator, a tiny device that had the power to convert ordinary sunlight into a laser beam.

One idea was to set the story — and indeed film it — in Iran. Which only goes to show how quickly the world changes. The production team made a recce to Iran, then ruled not by ayatollahs, but by a secular regime under the dictatorship of the wealthy but utterly disgusting Shah. The Bond gang went out into the desert to what they imagined was the lost city of Bam. However, it turned out to be another city entirely. Sadly, Bam is entirely lost now, having been largely destroyed in an earthquake in 2003.

So where was the colour to come from? For Scaramanga's secretive base, Guy Hamilton settled on the Far East and Thailand, having been fascinated during the war by the mushroom-like islands poking out of the sea at Phuket. Phuket at the time was not a holiday resort for braying trustafarians on 'gap years'; in fact, hardly anyone went there at all. It was a top spot. But it was the only top spot of the film.

Now, this might simply be imagination, or a result of super-inflation, but this is the first and I think only Bond where it looks as though the team were beginning to cut corners a little on production costs. The sets, again not by Ken Adam, but by his colleague Peter Murton, were disappointingly unimaginative. And the set-pieces, once so exuberant, seemed a little flat. Back in 1965, Hamilton had declined to direct *Thunderball* on the grounds that *Goldfinger* had drained him of ideas. Now, by 1974, and after *Diamonds Are Forever* and *Live and Let Die*, this was his third Bond film in a row.

The same was true of screenwriter Tom Mankiewicz. Given that this production line was turning them out at a rate of one every eighteen months, could it be the case that everyone was suffering a little creative exhaustion?

The teaser this time featured Scaramanga on his private Thai island, with his lady Andrea (Maud Adams) and his dwarf Nick Nack (Hervé Villechaize). An American hood — the droll hearse-driving chap from *Diamonds Are Forever*, in fact — shows up for an assignation. The hood is under the impression that Nick Nack wants his master killed. The hood, however, is sadly mistaken. He is swiftly trapped in a stylised and disorientating fairground fun house, there to be used as live target practice for Scaramanga. He is shot between the eyes, and as a *coup de grâce* Scaramanga turns on a waxwork model of Roger Moore, shooting its waxy digits off.

This waxwork is unfortunate, for it gives critics an instant opportunity to sarcastically praise Roger Moore's most convincing turn.

The film's title song is so extraordinarily kitsch that it is now played ironically in clubs for laughs. 'He has a powerful weapon!' avers Lulu. 'He charges a million a shot.' Then, immediately afterwards, a moment of sublime lyrical bathos: 'An assassin who's second to none/the Man with the Golden Gun'. The tune, at least, is nice enough, though one senses that John Barry's heart is not quite in it. Nor do Maurice Binder's titles appear to be on form: ripply, watery shots of girls sliding past, and a naked silhouette dancing against the backdrop of a firework. Motions are simply being gone through.

I must point out in the interests of fairness that I know several people – eminently sensible, critically clued-up people – who adore this film, Bond who ignore all of these gripes. Who cares, they exclaim, if almost every set in the film appears to be brown? And what is more, the argument goes, what about Christopher Lee, hmm? This fine actor finally gets the chance to throw off his Hammer Dracula image to turn in a bravura Bond villain, all silky menace and cheerful articulacy.

'It was a well-written part in a good story,' said Lee. 'Better than the book. In the book, Scaramanga's just a thug. The screenwriters took the character and changed him into a civilised lethal man with a sense of humour and a lot of charm.'[1]

Well, all right, let's give the film that one point. Lee is unquestionably very good, and rather disconcerting in one scene with his mistress Andrea, when he caresses her breast and then her lips with the barrel of his golden gun. 'Love is required whenever he's hired,' as Lulu helpfully pointed out at top volume in the opening title song.

Lee is also rather good in his set-pieces with our Roger, insisting that he and Bond are two sides of the same coin and are in many senses equals. And there is another good, mildly unnerving scene as Scaramanga quietly assembles his golden gun from various components – a pen, a lighter – while talking lightly with his unwitting victim, the wealthy industrialist Hai Fat. So yes. It's not all bad.

Incidentally, Christopher Lee received a visit from a most distinguished fan while filming his scenes at Pinewood. The world champion boxer Muhammad Ali came to have a look at him in action on set, and was so impressed by meeting the actor in the flesh that he pledged to dedicate his next fight to him. Everyone around thought that was a bit of polite hyperbole; but in fact, after one subsequent fight back in America, victor Ali did indeed shout out: 'This one's for Christopher Lee!' So there we are. That is now two *Golden Gun* fans that I can think of.

But almost from the off, the film is sabotaged by its lowering visuals. Bond sets off on Scaramanga's trail, first popping into a Beirut belly-dancing club. Except that we can see that it is very obviously a rather shabby corner of Pinewood. Then it is off to Hong Kong and Macau where, as previously mentioned, almost everything is brown: walls, bedsheets, bathroom fittings. Even the interior of the partially sunken *Queen Mary* in Hong Kong harbour, now transformed into a field office for MI6, is a symphony in beige. While all the sloping, crazily angled walls and furniture are a nice, semi-surreal touch, it is all so drab that we want to be shot of the place within seconds.

So, yes: Scaramanga is after the Solex Agitator, as indeed is Bond. Bond trails Scaramanga's mistress Andrea, and surprises her in her hotel shower. What follows is a scene that still leaves one frowning deeply with disapproval – and that goes for Sir Roger Moore too. Having allowed her the courtesy of putting on a bathrobe, Bond throws Andrea face down on a bed and threatens her with a broken arm if she does not tell him of her lover's whereabouts.

A moment's further stubbornness on her part earns her a hard slap around her face, with Bond raising his hand to strike again. So Andrea talks. It's really not on, is it? Sir Roger, speaking recently, certainly did not think so, blaming the influence of director Guy Hamilton, and claiming that fellow Bond director Lewis Gilbert would never have had him doing that.

The production team would doubtless have argued – except that no critics at the time seemed to object – that this is what the Bond of the novels would have done. On another occasion, director Guy Hamilton said: 'Bond does beat up the dollies and I see nothing wrong with it if they are villainesses.'[2]

That much is debatable. I can't offhand recall any scene where literary Bond hits a woman. And nor was the character Andrea a 'villainess'. But the main point is that it is Moore on the screen, who is quite a different kettle of fish. He was best known for his impeccably behaved years on *The Saint* (and before anyone snorts that that was just a television series, bear in mind that it was sold worldwide, and that Frank Sinatra was a big fan, subsequently becoming friends with Moore). On top of this, the Bonds were always family films, first and foremost, and Moore, perhaps more than any of the other actors, was keenly aware of this.

He knew that he was a hero to children. And as such, it was up to him to set an example. We did not pay our shekels to see Roger dishing out domestic violence. His feet were very firmly put down after this incident.

Furthermore, this scene – and subsequent episodes involving Britt Ekland as dopey secret agent Mary Goodnight – gives us a chance to ask how exactly it was that in 1974 – when the Women's Lib movement had reached its height both in the US and across much of Western Europe, and when the British government was about to pass the Sex Discrimination Act – Broccoli, Saltzman and Mankiewicz felt that now was the ideal time to have Bond aided by a passive victim and by a blockhead. They must have been aware that women make up a significant proportion of Bond's audience: so what is the reasoning behind Andrea – the original Woman Who Loves Too Much – and scatterknickers Goodnight, hopping into Bond's hotel wardrobe wearing naught but a baby-doll nightie?

Equally, the publicity shots for the film do no one any favours. Moore leans forward with gun in a quite extraordinary white safari suit, flanked on either side by Maud Adams and Britt Ekland, holding on to him desperately, both in itsy-bitsy, teeny weeny bikinis. In these sunnier days of post-feminism, a certain amount of ironic leeway is allowed when images of this sort are displayed. No irony was intended in 1974. This is exactly what the production team thought of women.

So, anyway. After being threatened with a broken arm, Andrea clearly decides that she fancies Bond; Bond has made an assignation with Goodnight but Goodnight must take second place to Andrea who visits Bond's suite, consigning Goodnight to a hiding place in the wardrobe. In due course, Andrea's jealous and abusive lover Scaramanga – well, I'd call the caress of a golden gun pretty damned abusive – kills her for this betrayal, later informing Bond in all solemnity that 'a mistress cannot serve two masters'. Meanwhile, superspy Goodnight attempts to plant a bug in the boot of Scaramanga's car and ends up getting locked in that boot, as Scaramanga makes his escape.

Goodnight's role at the villain's island HQ is largely to wear a floral bikini and to behave in as dimwitted a fashion as is humanly possible. At one stage, she accidentally almost injures Bond with a laser beam by unwittingly backing into the laser button and pressing it with her bikini'd bottom. Was this really around the same time that the magazine *Spare Rib* had launched? Or at a time when Erica Jong and Angela Carter and Marilyn French were among the most influential authors?

Oddly, neither Maud Adams nor Britt Ekland seemed immensely fussed by this aspect of the script; possibly they thought all Bond films were like that. Britt Ekland had first made a name for herself as the wife of comedian Peter Sellers. In 1973, she turned in a very likeable performance as Willow, the landlord's daughter, in the sublimely sinister *The Wicker Man*, in which she once more played opposite Christopher Lee.

A couple of years before that, she was called upon to writhe topless on a hideous floral bedspread while indulging in a primitive form of phone sex with Michael Caine in *Get Carter*. She was later to state that she found the character of Bond 'a total male chauvinist pig'; in terms of *Golden Gun*, that was putting it mildly.

She added: 'When I auditioned for the film, I was up for the role of the bad guy's mistress. But the director had seen a picture of me in a bikini and decided I should be . . . Mary Goodnight instead. It was great fun, the best job I've ever had.'[3] Poor Britt! Really?

These days, she is less willing to talk about it. Indeed, her charming agent told me that Miss Ekland would be willing to discuss *anything* else – anything at all except Bond. Although Miss Ekland did tell the *Manchester Evening News* recently that 'the role didn't do a lot for my career'.

Well, it did one thing: it fixed for ever her position as an icon of old school crumpetdom. You sense that whatever now transpires in her life, she will always be haunted by this bikinied doppelgänger.

Maud Adams, meanwhile, was a successful Swedish model and this was her first big film break; according to her, she and Ekland formed a giggly Nordic bond on set.

The other point was that no matter how shabby and off-putting it all seems on screen, to star in a Bond movie was a very big deal for an actor; you were treated, as all attest, like royalty. You stayed in the finest hotels, ate the finest food, got driven everywhere and, in the words of Yaphet Kotto, 'got to live the life of James Bond'.

That is, except for the few days when the crew moved to Phuket. Continuity director Elaine Scheyreck recalls with a laugh the primitive hotel 'that was actually a bordello' and its distinctly rudimentary facilities. Happily, after Phuket, when the crew moved to Hong Kong, Eon more than compensated the team by putting them up in hotels of the very greatest luxury. As ever, Broccoli and Saltzman were assiduous about maintaining the film's family atmosphere. Much the same appears to apply today, but then of course it is still a family concern.

In the novels, Mary Goodnight is a semi-recurring character; she is

Bond's sometime secretary back at HQ, and she and Bond have a gentle and rather dignified pash for one another. Quite why the producers decided to reinterpret the character as such a dopey Dinah might be something to do with the tenor of the times. As mentioned, the first editions of *Spare Rib* magazine were appearing, and feminists were becoming increasingly militant, not only over issues of equality, but also over the treatment of women in the media.

It was common at that time to see such things as adverts for Outspan oranges that would feature a young woman running in a tight T-shirt, the camera unambiguously focusing in on her breasts. All popular comedy appeared to be based on the premise that nothing was funnier than a pair of what used to be termed bristols. The feminists were vocal in their insistence that such imagery was intensely demeaning. It took an extraordinarily long time for their view to prevail. But it did, and now when we look back, it does seem as though Britain in the 1970s was in the throes of some national menopausal sexual fever.

The curious thing about the Bond oeuvre is that while the films are often silly, they are very rarely reactionary. But this one very obviously *was*. After all the bra-burning and boycotts of Miss World contests – a bag of flour thrown at host Bob Hope one year at the Royal Albert Hall – women, it seemed, had to be put in their place. The leading ladies in all previous Bonds – even *Diamonds* – had been allowed their dignity, even if the roles weren't up to much. We think of Pussy Galore, and Tracy, and Honey Ryder. Here, dignity amounted to Britt Ekland running through the villain's generating plant in a bikini and high heels and falling over at the merest suggestion of a loud bang. Interestingly, no subsequent Bond film would treat its female characters with such contempt.

The problem here is exacerbated by the sheer lack of other characters, and this is where one gets another sniff of cost-cutting. In every previous Bond, the screen is always jammed with characters greater or lesser, from hero to cocktail waiter, by way of smarmy casino croupiers and people there to perform double takes at stunts. Not here. The street outside the frankly embarrassing Bottoms Up club, where one of Scaramanga's victims is killed, is not bustling, but strangely and disconcertingly quiet – even the assassination seems to draw only two or three onlookers.

Elsewhere, the horrid Hong Kong hotel in which Bond stays seems eerily empty, the corridors stretching on illimitably without a soul in sight. In the film's signature car chase, the protagonists quickly leave the semi-busy main road and head off into an utterly deserted countryside – no comical double takes there.

Then finally, at the climax on Phuket, Scaramanga's big set – the generating plant – features not the usual teams of boiler-suited extras, but just one lone, very ugly maintenance man, who attempts to get fresh with Britt. Other than that, it is just Bond, villain, girl and dwarf. There is no sense of spectacle at all.

In an earlier chapter, we mentioned how the producers were keen to reach over and help themselves to the newest cinematic crazes. This time around, after 'blaxploitation', the theme was clearly martial arts, in the wake of the craze for all things karate kicked off by Bruce Lee in 1973's *Enter the Dragon* and imitated by countless others.

And so it is that rather than kill Bond in the traditional fashion after his bruising encounter with two sumos, Hai Fat orders him to be taken to karate school, to be killed there. Bond awakens to find himself in karate outfit. All the black-belts arrive. Bond takes one out with an easy kick; he is almost overcome by another before making an easy escape by jumping through a flimsy wooden lattice.

Here, the schoolgirl nieces of his ally Lieutenant Hip (Soon-Tek Oh) are on hand to deliver a comedy kung-fu sequence, where they take out every single one of the bad guys with a series of kicks, punches and chops. I distinctly recall this clip being shown on children's television when I was seven, clearly intended as a mouth-watering inducement for all us kids to nag our parents into taking us to the latest Bond. I also recall that it had the opposite effect on me, for karate was dead boring, and I was not to see the film until it was rereleased in double bill with *Live and Let Die*.

This sequence, incidentally, played out against a lowering Thai backdrop, was immediately followed by a grim boat chase along the 'glongs', or canals, which all the cast, and Roger Moore in particular, recall as being utterly filthy.

Here we see the return of Bond's old racist friend Sheriff J.W. Pepper, here on holiday with his wife. It says something for the film's exhausting flatness that Pepper lights the whole thing up. Not even the gambit of Scaramanga having three nipples, leading to Bond being fitted with an extra false nipple for disguise purposes – 'most titillating', as Moore observes unblushingly – could quite pull off that trick.

Now, as a final point on cost-cutting, is it unfair to point out that in Scaramanga's fun house, it is possible in one shot to see what appears to be sticky tape on the set? There it is, on one of those angular white cardboard triangles on the black background. Too nitpicking? Not really, because as soon as you notice it, your eye is taken off the final duel between Scaramanga and Bond in this deadly maze, and on to other parts of the set; indeed, you notice that it is all a little scuffed and scruffy. Perhaps this is something to do with the unforgivingly sharp definition of DVD, because in fairness, I can't remember spotting it on the big screen. But I think it is also symptomatic of a period in which the very form of cinema itself was widely predicted to be on its last legs.

The duel itself is reasonably suspenseful – the fun house includes mock-ups of a Wild West saloon bar, Al Capone's garage, skeletons and revolving trick mirrors – even though this scene gives comedy critics a second shot at the same gag by having Roger Moore pose as his own waxwork in order to finish Scaramanga off.

But there it is: we say goodbye, at least, to one of the films' more memorable villains. Christopher Lee argued that one of the reasons he was so well suited to the role was that he was actually a cousin of Ian Fleming. More than that though: in the scene where Scaramanga and Bond have lunch seated around the villain's glass-topped dining table, the villain comes across as having a shade more taste and elegance than the hero, who at that point is attired in a hideous checked sports jacket. Bond can claim as much moral high ground as he likes over the assassin but we can't pay attention to a single word while under the hypnotic spell of this garment. It ought to be on display at the Victoria and Albert Museum.

And sorry to keep banging on about nasty 1970s aesthetics, but the final scene set in the boudoir of Scaramanga's junk: just how brown is that bedroom? Sheets, pillows, walls, carpet, smoky mirrors . . . it is a powerful reminder to those of us of a certain age that in 1974, everything was either brown or orange. But mostly brown. Like Scaramanga's unforgivable brown car.

That final scene on board Scaramanga's boat also shows us another uncharacteristic outburst of ill temper from Moore's Bond, as he is forced to deal with the midget Nick Nack. Finally, after much wearying smashing of tables and glass, Bond succeeds in scooping him up in a suitcase, then putting him in the boat's crow's nest. A later Roger would have found all this wildly amusing (even if the shorter people in the audience didn't). But this Roger is simply peevish.

Indeed, as a general note, having found his feet in *Live and Let Die*, Moore appeared temporarily to have lost them again. Bond this time round is a surlier creature, being not only aggressive to Andrea, but rather rude and dismissive to Goodnight all the way through and positively beastly to Nick Nack. In one chase scene, a little boy helps Bond by restarting his boat as the villains loom into view; Bond rewards the boy by pushing him into the water.

It looks as though Moore is being told to play it with a harder edge, to tone down the twinkliness; this certainly happened in his later Bonds. But the result is very off-putting, rather like seeing a favourite uncle get uncharacteristically drunk and start a fight in the street.

But heroes were getting tougher generally. By 1974, we had had two *French Connection* thrillers featuring Gene Hackman as a grizzled and tough-as-nails detective called 'Popeye' Doyle; there was also a voguish craze for disaster movies, such as *The Poseidon Adventure* (1972), *Earthquake* (1974) and *The Towering Inferno* (1975), in which the ordinary men who stepped up to become heroes, such as Steve McQueen and Paul Newman, were also rough-edged and laconic.

The camp escapism of the 1960s had given way to an attempt at greater realism, in Hollywood at least. In Britain, where by that stage we barely had any form of film industry left, the main leading men were to be found on television in the form of John Thaw in *The Sweeney* and Edward Woodward in *Callan*. All very grim.

And across the Atlantic, America was reeling. In 1974, President Nixon resigned, the first time a serving US president had done such a thing. He had become engulfed by the Watergate scandal and was about to be impeached. On top of this, the States had lost in Vietnam and was beginning the messy process of withdrawal.

All these things, combined with the recession caused by hikes in oil prices, made it an unusually troubling year. Though one can hardly psychoanalyse a nation, it is temptingly easy to hear echoes of a form of national neurosis, or trauma, in the popular culture of the day. All these tough, violent thrillers and disaster movies, where helpless people are taken to the edge of endurance, seem now to be the very opposite of escapism.

In Britain, where Harold Wilson had squeaked back into power heading a minority Labour administration, things were scarcely any better. In an economy that was mostly nationalised, the government was vulnerable to the spread of industrial action. Wilson's main gambit in this period was the so-called 'Social Contract', a form of agreement with the unions that wage demands would be reasonable as long as prices were brought under some semblance of control.

The cycle of boom/bust, inflation/unemployment seemed wearily unbreakable. Britain's story appeared to be very much one of decline – the once proud hub of empire deflating into this sorry, shabby, profoundly ugly country, with its badly planned city centres and cheaply built council estates and chaotic railway system and strike-prone, loss-making heavy industry. Bond was supposed to be our hero, the one who could help us escape all this: but even Bond, it seemed, was struggling to keep his good humour in 1974.

This did not escape the attention of some of the more high-minded critics.

'It is so much the mixture as before that one wonders if the makers of the Bond films haven't finally switched the series on to autopilot,' sniffed the *Financial Times*. 'Roger Moore's charm school Bond is beginning to prove a depressingly plastic successor to Sean Connery.'

Elsewhere, *The Observer* felt that it could not hold back. 'This series, which has been scraping the barrel for some time, is now through the bottom . . . there are depressing borrowings from Hong Kong kung-fu movies, not to mention even more echoes of Carry On smut.' That final point is quite unfair; the *Carry Ons* were much wittier, as doubtless Sean Connery would agree.

Good news, though, for Christopher Lee from the *Evening Standard*. 'Lee gives an authority to the part . . . that evens up the confrontations between him and Bond and for once gives 007 an adversary worth his attention.'

If anyone at Eon was crying, they wouldn't have been doing so for long. The following year, the entire series received an unexpected boost by the simplest of means: Eon Productions had sold the rights to show the films on television. Thus it was in October 1975 that eighteen million viewers in Britain sat down to watch the ITV premiere of *Dr. No*.

My eight-year-old self was among those breathlessly jammed next to the screen, ignoring parents' injunctions to watch it from the sofa nicely. In an era of three television channels and no video recorders, the idea of something as exciting as this playing in our homes was the most unbelievable treat. The talk in the playground the following day was of nothing else. The tarantula! The countdown! The metal hands!

And the reason these and subsequent transmissions were so important to the series was this: for older viewers, they were semi-regular reminders of just how enjoyable these films had been first time around. And for younger viewers, an entire new generation of eight-year-olds was introduced to films made before they were born, and thence made eager to see more.

There is also something about the intimacy of television that made Bond even more of a central pop-cultural figure than he was already. For it was not too long before ITV began the tradition of the Christmas Day Bond screening. It is an accolade awarded to few heroes. Throughout the 1970s and early 1980s – before the advent of home video and then satellite television – Bond became as much a part of family ritual as turkey, crackers and the Queen's Christmas broadcast. In those days, households would only have one television. And God, how I remember the family row that broke out in 1978 when the BBC scheduled the premiere of *The Sound of Music* directly against the ITV premiere of *Diamonds Are Forever*. But in general, these screenings were to have the effect of making audiences much more eagerly expectant of future Bond films at the cinema.

By the time ITV screened *Goldfinger* for the first time in November 1976, the vast TV audiences were being reminded of films that they had not seen for over ten years; even though the Bonds were sometimes reissued at the cinemas, they tended to be the more recent ones.

Also, thanks to the innovative nature of Ken Adam's set designs and the careful choices made by the costume departments, the older films did not look dated. A similar effect can be seen among American audiences. Putting Bond on the small screen made him even closer to viewers than he had been before.

Funnily enough, cinema managers were deeply concerned when news of the TV rights first came through in 1974, imagining that such broadcasts would have exactly the opposite effect, and that by showing them outside of theatres, Eon Productions were 'not only killing the goose but also selling off the golden eggs'.[4]

Three decades on, and in Christmas 2007 one of the biggest billboard ad campaigns was for Sky TV; the image it featured was that of Daniel Craig as Bond in *Casino Royale*. The satellite station was pushing this film as its main

Christmas TV highlight. In the meantime, that same year, ITV scheduled one Bond film after another from Boxing Day onwards. So while DVD will have chipped away at terrestrial TV audiences, the films are still regarded as a traditional part of the British festive season.

Back to the mid-1970s, and happily the films and the character were about to regain their lightness of touch. In 1975, after Harry Saltzman was bought out of Eon, Cubby Broccoli sat back and had a good, long think. Actually, he was forced to. A court action had been brought by rival producer Kevin McClory of *Thunderball* fame, who claimed that Eon's idea for the next Bond was the same as his, a screenplay entitled *James Bond of the Secret Service*. With this enforced break – Eon won the case, by the way – the team had a chance to go back to the drawing board. Rather than rush into the next Bond picture, in the desperate hope of keeping interest in the franchise alive, it would instead be a better idea to play it cool and take a little longer in order to revive the spirits of the entire series.

Thank the heavens Broccoli did so; for the film that was to follow was among the finest, frothiest two hours of escapism ever committed to celluloid, and still stands as one of the ornaments of the entire series.

I t was not Britain's sunniest summer. That honour fell to 1976, with its
famous drought and government minister Denis Howell saucily advising
people to save water by sharing a bath. Come the summer of 1977, and the
weather was a little drabber, but that didn't matter, for the nation had gone
quite mad with nostalgia for a time when the skies were always blue.

While preparations to celebrate the Silver Jubilee of Queen Elizabeth II
were being hammered out earlier that year, there was some anxiety in royal
and government circles that the whole idea would be treated with disdain
by the British people. The country was, after all, widely regarded as being in
a terrible state. The previous year, chancellor Denis Healey had been
famously forced to go 'cap in hand', as they always say, to the International
Monetary Fund; spending and inflation were so wildly out of control that
Britain needed bailing out. The IMF agreed a loan but only under condition
that state spending was substantially reduced; thus it was that a Labour
chancellor had to introduce an early form of monetarism.

In 1976, Prime Minister Harold Wilson had suddenly resigned, to much
general shock, and dark rumours. The truth was that he had planned his
departure long in advance. But Wilson himself added to the dark rumours
by briefing two journalists that the security services had long been plotting
against him; all of which was a sensational reminder of Hugh Gaitskell's
mysterious death, and of Wilson's alleged Soviet links. By 1977, James
Callaghan was Prime Minister, and while his avuncular style seemed
reasonably popular, the political problems were piling up, not least Labour's
parliamentary minority, which forced him into an alliance with the Liberal
Party.

In terms of pop culture, the headlines were being made by the Sex Pistols,
a pogoing, gobbing, safety-pinned band assembled by impresario Malcolm
McLaren; via an encounter on an early evening ITV current affairs
programme called *Today*, the country came to know the faces of Johnny
Rotten, Glen Matlock and, in the background, their pal Siouxsie Sioux, as
irritated presenter Bill Grundy invited them to say something shocking,

Keeping it amusingly cool as always, Sean Connery takes time out from tussling with Bambi and Thumper in Nevada in *Diamonds Are Forever*. **Rex Features**

Possibly the most gruelling aspect for Connery of preparing for his debut 1962 Bond outing *Dr No*: endless Savile Row fussing over 007's suits. *Rex Features*

Connery and Honor Blackman bonding on the set of *Goldfinger*; the actress told the press that she thought 'Pussy Galore' was 'a lovely name'. *Rex Features*

Bond and Goldfinger hit the tees. In reality, Connery and Gert Frobe were golf novices. But Connery later became a pro-celebrity stalwart. *Rex Features*

A startlingly coiffed Lois Maxwell briefly escapes her Miss Moneypenny duties to link up with future Bond (and drama-school pal) Roger Moore as a guest star on *The Saint*. **BFI**

Daniela Bianchi, Ian Fleming, Lois Maxwell, Lotte Lenya and Sean Connery celebrate *From Russia with Love*. One wonders what the serious Connery discussed with Lenya. **BFI**

Luciana Paluzzi brings a little fire to the screen as archetypal Bond Bad Girl Fiona Volpe, in the otherwise wholly un-fiery *Thunderball*.
Rex Features

Harry Saltzman, Dana Broccoli and Albert R. Broccoli meet the Queen at the *You Only Live Twice* premiere - Her Majesty presumably still in shock over Connery's resignation.
Rex Features

Foreshadowing Daniel Craig's famous blue bathers, George Lazenby wears similar - though somehow weirder - items while off-duty in Portugal in 1969 for *OHMSS*.
Rex Features

At the opening gala for *OHMSS*, bearded George Lazenby meets the Duke of Kent; perhaps they are discussing the multiple layers and meanings in the narrative.
Rex Features

Desmond Llewelyn, as gadget-master Q, inhabited the role from 1963 to 1999; pleasingly, his own aptitude for technology was almost non-existent. *Rex Features*

With an admirable disregard for ridicule, Jane Seymour eases herself into the role of Tarot priestess Solitaire for her film debut *Live And Let Die*. *Rex Features*

They sure don't make them like they used to. In 1974, Britt Ekland, Herve Villechaize and Maud Adams gather for *The Man With The Golden Gun*. *Rex Features*

A bearded Moore and his then wife, Luisa. The ever-vigilant Luisa was always there to cast a beady eye over Moore's romantic scenes. *Rex Features*

The film may be filled with futuristic imagery; but – as is not commonly known - the premiere for *Moonraker* in 1979 revealed that the space shuttle was launched into orbit from the back of a Ford Transit. *Rex Features*

A traditional 'bevy of bikin'd beauties' shot; in the days before post-feminism was invented, such images found deep disfavour with the sisters. *Rex Features*

With a startling swerve in style, Timothy Dalton made his Bond a more serious, rounded human being and gave *The Living Daylights* an unusually romantic edge.
Rex Features

Commander Pierce Brosnan perfectly at ease in his second Bond, *Tomorrow Never Dies*. Brosnan brought a lighter sense of comedy to the role.
Rex Features

A huge popular and critical success though his new Bond has been, Daniel Craig's introduction to the world's press in 2005 - complete with girly life jacket - was the source of much impolite comment. *Rex Features*

and Johnny Rotten (né Lydon) did. The tabloids seized on this with vehemence, the *Mirror*'s headline proclaiming: 'The Filth and the Fury!'

For an older generation, it seemed inconceivable that Britain – which just thirty years previously had won the war – was now producing frightening foul-mouthed nihilists like this. Of course, these days, the band's artful dissonance and arrestingly Blakean lyrics – oh, go on, 'England's dreaming' is a wonderful phrase – are appreciated as an artistic landmark. In the summer of 1977, as the Jubilee celebrations drew closer, they were regarded as a disgusting affront to decency, banned from the playlist of BBC Radio One.

For while the Pistols were singing 'God save the Queen, her fascist regime', the rest of the country was festooned with red, white and blue, from souvenir trays and mugs to newspaper pull-outs, to little flags, even to the extent that some red London buses were painted silver to mark the Jubilee. Magazines were full of Twenty-Five Things You Never Knew About The Queen. Even children's comics had special red, white and blue Jubilee editions.

Beacons were lit across the country. There were street parties – a peculiarly British phenomenon not seen since the Coronation of 1953. In spite of the lowering economic conditions, and the outrageous nature of pop culture, it seemed that the entire country united in heaving one great nostalgic sigh for the days when Britain was Great.

And in July 1977, serendipitously zooming into this mood of national celebration, was 007 – unforgettably skiing off a dizzying cliff, free-falling a heart-stopping distance, and then, finally, cheekily opening a Union flag parachute. The Queen had revived national spirits, and now James Bond was back to save us all.

He had taken his time about it; the longest wait between Bond films, this one of two and a half years, but the time had been used well. A number of screenwriters entered into discussion with Eon, including veteran Richard Maibaum, Stirling Silliphant and novelist Ronald Hardy. Also among the prospective writers was, startlingly, an enthusiastic Anthony Burgess, then best known for his novel *A Clockwork Orange*.

Burgess, who was later to gain yet greater literary appreciation with novels such as *Earthly Powers* and *Any Old Iron*, was a fascinating writer for the Bond people to be talking to. He was brilliant at a certain sort of textured, learned pastiche. His 1964 novel *Nothing Like the Sun* conjured the voice of

Shakespeare, while later in 1993, *A Dead Man in Deptford* was written, with fantastic intellectual deftness, from the point of view of the playwright Christopher Marlowe, famously murdered in a tavern brawl. Not only could Burgess make language dance, his imagination was unusually rich.

What one wonders about Burgess now is, if his collaboration with Broccoli had been taken any further, whether his approach to Bond would be that of a similar literary tribute. But what Burgess, and earlier Kingsley Amis, also show us is that the very notion of writing a Bond story seemed – and seems – irresistible to a certain class of author.

One immediately thinks of *Birdsong* author Sebastian Faulks turning his hand to the Fleming centenary Bond novel *Devil May Care* in 2008. One of the consistently beguiling elements of both the films and the novels is the way that they have crossed the usual audience dividing lines, attracting highbrow and lowbrow alike.

And Anthony Burgess was clearly enamoured of Ian Fleming's work. He once said of it that Fleming had 'a sort of Renaissance gusto which contradicted the socialist austerity of the fifties and yet did not endorse the permissiveness of the sixties'.

Broccoli, on this occasion, was not keen on the idea of a bunch of anarchists being the villains. He said at the time that he felt uneasy about the Bond films acknowledging real-life terrorist groups (and rightly so – talk about the oxygen of publicity). So we are left with daydreams of what might have been; and by curious coincidence, what springs to mind is an image of Burgess's putative Bond villains as terrifying young Droogs; snarling, staring-eyed nihilists led perhaps by John Lydon, with various pierced, rainbow-haired colleagues, Bond now coming to represent the forces of the old Establishment attempting to defeat a sickly new generation of delinquent psychopaths.

But the reality of the film world, and of the Bond film world in particular, is that daydreams won't do. Broccoli – now the sole producer – was in the business of proving to a worldwide audience that Bond was still relevant in the 1970s, and perhaps beyond into the 1980s. He needed some means of showcasing all the best elements of the series to their finest advantage.

He was helped a little by the fact that Ian Fleming had stipulated that no part of his novel *The Spy Who Loved Me* could be used in screen adaptation. *Spy* had been an excessively sore point for Fleming. The most unusual of the oeuvre, the story focused not on Bond but on a Canadian woman called

Vivienne Michel. Told in the first person (brave of Fleming, this), Vivienne gave an account of her recent life and how it had led to her being held hostage in a deserted North American motel by two thugs called Slugsy and Horror. Worse than these thugs, in terms of taste, this female narrator tells the reader of a queasy, fumbling sexual relationship with an Old Etonian sixth-former not a million miles from young Master Fleming – the sordid episode in the Windsor cinema is especially flinchworthy. She then tells of a subsequent relationship with a chilly German publisher, hilariously pointing up all of Fleming's prejudices towards that nation; then, after these ordeals, Vivienne is more straightforwardly at the mercy of these two thugs. And by complete chance, James Bond shows up.

A night of to-ing and fro-ing ensues; Slugsy and Horror are scuppered and in the meantime, Bond and Vivienne have taken the opportunity to enjoy a saucy interlude, with Vivienne asserting that all women are rather partial to 'semi-rape'. The general tenor of the contemporary reviews was: Whatever can Fleming have been thinking? Critics poured especially boiling scorn on his attempts to get inside the mind of the modern, independent woman.

Strangely, as a whole, it doesn't read so badly now; Fleming is a good enough writer to convince for most of the time. And his Bond is again a slightly more layered creature than the popular image suggests. The thriller aspect of the plot is no good at all, however; Bond confronts Slugsy and Horror in this dreary deserted motel, nothing happens, then there is a fight and some running through some woods, then another fight, and that's it. You would be hard-pressed to get a half-hour television episode out of it. It is the work of a very tired, very ill man. 'Spy,' said Ian Fleming in a later interview, 'was an experiment that had gone very much awry.'[1] But it has to be said that Horror is one hell of a name for a bad guy.

And Horror was the sole element from the book that Broccoli thought he might be able to use. Certainly there was nothing else in there that could get anywhere near the screen. And so, having defeated Kevin McClory in the courts (but with the side result that Eon could not use the name 'Blofeld'), Broccoli started assembling his team.

Before the enforced hiatus, director Guy Hamilton had been due to return again. The delay meant that he could not. So experienced director Lewis Gilbert stepped up to the plate. In pre-production with Broccoli and his stepson Michael Wilson, they explored the idea of doing another adventure in the Far East, with perhaps the notion of a Japanese marine laboratory that could rise up and down beneath the waves as a starting point for the villain's lair. Luckily, the Far East was abandoned in favour of Egypt and Sardinia.

And Lewis Gilbert was a very fine choice who understood especially well what made the Bond films tick. 'Part of the charm of a Bond picture is you know what you are going to get,' he said.

> Audiences in a Bond film aren't looking for great acting – they want to be overwhelmed by physical things . . . Bond films are very, very different from any other kind of film made. They've disproved every law in the cinema, they've done everything wrong, and they're huge successes . . . I mean in story elements, in characterisation elements, things like that – the anti-climactic bit they always have at the end which you wouldn't dare do in other pictures where they have a huge big ending and then suddenly, the film starts up again . . .[2]

Gilbert brought on board the screenwriter Christopher Wood, who had made something of a name for himself with the script for *Confessions of a Window Cleaner* (1974). Even now, *Spy* is renowned for its exhausting quantity of double entendres. But Wood was also young and clever and brought a great deal more than that.

As indeed did production designer Ken Adam, triumphantly back after having won the Oscar for *Barry Lyndon* (1975), a collaboration with the famously intense Stanley Kubrick that had induced a near-nervous break-down in Adam. *Lyndon* was an adaptation of a William Thackeray novel; it was an eighteen-month shoot and Kubrick wanted the eighteenth century portrayed not as conventional period drama but almost as 'documentary', which meant, for instance, lighting huge rooms with nothing but candles. Kubrick would confide only in Adam; as the weeks wore on, his dependence on the designer grew more and more intense and Adam felt himself warping under this perfectionist, near autistic, pressure. Eventually he booked himself into a Scottish clinic for a short while, for rest and recuperation.

Sir Ken now says that it was a frightening period; he lost all of his artistic confidence, and had to ease himself back into film slowly, with small sketches. He also gives Bond credit for having a certain therapeutic value, giving him licence to stretch out his imagination once more. Indeed, it is doubtful if *Spy* would have been half so successful without his brilliant aesthetic flights of imagination. It is one of the most beautiful-looking films of the entire series, and a vast relief after the visual indifference of its two immediate predecessors.

It also seemed at last that the insistence of the feminist movement had percolated through to the Eon production offices, for it was decided that the new Bond girl would be, in some ways, Bond's equal. Russian agent Triple X — Anya Amasova — was, according to director Lewis Gilbert, quite a hard role to cast. Broccoli himself had strong views about the wisdom of hiring what he termed 'well-known ladies' such as 'Dunaway' and 'Streisand'. He felt that very few actresses had sufficient box-office draw to make any difference to a Bond. What he did not say out loud was that you would not want any such dame coming in and trying to upstage his leading man. The then unknown Barbara Bach won the part. And actually, I think we can all agree with Broccoli; she was much, much better than Barbra Streisand might have been in this role.

The leading man, I am quite sure, would have taken anyone in his stride, for here was Roger about to embark upon his third Bond adventure, and finally looking perfectly happy and relaxed in the role. Moore has said that he and Lewis Gilbert share the same sense of humour, and certainly this is the film where Moore's great talent for light comedy — a million times harder to do than it looks — is encouraged to the fore. No longer does he have to pretend to have the hard edge of Sean Connery.

So, with the story, it is very much back to basics, with British and Russian nuclear submarines apparently disappearing into thin air, and the atmosphere of detente between the two great nations being placed under strain. Not for long though; M and his KGB counterpart General Gogol agree that their agents must join forces. And this Bond and Anya do, pursuing a brilliantly colourful trail through Luxor and the Pyramids and Karnak up to the Mediterranean and 'Atlantis' — the huge underwater laboratory/city constructed by weirdo Karl Stromberg (a husky Curt Jurgens), who has webbed hands. The diabolical plan this time is to fire kidnapped nuclear missiles at New York and Moscow, precipitating an atomic conflict that will put an end to humanity. Only Stromberg and his chosen few will survive, in his city beneath the waves.

It makes very little sense, and we do not care. Because right from the start, this is an elegant and witty and pacy return to the cartoon of *You Only Live Twice*. The pre-credits sequence prior to the breathtaking ski jump has one of my all-time favourite Bond lines. Bond is canoodling with a blonde in a ski chalet, when suddenly his naff Seiko digital watch chatters into action, spewing out a plastic ticker-tape strip ordering him to return to base. 'But James, I need you,' cries the blonde as Bond clambers into a banana-yellow ski suit. 'So does England,' replies Roger as he heads for the door, delivering the line with such a perfect blend of irony and self-deprecation that it makes me yelp with laughter every time.

And after that magnificent stunt – no CGI work in those days, it was all for real – we head into Maurice Binder's finest title sequence – naked women wearing Soviet military caps, and other silhouetted women performing gymnastics on giant guns. Not to mention one of the best Bond songs – a cheeky, chirpy ditty by Marvin Hamlisch called 'Nobody Does It Better', sung unforgettably by Carly Simon. It is one of the few Bond songs to have really been a monster hit on *Top of the Pops*, succeeding in reaching number two.

When Gogol is briefing Anya, we are given the real emotional hook of the film: in that pre-credits sequence, Bond turned and shot one of his pursuers. The man, it seems, was Anya's lover. At this stage, she doesn't know that Bond pulled the trigger. Thus the usual travelogue to-ing and fro-ing is given an extra level of suspense, for we know that inevitably at some point, she must discover the truth.

Bond is given an unusually pleasing briefing, up in a Scottish submarine base. He is in full naval commander uniform. In one shot, we see him walking along the edge of the Holy Loch quay with the defence minister, a Polaris submarine gliding through the water beside them as they talk. What we also see, accidentally, is a small bunch of real sailors standing on top of this submarine, rubber-necking James Bond visiting their base.

It is a strangely post-modern moment; the real defenders of the realm scrambling to have a look at their base being blessed with a visit from a fictional defender of the realm. It all helps to establish Moore further in the role. In fact, this is the point where you forget all about Connery. Moore completely inhabits the part.

So: someone has developed a nuclear sub tracking device. But who? Well, Q says in one scene that it is very simple to do – so presumably practically anyone, including you and me. But never mind him. This is one of those script constructs where a tiny lead – this time some Egyptian nightclub owner – is teasing the secret service with the name of a possible contact. So off Bond goes to Cairo. These days, MI6 must look at the departmental budget of their fictional counterpart and weep.

Lewis Gilbert and Ken Adam have recced Cairo beautifully, for the location work is wonderful, especially the house of shady local operator Aziz Fekesh, where Bond snogs a lady who is then accidentally shot by a heavy; and where Bond takes to the roof to fight this heavy. (That snog is slightly off-putting, but it is something Moore always does: when he locks lips with any actress, he suddenly sucks his cheeks in, and it looks as though the woman concerned is sucking all the air out of an old paper bag. It always gives rise to the disquieting thought that the lady, in all her enthusiastic inhalation of Roger, has created a vacuum from which neither will be able to escape without injury.) The house is all elaborate arches and tinkling fountains and the ululating cries from the minarets and dazzling light, and usefully diverts attention away from the fact that the scene is pure Bond-filler – all he learns is where Fekesh will be tonight.

The pyramids, as it happens, for the night-time *son et lumière* presentation, and what a brilliant scene this is. Against the gothic green-lighting and booming narration of the show, poor Fekesh is chased into a hieroglyphed tomb by Stromberg's henchman Jaws and bitten to death by the hench-man's steel teeth. I recall, as a child, finding this scene almost unbearably suspenseful, for at the start of the film, Jaws (Richard Kiel) is one of the most implacable and creepy of the menaces Bond has ever had to face.

The critics thought so too. 'He will be the hit of the film,' said the *Evening Standard* reviewer Alexander Walker, noting the character's resemblance to 'Karloff's monster', while the august *Spectator* paid tribute to this 'Charles Addams monster with stainless steel teeth and the unstoppability of the Life Force itself'. The name 'Jaws' was of course amusing tribute to the Spielberg blockbuster of 1975; the idea was to invert the whole thing so that the man could bite the shark. Originally Jaws was to have been called Horror, as per the novel. But it would have been harder to infuse the role with any comedy later in the film, as Gilbert and Kiel rather skilfully did.

Anyway, Bond races off to that green-lit tomb only to meet Jaws; disconcertingly, the lights go off and when they go back on, the henchman has disappeared. In his place, though, is Anya, and a couple of male Russian agents, who Bond gets into a scrap with prior to heading off for the Egyptian nightclub.

And here we are in the wonderfully elegant Ken Adam-designed club, where Bond and Anya meet socially for the first time. It's a nice little piece of scripting; Agent XXX knows as much about Bond as he knows about her, and it also gives Moore a chance to display sensitivity over the issue of poor dead Tracy. Cocktails are swigged, microfilms brandished (those were the days – now, emails and PDF take the fun out of everything), another Egyptian – the nightclub owner, Max Kalber – is vampirically bitten by Jaws, and it's off into the desert for Bond and Anya in the back of Jaws's old truck.

Again, none of it makes any sense: why would Jaws drive these two all the way to the mighty ruins of Karnak when he could have killed them in Cairo? Never mind, the scenery is breathtaking. What is also amusing – and I think this is the first time it happens in the films – is the idea of a world-famous tourist destination being used specifically as a playground by the Bond team. Some have taken offence at this aspect of the series, claiming that it underscores a sort of old-style imperial racism inherent in the films, but I don't agree.

Certainly the ancients who built this extraordinary place might have been a little surprised if told that in the far future, these mighty pillars would be stalked through by a man in a flared dinner suit, a woman in a cocktail dress and a giant with metal teeth. But it did absolute wonders for the tourist trade. In 1977, Egypt was still seen by most as an unattainably exotic destination. *Spy* was a mouth-watering advert that said subliminally: if Bond can enjoy this beautiful land, then so can you.

The advert is heightened romantically as Bond and Anya walk through the desert (Maurice Jarre's *Lawrence of Arabia* theme playing in the background) and cruise down a sunset Nile on a handy fishing skiff. The by-play is unusually subtle, revolving around 'shared bodily warmth', and Anya's fake cigarette, through which she blows knockout powder, is a good, knowing joke. To then have M and Gogol share a base beneath a pyramid is an even finer joke, especially when one considers the real-life possibility of any such thing happening; audiences in 1977 would still have strong memories of Britain's 1956 Suez humiliation.

This pyramid base scene is somehow even more uplifting than usual because of the sheer optimism of its premise: the British and the Russians joining forces, and the top agents of both sides beginning to fall for one another. The competitiveness is still there – Anya got the microfilm but Bond saw that it contained nothing of interest – but the good humour is rather warming. Walter Gotell is the actor playing Gogol and he would become a series regular until 1987. If he is meant to represent the hard face of the Soviet Union, then surely detente is thawing the Cold War rapidly.

Things, naturally, were not quite so simple in real life – at this point, we were all still reading the revelations of exiled dissident Alexander Solzhenitsyn, in his *Gulag Archipelago*; but in Bond, any such reference is reduced to one small quip as Anya explains that she went on a survival course in Siberia. 'I understand a great many of your countrymen have done the same,' Bond says deadpan. She ignores the quip.

Also, in the real world, various top secret hostile skirmishes were still taking place between the two nations. MI6 sometimes used deep-sea trawlers as secret monitoring vessels – with intercept officers among the fishermen – and one such boat, the *Gaul*, was sunk with all hands in the Barents Sea in 1974, to the tremendous grief of the trawlermen's families. The official line was that this sinking had nothing to do with Soviet action; an inquiry many years later explained that the sinking might have been due to insufficiently battened hatches. But it could not dispel the suspicion that the boat had been sunk as a result of espionage, and Russian retaliation.

On top of this, there were incidents involving submarines, with Soviet vessels occasionally aggressively pursuing British craft. On one occasion, in 1981, a British sub was almost sunk when a Soviet vessel scraped alongside it. The crew were instructed to say that the marks on the British vessel were caused by an accidental collision with an iceberg.[3]

But we are in the altogether made-up world of Bond; and it's all aboard for a train sequence which, as we know from *Live and Let Die* and *From Russia with Love*, is always going to mean trouble. And so it does, following a sweet – and unusually teasing – scene in which Bond and Anya make much of their separate sleeping quarters. But Jaws is lurking in Anya's wardrobe and Bond must come along and save her, which he does after a spectacular fight involving a broken electric light.

Having rescued Anya from her biting, the code of the Bond films is that Bond is now entitled to a nibble himself, and this is what he gets as the narrative swoops into Sardinia. Once again, this is a wonderfully chosen location; the sandy mountains and the deep blue ocean are calculated to lift the spirits. Even the hotel is reasonably un-horrid, although the same cannot be said for the weirdly teutonic flounce 'n' bosoms get-up sported by receptionist Valerie Leon. Posing as amateur botanist James Stirling and his missus, Bond and Anya get an unlikely entrée to meet Karl Stromberg aboard his magnificent oceanic laboratory.

Here, he recalls, Sir Ken Adam made quite a sharp change of direction, as he found his creative strength resurging after the depredations of *Barry Lyndon*; he started designing sets with curves rather than these forced perspectives with straight edges. Atlantis has a more organic feel – even the corridors have curves as opposed to right angles. And the lighting is ingenious. Once seen, Adam's circular shark pool chamber, with its cruciform walkways, and spotlights built into the gleaming aluminium walls, burns itself into the memory. But crucially, it never distracts from proceedings – merely highlights them. The point about this chamber is that you know no good can come of it, and that is before we even see the first shark fin emerging from the water.

Naturally, Stromberg must live in a luxurious villainous aquarium, and wear unflattering unisex blouses, matched with unbecoming slacks. He must also obviously rumble Bond. But Bond is clearly no actor, for the web-handed industrialist is on to him after only about three sentences. And that's even with Bond showing off about his knowledge of fishes. But in one black mark against this otherwise ingenious mastermind, he leaves a scale model of a supertanker on display to be clocked by beanie-sporting Anya.

Back on dry land, a rather stylish and slick mountain-top car chase ensues, involving a helicopter and a motorbike with missile sidecar. But Bond is in his super swanky, specially modified Lotus Esprit – a white sports car tooled up by Ken Adam and yearned after by every male who saw the film. Despite ingenious evasions involving a lorry carrying a consignment of feather mattresses, Bond is forced to drive the Lotus along a wooden pier and thence into the sea.

Now, in the 1970s, there was not much around in the way of spoilers: the internet was not even a far-off dream, while newspapers and magazines were slightly more old-fashioned and, like the film-makers, thought that it would be quite nice to keep surprises for the audience. So when we in the cinema auditorium saw Bond plunge off that pier, we all thought: 'What in blue blazes is he playing at?' How could we know that he would flip over the dashboard to reveal submarine controls?

That's right: the car is now a submarine, allowing Bond and Anya to take an undersea gander through a porthole at Stromberg's secret control room;

then, in a bravura and sublimely silly moment, the car emerges from the sea on to a beach packed with sunseekers who gather round as Bond drops a fish from his window.

Sometimes with Bond films, the structure would get a little lumpy; but here, it flows as smooth as Guinness. A solid fifteen minutes of funny, kinetic excitement is followed by a scene that, ingeniously, we had all been tricked into forgetting about; and that is the point at which Anya twigs that Bond was the man in the banana-yellow ski suit who shot her lover in Austria. She pledges revenge as soon as the mission is over; for once, the production team have worked out that, occasionally, the obligatory spectacle of villain being defeated in mass of explosions might not be quite enough on its own. Now we have a further element of suspense, for shouldn't Anya be copping off with Bond rather than killing him?

Still, defeat Stromberg they must, so Anya and Bond board the next sub due to disappear into thin air. The American sub captain is played by Shane Rimmer; an itchingly familiar face who has been cropping up in these films in tiny roles since *You Only Live Twice*, presumably because he was an American based in London. There is hardly enough time for crewmen to comically ogle the silhouette of Barbara Bach in the shower; for they have been overtaken by – yes – a supertanker, with wide bow doors. And duly, sub and crew are swallowed up. This is not really such a huge surprise.

The interior of the supertanker is, though, a very, very fine effort from Sir Ken Adam, all clean perspective, metallic surfaces, working lifts, water, submarines in docking bays, a walloping great control room at the back and a working monorail, Lord be praised. Indeed, not just any old monorail, as Sir Ken told me, but one worked by the then revolutionary magnetic levitation (maglev) principle that the Japanese were later to try out on parts of their rail network. In terms of materials, copper makes a welcome comeback in the form of the CCTV globes that run back and forth. Adam kept secret the fact that his old collaborator Stanley Kubrick visited the set one Sunday, when no one else was there to spot him, to advise Adam how to light the place.

It is the sort of set that makes you wish you could actually have been there, in the specially built 007 Stage at Pinewood (they had to build their own studio at that point because the demands of the supertanker set could not be met in any other way). The extras look tiny against its vast scale. It is little wonder that Sir Ken's designs for this film were nominated for an Oscar. It is an outrage that they did not win.

The missiles from the kidnapped subs are aimed at New York and Moscow. Bond and his men must find a way of storming Stromberg's control room to prevent nuclear Armageddon. Not only this, but Anya is now tied to a recliner in Stromberg's luxury aquarium. So much for equality, by the way; it is all very well these women getting ideas but as we know, Bond must always finally be in the position to save them. Look at Halle Berry in 2002's *Die Another Day* — here we have the most apparently equal Bond girl of all time. She runs around shooting people, dives off precipices, is nifty with a sabre. But Bond has to come to her rescue not once but twice, first to save her from a laser beam and secondly to save her from drowning. It's the way it works. Whatever the prevailing ideological mood of the day, the heroine must always end up tied to the railway tracks.

Whumph! Up goes the big Ken Adam set. Whumph! There goes the exquisite model of the supertanker built by the film's modelling genius, Derek Meddings. Hooray! There goes Roger, setting off on a jet-ski to pluck Anya from Atlantis. Time for a final exchange with Stromberg in his vast reproduction dining room, with the longest refectory table in the world. Ken Adam, by his own admission, was big on refectory tables. The villain thinks Bond has failed to notice the pipe on the table's underside, through which his bullet will speed. But Bond has noticed; and Stromberg is hoist with his own petard. Thence on to a valedictory fight with Jaws in that wonderful shark chamber — the giant is defeated by means of an industrial magnet, to which his teeth are drawn. Then, as Bond and Anya escape, the base falls beneath the waves.

A moment of tension in the improbably camp escape capsule, complete with pink ruched curtains (who the hell was originally intended to escape in that?). Anya points her gun at Bond. But when he blinks at a popping champagne cork, she forgives him and snogs him instead — all four cheeks sucked in madly. Just time for M to look in through the capsule window, and for Roger to insist that he is 'keeping the British end up' and you have the end to one of the most amazingly assured productions in the entire series.

'It's Bond — and beyond!' yelped the stylish posters for the film — a vaguely Art Deco montage of images showing Bond, Anya, pyramids and supertanker. And by golly, it all worked a treat. The public piled into the cinemas, in Britain, in the US and of course right the way around the world. 'Unqualified joy,' declared the *Daily Mirror*. 'Since Roger Moore took over the role three years ago, the Bond image has undergone a face-lift. The flab has been removed and the chap is getting more fun from his job. Cinema entertainment at its very best.' It was with this film that it was estimated that half the population of Earth had seen a Bond movie.

The *Sunday Times*'s Alan Brien was a lonely voice of disapproval. Looking to the future, he sweetly imagined that in years to come, we would all disapprove as well. 'Some day around 2001,' he wrote on 10 July 1977, 'the National Film Theatre is going to run a retrospective of Bond films. A new generation will stare aghast at these grandiose, megaloptic visions of space age hardware and teenage soft porn, slapstick death and clockwork sex, saloon bar smut and playground fantasy, credit card high life and travelogue low jinks . . .' Stare aghast? Hardly. And he makes it all sound rather juicy.

But he was wonderfully right about the art-house retrospectives. Without a hint of a blush, London's Barbican Arts Centre held a Bond season in summer 2008. Moreover, their art-house regulars were asked to vote for their favourite entries, to determine which Bond would be shown. One knew fine well that in spite of Alan Brien's prediction, the 'space-age hardware and teenage soft porn' would be applauded.

Back in 1977, Brien added, 'Roger Moore is a sort of Alan Ladd with legs plus a remote control whimsical smile.' But there was nothing remotely remote about it. Roger was enjoying himself very much.

'Roger was much easier to work with than Sean,' observes Sir Ken Adam. 'Because, I think, he was pleased to have the job. Sean was always concerned about the money.'

Ah. The 'M' word once more. Certainly in 1977, all may have been proceeding smoothly in these terms, but a familiar theme was to reassert itself in the following years: that of the Bond actor sensing that perhaps he ought to be earning a little more, and that of Bond's producer becoming rather irritated by what he regarded as excessive demands.

It has also been noted by screenwriter Christopher Wood that it was in *Spy* that we saw Moore at the height of his physical powers – a handsome, dashing, mature fellow. What we tend to forget now is that *Spy* cemented Moore as one of the biggest film stars in the world. Hollywood had turned out a laconic new generation of actors such as Jack Nicholson, James Caan and Burt Reynolds, but Moore held sway in straight heroic status. Also bear in mind that *Spy* was released just weeks ahead of another film made in

Britain, a film entitled *Star Wars*. In the summer of 1977, Bond was the peak of family entertainment.

Moore was still also very much regarded as a 'sex symbol'. During production of *Spy*, he attended a '*Woman's Own* Meets James Bond' lunch at Pinewood, organised especially for lucky female readers of the magazine who had won a competition to meet him. If this seems a little difficult to imagine now, bear in mind that around the same time, huge numbers of British women were taking part in a *TV Times* magazine competition to emulate the mushroom bob hairstyle pioneered by New Avenger Joanna Lumley. Perhaps all those hot summers had made the ladies a little addle-headed.

What is also notable about Moore the superstar is how very nice he was (and is). No strops, no tantrums, no weird starry obsessive-compulsiveness. Nor did we see him tumbling out of nightclubs at 2 a.m. or conducting strings of affairs or behaving badly in any way. His was the quiet family life; and I think part of this is that Moore, perhaps more than any other actor who has taken on the Bond mantle, was aware that he had to set an example to the young; children looked up to him as a hero and he had to conduct himself accordingly, both in the films and – to a certain extent – in real life.

It was with *Spy* that Cubby Broccoli found that he was fine as solo producer, that the whole thing did not crash and burn because of the absence of Saltzman. Indeed, as well as securing a mammoth box-office success – the best since *Diamonds* – Cubby further endeared himself to the film's crew, who often stayed the same from production to production. Out in Luxor, the crew was hit by a catering crisis; the food on offer was awful. Cubby tried to have supplies sent out but they rotted in an accidentally unrefrigerated lorry. So Cubby flew out himself.

There is 16mm footage of this large man wearing a cowboy hat stirring a ladle in a vast cauldron of spaghetti bolognese that he himself has made, and footage of him dishing it up. The clear message was: you wouldn't have got that with Erich Von Stroheim. The images project Broccoli as daddy; a father figure to his Bond family. For after *Spy*, that is exactly what it was. And in the increasingly tight economic climate of the 1970s, which had seen practically the whole of the British film industry wiped out, it was a strikingly unique set-up.

CHAPTER FIFTEEN ONCE MORE ROUND THE WORLD

The artistic career of Roger Moore outside of Bond was, in the 1970s, a mixed affair, and to watch some of his other films now, one must have quite a high tolerance level for unintended kitsch. I refer mostly to the 1974 epic *Gold*, in which he starred with Susannah York, Ray Milland and John Gielgud. There was a rumour – wholly unsubstantiated – that this South Africa-based thriller, directed by erstwhile Bond hand Peter Hunt, was made with financial assistance from the apartheid-era South African government, presumably on the grounds that it would boost tourism.

There was rather more comical ground to be covered as Moore co-starred with Lee Marvin in a period adventure called *Shout at the Devil* (1976), attempting to foil the villainous Hun in Africa during the time of the Great War; Moore also put on a deerstalker for *Sherlock Holmes in New York* (1976) alongside Patrick Macnee as Watson.

And anyone who has ever stumbled in late from the pub and switched on the television will doubtless be familiar with *The Wild Geese* (1978), which always seems to be on BBC1 after the late night local news. In this, a cigar-chomping Moore played alongside Richard Burton and Richard Harris as a bunch of superannuated mercenaries. The scenes in London in which the men are gradually pulled in to the story are a vivid illustration of how very grim the late 1970s were in aesthetic terms.

Elsewhere, there was the wartime escapade *Escape to Athena* (1979). And who could forget the excitement generated by 1980's *North Sea Hijack*, in which Moore played a hero called Rufus Excalibur Ffolkes, pitted against the villainy of Anthony Perkins? Well, practically everyone could forget it, apparently, although the film did what it said on the tin. I saw it in a village hall on the Isle of Arran just off the coast of Scotland. The projectionist accidentally played the start of the second reel upside down. No one seemed too bothered.

The same year, 1980, also brought the genial slapstick comedy of *The Cannonball Run*, one of those American all-star caper movies involving an epic car race; Moore played a man who was convinced that he was . . . Roger

Moore. But with a Jewish mother. Now, you might think, we never see these films any more (unless they are given away free as DVDs by newspapers) and there must be a reason for that. But really, at the time, Moore was a big deal. And the above list gives a good idea at least of what a hard worker he was across the years.

Could his reflexive self-deprecation have done him out of weightier roles? In 1979, Moore declared: 'I may not be Olivier, but I'm taller. I have my three expressions. 1) Eyebrow raised. 2) Eyebrow lowered. 3) Crossed eyes when the villain Jaws grabs me by the kidney stone.'[1]

Indeed, whether he was being ironic or not, Roger was always drawing attention to his acting deficiencies. 'Have you ever seen a single film I was ever any good in?' he asked one interviewer humorously.[2]

Now I know that Sir Roger has no need of my counsel, and it is probably a little late now anyway; but come on, Rog! You're so much better than that! You would never have heard Connery talk like that!

As mentioned before, 1977 brought a cinematic event that – along with 1975's *Jaws* – finally demonstrated that cinema was still very much a live and kicking medium. The response to *Star Wars*, as the entire galaxy knows, was phenomenal. Whatever anyone might now say about the grown-up golden age of the early 1970s, in which Hollywood films were the layered, mature products of serious artists, *Star Wars*, in all its wilful nostalgic childish hokiness, was the film that saved cinema. It was only natural that it should generate huge repercussions through other productions. And not just in terms of other studios scrambling to produce their own space cobblers.

The original idea for 1979 was that *For Your Eyes Only* would be the next Bond in line. *Star Wars* clearly did away with that; handily, the title *Moonraker* was also knocking around. Unhandily, Ian Fleming's plot was closer to *Quatermass* than Luke Skywalker. In Fleming's 1955 original, vulgarian parvenu Hugo Drax is building a missile installation near Dover with what appears to be his own private workforce. He says it is for the defence of the realm. Now, if you were the head of the British secret service and this was going on, what exactly would you do, hmm? Well, *you* would, but *they* don't. It is only when Bond sees Drax cheating at cards that he senses that he might be on to a wrong'un.

And what a wrong'un! Drax is in fact a former Nazi; his workforce are Nazi 'werewolves'. And his bloody nuclear missile is pointing at London. D'oh! Well, of course Bond saves the day, with the help of working-class policewoman Gala Brand, and following close shaves involving searing rocket exhaust and indeed a car chase down the old A2 from London to Dover which now reads like a scene from *Genevieve*. In other words, it is a terrific – and incredibly quaint – read. But it obviously wouldn't do for the screen.

Having enjoyed such a monster success with *Spy*, it was natural for Broccoli to turn once again to Lewis Gilbert, screenwriter Christopher Wood and production designer Ken Adam. And it was clear that they were going to have to take Bond into space. There was no choice. Everything was in space. Spielberg's *Close Encounters of the Third Kind* (1978) had cleaned up after *Star Wars* and now, if you didn't have rockets and lasers, you were nothing. The question was: how would they get Bond out there and what would he do with himself once he was there?

It couldn't be completely science-fictional, because it wouldn't be Bond. Somehow, it would have to try and stay within the limits of belief. And that is when the production team got on to NASA, and were given privileged access to an exciting new project called the Space Shuttle. The real thing – SS *Columbus* – made its maiden voyage in 1981. In this respect at least, Bond was a couple of years ahead of his time.

Actually, it was a nifty and timely piece for PR for NASA. Throughout the 1970s, after the excitement of the moon landings had died down, people were beginning to ask what exactly the point of the space agency was; and more crucially, politicians were starting to wonder if it was really worth the billions of dollars a year being thrown at it, especially at a time when the economy was ailing. Acutely aware of such questions, NASA chiefs must have whooped with relief when Albert R. Broccoli came knocking.

Though thinking about it now, the *Moonraker* exercise does not work entirely in NASA's favour: it meant that the general public's first look at the Space Shuttle was as a craft being used by a rich psychopath to transport his Aryan super-race into space, prior to exterminating all remaining life on Earth. Still, no such thing as bad publicity, I suppose.

The other thing that Broccoli seemed to have learned from *Spy* was that it paid to throw money at the screen; huge quantities of it. The budget of *Spy* had clocked in at a handsome $13 million. *Moonraker* was to go further at a cool $25 million. It's interesting that periods of tremendous Bond profligacy always seem to coincide with profligate Labour governments; the budget for the Bond to follow, *For Your Eyes Only* in 1981, was trimmed quite a bit, which was somehow in keeping with the monetarist early years of the Thatcher Conservative government.

Moonraker had to be expensive, though, for outer space was to be only one of the locations: also in the frame were Venice, Rio de Janeiro and the Brazilian rainforest. Indeed, everything about the film seemed designed to both mirror and exceed its predecessor.

The pre-credits teaser is still a fantastic spectacle. Bond is in a private jet, snogging a stewardess with his cheeks sucked in, when suddenly the pilot emerges from the cockpit with a parachute for himself and the stewardess and announces that Bond is to stay put as the plane plummets to destruction. We are never told quite why. Perhaps Bond is being punished for his white polo neck/blue blazer combo. Anyway, a fight ensues, and Bond is pushed out of the jet. Without a parachute! By returning villain Jaws! It is a breathtaking and funny cliffhanger. How in the name of anything can Bond – spinning and flailing through the sky, the hard earth thousands of feet below – get out of this one?

By skydiving through that wonderful blue sky after the captain and wrestling his parachute off in mid-air. It is gob-smacking, audacious and very funny. Then a quick mid-air tussle with Jaws – it really is terrific, all those somersaults, conducted in thin air, filmed for real with no trickery. Of course the stunt doubles are wearing parachutes under the costume facsimiles and in a couple of shots, this is all too clear. But the first time you see this sequence, I swear you don't spot them. Suspension of disbelief is so total as to create a form of optical illusion. Clever old Bond!

Meanwhile, a Moonraker shuttle has been stolen; it belonged to squillionaire industrialist Hugo Drax, who lives in a chateau that has been imported stone by stone from France to California. This is a very neat idea, drawing a veil over the fact that this was actually filmed in France. The taxes for big earners in Britain were by this stage just a little too high for the taste of both Broccoli and indeed Roger Moore. And production costs were impossibly high. So they shunted production over to Paris. Anyway, Bond is sent by M to suck up to Drax – a very nicely understated and darkly comical performance from French actor Michael Lonsdale – and convince him that the secret services will find the shuttle, but as soon as they meet, it is very clear that Drax is a wrong'un.

This becomes even more clear when Bond visits the Drax space mission control and is invited to have a go on the pilot-training centrifuge machine.

Practically nothing could be more guaranteed to end in tears. But in Bond climbs, along creeps the saboteur, and then round and round Bond whizzes, the G-force rippling his cheeks and threatening to rupture his heart. Thank the Lord for his dart-firing wristwatch.

Possibly, on another level, Bond is being paid back for the previous scene, in which he meets the astrophysicist Dr Goodhead (Lois Chiles) and, having expected the scientist to be a man, exclaims 'A woman!', as though the suffragette movement had never happened. Actually, with a name like 'Goodhead', perhaps it didn't. In real life, Moore himself was comically disingenuous about the character's name. 'Whatever *can* that mean?' he said, one eyebrow characteristically raised. Anyway, a permanently sceptical-looking Dr Holly Goodhead is another of these women who seem to think that they are equal to Bond. Where can they get such ideas?

After Drax's PA Corinne is torn apart in the woods by his dogs as punishment for snogging Bond and showing him the wall safe (when this scene was played at the royal premiere, Prince Philip apparently involuntarily exclaimed 'Don't go into the woods, you stupid girl!' and leapt from his seat with the suspense), the action moves to Venice where, as Moore remarked, 'it is impossible not to get a beautiful shot, every time'. It's all something to do with a glassworks, and a mystery laboratory in an old palazzo. And yes, it is hypnotically lovely to watch. So much so that this film really benefits – on second viewing – from being watched with the volume down. The fusion of Ken Adam's intricate set designs, and the location, make this the most aesthetically pleasing Bond film of the lot.

That's once we get past the product placement. Product placement is something that the Bond films are especially noted for. Director Guy Hamilton recalled arriving early on the studio set of Goldfinger's private jet in 1964, to see producer Harry Saltzman pottering around in the bathroom section. A bemused Hamilton asked him what he was doing, whereupon Saltzman turned to reveal his hands full of branded luxury bathroom items, which he was carefully positioning on the shelves. According to Hamilton, he had these removed.

Even the world's favourite car, the *Goldfinger* Aston Martin DB5, was a cheeky advertisement in return for getting the car for free. As Sir Ken Adam recalled, Eon had explored the idea of various other cars, including Lotus, but Adam lobbied for the Aston. In fact, the car company was, in 1964, not doing terrifically well. At first, its directors were reluctant to help Bond out.

But the fact that they did was a life-saver for their balance sheets. After the release of the film, according to Adam, their sales went up by 47 per cent.

In *Moonraker*, one sequence alone – Bond and Holly trapped in an ambulance winding along a country road outside Rio – clocks up gigantic billboard advertisements for Dior, Marlboro cigarettes and British Airways. The climax of the cable car fight sees Jaws crash through a towering poster for 7-Up. Every television screen in the film appears to be made by Sony (this was the case for many of the Bond films in this period).

And what's new? Wind forward to the modern day and you find critics howling about an ostensibly outrageous line in 2006's *Casino Royale* when Vesper (Eva Green) asks Bond (Daniel Craig) if the watch he is wearing is a Rolex. 'No, Omega,' he says. 'Magnificent,' she says. But what makes it all slightly better is the way that both actors noticeably struggle to hide laughter in this part of the exchange.

And this film was not the worst offender. In 2002, *Die Another Day* featured so many branded products that one wag renamed it 'Buy Another Day.'

But it really is nothing new, and the producers were only taking their lead from Ian Fleming himself, whose Bond novels were jammed with product placement; everything from super-posh Floris soap to Tiptree marmalade. Rupert Hart Davis commented: 'Ian's are the only modern thrillers with built-in commercials.'[3]

And let's face it, the commercials don't get in the way of the fun. Nor, after watching *Moonraker* innumerable times, have I ever been tempted to raise a bottle of 7-Up to my lips. Or buy a Sony television. Or a packet of Marlboro. I have clearly been concentrating too hard on the story which, this time around, is not dissimilar to *The Spy Who Loved Me*; bonkers misanthrope Hugo Drax has built a space station (as one does) which he plans to staff with his new hand-picked master race; the aim is to destroy all current human life on Earth with a deadly pollen derived from a rare South American orchid. Once the planet has been thus cleansed, said master race can nip back down to Earth and get breeding.

The pleasure of this film is not the plot – well, it wouldn't be, would it? – but the ingenuity with which plot points are crowbarred in to fit with the locations; thus we are taken on a tour of Venice and its glassworks because Drax is having some special outer-space-strength glass manufactured. These strange glass globes are being flown to Rio de Janeiro; and it is deep within the Brazilian rainforest that Drax has his rocket-launch lair and where also, handily, the deadly orchid may be found. See? Locks together like a jigsaw.

For some regretful critics, including Dilys Powell, this was the film where 'the hardware really took over', although the critics had actually been saying this from *Goldfinger* onwards. What caused dismay among Bond fans was the sheer profusion of broad humour. The scene in which Bond's motorised gondola suddenly leaves the water and takes to dry land in St Mark's Square like a hovercraft caused particular distress.

The original boat chase through the canals, sparked by an assassin hiding in a coffin barge, had come from nowhere; and this, the fans howled, simply made Bond look like an absurd popinjay. What they forgot — and what I have to repeatedly point out — is that unlike the novels, Bond films were for all the family. And the children in the audience would have been utterly delighted by this scene.

And the fans forget another set-piece — the terrific fight in the glass museum between Bond and Drax's martial arts sidekick. As well as the gleeful quantity of destruction contained therein, the fight moves upstairs to behind the big clock in St Mark's Square. It is recreated in rich, loving detail by Ken Adam, the blues and the reds of the delicate stained glass and the gleaming brass of the clock mechanism, utterly rich and mesmerising. All the more so for you know it will be a matter of moments before Drax's henchman is sent flying through it into the square below.

So it's off to Rio for the carnival; these sequences were filmed almost a year before the rest of the production, which goes to show what a mighty work of organisation a Bond film is. Script and scenario had to be nailed down at the earliest available opportunity. As spectacle, it is wonderfully gratuitous. The actual piece of story development that takes place in Rio might just as well have been set in Blackpool for all the difference it makes.

But mustn't grumble, for we have a scene that combines gaudy costume, loud music and a surprising sense of the macabre: Bond's Rio ally Paula is waiting in a dark alley just off the main carnival drag while Bond explores a warehouse.

We become aware of her being watched from the nearby throng by one grotesquely tall carnival figure, with a vast carnival head. Then, slowly, this grotesque figure detaches itself from the parade and walks implacably down that alley towards the increasingly frightened girl. Listen, I was twelve when

I first saw that and it genuinely spooked me. The fact that the figure turns out to be silly old Jaws is neither here nor there.

As the first recurring henchman to be used in the films, Jaws actor Richard Kiel has received a great deal of fan attention across the years. Not all of it has been hugely complimentary – the more earnest devotees have become overheated by the transformation of this serious and creepy menace into cute comedy figure by the end of the film. But actually, the blend of heaviness and broad comedy feels perfectly natural, and very much in keeping with the cartoonish spectacle on display.

We see this in the terrifically amusing cable car scene, where Bond and Holly find themselves trapped many hundreds of feet in the air near the Sugar Loaf mountain in a swinging gondola as Jaws attempts to grab them. It is pure *Perils of Pauline* – especially the silly escape made by Bond and Holly, as they use a chain to slide down the cable, Jaws in the gondola in hot pursuit. At the end of the sequence, the cable car crashes and, emerging from the wreckage, fastidiously dusting himself down, Jaws is helped by a pretty blonde girl; their eyes meet. And the music swells to Tchaikovsky. It's love.

Which is why, I suspect, the world will always be divided into two tribes: those who believe that the Bond films should be essentially serious and 'stick to the spirit of the original Fleming'; and those who believe that the films are there as daft, fun, escapist nonsense. And I'm not just talking fans, I am literally talking everyone who has ever seen a Bond.

One might quickly go back to the novels and ask what exactly the 'spirit' of Fleming is: can it be most accurately found in the intricate, chilly plotting of *From Russia with Love*? Or do we find a more representative spirit in the bonkers moment where Bond fights it out to the death with a giant squid at the climax of *Doctor No*? Is the spirit somewhere within the gloom and oppression and anger of the short story 'The Living Daylights'; or in the schoolboyish earnestness of *Moonraker*, with Bond and Gala enjoying a skinny-dip in the English Channel prior to having a white cliff fall down around them?

So we had better get on with the silliness. M and Moneypenny have set up office in some kind of South American gaucho monastery, with Q establishing an outdoor gadget testing ground featuring various hombres. Is it strictly necessary for Miss Moneypenny to be there? One slightly suspects that all this is a result of kindly Cubby Broccoli allowing actress Lois

Maxwell to fly out on location with everyone else. Thus from this point, Bond is pointed towards the rainforest, and sets off upriver in a fancy boat. We will ignore the boat chase that follows, for it is even duller than the rest, and concentrate on the lush, beautiful and almost wholly pointless sequence that follows.

Bond traipses through the jungle and is lured along by a distant blonde beauty in white, who is heading for some kind of Inca pyramid. Once inside, Bond finds himself surrounded by countless lovelies in white. Then he is tipped into water for a fight with a giant python. 'Roger hated getting wet,' confided one crew member. But Moore himself is now more sanguine about the scene. He said in an interview: 'People often asked me how you act out fighting with a giant snake. I said, first you fight with the snake, and then you laugh all the way to the bank.'

In any case, with the novels filled with deadly stingrays, octopi, etc., surely Fleming would have applauded this scene!

What makes all of this exceptional is the aesthetic wonder of it; first, the fantastic rainforest locations, which Moore complained were so remote 'that they could only be reached on foot'. Given that he was having kidney stone problems at the time, you can see why he might have been reluctant. Secondly, the interior of that pyramid: it is the very height of Ken Adam's work. It is only there on screen for about three minutes but the scale and the detailing of that interior are extraordinary. The authentically dated bas-reliefs on the walls, the beguiling angles, the realistic-looking rock over which the water splashes . . . no other Bond before or since has boasted such consistently amazing production design.

And this goes most especially for the finest villain's lair ever, as inhabited by Hugo Drax. The pyramid angles inspired by the exterior, this is a toweringly vast control room, predominantly shiny black, dominated by vast Mondrian-style screens. Again, what makes this doubly astounding is that it is only on screen for about three minutes. Other films would have spent simply hours in there. Its sole purpose here is for droll Michael Lonsdale to inform Bond that all the Moonraker shuttles are blasting off for the space station, and that Bond himself will not be going with them, owing to the one cliffhanger that he has managed to filch directly from the original novel. That is, for Bond and Holly to be trapped in the backblast of the final craft.

For the ten-year-old *Star Wars* fans who had been lured along by the promise of space and lasers, the long wait was finally over. For Bond and Holly – luckily, she can pilot a Moonraker, even though she is a *woman* – trick their way on board the final ship and strap themselves in. Here, Roger is seen to be wearing a space suit and a sort of astronaut swimming cap, which caused the actor very great annoyance at the time. He felt that it robbed Bond of a certain quiet dignity. When it comes to unusual hats, actors are a little like dogs; they whine and fidget and ineffectually try to get the damned things off.

I am sure that Broccoli would not have denied that the climax of this film owes absolutely everything to *Star Wars*; from the scene in the shuttle where Drax's space station slowly looms into view (echoing Han Solo's *Millennium Falcon* approaching the Death Star); to all the running around in corridors with laser beams; to the grand climax, where Bond and Holly, skimming over the Earth's atmosphere in a shuttle, must race against time to catch up with the lethal death-globes hurtling towards the surface and destroy them with a laser beam (echoing Luke Skywalker's countdown mission to destroy the Death Star).

What is nice, however, is John Barry's wonderfully elegant, doomy score, reaching comically Wagnerian heights on board the station; and the jokes, which, although fairly awful, none the less evoke yelps of laughter. There is Drax's final line, as he points a laser gun at Bond: 'Let me put you out of my misery.' Then, as Bond and Holly canoodle weightlessly in a returning space shuttle, Q naturally fixes up a video link so M and indeed the Queen can see them. Surely by now we all know Q's line: 'I think he's attempting re-entry, sir.' But what really clinches the laugh is Roger in close-up, eyebrow saucily aloft.

We fade out over Shirley Bassey's rendition of the title song. This song had originally been offered out to others. Frank Sinatra was one. It somehow seems very difficult to imagine, not because of this slow, romantic song itself, which you can actually hear him singing, but because it seems like too much of a collision of eras and styles. The song was also apparently offered to Kate Bush, who would only have been about nineteen back then, and fresh from her hit 'Wuthering Heights'. Again, this song might have lent itself to her ethereal ululations. But you can also imagine that bookish feminist Kate would have been repelled by the entire notion of Bond. So the ever-dependable Shirley it was; this was the last of her Bond songs.

It had been a tough old shoot for Roger Moore who, let us not forget, had now passed the milestone of fifty. Moore, it seems, is a martyr to his health – his proposed autobiography back then was entitled *Out of the Bedpan*, but he said he lost the manuscript – and on this film, the problem was kidney stones. The condition caused him to collapse prior to being flown out to the Rio location; he had to spend a couple of days in hospital. Even now, when looking at that Brazilian boat chase, you can see in Moore's bloodshot eyes just how much strain he was under. In fact, in all his subsequent films, despite being older, he looks considerably better.

That marvellous old journalistic hand Victor Davis was out there on location, as ever, to capture the feel of the shoot. He found Roger in his canvas chair, 'puffing lazily on his favourite Monte Cristo cigar' and musing on press speculation about his wages for Bond. 'Now, how could I live on a million pounds?' Roger said.

Mrs Moore was on hand to be fierce. 'Of course he should stop playing Bond,' she declared. 'Look at him sitting there, cool, calm, playing his debonair part. It is all a big act. You should see the man who comes back home at night, tense, slamming down the phone if he can't get through.'[4] Phone-slamming, eh? We are reminded, suddenly and without warning, of Roger confessing to an earlier rage when he threw some toast across the room. It must have been all go chez Roger.

Broccoli was naturally also there. 'What's that son of a bitch actor saying?' he asked of reporter Davis. 'Actors are always asking for more money or threatening to quit.'

Joshing aside, though, the physical stress of these five-month-long Bond schedules caused Moore to wonder seriously whether he shouldn't pack it in after *Moonraker*. While he was busy pondering that, production designer Ken Adam had decided definitely that this would be his last.

According to some reports, rising expenditure had caused tension in the production office, and Adam ended up getting some of the flak from Broccoli. It seems utterly absurd that he should have done so, for it was Broccoli's decision to reroute production from London to Paris; every single film studio in the city had to be booked in order to ensure that the team had enough room to realise everything from the space station to the pyramid. How could costs not have been colossal? Adam, rightly, felt that he didn't have to be treated like this.

Now, to this day, he continues to speak very warmly both of the Bond films, and of the Broccoli family; and he clearly has a great deal of admiration for both. But one also senses that there was some hurt at the time. He was obviously not short of work and as well as divergent productions such as *Pennies from Heaven* (1980) and *Addams Family Values* (1992), Sir Ken also picked up an Oscar for his production design of Nicholas Hytner's *The Madness of King George* (1994).

Though Eon Productions own the copyright to Sir Ken's finished designs for the Bond films — everything is there in that Bond vault — Sir Ken still has the sketches for everything, neatly filed, from the 'tarantula room' of *Dr. No* to Blofeld's escape sub in *Diamonds Are Forever*. They make you wonder why we can't see anything like that in films nowadays.

Roger decided: he was going to stay. But Cubby Broccoli, who apparently felt that *Moonraker* had taken Bond too far into the realms of pure fantasy, decided with new executive producer (and stepson) Michael G. Wilson that when Bond returned in 1981, he would, to use that great old phrase, be 'much closer to the spirit of the original Fleming'. Funnily enough, in that interregnum between '79 and '81, both Britain and America experienced seismic political changes that would make a more sombre, grittier, straighter Bond look strangely prescient.

CHAPTER SIXTEEN THE SMACK OF FIRM ESPIONAGE

I t has been claimed by some critics that it is possible to detect a right-wing sensibility in the twelfth Bond entry, *For Your Eyes Only*; that the film's harder, more pared-back, less comic style is an echo of the first two years of Margaret Thatcher's Conservative government. On first glance, perhaps. But actually, there is something rather more complex going on beneath this production, which would have been much less to Margaret Thatcher's tastes than the critics suppose.

Also, I think in most circumstances that one can exonerate Eon from any sense of political bandstanding in the Bond pictures. The reason for the unaccustomed feel of *For Your Eyes Only* is rooted in something quite different. For the producers are doing something entirely new with the character, something that they would never really try again. It is less to do with political positioning than with fixing Bond's role as a fictional figure within a recognisably real world. Instead of a smirking superhero operating against a lurid backdrop, Bond is once more simply an English secret agent, dealing with more realistic adversaries and allies. He is even seen to go shopping in a Greek market. When you look at the film again now, you see how beguilingly anomalous this approach is.

We can sketch out the backdrop fairly swiftly. After his tax-fleeing flight to Paris, Broccoli returned to production at Pinewood; this at least we can directly attribute to Mrs Thatcher. In her Chancellor Geoffrey Howe's first budget, the top rate of income tax had been reduced from 83 per cent to 60 per cent. And Broccoli's view was that both economically and for the sake of change, the new Bond film would go in an entirely new direction.

The veteran screenwriter Richard Maibaum was lured back and was teamed up with rising executive Michael G. Wilson, who had been working on the production side since *Goldfinger* in 1964. Wilson and Maibaum wove a story that plunged Bond back into Cold War anxieties, but as filtered through the manoeuvrings of shady Mediterranean players.

This time around, there would be no cartoon megalomaniacs, no vast lairs and no comedy chases on gondolas. Instead, this would be a tale of missile destructor codes, crossbows and an amazingly low-key climax in a disused monastery. There would be old wartime friends turned enemies, a young woman seeking to avenge her murdered parents, and in the midst of it all, an older, reined-in Bond.

One of the few touches of extravagance came in the pre-credits sequence as Bond is trapped in a remote-controlled helicopter being guided from a London docklands rooftop by a bald figure in a wheelchair with a white Persian cat. Remember, after the court case of 1976, Eon could not call a character 'Blofeld'. But they could get away with this rather cheeky and thrilling set-up. The various shots of the helicopter hurtling between and through crumbling riverside depots, as Bond hangs desperately on to the side-strut, are tremendously exciting; there is a reckless, swooping beauty as the helicopter dives towards the Thames and weaves through decaying industrial chimneys. But the sequence is slightly jarring too. It took me a long time to work out why. When, out of curiosity, I visited the location recently, it became clear.

The helicopter scene was filmed in 1980 in and around the site of the Beckton gas works, in east London, some four miles downstream of where the mighty Canary Wharf complex now stands. Before Canary Wharf came, these were miles of silent and creepy industrial desolation. The old docks had been closing down since the 1970s, business moving downriver to larger facilities at Tilbury. By 1980, there was nothing left, save the vast monuments of abandoned warehouses and twisting mazes of rusting pipework.

But one of Margaret Thatcher's young ministers, Michael Heseltine, was backing a government-funded quango, the Docklands Development Corporation, to find ways of bringing new life to the dead area. Unlike many in those chilly monetarist days, Heseltine believed that this sort of regeneration was very much the government's responsibility. The results are not quite what anyone back then would have expected.

These days, the area around those old Isle of Dogs quays is like Manhattan; a gleaming techno-city inhabited by Euro-bankers living in luxurious penthouses. Down in Beckton, after many years of disintegration, the location of Bond's helicopter cliffhanger is now a smart retail park. There is a branch of the music store HMV that sells classic films on DVD. Where once was grimy industry is now an area where consumers can park with ease. When you look at *For Your Eyes Only*, this is not necessarily the transformation you might have anticipated.

The point is that this was the first time that an action scene – or indeed any other kind of scene – in a Bond movie was located so unequivocally in the real world, against a real backdrop of what many saw as economic failure and despair. I have no doubt that new director John Glen – promoted from his sterling second unit work – was drawn to it simply by the spectacular possibilities it afforded for buzzing a helicopter through cavernous warehouses. And indeed the minimal cost of securing the location. But after all these years, what the sequence does is locate Moore very firmly in Thatcher's Britain.

The climax of the sequence – where Bond regains control of the helicopter, hoists Blofeld's wheelchair aloft, and drops him down a vast industrial chimney – might loosely be read as Bond taking a villain from the bad old days of consensus politics and burying him in a soon-to-be-demolished landscape. Go on, admit it. It's there.

That wheelchair was the source of terrific embarrassment at the gala royal premiere of the film in June 1981. As my own dear father Peter McKay noted in his newspaper column at the time, one of the charitable concerns benefiting from this lavish occasion was the Year of the Disabled. 'A number of disabled people will be present at the Odeon Leicester Square premiere ... I hear from a production man that, in the light of all this, the opening scenes in the film could be seen as unfortunate.'[1] Happily, everyone was amused. It's quite difficult to take offence at anything that involves Roger Moore.

Various other production companies managed to squeeze several more films and pop videos out of that entropic docklands vista; among them were the Richard Burton/John Hurt version of *1984*, Kubrick's *Full Metal Jacket* (1987) and an Oasis song. For some incorrigible London nostalgics, the recent demolition of these haunted industrial monuments was a source of very deep regret. All that remains are the fragments of a brick archway that lead into Winsor Terrace.

Anyway, thence from the pre-credits into an unusual title sequence from Maurice Binder featuring, for the first time, the chanteuse belting out the title song in shot. The singer in question was Sheena Easton, a bonny Scottish lassie who not long previously had won a TV talent competition overseen by Esther Rantzen. It's very striking, all those shots of Sheena apparently standing in an aquarium into which bubble bath has been poured, and surrounded by naked swimming silhouettes. And she has a fantastic voice. But the song – and I know I am very much in a minority on this one – is simply awful.

It sounds tinny, the tune is supremely unmemorable, and the lyrics make the toes curl so far that they practically retract into the foot. 'For your eyes only/can see me through the night' is the opening gambit. But clearly I am wrong because the song, composed by Bill Conti, was nominated for an Oscar the following year. So was Dolly Parton's 'Nine to Five', if memory serves.

Bill Conti, brought in for the absent John Barry, was an American who had composed the *Rocky* theme and went on to compose the title tunes for the glossy soap *Dynasty* and the cop show *Cagney and Lacey*. To the score of Bond he brought a sort of electronic late-disco feel; but these were the early days of synthesisers, and among the real drums and trumpets were some terrible squealy Stylophone noises.

Happily, the action on screen felt rather more energetic and authentic than of late. Once again, we must doff our titfers to Broccoli for his prescience, and his nose for sniffing out the changing tenor of the times. For the tone of the adventure that Bond is about to be plunged into very much accords with developments in the world outside.

First, there was the curious sense, in those first austere years of Thatcher, that a certain sense of British masculinity had been restored. The event that sparked this mood was a siege of the Iranian embassy in Kensington, west London in May 1980. To general astonishment and acclaim, the crisis was brought to a sharp conclusion when the building was stormed by members of the SAS. This was the first that the wider public had really heard about this military elite division, with its stirring motto 'Who Dares Wins'. And such a victory against terrorism – in an era when the IRA was regularly responsible for unstoppable bomb outrages – seemed utterly extraordinary. Did Britain truly still have that sort of spirit?

Among those brimming with admiration for the SAS boys was Margaret Thatcher, who met all the operatives concerned for a special reception one evening and was reportedly sparkling-eyed at this assembly of macho British manhood. Later that evening, she had to join a group of senior Whitehall mandarins for dinner; by contrast, their effete, fussy Oxbridge ways were said to have filled her with distaste, and added fuel to her campaign to bend the civil service to her will.

It was not until 1982, and the expedition to the South Atlantic to reclaim the Falkland Islands from an invading Argentine force, that this resurgence of national bellicosity was to find its apogee. But even by 1981, Mrs Thatcher – despite the depredations of her zeal for monetarism, and the mass unemployment that resulted – was becoming associated with a sense of a revival of bulldog pride, the sense that Britain had been in a terminal nosedive but now was being pulled out of it. In other words, it was jolly lucky for the character of Bond that the producers chose this national moment to toughen him up.

Those years also saw a curious outbreak of nostalgia for the notion of 'Englishness'. In 1981 came the release of Hugh Hudson's Oscar-winning *Chariots of Fire*, an unashamed retelling of the 1924 Olympics when running glory was sought by two British men. It also saw a marvellously bad film called *Who Dares Wins*, which was obviously based on the Iranian embassy siege and starred Lewis Collins, of TV's *The Professionals*, as the chief SAS hero going in with both balls blazing. The villains this time were irredeemable Marxists. It is now a masterpiece of right-wing Thatcherite kitsch, a 'one of us' wet dream. For a time, Lewis Collins was a British tabloid favourite to inherit the role of Bond. Ah well.

In another vein, the same year saw the hugely successful and influential adaptation for ITV of Evelyn Waugh's *Brideshead Revisited*, which depicted a between-the-wars England of unabashed poshness, dreaming spires, teddy bears, champagne, exquisite cars and grand houses. Meanwhile, 1980 had seen the advent of the 'Sloane Ranger' phenomenon, amusingly identified by Peter York and Ann Barr; through the medium of a humorous best-selling Christmas book, York and Barr introduced the rest of the world to the tribe that lives within one square mile of London's Sloane Square, of whom Lady Diana Spencer was a leading figure.

It was this – for better or worse – that brought a subsequent middle-class craze for green waxed jackets and wellingtons and tweed and pearls and old jumpers and phrases such as 'OK, yah'. The very essence of this and the *Brideshead* cult, emulated by 50 per cent of all Oxford students during that period, seemed to be a backward-looking yearning for a P.G. Wodehouse world, where one could escape the Smoke at the weekend and stay in one's friends' country piles. It was a defiant redefinition of Englishness intended to stand apart from the images of Labour's era: the unions, the strikes, the steady decline.

We might now debate why this snob nostalgia suddenly became so popular at a time when the country was riven with economic and social problems not seen since the 1930s. But we can see how the toned-down, slightly tougher Bond of *For Your Eyes Only* would himself stand for a certain sort of nascent British pride.

Internationally, another influence on the film may have been the re-freezing of relations between the Soviet Union and the West, in the wake of Russia's 1979 invasion of Afghanistan (no, it is all right when *we* do it). The 1980 Olympics were held in Moscow; Mrs Thatcher's insistence that British athletes boycott the event caused tremendous ill-will. Many ignored her.

That same year, there was ruthless Soviet-inspired repression of the Polish trade union Solidarity, led by Lech Walesa. Once again, there were inter-national protests. Then, in the US in January 1981, the Republican President Reagan was inaugurated. Like Mrs Thatcher, he regarded Communism as inherently evil. Thus the era of missile talks and trade agreements was at an end. Both Britain and the US sharpened their rhetoric, and the Soviet Union responded with equal vehemence. For the first time since the Cuban missile crisis, the world had once again become tense and nervy.

So here we are in the Ionian Sea, with a shot of a trawler called *St George's*. This, like the real-life trawler supposed to have been sunk by the Soviets in 1974, is the cover for a spy vessel, holding a secret control room with an ATAC missile guidance system on board. This boat, however, is not sunk by enemy action, but by accidental collision with a sea-mine. The drowning of those on board is an unusually harrowing Bond scene.

Meanwhile, beautiful Melina Havelock (Carole Bouquet) is flying out to the yacht of her Greek mother and English father. Their reunion is cut short when Melina's pilot unexpectedly flies back, swoops in, and unleashes a volley of machine-gun bullets. Melina is unhurt; but her parents are dead. It is another unusually shocking scene. But how can the events be connected?

As ever, when Eon goes back to 'the spirit of Ian Fleming', the plot becomes fiendishly complicated; but it is not long before Bond is on the trail of a sinister killer called Locque in Spain, implicated in the Havelock murders. Melina is out for vengeance with a crossbow; she and Bond are obliged to use her battered old 2CV to escape a platoon of bad guys.

It is a blissfully funny and exciting car chase; without his invincible Lotus (blown up when a bad guy tries to break in) Bond is forced to rely on his wits and the bumpy hillside pursuit is fantastically arranged. 'I do love a drive in the country,' quips Bond as the car rolls unstoppably through an olive grove.

And having made the acquaintance of Melina, it is surprisingly uncertain in the scene that follows as to whether they sleep together or not. All we see is the pair of them fully dressed in a hotel room preparing to leave, with Bond handing out some sage Confucian advice about the inadvisability of revenge.

Carole Bouquet was later to become the face of Chanel; for many, she is the queen of knockout Bond girls. Mesmeric beauty aside, what is interesting about her character is that at long, long last, Bond appears to have accepted the notion of sexual equality and treats her as a grown-up human being as opposed to a walking double-entendre generator. For most of the film, Melina is either angry, or solemn and grave. The scenes where she at last relaxes with Bond and smiles are all the stronger for it.

Bouquet herself was only slightly unhelpful when she remarked warmly of her co-star: 'Roger is very nice. He reminds me of my father.'[2]

The casting for the villain Kristatos – beautifully played by award-winning actor Julian Glover – tells us much about the inner workings of Eon Productions at that time. 'I had done a drama documentary about the Czechoslovakian president Alexander Dubcek which made a big stir at the time,' Glover says. 'Cubby Broccoli was looking for someone who could seem really nice and credible so everyone would be fooled. I was actually filming Alexander the Great in Greece when I got the call to see Cubby on a Sunday. The call came on a Saturday.' There was, it seems, little choice but to obey the great summons and so, after some awkwardness, Glover managed to get a flight out that afternoon. 'I got to London via Frankfurt and Paris,' he says.

'At 10.30 a.m. that Sunday morning at Eon, Dana [Broccoli] was there and everyone was assembled. I was advised by one of the team not to smoke. After a talk, someone took me aside and said "You've got it." How did he know? "I can tell from Dana's face."'

The Eon way was every bit as lavish as legend had it. 'When I arrived at the first location in Corinth, Greece – first-class ticket – I was given an envelope containing £525. Marked "Expenses". I couldn't believe this paradise. It really is another world, doing Bond. And on a Bond film, everything works. They are the most meticulously planned productions.'

Another of the ritzy locations Glover got to go to was Cortina,

Switzerland, where Bond initially meets Kristatos, at that stage ostensibly a good guy. God knows why the two of them are there, really – it's one of those journeys where Bond appears to get just one tiny clue from one brief conversation – but we know we are in for a treat because the snowy backdrop can only lead to a ski chase.

Bond meets Kristatos's young protégée, a nymphomaniac teenage ice skater called Bibi (Lynn-Holly Johnson). Her attempted seduction of Bond – and Bond's amused insistence that he will instead 'buy her an ice cream' – is another surprise. What has happened to the eyebrow-wiggling Lothario who, let us not forget, was quite happy to deflower the virginal Solitaire? It is a shrewd and amusing acknowledgement of Moore's middle age. But it also has the effect, once more, of rooting the film in a stubborn reality that we have never seen Bond in before. The effect is mildly disconcerting.

Lynn-Holly Johnson's breathless Bibi is a lovely light touch at this point in what is already a rather complicated film. 'When I auditioned for Cubby, I did all my own skating and skiing,' she said in an interview, adding that it was fun to have joined the now-famed pantheon of Bond girls.[3] Having been knocked back by Bond, Bibi sets off in artless pursuit of Olympic cross-country skier Eric Klieger; a blond and rather menacing-looking chap who, first of all, doesn't seem interested and second of all, is actually a bad guy.

This is all by means of setting Bond up for the brilliant ski chase – every bit as good as those in *On Her Majesty's Secret Service*. It comes courtesy of a wonderful cliffhanger atop a vertiginous Olympic ski jump, where Bond has been pursued by Locque and his bad guys. He has no choice but to ski down it; below, Eric Klieger is waiting with his rifle. As Bond launches himself down the slope, so does another henchman. After a jaw-dropping fight at 100 m.p.h., Bond zooms off and heads for the hills, being followed on skis by Klieg plus armed motorcyclists with spiked wheels.

It is a sequence that I don't think they have topped. Whether causing havoc on the nursery slopes, or skiing down a bobsleigh run, the sheer pace and energy and inventiveness of this chase leave one breathless with both excitement and laughter. In fact, a shadow hangs over this scene, for during filming, one of the stuntmen had a terrible accident and was fatally injured. The crew, naturally, were in shock, but the shoot went on. It is worth bearing in mind that no matter how dazzling the special effects of today's multiplex blockbusters, very few things these days are actually performed for real in front of the cameras. Broccoli once said that the welfare of the stunt artists was paramount. We also know that he was attentiveness itself when accidents happened. During filming of 1967's *You Only Live Twice*, one of the helicopter cameramen had his foot accidentally severed. Eon made sure he got the most expensive medical treatment available.

The plot of *Only*, loosely based on a conflation of the Fleming short story of the same name and another called 'Risico', is a carnival of confusion, and I have to admit that I didn't fully get it the first time around. Kristatos fingers his one-time friend and now dear enemy Columbo (Topol) as the smuggler who is after the sunken ATAC system, and who wants to sell it on to the Soviets. But then Bond meets Columbo, who tells him that in fact Kristatos is the bad guy – a heroin smuggler and full-time Kremlin nark.

But . . . oh, who cares, for in the Greek section of the film, we have even more intrusions of the real world. First, Bond encounters Columbo's mistress Lisl (Cassandra Harris, who was Mrs Pierce Brosnan), who would appear to be swanky sophistication itself; but after a couple of glasses of champagne, her Liverpudlian accent slips through. It's a wonderful moment, this typically exotic Bond girl suddenly owning up to her humble social roots. And again, rather than the *Carry On* double entendres, we instead have Bond engaging in something closer to real conversation.

At the time, there was some reaction against this removal of broad humour; but the change of pace suits the film rather well. Alas! Next morning, out on the sand dunes, Lisl is brutally run over by one of Kristatos's thugs. Bond is rescued – then knocked unconscious – by Columbo's men, taken aboard his yacht and subjected to a heavy dose of exposition, as delivered by an amused-looking Topol.

It really is all too confusing, especially for those of us used to camp Euro-actors wearing Nehru jackets. But the main thing is that this new 'real' Bond keeps us watching. Much later on, Melina takes Bond on a shopping expedition to stock up for her crew. We see them both wandering through a marketplace, sampling pomegranates. It is an astonishing shift – we have never seen Bond conduct so basic a form of economic transaction before – but the shift feels right, for Moore seems insouciantly at home in this more down-to-earth mode. It's slightly trickier to imagine Connery in the same circumstances.

An earlier scene in which Kristatos and Bond have dinner outside a Greek casino featured in the background rich jet-set onlookers who wanted to be 'extras'. They found it was all rather less glamorous when we went for more retakes at two o'clock in the morning,' recalls Julian Glover. 'Some of these glamorous people got obstreperous. No one quite knew what to do. Then a waiter came along and tipped a dish into Roger's lap. It was a moment of horror. But then the "waiter" actually turned out to be Roger's wife in a wig and moustache – they had set it all up to lighten the mood and bring everyone back on side. So deeply silly, but Roger always keeps the atmosphere on set so comfortable.'

Back to the fundamentally unsilly plot, which we must remember centres on ATAC. Unfortunately, the rescue of same from the sunken *St George's* entails an underwater sequence involving a rival diver, an airpipe being cut, and a surprise shark, as all underwater sequences must. And like all such sequences, it goes on for what seems like two and a half hours. Happily, Bond and Melina are then captured by Kristatos and put through an ordeal originally found in the novel *Live and Let Die*. They are hauled through the water behind his yacht, dragged over sharp reefs, the idea being that the sharks will be attracted by their blood. More paring down: in all previous Moore films, one might have expected Bond to escape using a gadget. Not this time: instead, he has to dive underwater and try cutting the ropes on the sharp reefs, all the time holding his breath until he is blue. It is genuinely thrilling stuff.

And thence on to the climax, set in the fictitious mountaintop monastery of St Cyril's, where Kristatos has taken the ATAC machine and is due to rendezvous with General Gogol. In order to thwart him, Bond must scale the side of the mountain and effect entrance to the monastery for his attack squadron, which includes Topol and Carole Bouquet. Only in a Bond film. Anyway, it sounds most un-Bond-like: a lengthy ten-minute sequence of suspenseful mountaineering, with a bad guy at the top pushing him back off the precipice, leaving Bond dangling by a rope while the bad guy attempts to knock out all of his pitons. No explosions, no countdowns, no tannoys, no stuntmen performing somersaults. Yet – perhaps because it is so unusual – it really is exciting and tense. Director John Glen's overall idea for the film was to recapture some of the feel of *From Russia with Love*; but actually, this was much more pulse-pounding than that film's flabby climax.

Afterwards, that surprisingly low-key climax: the capture of the monastery, Kristatos and Columbo slugging it out, and the final encounter with General Gogol. Yet here we once again see the measure of Broccoli's fantastic shrewdness. Just as Gogol emerges from the helicopter to claim his prize – which would give Russia full access to NATO nuclear missile codes – Bond manages to grab the ATAC machine. There is a brief stand-off as Gogol's bodyguard points a machine gun at Bond, before Bond hurls the ATAC contraption over the side of the cliff. It falls thousands of feet and is smashed to pieces. 'That's detente,' Bond tells Gogol. 'You don't have it, we don't have it.' At this, Gogol smiles reluctantly, then leaves.

With hindsight, this is a fascinating and rather puzzling ending. For in a period where East and West were once more seriously squaring up to one another, and engaged in a new arms race, here is the West's premier fictional defender apparently not acting in the interests of his nation. What would Mrs Thatcher have made of his gesture? I think we can say with some confidence that she would have gone stark staring mad.

On whose authority does Bond act here? His mission was to bring the bloody device home, not unilaterally deprive his government of it. One might say that Bond at this point is being threatened at gunpoint by Gogol's guard; but since when has Bond been so intimidated by a single gun? And in any case, so what? That is his job, and surely Melina with her crossbow could have provided covering fire. Bond's destruction of ATAC can only be interpreted as a peace-keeping gesture, curiously out of kilter with the times. You would not have caught Mrs Thatcher's beloved SAS boys making such a move. In real life, Bond would at the very least have been fired.

In the end, cinematically, it is always a question of commercial considerations; Bond had to sell to as many countries worldwide as possible. And that meant that to avoid giving any possible offence to anyone, Bond in one sense had to stand above everyday tensions.

'There was a feeling of detente,' said executive Michael G. Wilson in an interview. 'Bond had always been leading the idea that the Cold War would eventually end and there was no point in stirring up hostility because there wasn't that much difference between us and the Russians or anyone.'[4]

This very sentiment alone would have made Thatcher mauve with rage. She – and to a similar extent, the newly inaugurated President Reagan – were Manicheans, believing firmly that the West was engaged in a struggle against an evil ideology. Indeed, from 1980 to about 1983, they intensified the hostile rhetoric, which in turn had the effect of making the Kremlin more paranoid and twitchy and wrathful. It is now argued that that period was actually the closest that the world came to an all-out nuclear conflict. For Thatcher, 'detente' would be a term equivalent to 'consensus politics'; figures such as General Gogol should be treated with disdain, not knowing grins and friendly gestures.

This is Bond though; and in a meta-fictional sense, Mrs Thatcher is perfectly delighted with Bond's actions, incredibly unlikely though this may seem. For in the film's final scene, the Prime Minister, played by Janet Brown, is given the honour of being the only real-life politician ever acknowledged in the films. Bond is aboard Melina's boat, being patched through by phone to Mrs Thatcher's kitchen in Number Ten. Also present beside her is husband Denis (played by John Wells).

Any male Prime Minister would have been depicted in the Cabinet Room; throughout her time as Leader of the Opposition, Mrs Thatcher carefully propagated this image of herself as a housewife and mother of two, eager to bring a sense of household thrift to the nation's finances with good homely common sense.

Thus it is that the film portrays her not only in the kitchen but also wearing a pinny and in the middle of preparing some meal, slapping Denis's hand as he tries to filch from a bowl. Instead of Bond, Melina's parrot comes to the phone and tells Mrs Thatcher 'Give us a kiss, give us a kiss.' Mrs Thatcher pats her hair, clearly flattered. How very strange it all seems now. When the film was released in the summer of 1981, she was, according to polls, the least popular Prime Minister of the twentieth century.

Her hardline pursuit of monetarist theory, slashing public spending and subsidies and leading to the closure of thousands upon thousands of businesses, had wrought economic desolation throughout the old industrial heartlands of the north of England, and Scotland, and Wales, and unemployment had risen to a breathtaking three million. In the spring of 1981, there were riots in Brixton, south London, and Toxteth in Liverpool. Mrs Thatcher and her cabinet furiously denied that these blazing confrontations with the police had any connection to the recession; they were simply ugly outbreaks of law-breaking from shiftless youths.

But in contrast to this, and the deepening gloom of the recession, the summer of 1981 also saw the nation once more putting on Union flag plastic bowler hats, this time for the royal wedding of Prince Charles and Lady Diana Spencer. The national effusion of royalist enthusiasm matched that of the Silver Jubilee; the wedding itself, broadcast all over the world, leading to a sudden gust of patriotic fervour, more street parties, a bit of tinselly escapism amid the grey economic backdrop.

It was this Britain that *For Your Eyes Only* seemed calculated to appeal to: a country where a bit of grit and determination could restore Britain's position in the world. No wonder the newly married Prince and Princess took this film on board the Royal Yacht *Britannia* for their honeymoon.

There was one scene in *Only* that caused Roger Moore some distress. It comes in his final confrontation with the icy (and dialogue-free) hitman Locque. Locque is at Bond's mercy: he is sitting in his car, precariously angled on a cliff-top. Just one move could send him over the edge. He looks up at Bond in silent appeal. Bond simply tosses a small badge found on the murdered body of his fellow agent Ferrera; and then he kicks Locque's car over the edge.

Moore's view was this: it was all very well to make Bond harder and tougher but a scene like this would send out an appalling message to any of the children in the audience. Wouldn't it be better if the car went over simply as a result of the weight of the badge? But director John Glen was having none of it. And after a great deal of debate, Glen prevailed.

It was an interesting power struggle for the new boy. When he had originally got the job, Glen described it artlessly as 'the most exciting day of my life'. Lynn-Holly Johnson said of him: 'You could really tell that this was an editor who was directing. He was really meticulous and neat.' But his authority on set had to be matched to that of the leading man who, by his fifth Bond picture, was entitled to feel that he had a firm handle on the character.

Both men have made elaborate bows to one another across the years. 'You had to devote ten minutes a day to Roger's practical jokes,' said Glen fondly of *Only*. 'He is a fantastic actor, rarely fluffs.'[5] Equally, Moore has said that he had a very good time with Glen and that they 'laughed a lot'.

It must have been a slightly tricky period for Moore. Here he was, now at the age of fifty-three, still heading up an amazingly lucrative film series that was, at the same time, making greater and greater physical demands of him. The actor has cheerfully and winningly confessed that one scene – where Bond is seen running up a vast hillside flight of steps in pursuit of a bad guy – was performed by a stunt man, with Roger dubbing on the puffing sound effects. And indeed, before production began on the film, he was genuinely in two minds about whether he should carry on.

The subject of money sparked off an amusing spat between Broccoli and Moore. Moore's fresh demands had clearly nettled the old man. In 1980, as negotiations were going on, Broccoli – doubtless with a twinkle in that roguish old eye – had this to say of his leading man and friend: 'I thought we were scraping the bottom of the barrel when we first took him on. But when we dieted him and got rid of those damn eyebrows he would keep wiggling up and down in *The Saint*, he was fine. Roger is good in a different way from Sean,' he added. 'But he has never managed to be cruel, and cruelty is an important part of Bond's make-up.'[6]

This prompted a querulous response from the normally amused Moore. 'Cubby and I were having some tough negotiations over money,' Moore said. 'The reason we broke off talking is because I learned they were testing other people to play Bond. I was irritated. I felt insulted. But then we started talking again.'[7]

Director Glen pronounced himself delighted about Moore staying on, for he was anxious about the idea of bearing the responsibility for introducing a new Bond.

Nor did he want to introduce a new M. Actor Bernard Lee had not been well in 1979's *Moonraker*, even though he did get to go on location to Venice and South America. This time around, sadly, Lee died before shooting was under way. It was too sudden to think of parachuting another actor in there, so M's role was given to the character Freddie Gray, the Defence Minister, as played by Geoffrey Keen. He was flanked by those excellent character actors James Villiers and Graham Crowden.

And the scene in which Bond walks into the confessional booth of a Greek Orthodox church, originally intended for M to give a bit of exposition from behind the screen, was instead given to faithful Desmond Llewelyn as Q. It is as well the old boffin was given something to do, for this time around, Bond had been determinedly short of gadgets, instead using such items as poolside umbrellas to effect his ingenious escapes.

Broccoli's gamble of bringing Bond down to earth appeared to have done the trick, for while the receipts did not quite match those of *Moonraker*, the film had still performed extremely handsomely, enough to be able to look forward to a new decade with some confidence.

The reviews, too, were broadly enthusiastic, though an occasional note of sarcasm and satire was beginning to creep in. Thus the magisterially highbrow journal *The Times Literary Supplement*: 'Instead of haplessly falling prey to discontinuity, the screenwriters have consciously sought it out,' wrote T.J. Binyon. 'Their aim, skilfully achieved, has been to produce a kind of kinetic mosaic: a series of chases and fights arranged in a purely aleatory order – there is very rarely a logical narrative reason why one should precede or succeed another. Each individual chunk of pattern, examined closely, reveals itself as an extended vermouth advertisement.'

In *The Observer*, wise old Philip French logged the meaning of the series's change of direction. 'The final comic touch is typical of the way the series has cannily moved with the times, as also is the hiring of Sheena Easton to sing the title song,' he wrote. 'Displaying the wonderfully confident show-business timidity that has made them rich, the producers know that the Thatchers can be mocked and that Ms Easton must be taken seriously.'

Meanwhile, speaking up on behalf of the youth of America was *Rolling Stone* magazine: 'Roger Moore is a slick English smarty-pants with all the resonance of a glockenspiel.'

I expect it did not take Broccoli long to dry his tears after reading that. And there was a further boost for Broccoli in the spring of 1982: at the Oscars, he was given the Irving J. Thalberg Award, an acknowledgement of his achievement as producer of these films. Broccoli was, according to several accounts, more nervous of receiving this award than anything else he had come across in his professional career. The statuette was presented to him by Roger Moore. Clearly, Cubby was slightly overwhelmed by the whole thing.

But as the new film, *Octopussy*, went into pre-production, it looked as though Bond was about to be hit by two vast setbacks. Kevin McClory had at last got himself together and was planning to bring Sean Connery back as Bond in a production called *Never Say Never Again*. Worse than this, though, perhaps for both productions, was that the tide of fashion was starting to move against Bond. For the first time ever, the invincible agent was to face not merely charges of sexism but – more damagingly – the accusation that the character was becoming naff and outdated. For both Broccoli and McClory, 1983 was going to be the crunch year. Only one of them would get through it with head held firmly aloft.

'The battle of the Bonds!' bellowed the headline of a piece written – well, actually written by my own dear father, now I recall, for the *Daily Express* in the days when it was still a newspaper. This was in the spring of 1983 when the world was becoming aware that not one but two Bonds were heading for the cinema screens that year. In one corner, Roger Moore would be back, in a film intriguingly entitled *Octopussy*; in the other, the sensational return of Sean Connery to the part that he vowed he would never play again. Hence the title, suggested by Connery's wife Micheline: *Never Say Never Again*.

I detected a pro-Connery bias in my father's piece, which analysed the key points of each contestant; first because of his shared Scottishness with Connery, and second, because for people of my father's generation, Sean was the governor, the real Bond, never bettered. For us younger folk, it wasn't so clear cut: we had grown up with Roger, and liked the jokes. But it is interesting just how much pro-Connery coverage there was.

Indeed, when it was first officially announced in 1982 that he was returning as 007, newspapers ran the obligatory publicity shot – Connery with gun and new grey barnet – with some extraordinary drooling captions about how at fifty-two, the original Bond was sexier than ever. Well, perhaps he was and perhaps he wasn't. But it must have been an anxious few months for Eon Productions.

Actually, rather sweetly, despite all the grinding court cases over the years, Kevin McClory and Cubby Broccoli were on perfectly friendly terms, and would occasionally meet to play backgammon. Much in the same way, come to think of it, that Broccoli was friendly with Charles Feldman, the producer of the 1967 *Casino Royale*, and came to worry about Feldman's health as that film's production nightmares escalated.

None the less, Broccoli must have been at least disconcerted by the production that former tax lawyer Joseph Schwarzman was putting together with McClory as executive producer, financed by Warner Brothers. As well as Sean Connery, they had enlisted Max von Sydow as

Blofeld; European art-house star Klaus Maria Brandauer as Largo; Kim Basinger as Domino; and Barbara Carrera as exuberant bad girl Fatima Blush. Stepping up to play M would be Edward Fox; Q would be essayed by Alec McCowen. And Pamela Salem would be Miss Moneypenny.

That wasn't all. They had hired the formidable talents of Lorenzo Semple Jr to write the script (he was the man who had given TV's *Batman* its camp comic bite, as well as scripting hits such as 1973's *Three Days of the Condor*) and veteran director Irvin Kershner, late of *The Empire Strikes Back* (1980), to take the helm. Unlike the neurotic overexcitement of Charles Feldman's *Casino Royale*, this was going to be a serious, proper, spectacular production that would feature locations from Nassau to North Africa.

Now, the point here is that McClory only had the right to draw on one Bond plot, and that was the plot of *Thunderball*. However, lessons had clearly been learned, for in the tweaking of the storyline, much of the soggy underwater stuff was jettisoned, thank the Lord.

But the end result was genuinely weird – a real curiosity. Released several months after Eon's *Octopussy*, which may have damaged its box office somewhat, it stands now as a sort of alternative-dimension Bond, the Bond we would have had if we were to slip between universes, or go back in time and tread on Ian Fleming's toe in 1933. This is not to say that it is wholly bad; not at all, in fact. It is simply down to a question of taste. But before we get on to the Cold War genius of *Octopussy*, we must assess its competitor to get it into perspective.

Never opens directly on to the title song, and at this, the Bond aficionado's antennae start quivering. Thanks to poor synthesiser reproduction, the opening bars quaver like a bad primary school recital. Then some woman sings a 1970s loungecore cabaret song that automatically puts one in mind of the musical interlude that they would have every week in *The Two Ronnies*. 'Never say never again. Never. Never say never again,' croons the woman, just in case anyone was thinking of doing exactly that. Against this, no dancing silhouettes; merely the credits picked out against an aerial shot of some unspecified rainforest.

Mercifully, the song is over quickly and hooray! here is Sean up a telephone pole. He is apparently in South America, and apparently in the process of saving a woman held prisoner in a shack from a bunch of desperadoes. He's not looking bad for fifty-two years old and the special effects hair is a huge improvement on the strange barnet seen in *Thunderball*.

But this is a training exercise and Bond has failed! He is summoned before a shouty new M, who orders that he be sent on a mission to get rid of 'the free radicals'. Yes, he's off to a health farm.

In other words, it is exactly the same cobblers as *Thunderball*, but this time around, they have made the health farm segment rather amusing. What helps enormously is a) Connery's comic performance and b) the early introduction of Barbara Carrera as the killer Fatima Blush. From the moment she struts on to the screen in a ludicrous vampish cape, you can see that she has hit exactly the right note; when not visibly devouring the scenery, she gnaws noisily at it.

And we swiftly see something else quite remarkable. In the twelve years since he last carried the Walther PPK, Connery has somehow turned into Roger Moore. Both the script and Connery's wry approach to it are as broad and humorous as any of Moore's outings. Indeed, if not more so. At one stage, Bond gets into a terrific gymnasium fight with a heavy. This rages on all over the health farm until both protagonists crash into a medical repository. In a moment of inspiration, Bond hurls a urine sample into the heavy's face. The heavy collapses. The urine sample was Bond's. The fact that the man has also been impaled on some surgical instruments is neither here nor there. The gag is a top one.

And Connery's self-deprecating facial expressions are a further bonus. It is here that we can see most clearly how he would always have preferred Bond to be: that is, a light-hearted Roger Moore figure. It works.

Indeed, in the spring of 1983, before either *Octopussy* or *Never* was released, both Connery and Moore repeatedly crossed the street to hose each other down with the warm treacle of praise. They met for dinner, then discussed posing for publicity shots together. When speaking of the competition, Moore said: 'I'm not going to get hot and bothered. The more the merrier, say I. Does Gielgud complain because Olivier is playing Hamlet at the same time?'[1] Well, yes, I expect he did – if it had ever been the case, he would probably have screamed blue murder.

But actually, in terms of interpretation, Moore and Connery were not in competition – for they had both seen that a super secret agent played without humour had the potential to be a colossal bore.

Back to the film. What doesn't work in *Never* – among many other things – is Edward Fox's M. Why won't he stop shouting? It is incredibly tiresome. Never mind, for here comes bearded, bow-tied Blofeld, with a

Persian cat. SPECTRE's secret base appears to be beneath a bank depository. Here, Max von Sydow's remarkably genial-looking criminal genius outlines the usual blithering blah about stealing nuclear warheads. But we are transfixed by his handling of the Persian cat, which is perfect. The cat sits on his lap, good as gold – no struggles, no cat-scratch bobbles on Blofeld's suit. Perhaps it was actually von Sydow's cat in real life. Or perhaps the creature was drugged.

Anyway, those bloody warheads are snaffled, as per, and Fatima disposes of the accomplice RAF pilot by throwing a snake into his car, thus panicking him into a crash. Fatima then returns to the wreckage, but only to retrieve her snake, which she wears around her neck like a scarf.

Now it is time for us to meet Largo (Brandauer) – a terrifically unusual Bond baddie in that he appears to be playing it for real. Largo is young, seemingly affable, yet psychopathically able to switch mood in the flicker of an eye. He is stepping out with leotard-clad aerobics fan Kim Basinger. Indeed, he is besotted, because he gives her an ornamental pendant so hideous that it can only be there for a future plot purpose.

And on to the Bahamas, quite familiar Connery territory, but not before Bond has an encounter with a radically different Q; Alec McCowen plays him as a mockney rebel complaining of cutbacks and glad of Bond's return with all its promise of 'gratuitous sex and violence'. It is all so very wrong, like Lady Macbeth played by Cilla Black. A radical reinterpretation is one thing but McClory appears to have ignored the fact that Q was a major, and most unlikely to carry on in this fashion.

Never mind, here is a bit of tiresome underwater nonsense with Fatima attaching some form of shark-attracting device to Bond and Bond having to swim for his life through the wreck of a boat. What makes it doubly irksome is the random oompah music that otherwise hugely talented composer Michael Legrand has decided should form the bulk of the score. It makes Bill Conti sound like Thomas Tallis. Again, it must have been a conscious effort to get away from the rich, stylised harmonics of John Barry; but all this music does is itch away at the back of your head until finally you are forced to leave the room.

Rather like its predecessor *Thunderball*, very little of the Bahamas stuff makes any narrative sense; hotel rooms are blown up, Bond meets a comedy embassy official played by the young rising comedian Rowan Atkinson. And the tone of the script is relentlessly arch and comic, which means that there is little time for us to enjoy the scenery. Broccoli always ensured that his audiences enjoyed the scenery.

Anyway, for some reason, the action now moves to the exquisitely naff south of France, where McClory appears to acknowledge the inherent vulgarity of casinos by filling his opulent gambling den with slot machines and video games. This is prior to Largo challenging Bond to a video game of his own devising called Domination, in which the loser is subjected to violent electric shocks. I seem to recall at the time that many critics were full of praise for this artful blend of special effects and up-to-the-minute suspense. It has dated hilariously, so much so that it might now have the same retro appeal as the primitive computer game *Hungry Horace*.

And it is also interesting that at a point when Eon were trying to crowbar Bond into a more realistic-looking world, McClory put the character straight back into a glossy cartoon. These onlookers in the casino – are they supposed to be real people? They might as well be *Blade Runner* androids for all the verisimilitude they give off. Similarly, the jet motorbike chase through the back streets of what might be Monte Carlo or Nice or any other of those weird rich towns is distracting but somehow abstract.

The same goes when the narrative shunts off to north Africa, where the whole thing seems to take on the flavour of Hergé's adventures of Tintin: there's a fortress, and turbanned natives on horses, looking shouty and cross and there chiefly for the purposes of racism, haggling over a bound Kim Basinger.

Now, to be clear: in her later career, Kim Basinger matured into a very fine actress. But here, in her early days, she appears to be little more than a gesticulating leotard. As we have seen before with the part of Domino, it doesn't help that the script makes her insipid from the start. But Basinger contrived to add a further layer of blandness to this. So in that scene when she is about to be carted off into white slavery, it is almost impossible to convey in words just how little one cares.

Similarly, the scene when Connery pretends to be her masseur and tricks her into blurting information while rubbing her down should have been amusingly sexy. Instead, you find your feet moving, seemingly of their own volition, towards the kitchen to make a cup of tea.

There are more comic-book thrills, which come chiefly in shots of the hijacked missiles zipping through the air above coastlines and over the ocean. We could watch these all day. Irritatingly, though, what goes up must come down and we must go through this *Thunderball* rigmarole once more of warheads hidden underwater. But all in all, this parallel-dimension Bond has been a fascinating exercise.

The point is this: without his much-loved familiar trappings – an M and a Q and a Moneypenny that we know, plus Maurice Binder's naked silhouettes, plus John Barry, plus the 'gunbarrel view' at the beginning – is Bond really Bond? Does it work if the formula is bent too far out of shape or if we don't hear those familiar musical leitmotifs?

On the evidence of *Never*, the answer is no. Although Connery is as authentic as one can get, nothing else in the film seems to hold that same conviction. The uncommonly straightforward approach of Klaus Maria Brandauer clashes confusingly with the howling camp of Barbara Carrera; while it is nice to see Max von Sydow as Blofeld, you wonder why he is addressing his fellow criminals while sitting on a throne in what appears to be a downmarket auction room.

And when it is not possible for us to take M seriously, then it's also a little difficult to get worked up about any threat that we are supposed to be facing. In other words, it seems as though director Kershner was not entirely clear whether he was making the ultimate Bond movie or the ultimate Bond movie spoof.

This uncertainty caught critics on the hop as well. It was clear that many of them were passionately pro-Connery and passionately anti-Moore, and obviously wanted Connery to win through. Much was therefore made of set-pieces like the tango scene, in which Bond uses a particularly showy dance to impart some crucial exposition to Domino, and the blowing up of Fatima Blush after she threatens to castrate Bond with her first bullet.

And naturally, many of the critics were in raptures about Connery himself – their Bond had come back to show that no one did it better than him. Certainly the amused confidence that he wears throughout the entire picture is very engaging. But then, much was true of any other picture that Connery had been involved with in the 1970s and 80s, from *The Man Who Would Be King* onward. And here he was, being 007 in a film that just wasn't a real 007 film.

The public were not quite so convinced as the critics and the film made less than half the money of its direct competitor *Octopussy*. This wouldn't discourage Kevin McClory from thinking of giving it another go in the 1990s. Actually, when 1997 came, there was an even more lethal competitor on the block in the form of an 'International Man of Mystery' called Austin Powers. But the fact of the matter is that all such films show that Bond – real Bond – is as much a matter of tone and attention to detail as of who plays the leading man. Perhaps this is why in 1983, Eon Productions almost replaced Roger Moore with American James Brolin.

CHAPTER EIGHTEEN **MOST DISARMING**

It has recently been argued by some modern historians that in terms of sheer, sweaty, five-minutes-to-midnight nuclear tension, the worst period was not in fact the Cuban missile crisis of 1962, but the autumn of 1983. Against the backdrop of an increasingly hardline-sounding US President, and a reactionary gerontocracy in the Kremlin, there was one false alarm in particular – one night in October 1983 when Soviet computers appeared to detect that the West had launched a pre-emptive nuclear strike – that brought us all within a whisker of Armageddon.

That incident, a result of Soviet satellites misinterpreting sunlight bouncing off high-altitude clouds, was kept firmly under wraps at the time. But it was clear to pretty much everyone in Western Europe during this period that nuclear tension was at its height.

In 1982, Soviet leader Leonid Brezhnev – who had made determined efforts to keep the arms race under control – died; he was replaced by the elderly and ailing KGB man Yuri Andropov. This was not a propitious time for dialogue. There were American air force bases throughout Britain and West Germany, intended to match Soviet military bases dotted across East Germany and Eastern Europe. In Britain, there was domestic controversy about the proposed siting of the new intermediate range Cruise and Pershing missiles.

In the meantime, President Reagan was upping the rhetorical ante, deliberately dubbing the Soviet Union 'the Evil Empire', knowing how much this would anger and upset the Politburo. Non-Republicans, and left-wingers over here, flinched at the language, which they felt had been filched from the 'Empire' of the simple-minded *Star Wars* films. They flinched further when he announced plans for a 'Strategic Defence Initiative' which would consist of satellites destroying Soviet missiles from space – a project that was immediately referred to as 'Star Wars'.

Margaret Thatcher, meanwhile, stood by the President shoulder to shoulder; it was an unusually close special relationship between Britain and the US, not matched until the advent of George W. Bush and Tony Blair.

For many, it was not a reassuring relationship. In other words, the people of Western Europe saw themselves as the first target in any potential war.

Such an idea had been seeping through pop culture for several years. In 1980, Kate Bush had a hit with 'Breathing', a ditty sung from the point of view of an as yet unborn baby as the first nuclear bombs start raining down on Britain. Later, we would have Nena's '99 Red Balloons', a catchy song about a nuclear disarmament protest that goes wrong when the ninety-nine balloons of the title are released into the sky and show up on radar as missiles, thus accidentally starting a full-scale nuclear exchange.

For those of us who lived in London at this time, every other car sported a CND bumper sticker. The Campaign for Nuclear Disarmament was enjoying a surge of support in the early 1980s under the leadership of Monsignor Bruce Kent and it staged successful demonstrations and marches. CND in turn had shown support to the women of Greenham Common, who were camping outside the base of that name in Berkshire in protest against the siting of Cruise missiles. In 1983, CND held its largest ever protest march – 200,000 people in Britain, 600,000 in Bonn, West Germany.

The imagery of nuclear destruction was everywhere. Newspapers such as the *Daily Mirror* published spreads detailing the most likely targets of the Russian bombs, and what the immediate effects on the cities targeted would be. Everywhere one looked, there were mushroom clouds – in magazines, on T-shirts, on mugs.

In 1983 BBC TV broadcast a hugely controversial drama called *Threads*, which depicted the horrific aftermath of a nuclear strike on Sheffield. Many to the right of the Conservative Party found such material deeply unhelpful in the struggle against Communism. Lady Olga Maitland, a Sunday newspaper gossip columnist, started Familes For Nuclear Defence, and was regularly howled down on television chat shows.

And against all this – the dark murmurings of MI5 dirty tricks against nuclear protestors, the murky urban rumours of nuclear freight trains that would travel through London on what is now the London Overground route in the dead of night, and the booming market in private domestic nuclear shelters – the Bond team were sitting down, knitting together a screenplay for a film called *Octopussy*, wondering if Roger Moore would agree to return and in the meantime screen-testing an American actor called James Brolin, best known for successful television series such as *Marcus Welby MD* and for films such as *Capricorn One* (1978) and *The Amityville Horror* (1979).

It is said in some quarters that Charles Dance – who had played a non-speaking thug in *For Your Eyes Only* – had also been up for consideration, but that he had blown his chances by saying something mildly disobliging about *Only* in an interview. What was more, Dance was ginger-haired. No one would have been insensitive enough to say this out loud, I am sure, but a ginger Bond?

At this stage, the production team had also clocked the young Irish actor Pierce Brosnan, who had been with his wife Cassandra Harris on the set of *For Your Eyes Only*. In 1983, Brosnan began his stint starring in the American TV crime comedy *Remington Steele* opposite Stephanie Zimbalist. He was still a little young to be considered for Bond but it was interesting that he was on the radar so quickly.

In any case, it was all academic because Roger had one of his games of backgammon with Cubby Broccoli – Broccoli once more vociferously complaining that Moore had had the brass nerve to ask for more money – and Moore ended up some $4 million richer. Just as well really, because the weird charm of *Octopussy* could only ever have worked with him at the helm.

What the producers did this time was twofold. First, they decided to acknowledge that sense of rising global nuclear anxiety; second, they had very obviously seen Steven Spielberg's 1981 smash hit *Raiders of the Lost Ark*, a determinedly nostalgic period adventure starring Harrison Ford as Indiana Jones – and were equally clearly determined to snaffle some of that film's winning elements.

On top of this, Broccoli and the team were determined to incorporate as many elements from their source material – two Ian Fleming short stories, 'Octopussy' and 'The Property of a Lady' – as they could. What this meant was a film about nuclear tension, an octopus, a Fabergé egg, and Bond being menaced by a tiger. An excellently varied shopping list, but what sort of writer would be ideal to put all of these elements together?

The first person that Broccoli and director John Glen got on to was the brilliant novelist George MacDonald Fraser, writer of the *Flashman* series (who sadly died in January 2008). Flashman, of course, is MacDonald Fraser's wildly funny, exciting and sometimes moving extrapolation of what happened to the famous Victorian school bully after he left Rugby. The books threw the cowardly yet somehow rather loveable 'Flashy' into terrifying snakepit situations, some quite literally, as he found himself up against various emirs, warlords and insane warrior queens, all over the world from Afghanistan to Madagascar. Very often, these would be real-life historical figures. But the cliff-hangers were outlandish.

'Flashy' would find himself facing death by cobra, by molten lead, by flaying, by keel-hauling. But after each sweaty escape, there would be the chance of sex with whichever flashing-eyed temptress was sharing that particular narrative. If any man understood about the triple attractions of jeopardy, sex and comedy in a narrative, MacDonald Fraser was the man.

In his autobiography, MacDonald Fraser modestly suggested that he had been rather pressed upon Broccoli by an MGM executive. But this notoriously plain-speaking writer had nothing but kind words for the entire Eon family:

> There may have been nicer people in Hollywood than Albert 'Cubby' Broccoli but I never met them. As his nickname implies, he was plump and cuddly and gentle; he was also generous and considerate, and his staff and colleagues regarded him with an affection which I suspect was unique towards a movie tycoon. He had a modesty and an innocence and an air of vulnerability which seemed to inspire a protective feeling in those around him. They showed him a respect that had nothing to do with fear of a man who controlled the most successful series of films in the history of cinema; it was simply that they liked him.[1]

After some initial consultative meetings in Los Angeles, Macdonald Fraser got to work and was pleased to note that, against his expectations, much of his material was retained. It is one hell of a complex plot though, so here is the thing in the plainest possible nutshell. If I get things wrong, well, you can't entirely blame me. I had to see the film about six times before it really sank in.

After a forgettable pre-credits sequence (involving a Cuban airfield and Bond getting away in a foldaway plane), the thing begins properly in the British embassy in West Germany where, during a grand reception, the windows crash open – and a circus clown staggers through, collapsing dead on the marble floor. He has been stabbed. Out of his hand rolls an exquisite – and priceless – Fabergé egg. The clown was agent 009.

Such an invaluable ornament could only have been spirited from the secure vaults of the Kremlin; but it's a fake. And Bond is put on the trail of the real egg up for auction at Sotheby's. This leads him, through various twists and turns, to a pursed-lipped gentleman called Kamal Khan (Louis Jourdan); and a beautiful international jewel smuggler called Octopussy (a returning Maud Adams) who, while not running a crack squad of leotard-clad fighting women, also runs a travelling circus, the means through which she carries out her smuggling operations.

Octopussy and Bond apparently have history; her father was a traitor and Bond gave him the chance to salve his dishonour by taking his own life. Octopussy is grateful. But she also has dealings with the villainous Kamal Khan. Khan, in turn, is in cahoots with a deranged rogue Russian general called Orlov (Steven Berkoff), who has been pilfering Kremlin treasures such as the Fabergé eggs in order to finance a particularly psychopathic scheme. Through a dizzying chain of circumstances, Orlov plots to smuggle a nuclear bomb into Octopussy's circus on the occasion that she performs at an American air force base in West Germany.

Orlov's idea is that the bomb will go off and the general public will think the explosion was caused accidentally by the Americans. The resulting outcry will force NATO into unilateral nuclear disarmament; and then the way will be clear for the Soviet Union to pounce . . .

What sounds grindingly complex on paper actually makes one of the most diverting and richly entertaining of all the Bond films. And interestingly, it is made quite plain from the outset that Berkoff's Russian general is shunned by the Politburo as a crazy and dangerous loon.

That Politburo is rather flattered by production designer Peter Lamont, who has given these old warhorses a hi-tech conference chamber, with laser-illuminated maps and a revolving dais. Quite a distance from the real-life makeshift conference table that was in fact to be found at Yuri Andropov's hospital bedside for much of that time.

In this early scene, we are reintroduced to our old friend General Gogol (Walter Gotell) who, very surprisingly for a Bond movie, sets out what he believes to be the Soviet military strategy; that is, to maintain defence while actively pursuing multilateral disarmament. Steven Berkoff's Orlov is having none of it; in a performance that must win some form of Bond award for scenery guzzling, he dims the lights and outlines his belief, via laser map, that with a swift invasion, Western Europe would be theirs, and that NATO would be too 'decadent' to respond with a nuclear strike.

Gogol — and the Brezhnev lookalike who is clearly supposed to be General Secretary — react with rage and horror to the very suggestion. Why, it would be madness! Thus we the audience are left in no doubt that when Orlov sets his mad plan into gear, he is acting without the approval of a single living soul in the Kremlin.

All this makes it sound rather heavy going. But in fact, structurally and in terms of tone, this is one of the lightest and most assured Bonds of the lot. What works best is the clever meshing of Cold War fear and colourful, shamelessly old-fashioned derring-do in India.

The set-up, at the start, is pleasingly *Avengers*esque: the 009 clown fleeing through some woods in terror, pursued by twin trick knife-throwers. And after some to-ing and fro-ing in London – Miss Moneypenny now has a new, younger assistant called Penelope Smallbone (Michaela Clavell, daughter of novelist James) who is *very* obviously there to take over should Lois Maxwell decide at last to call it a day – and some sleight-of-hand auction comedy, where Bond substitutes the fake Fabergé egg for the real one, it's off to India, and some of the loveliest location work in the series.

Some critics, Simon Winder among them, have claimed that out of all the racist James Bond films, this one is especially bad. Attention is drawn to the put-put chase through the streets of Udaipur; at one point, as a diversionary tactic, Bond takes all the money from his pockets and throws it up in the air into the bustling crowds, with a cry of 'Rupees!' The crowd go mad, thus detaining the pursuing villains. Is this intrinsically racist? There was, after all, a very similar scene in a recent *Doctor Who*, but this time the money-grabbing crowd were in a London street. So no. Also up for question are the marketplace shots involving snake-charmers, sword-swallowers, fire-walkers and a comedy fakir with a bed of nails. Well . . . again, is this very much worse than Austin Powers's Mike Myers depicting Carnaby Street as being full of Beefeaters?

All right. Less happily, we have a moment where Bond takes his backgammon winnings from Khan and hands the wads of cash to the Delhi equivalent of M with the line: 'That should keep you in curry for a while.' Clearly it wasn't meant as racist but it has the effect of making one jump up and run from the room with embarrassment.

However, it was by no means the worst offender in this period of cinema. Ladies and gentlemen of the jury, I draw your attention back to the aforementioned *Raiders of the Lost Ark*. Now clearly one is not supposed to take this narrative entirely seriously; the Nazi villains, for instance, are as camp as pink poodles. Yet one cannot help noticing the role assigned to Arabs in this film, and that is largely as jabbering slaves either of Germans or indeed Indiana Jones himself.

In one desert scene, at the site of a dig, Jones is more imperious than dear old Bond ever was, peremptorily whistling to some Arab workers and instructing them to shovel sand. In the context of this story, Bedouins are there chiefly to be untrustworthy, greedy, thick and servile.

I also draw your attention to 1984's *Indiana Jones and the Temple of Doom* – set in India. Here, in a remarkably tasteless film, we have starving Indian peasant villagers, a cruel boy maharajah who serves his guests snakes and sheep's eyes (funny foreign food, eh?) and child slavery. Anyone in a turban is a bug-eyed bad guy. And in the thrall of a barbaric death cult. Next to all this, *Octopussy* looks like *Midnight's Children*.

One final word of defence: *Octopussy*'s portrayal of India at least did not involve English actors 'browning up' – unlike David Lean's 1984 adaptation of E.M. Forster's *A Passage to India*, in which the actor Alec Guinness was required to do exactly that; for according to David Lean, 'Hindus could not act.' It is a pity we cannot now ask George MacDonald Fraser about the race issue, for his *Flashman* novels often had similar charges levelled at them, which he would dismiss impatiently.

Bond encounters Kamal Khan, who as we have seen is cheating at backgammon with some loaded dice; Bond spots this and out-diddles him. Khan's turbaned heavyweight sidekick furiously crushes the dice in his fist. Later, Bond gets entangled in a romantic assignation with a beautiful blonde with a most unusual tentacular tattoo. 'What's that?' asks Bond. 'That's my little octopussy,' comes the pertly delivered reply. As Eric Morecambe used to say: 'There's no answer to that.' Said blonde then makes a moonlit flit by using her sari to drop from Bond's balcony.

All of which seems to lead us to Octopussy's island, and also to the film's stickiest wicket, for this was the period when the series came under the fiercest scrutiny from the feminist movement. Here is what happens on the island: feverishly attractive women bathe nude in ornamental ponds, to the accompaniment of much tinkling laughter and, with the presence of Roger Moore, what the feminists used to describe as 'the male gaze'. And as mentioned, when Octopussy's girls are not bathing and laughing, they are dressed in skin-tight leotards, the better to do their mistress's bidding. One of them is apparently called 'Gwendolin'.

Those of us who grew up as 'right-on' teenagers in the 1980s will still find part of this a little flinch-worthy – chiefly, a parade of flesh intended for the drooling delectation of middle-aged men. What makes it very slightly worse is the film's implied defence that the women of Octopussy's gang are somehow 'empowered'. They are just *so* not. Yes, I know, they fight with Khan's thugs at the end, but the flavour of the fight is comic; all acrobatic leaps and feigned belly dancing and high-kicks.

This was at the dawn of what became known as the 'political correctness' movement on American campuses. In Britain, militant feminism was often associated with left-wing urban councils, which provided funding for organised groups. And it was films such as *Octopussy* that came under the beady eye of the sisters.

Thus Roger Moore on those very sequences: 'I suppose today we'd say it's sexist,' he said, 'but part of Bond was to have young attractive people sitting around a swimming pool. The way to get a publicity picture into the newspapers was to have a pretty girl.' He added: 'I had to carry the mantle of being irresistible to the opposite sex. A rotten job but someone's got to do it.'[2]

And the film did have one rather brilliant element that could simultaneously snatch the wind from furious feminist sails while helping it to become one of the most popular entries among older women: that is, the figure of Octopussy herself, as portrayed by Maud Adams, returning after the misogynist debacle of 1974's *The Man with the Golden Gun*.

Octopussy's name aside (as P.G. Wodehouse's Wooster once observed, 'there's some raw work pulled at the font'), this leading-lady role is unusually prominent and proactive for a Bond film. Octopussy is an intriguing prospect; as a smuggler, she should strictly be termed a criminal but there is something about her that suggests the more ambiguous term 'outlaw'. When we first meet her, she appears to be fully in cahoots with the villainous Kamal Khan; but her first meeting with Bond changes all that. And in casting terms, it makes perfect sense to have fifty-five-year-old Moore playing opposite a slightly more mature woman. It's not quite grand sizzling passion but it is rather pleasing romance. 'I was delighted that Maud was back with us after *Golden Gun*,' said Roger. 'She has a very good sense of humour.'

It seems that Faye Dunaway had originally been up for the role. In 1982, she told the *Sunday Express*: 'I'd love to do the film. I've always admired the expertise of the Bonds. And I'd love to work with Roger.'[3]

As it happened, though, Maud Adams was just the ticket. And, in all senses, this is one of the most romantic Bond films of the lot.

So much is signalled from the opening title song. Perhaps wisely avoiding having some chanteuse shriek the word 'Octopussy!' at top volume, John Barry and lyricist Tim Rice instead concocted a rather sweet, smoky slow number called 'All Time High' sung by Rita Coolidge and which, by the standards of most Bond songs, was positively demure. The main theme from this song was then used throughout the film as the chief romantic leitmotif, all swirling strings. In 1998, Jarvis Cocker recorded a rather breathier cover version of the same song.

Even the film's 'snakepit situations' seemed romantic in the sense that they were so curiously anachronistic. In one scene, Bond manages to escape from the mountain palace of Kamal Khan – but finds himself being used as human safari quarry through a jungle teeming with an extraordinary amount of biodiversity. In his bid to outrun the elephants and the rifles, Bond first accidentally runs into a huge web of tarantulas. With a curiously unBondlike exclamation of 'E-urgh!' and a bit of frantic safari-suit brushing, he continues on his way.

Next up is a sudden brush with a prowling tiger. 'Sit!' he commands, hand held high, in a reference to cult dog-handler Barbara Woodhouse. The cat does so. Thence a bit more running, a dive into the undergrowth, and a meeting with a huge cobra. 'Hiss off,' Bond tells it. The villains grow closer and, spotting some vines in the trees, Bond sees an opportunity. Seconds later, we hear a Tarzan yodel as the safari-suited figure swings through the branches before comically plunging into a river. This leads to Bond being covered with leeches, which have to be removed by means of a cigarette lighter. Finally, as he wades through waist-high water, an alligator gives chase.

In other words, this blend of imperialist-era peril and light wisecracking is quite a distance from the hard-edged espionage of *For Your Eyes Only* and quite a bit closer to the retro hokum of *Raiders of the Lost Ark*, the opening sequence of which featured a jungle chase, tarantulas and blow-pipes.

The sense of nostalgia is reinforced in the film's final quarter, as Octopussy's circus – travelling by means of thunderingly theatrical steam engine – heads through East Germany towards that American base in West Germany. The steam train is yet another deliberate throwback, which enables Bond not only to hang on to the side of it, but also to have a thoroughly traditional fight with a heavy on the top of it.

A props van on the train carries its deadliest secret; hidden inside the cannon used by the Human Cannonball is not a stash of smuggled jewellery, as Octopussy supposes, but a ticking nuclear device. Bond realises this only after he has disguised himself in a gorilla suit, yet another trope that harks back to the 1920s.

But towards the end, this sense of cosy nostalgic fun is replaced by something more remarkable: a contemporary James Bond climax of real, genuine, sustained, nail-biting suspense. The device is steadily counting down and must be defused. But Bond has been hurled off the steam train before he has been able to give warning. Remember, this was before mobile phones had been introduced. Somehow he not only has to find a way to that air force base many miles away, but also then find a way into that base – and all within the space of a few minutes.

By this stage, we in the audience have been fully apprised of Steven Berkoff's scheme and now it suddenly seems to have a ghastly plausibility about it. Previous countdowns to doom in *You Only Live Twice* or *Diamonds Are Forever* have always been rather fantastical and abstract. This one, however, with its resulting political consequences, is uncomfortably easy to envisage.

Bond manages to steal a car and thunders down the autobahns. But that nuclear clock is ticking away – just minutes to go – and Octopussy's circus, performed for the American servicemen and their families, is in full swing. Bond smashes through the air force entrance barrier and before the guards can catch up with him, has ducked into a clown's caravan. The stage is thus set for what I think is one of the very finest Bond denouements.

Bond is dressed as a clown, complete with make-up, silly costume, the lot. And so he makes it into the circus ring. But his attempts to get near the cannon are thwarted by other clowns, who insist on throwing him around in slapstick fashion. Less than a minute to go! Bond desperately tries to appeal to a general in the audience; the general, however, thinks that this is merely ingenious clown comedy. By this stage, the cinema audience is raking the arm-rests with their fingernails.

Bond tells the general where they all stand – there's a nuclear bomb and he has to defuse it. But still they won't believe him! Just as a desperate Bond is being pulled away by guards, an incredulous Octopussy takes aim at the cannon, breaks it open – and the bomb is disclosed. Fourteen seconds to go! Hurry, hurry! At least four seconds are wasted as everyone simply stands there gawping with horror. Happily, Bond has had experience of this sort of thing and removes the detonator with one second to spare.

As a *coup de grâce*, the Human Cannonball emerges crossly from his tube to ask why he hasn't been fired. It is a bravura sequence, curiously under-rated today; and it is largely down to the sparky and comic imagination of George MacDonald Fraser, though he in turn acknowledged Michael G. Wilson as an 'inspired ideas man'. As MacDonald Fraser wrote in his autobiography:

> It was a tough, exhausting process, but from the writer's point of view it had immense advantages all too rare in the film world: you knew it was going to get made, that no expense would be spared, that you would have no problem about money, hotels, transport or expenses, all of which were cut and dried, that the whole operation would be managed with a professionalism second to none, that it would be a happy ship (Roger Moore gleefully crying 'Commiserations!' when I was introduced as the writer), and that it was simply the most important thing in Hollywood.[4]

MacDonald Fraser was also aware that he was pushing things a little in Bond terms, for Broccoli was vehemently insistent that nothing should compromise the dignity of the leading man.

> I may have been imagining that Cubby had misgivings about me. Possibly he was wary of writers, unpredictable creatures who might not treat 007 with the deference Cubby thought he deserved. I may have seemed unduly casual and flippant, as when I had Bond assuming the costume of a circus clown, and absolutely horrifying Cubby by later proposing an even more bizarre disguise for his hero; I can still hear his cry of outraged disbelief: 'You want to put Bond in a gorilla suit?'[5]

Some reports say that Moore himself was initially unsure about the clown stuff, but that he soon saw his way into it. 'You don't argue, you just get on with it,' he said in a later interview. 'James Stewart had been a clown and you couldn't have a better role model.' He added ruefully: 'I could have had a nicer shade of lipstick.'[6]

There were other nice MacDonald Fraser touches, including the lethal and macabre weapons utilised by Khan's men: stainless steel razor-edged yo-yos. During the scene when Bond's tennis-playing ally Veejay is held by the thugs, while one above prepares this device, you could hear the audience in the cinema gasping. It was a device that would have worked well within a *Flashman* novel. Indeed, most of the elements, from Khan to Octopussy, would have been equally at home within one of those books.

One of the few disappointments is Louis Jourdan; clearly, with Steven Berkoff's Orlov breaking bits off the scenery and chewing them with his mouth open, it was obvious that his villainy would have to be silkier and more understated. However, veteran Jourdan went a little too far in this, and his character seems less a wicked Afghan prince, more a petulant French hairdresser trying to persuade Madam into having a perm.

A pity, because even though Jourdan was best known for roles in light entertainments such as *Gigi* (1958), he was capable of exuding menace, and he did so rather successfully as the eponymous Count in the BBC's 1977 adaptation of *Dracula*. The problem here is that we never quite believe he is capable of conniving in the nuclear obliteration of thousands of innocent people.

There is one nice moment, and it comes in one of those characteristic post-climax climaxes that, bafflingly, the Bond movies still had to have. Nuclear horror averted, and with foaming Orlov shot dead on the railway track on the orders of our dear old friend General Gogol, Bond has to skedaddle back to India to rescue a kidnapped Octopussy from Khan's clutches. As the Octopussy girls raid Khan's palace, Bond finds that Khan has hot-footed it to his private jet, with his henchman and Octopussy over the henchman's shoulder. It is left to Bond to catch up with the taxiing plane, then clutch on to its roof as it takes to the air.

Jourdan, at last, notices that Bond is outside. 'Get out there and deal with him,' he snaps to Gobinda as Gobinda stares back at him with horror. It got a good laugh in cinemas. After a nicely filmed aerial fight – having written it, MacDonald Fraser was aghast to discover that stuntmen were going to fly thousands of feet up in order to do it for real, rather than mocking it up in the studio – Khan is killed in his plummeting plane, while Bond and Octopussy manage to jump out at exactly the right moment.

Roger Moore, however, was very much in favour of Jourdan, if only because he was such an affable presence on set. 'We played tennis,' Roger said in an interview. 'And he loved to serve herring. Pickled herring. He loved to be in charge of catering.' So there we are. Jourdan did at least have one fan.

On the basis of purely anecdotal evidence, this is a Bond film that turned out to be extremely popular with women (that, and 1987's *The Living Daylights*, as we shall be finding out before long). Why is this so? I think it is not merely that a mature Bond has a slightly more mature lady friend, with an interestingly fleshed-out relationship; it is that the whole thing offers a form of escapism which seems more human and is largely free of clanking hardware. There are no supercars, and the gadgets are forgettable.

Apart from one, which caused winces of distress among die-hard fans: and that was the crocodile. Bond must get to Octopussy's island undetected – and happily Q has a one-person submersible shaped like a crocodile, the jaws of which lift up to allow the driver to see out. All right, so we know that Ian Fleming would not have considered such a thing: but lighten up. It's a good visual gag, the sort of thing that only Roger Moore, among all the Bonds, seemed to be able to pull off completely. And in any case, in this world of timeless jungle threats and steam train peril, who needs futuristic gizmos?

The box office was extremely healthy – the film hauled in $183,700,000 worldwide. But first reviews in 1983 were mixed. Some American critics were a little more, shall we say, squeamish about the title than anyone might have expected. 'I discussed it on a breakfast show over there,' recalled Moore. 'I said, "What's wrong with a little pussy?" *Grande scandale.*'[7]

Novelist Peter Ackroyd, writing for *The Spectator*, thought he detected a strong political undercurrent, as well as naked racism: 'Victorian values have been brought bang up to date as our most famous secret agent cuts a swathe through various brown people,' he said. 'The whole enterprise has finally found its spiritual home in Mrs Thatcher's Britain . . . if we are moving into the era of rule by the lower middle classes, in these films we have a bright image of the fantasies of that class.' Snobbery of this sort – identifying Thatcher with the net-curtain classes, and finding both 'ghastly' – was surprisingly common in this era. Ackroyd continued waspishly: 'Roger Moore has grown old in our service. Perhaps the film should have been called "Octogenarian".'

Elsewhere, the *New Musical Express* offered up the sort of review that the 1980s specialised in: 'The Bond films have degenerated into racist, sexist bombast in which a dummy western civilisation is regularly rescued by a dummy Bond.' Bless them! Doesn't that take you right back to a donkey-jacketed era of polytechnics and protests? Talking of which, here is the view of the *Morning Star*: 'Blatantly jingoistic and anti-Soviet.' But the film isn't. It *so* isn't!

There was a more insidious critical danger, and that was of the entire Bond set-up – the dinner suits, the globe-trotting, the martinis – being seen as slightly stale, repetitious and naff. Who those days apart from snail-trail-suited oil sheikhs went to casinos? And with the coming of the age of the sophisticated wine bar – and concomitant spreading knowledge about different grapes and styles – whoever drank cocktails? No matter that a 1983 TV special on *21 Years of Bond* featured enthusiastic filmed contributions from the likes of President Reagan; there was an opposite view that Bond was starting to look like a hero out of his time, especially to an upcoming younger generation reared on Space Invaders and Atari consoles.

The future was looking computerised. Among 1982's releases had been the dazzling Disney sci-fi spectacle *Tron*, about a chap trapped in a computer game. If anything, it was slightly ahead of its time. But suddenly the world was filling with the imagery of *Hungry Horace*, *Donkey Kong*, and the curiously hypnotic, bleak musical style of electro-pop. Once Bond had led the way in terms of music, fashion, and youthful attitude. Now he was beginning to look middle-aged.

And in the intervening years, the reputation of *Octopussy* has stayed low among Bond devotees, doomed to be seen as one of the misfires. But it really doesn't deserve to be treated like this. Compare it, for instance, with another blockbuster entry of 1983: *Return of the Jedi*. For all those who have shuddered with disdain at Bond's mechanical crocodile, what do you say to teddy-bear aliens the Ewoks, who some cynics might suppose had been created with more than half an eye on subsequent toy sales?

There was another *Star Trek* film that year too, *The Search for Spock*, which did what it said on the poster and not a great deal else. And of course as we have seen, autumn 1983 brought the Connery effort *Never Say Never Again*. Of all these films, the one that you might be least inclined to revisit, with its Fabergé eggs and foaming Russians, is actually by far and away the most enjoyable.

Difficult thing to shake off, though, the charge of naffness. No matter what screenplay fireworks you set off, no matter how brilliant the acting and needle-sharp the directing, if a character is suddenly deemed to be unfashionable, the effect is a box-office slow death.

And that, sadly, appeared to be the background to Roger Moore's final hurrah in the role in 1985. Cruel thing, fashion. Especially when it can cause one, a generation later, to sit back with chuckling admiration as opposed to open-mouthed horror.

CHAPTER NINETEEN MICROCHIPS WITH EVERYTHING

In Britain in 1985, one of the most popular shows on television was a satirical comedy called *Spitting Image*, in which hideous latex caricatures of famous people – politicians, pop stars and actors – would be used in sharply written sketches. It is acknowledged by one of its targets – the former Liberal leader David Steel – to have had the most lethal effect. He said that the show's depiction of him as a tiny puppet sitting in the top pocket of Alliance colleague David Owen's jacket became the chief image that the voting public held of him – a pipsqueak in another man's pocket.

Another of the show's regular caricatures was of Roger Moore. In one sketch, this immensely unflattering wrinkled puppet was featured in an audition, with an off-screen director calling upon puppet Roger to demonstrate a range of emotions. The puppet Moore did so by raising one eyebrow, then the other eyebrow, then both eyebrows simultaneously. And this became the central joke about Moore (even though it was one that he had made quite happily himself some years back): that the only acting he ever did was with his eyebrows.

All terrifically unfair. Any bloody fool can play tragedy; it takes a special knack to pull off light comedy successfully. Happily, for *A View to a Kill*, Broccoli and the team were happy to indulge Roger's eyebrows to the hilt in an almost self-consciously celebratory film that also tried to adjust itself to a fast-changing world.

For this was to be Moore's final go in the tuxedo. One always imagines that the passing of a 007 is akin to the death of King Arthur or some other mighty mythic figure, accompanied by fierce storms, keening and strange portents. Mr Albert R. Broccoli was on hand to deliver some portents to Roger in 1984.

'I said, "You realise, Roger, we're going to have to make a change,"' said Broccoli. '"I think you probably understand that. You've had a great run, but I think now we have to call it a day. I want this to be a businesslike arrangement. It would be better if it looked like your decision rather than ours. If you want to say, officially now, that you're not going to make any more Bonds, I'll happily go along with that." '[1]

Well, of course Roger knew. Every time the script called upon him to sprint up a staircase in the mid-1980s, he would have known. So to see him out, the producers gave him a familiar scenario of insane super-villain, but this time with a zeitgeisty microchipped twist.

The computer revolution was in its infancy in 1985. In offices, files still tended to be kept on paper, and stored in special filing cabinets. Imagine that now! Home computers were becoming more common but their range of uses was limited: namely, for games with primitive music and huge blocks of primary colours.

But in Britain, this dawning age of the microprocessor was a synecdoche for what seemed to be the condition of the nation – a nation moving gingerly into a post-industrial age. The previous year, the miners' union, led by Arthur Scargill, launched its last defensive battle against the Conservatives; a strike aimed at stopping closure plans. But Mrs Thatcher, who had seen where a miners' strike had taken the country in 1972, was prepared this time. Under the aegis of Coal Board chairman Sir Ian MacGregor, coal stocks had been secretly built up over the preceding months. This time the government was ready for what Mrs Thatcher described, for some unforgivably, as 'the enemy within'.

By spring 1985, after much violence, economic hardship and rancour on both sides, the miners' strike was broken. And this was symbolic of the wider dissolution of Britain's old industry.

In the wider world, there had been other changes. After the peak of anxiety reached in 1983, relations between America and Russia perceptibly improved. It is occasionally written that President Reagan had been deeply distressed by an American TV movie depicting the consequences of nuclear war entitled *The Day After* (1983). This does not ring especially true.

What was significant, however, was that within Russia, Yuri Andropov died in 1984, scarcely two years into his premiership. He was succeeded by the equally old and ill Konstantin Chernenko. In 1985, Chernenko died. The man who followed changed the geopolitical landscape.

As a junior Kremlin man, he had already been noticed by British diplomats as an unusually sharp and open figure, markedly lacking the fearful insularity to be found in the generation above him, formed after Hitler's invasion of Russia in 1941. This younger man came armed with different experience. And so it was that Mikhail Gorbachev became General Secretary in 1985.

It was Mrs Thatcher – with all her visceral loathing of Communism – who apparently was the first to see that Gorbachev was a man to do business with and a man under whom reform of the Soviet system might be a possibility. During talks, his manner was bright, questioning, and he kept careful notes. Thatcher began singing the praises of Gorbachev to Reagan. And so it was that the temperature of international relations became, from that moment, very much more comfortable. For the first time in a generation, there looked like there might be a serious prospect of the Cold War thawing for ever.

The cultural landscape that formed the backdrop to the new Bond was one of a colourful, ritzy nature. After several years of austerity and gloom, both music and fashion appeared to be becoming bright and exuberant again. From gaudy make-up to the insane puffball skirts, to new bands such as Frankie Goes to Hollywood and the Pet Shop Boys, to a minxish new American singer with a reedy voice called Madonna, to shouty 'alternative' comedy becoming mainstream, to the popularity of vulgar and opulent American TV serials *Dallas* and *Dynasty*, there was a new confidence and assertiveness in the air.

And thus it was announced to the world's showbiz correspondents that *A View to a Kill* would be Moore's final outing in the role. It was delicately suggested that he was knocking on (although if I look in such good nick at fifty-seven, I shall be jolly pleased). The title was drawn from the Fleming short story 'From a View to a Kill', but the storyline itself was completely new (just as well, for the original concerned little more than a tiny Soviet spying post hidden beneath the floor of a French forest).

Unlike its two cinematic predecessors, *Kill* was almost comically straightforward. Villainous Max Zorin (Christopher Walken), the psychopathic result of a Nazi eugenics programme, is also a microchip genius. And his plan is to corner the world market by flooding Silicon Valley in California and wiping out his competitors. But how will he trigger such a flood? By detonating an enormous underground explosion on the San Andreas fault, obviously.

There: simplicity itself, no? The original idea had apparently been to have Zorin pull Halley's Comet off course to wreak similar havoc but this was clearly felt to be a little too similar to *Moonraker*. Halley's Comet was a hot topic in 1985; it was due to pass by the Earth in 1986 and newspapers made much of various doomsday predictions, which were reminiscent of similar comet-as-harbinger superstitions of the Middle Ages.

But for Bond purposes, the comet would date the film too quickly. Once more up for scripting duties was the pairing of Michael G. Wilson and Richard Maibaum. And after the Asian adventures of *Octopussy* and the Mediterranean setting of *For Your Eyes Only*, it was decided to return to the United States for the bulk of the locations, with a quick drop-off in Paris.

And they assembled a rather wonderful cast. Although if feverish reports were to be believed, it could have been a shade more outlandish if David Bowie had agreed to take the role of Zorin. Also apparently approached was Sting, tantric lead singer of The Police. But Christopher Walken was by far the best of these options. Having won an Oscar for *The Deer Hunter*, he brought an amusingly perverse presence to *Kill*; the sort of amusing perversity, indeed, that he seems to have been purveying ever since.

He was teamed up with the statuesque model/pop star/gay icon Grace Jones. At this stage, she was best known for the album *Slave to the Rhythm* and, in Britain, for behaving badly on a chat show when she hit the host, a helpless nellie called Russell Harty, for not paying enough attention to her. Jones was to play the assassin May Day.

On the side of the angels was Patrick Macnee, who had of course played the absurdly insouciant Steed in *The Avengers*. Here he was racecourse expert Sir Godfrey Tibbet, drafted in to pose as Bond's batman when the pair investigate Zorin's winning thoroughbreds. And the chief Bond girl role was essayed by Tanya Roberts, who had previously portrayed one of the later Charlie's Angels in the TV detective series of that name. Here she was geologist (!) Stacey Sutton, under pressure from Zorin to sell her late father's oil company to him, a pleasingly antique scenario (swap oil company for gold mine) that stretches right back to the dawn of cinema itself.

According to Lois Maxwell, Tanya Roberts eccentrically insisted on having an entire crate filled with shampoo and beauty products sent over from California to Pinewood, as though, Maxwell said, Britain was in the dark ages.[2] Actually, Roberts sounds a thoroughly sensible girl to me. Always best to be on the safe side.

In terms of tone, after all the insistence on getting back to basics and back to reality, third-time director John Glen was clearly keen on the notion of allowing things to become frothier again. Hence the pre-credits sequence where Bond in Siberia is recovering a microchip from the body of agent 003 and is chased through the snow by Russian military. After he kiboshes a snow-ski, Bond improvises with the device and snowboards down a slope to his waiting submarine to the tune of 'California Girls'. It is absurd and not even tremendously exciting, but I still seem to recall it getting a huge laugh at the Odeon Leicester Square, where I was watching the film with two mates from our school sixth form.

Is it my imagination or is there a new hint of political correctness in Maurice Binder's cheerfully insane opening titles? For amid all the dancing women, caked with glow-in-the-dark make-up and pretending to be skiing, there are also random male silhouettes. Was this some form of concession to feminist feeling? Feminist feeling – or 'awareness', as we sometimes used to say – was reaching a widespread peak in 1985.

A good example of the flavour of the times: this was at the same period in Britain when the phenomenally popular comedian Benny Hill was becoming an embarrassment to Thames Television, which made his show.

The problem for his critics was that even though Hill was still getting high ratings, and indeed was very popular in America, his show featured the central joke of unattractive middle-aged men pursuing nubile under-dressed young women, a collective of whom went under the name 'Hill's Angels'. In other words, it was regarded in smarter circles and among young people as sexism of the most primitive and irredeemable sort. Often by people who never even watched the show. In the end, it was this smarter opinion, as opposed to a dearth of viewers, that saw Thames pull the plug on Benny Hill, thus ending his career. Poor old Hill, who died in 1992, never showed any sign of understanding of how it had happened.

Bond was very much in danger of falling victim to the same kind of smart opinion, both in Britain and the US. By this time, the phrase 'Bond girl' was emphatically not a term of approval; it was a put-down, a sneering insult, a badge of shame. There was nothing remotely clever or praiseworthy about being filmed in a bikini by the side of a swimming pool. That was a job for a vacuous airhead, not a modern woman.

In this modern age of lads' mags, it now seems odd to think back to a time when no self-respecting girl would ever strike poses semi-naked. And in Bond terms, it is funny how things swung back in subsequent years. In 2002, the Oscar-winning actress Halle Berry eagerly signed up to play opposite Pierce Brosnan, sporting a tangerine bikini in *Die Another Day*; the notion of her character Jinx rising from the sea in homage to Ursula Andress struck the actress as being a major honour, as opposed to a sexist outrage. 'I don't think any woman would complain about being called a Bond Babe,' she said. 'Especially as you age in life, the more you get called a babe the better.'[3] Had she ventured this view in 1985, she would have been chased down the street by a chanting mob of militant feminists.

So anyway, in *Kill*, things were a little less relaxed before they invented post-feminism so out went the semi-traditional poolside scene. To make up for it, though, Zorin's workforce appears to be composed chiefly of girls in tight jodhpurs, a slightly classier and more fetishistic form of sexism, made popular by the bonkbuster author Jilly Cooper.

In an echo of the novel *Moonraker*, MI5 gets on to Zorin's trail not merely by means of the stolen microchip, but also because of the scent of cheating – there is the mystery of how his racehorses just keep winning. So it's off to Royal Ascot for M, Moneypenny, Bond and Q. How ineffably sweet that the secret service should have corporate jollies like everyone else! Zorin's horse wins, then takes fright. May Day is on hand to calm the beast. Less the Horse Whisperer than the Horse Shouter. From this scene onward, you can see that Grace Jones has this role to a tee, even more so than Barbara Carrera. From start to finish, her gloweringly mad menace and yelpingly camp body language completely holds the screen.

So it's off to France – Paris, first, remarkably making its first appearance in a Bond film since the back-street scene of *Thunderball*. Bond is here to meet a man called Monsieur Aubergine. Really? Could I have heard wrongly? No. He really is called Aubergine. This reminds me of a very fine joke about lazy scriptwriting in the film comedy *Top Secret* (1984), where members of the French Resistance are variously named 'Croissant', 'Montage' and 'Déjà Vu'.

Anyway, Aubergine and Bond meet in a restaurant in the Eiffel Tower, where the windows are darkened for a curious entertainment involving a young woman on stage whistling a sweet John Barry composition while the air fills with fake fluttering butterflies on wires. (Why, incidentally, would one go all the way to the top of the Eiffel Tower for a meal only to have the magnificent view completely obscured by window blinds?) We can see that this scene is not going to end happily for tell-tale tit Monsieur Aubergine; and indeed it doesn't – a fake butterfly is lashed at his face and he is poisoned by a steel hook on its underside.

Bond sets off after the shadowy assassin; it is none other than Grace Jones, who in a wonderful moment throws herself off the side of the Eiffel Tower (well, the stuntman does at any rate). Her parachute opens a moment later. Thus begins a breathless chase as Bond nicks a cab to follow her descending figure through the streets of Paris. During the course of this chase, the roof is taken off the cab, and then the cab is cut in half. Looking at the scenes now, down on the banks of the Seine, you wonder how the production team managed to persuade Paris's notoriously fusspot local authorities into allowing all this.

Then it's off to Zorin's chateau; and there is some wonderful location work around the ethereally beautiful stables of Chantilly. The relationship between Bond and Sir Godfrey – neither of them spring chickens – is one we have never really seen before, and it is an eye-rubber for those of us who have fond memories of *The Avengers* on TV. In that show, Patrick Macnee utterly inhabited the role of secret agent John Steed, to the extent that one of the show's creators, Brian Clemens, said that if Macnee fell down a manhole, he could never be replaced by another actor.

Steed was a great figure, forever raising his bowler hat and lightly twirling his umbrella, and when you watch this character Sir Godfrey, all you can see is Steed. A tubbier version, perhaps, but unmistakably him. Same walk, same exclamations, same everything. So it is a mistake, really, to involve him and Bond in a fight with two heavies in the secret equine lab – where horses are injected with go-faster microchips – for it just makes us nostalgic for the days when Steed would deliver a light uppercut and then trip someone up with that umbrella. Instead, here, poor old Macnee is simply shoved backwards into a crate.

In real life, Macnee was not especially fond of the idea of Bond. Indeed, he told me: 'The very idea of a licence to kill is repulsive, especially to those of us who fought in the war and saw what it was like.' He added that the character of Bond 'was not a suitable role model', whereas Steed made do with 'insouciance and his umbrella and this feeling that you would only manoeuvre your way out of jeopardy at the very last minute'.

Here, his character Sir Godfrey fails to perform such a manoeuvre: he is assassinated by May Day in a car wash.

Macnee's feelings about the character of 007 might have been strong, incidentally, but the films in themselves were another matter, and Macnee was happy to return to record documentaries about them for American TV.

Interesting that the Americans felt that only his cut-glass Old Etonian tones would be suitable to narrate these efforts.

So with Steed gone, and after an attempt to drown Bond in a lake – Bond wriggles out of this scenario quite easily and villains are always too lazy to hang around and double-check that their target is dead – we are off to San Francisco, where the microchip trail seems to be leading.

Of all Bond's American adventures – and there have been a disproportionate number – this one seems the most romantically shot. Perhaps the air of San Francisco lends itself to this slightly softer quality. Even after the scene in which frogman Bond has just escaped death by underwater extractor fan, there is a rather splendid sunset as 007 emerges from the waves in pursuit of Soviet agent Pola (Fiona Fullerton) that makes us forget about his situation for a moment.

There is nice music from composer John Barry too – more of those slightly tilted military marches, with the addition of a neurotic electric guitar – and a pleasingly energetic title song, although the precise meaning of the lyrics remains as elusive as a seventeenth-century metaphysical poem. Performed and co-composed by the then stratospheric Brummie pop group Duran Duran, it features lines such as: 'Meeting you with a view to a kill/face to face in secret places/feel the chill'. No, me neither. But it proved one of the most commercially popular of all the Bond songs, reaching a hugely impressive number one in the US. Unlike the moronic song to *For Your Eyes Only*, this is a ditty that you just can't help liking, the sort of tune that gets an 80s retro night properly under way. As Simon le Bon sang in another of the song's inscrutable lines: 'A sacred why, a mystery gaping inside'. What? I mean, what?

So, Max Zorin is, in the manner of James Finlayson in *Way Out West* (1937), trying to menace Stacey Sutton out of the deeds to her father's oil company and now she lives alone in a big old empty house, having sold most of the furniture to finance her court battles. Bond senses that local geology is important to Zorin's plot; and having followed Stacey home from work, Bond is therefore available when some of Zorin's bad guys come calling at the big old house to apply extra pressure to her. In the aftermath of the fight – in which the heavies are comprehensively scuppered – Bond impresses Stacey by cooking a quiche.

This was a joke very much of its time. A couple of years previously, a humorous book called *Real Men Don't Eat Quiche* had been a huge bestseller (it was written by Bruce Feirstein, who ten years later would find himself writing screenplays for Bond). So it was a nice touch to have Bond reverse this quiche slur, and a nice hint also that it wasn't only bloody old agent Harry Palmer (Michael Caine) who was a dab hand with eggs.

For some reason, Zorin travels around in an airship, and it is out of this that he hurls an investor who displeases him. By the way, Zorin has to travel around in an airship, for without this curious device, the climax of the film would not be possible.

In the mean time, Zorin and May Day manage to trap Bond and Stacey in the lift shaft of the City Hall, to which they have set fire – a nice cliffhanger, for you can't really go wrong with a burning lift shaft, especially with an old-fashioned heroine who screams like a steam engine whistle. The pair are subsequently caught up in a wild chase around San Francisco, Stacey farcically at the wheel of a stolen fire engine, with Bond desperately hanging off the loose ladder behind.

This was 007 as Keystone Kops; all swerving trolley cars, while the roofs are knocked off trailer vans revealing illicit couples within and a couple of gay guys have their wigs blown off.

For some, the comedy was off-putting; personally, I think it's wonderful. It's Moore at his charming, engaging best. The same goes for the earlier scene in which he and Pola have shared a hot tub. While Bond is showering, she runs off with the secret cassette, back to General Gogol's waiting car (another appearance for Walter Gotell, deadpan as always in a beige trenchcoat). When he puts on the tape, they find it is not a recording of Zorin's voice, but actually some Japanese new age music. Bond has double-switched back. It's nicely played and I don't care what anyone says.

Moore reaches a height of post-modernism as he and Stacey prepare to smuggle themselves into Zorin's deadly mine – once again, you expect to see James Finlayson standing in the wooden-propped entrance – and Stacey is trying to find some workman's clothes to disguise herself with. 'Pity you couldn't find any that fitted,' says Bond as Stacey emerges from the hut clad in a tight, elegant Armani-style overall. Shake your heads with disapproval if you like, but I remember the roar of laughter that greeted that line in the Leicester Square Odeon.

Strange then that all of this stuff that plays to Moore's strengths is blended with a queasy increase in violence and even queasier lapses of taste in the script. I think we would all have accepted Zorin as the villain without being told of the experiment in Belsen that produced him; of how pregnant women were injected with steroids, and how most aborted, but Max was born a psychopathic genius. It's all wrong; you can't have a larky Bond villain then link him in with concentration camps.

You might see where this had come from, and indeed the provenance of the elderly Dr Mengele-style character who accompanies Zorin everywhere; 1981's *Raiders of the Lost Ark* had made the Nazis newly fashionable as screen villains. But that was acceptable because it was intended as a period piece; here, it smacked of a certain gratuitousness.

Talking of which, a scene near the film's climax caused Roger Moore a great deal of concern. Preparatory to blowing up the San Andreas fault, Zorin first floods the mine; those workers who are not drowned or electrocuted are picked off by him personally, with a machine gun, which he sprays all over the main mine set, laughing hysterically as he does so. Roger was absolutely right; there was something weirdly off-putting about an explicit massacre like this coupled to a fantastical plot. Moore was again concerned about the children in the audience. 'I thought it was wrong to have machine guns and brains spewing out all over the place,' he said.[4]

As we will come to see, in the next two Bond pictures Moore's advice on such matters was ignored to an even greater extent; the violence and brutality were to be ratcheted up further. And it is no coincidence that at this stage the films started to sink. Director John Glen would not accept this argument though, as he made plain in his autobiography:

Action films were changing a lot in this period. Arnold Schwarzenegger and Sylvester Stallone had become huge stars in films that were certainly a lot more violent than anything that had been depicted in the Bond films. In response to films such as *First Blood* (1983), we decided to toughen up our films a bit from here on . . . the world was changing, movies were changing. We had to keep up.[5]

Glen was wrong. Four years hence, his unusually violent *Licence to Kill* was trounced at the box office by the rather more innocent, old-fashioned adventure *Indiana Jones and the Last Crusade* (1989). A family audience is a family audience, as we can see just as well today.

But for the moment, let's relish Roger's final twenty minutes in the role of 007, for once we are past the machine-gunning, it is all very good fun again. Zorin has packed a vast underground chamber with dynamite, and set a helpful red LED countdown in the middle of it. Bond and May Day, almost swept away in the flood, decide to join forces. 'I thought that creep loved me!' exclaims May Day as she regards the drowned bodies of the tight-jodhpur-wearing women, her justification for suddenly turning from Ruthless Killer into Good Girl.

So it is that she lowers Bond down the hole on a rig into the vast dynamite chamber. Any attempt to defuse the main device will result in it exploding; so Bond has to bring it up out of the chamber and thence out of the mine. But there are only 120 seconds to go! Hurry, May Day, with that winch! Winch harder! Quick, get the bomb on that railway truck! Now there are only thirty-four seconds to go and Bond and May Day are still taking their time!

Then the moment when May Day stays on the railway truck with the bomb as it rolls out of the mine and we realise that she is going for grand self-sacrifice. Well, why not, after the fastest moral turnaround in cinematic history? And we are barely seconds after swallowing this when Zorin's airship swoops improbably down upon Stacey and she is borne into the skies, with Bond holding on desperately to the ship's guy-rope.

Zorin appears to have taken his San Andreas/Silicon Valley defeat with remarkable good humour; none the less, he pilots the ship in such a way as to try and dislodge Bond − scraping him against tall buildings and then bashing him against the Golden Gate Bridge.

At the risk of sounding tremendously old, there is something about the combination of studio mock-up, back-projection, and real location work that is more convincing to my eye than computer-generated effects ever will be. For instance, in the *Spider-Man* films, I never for one moment believe in this figure swinging between buildings or hanging off ledges. It's not only the non-naturalistic movement of the animated figure, it's the non-naturalistic camera angles that follow it.

But here − a fight to the death atop the main suspension cable of the Golden Gate Bridge − it is all somehow absurdly realistic, even if we know that that camera position is impossible. As cliffhangers go, it really doesn't get more old-fashioned; Bond hanging off the red pipe as Zorin advances upon him swinging an axe. Throw in a screaming heroine who is also dangling off the edge, and a crazy old man with a fizzing stick of dynamite, and you have something that would not have looked out of place in the days of Harold Lloyd.

Bond has tied the mooring rope of the airship to the red cable. I recall in the cinema that the female member of our party buried her head in her hands as we saw Bond and Stacey dangling with a back-projection of cars hundreds of feet below. My friend believed it. And there are real location shots of two stuntmen at the top of the bridge, slugging it out. It is blissfully old-fashioned and well put together.

Naturally, Bond must prevail; so Zorin plunges over the edge, down to a watery death. And thanks to the fizzing dynamite, his airship explodes. Bond hauls Stacey up on to the main cable, the wind whistling around them. 'There's never a cab when you need one,' Bond says, and you feel like cheering for the last time that 007 would ever be so light-hearted and mindlessly glib.

The critics, on the whole, weren't having it. Most pointed to Moore's very great age. Others detected a weariness in the very formula itself. The *New Statesman* magazine went a shade further: 'Time was when one could tune down the mind, lean back and enjoy,' its critic wrote. 'To submit to this tired old offer would be tantamount to accepting a mental rape.'

Speak for yourself, *New Statesman*! I don't think I accepted any such thing. And my larger point is, I think, proved by the film's double postscript to Roger's era; our old friend General Gogol is in M's office, desiring to award Bond the Order of Lenin. Glasnost indeed! Then Q uses a gizmo to spy on Stacey and Bond back in Stacey's house, taking a saucy shower.

Stacey gets to say 'Oh, James,' while Roger Moore's final utterance as 007 is – believe it or not – a Barbara Windsor-style 'Oooh!'

An entire glorious era summed up with one frisky monosyllable. I knew at the time that I would miss him. And I miss him still. But it was apparently time for Bond to wear a straighter face.

CHAPTER TWENTY DARLING MONEYPENNY

So farewell then, the most famous secretary in cinema history. If not the most famous secretary in history full stop. The retirement – or firing, to put it another way – of Lois Maxwell from the role of Miss Moneypenny in 1986 now gives us a chance to examine how she made the figure so very archetypal.

First let's have the swiftest, most sweeping historical overview imaginable, for younger readers not brought up in a world where dolly-birds would swing their mini-skirted legs on formica desks while 'taking a letter' for the randy junior executive. Right. Well, prior to the First World War, secretaries tended to be male. The depredations of that conflict, combined with the increasing use of the new-look typewriter, brought women flooding into office workplaces once dominated by men. We saw the rise of what was called 'the typing pool' – that is, a room full of women sitting at their typewriters, making neat grammatical copies of letters to be sent out. The very idea of 'the typing pool' established a swift hold on the male imagination. Not as strong, though, as the grip exerted by the idea of the personal secretary.

Even by the 1930s, the common image of a husband lured into temptation by his secretary had gained ground. By the 1950s, when Ian Fleming was tapping out Bond, he gave us two sides of this archetype: the pure, loyal Moneypenny; and the equally pure, though rather more flirtatious Loelia Ponsonby. Ponsonby was Bond's personal secretary, and he would often find himself musing on her good-hearted virtuousness.

Moneypenny, as secretary to M, was a much more grown-up figure. In the novels, Bond could always tell what sort of mood M was going to be in as he waited in the antechamber by the expression on Moneypenny's face, which could range from good humour to straightforward anger. If one might see M as the headmaster figure, then Moneypenny was matron.

She was the gatekeeper, the guardian of the portal. She was also the last line of reassurance before Bond was plunged into each fresh adventure.

The Moneypenny of the films was a rather different prospect. Canadian actress Lois Maxwell – her real name was Lois Hooker, which in those days might not have looked quite so becoming in lights, and indeed would not look so hot now either – had written to Cubby Broccoli asking him for a role in this new Bond film because she was in a sticky financial position following her husband's heart attack.

She was given a choice: she could either play saucepot Sylvia Trench, who seduces Bond after the opening casino scene; or she could play the secretary Moneypenny. What a stroke of good judgement it was for her to go for Moneypenny.

And it wasn't the immediately obvious choice because back in the 1950s, Maxwell had herself been a saucepot favourite for the British tabloid hacks. First she was spirited off to Hollywood by Jack Warner and appeared in a film called *That Hagan Girl* (1951); she then spirited herself back to London, describing her treatment in Hollywood in tones of perfect outrage: 'They put so much padding on my bosom that I nearly toppled over.'[1]

They would never have dared do such a thing to Moneypenny. Maxwell, Connery and Bernard Lee's M immediately made a memorable threesome; as well as being the gatekeeper, the screen Miss Moneypenny was, obviously, rather in love with Bond. Maxwell always portrayed this yearning with good humour – Moneypenny knows that it will never happen. But there is the occasional peep of poignancy too. Is Moneypenny permanently single? It would seem so. When Bond presents her with flowers and promises, is she really able to laugh it off as easily as all that? I have to confess that when I saw the films as a child, I always felt rather sorry for her.

As the films went on, so the humour of the character and of the relationship broadened. By *You Only Live Twice*, Moneypenny is more sceptical about Bond and his smoothie ways, showing especial impatience when he tells her of his degree in Oriental Studies from Cambridge. On this occasion, Lois Maxwell gets to wear a fetching naval uniform, since she and M are holed up in a secret submarine.

Incidentally, though he had struck a faint note of ambiguity when he greeted the news of Connery's casting, Ian Fleming gushed all over Maxwell: 'When I visualised Miss Moneypenny in the James Bond stories,' he told her, 'I saw her as a tall, distinguished woman with the most kissable lips in the world. You, my dear, are exactly the woman I visualised.'[2]

What an oily creep! But it was difficult to argue. By the end of the 1960s, Maxwell had made what was little more than a walk-on indisputably hers.

She made a few adjustments for the arrival of the new Bond, George Lazenby, in 1969. This more gauche, puppy-like 007 kicks off by appearing to goose Moneypenny, which is very, very wrong. That solecism aside, Moneypenny on this occasion appears to become more like a protective big sister – quietly defying, as we saw, Bond's headstrong dictation of a resignation letter and turning it instead into a request for two weeks' leave. Thus we see – in a nice warm touch – how both Bond and M regard her as utterly indispensable.

And the sexual spark has been replaced by something cosier; this now is Bond's surrogate family. In a sense, this is possibly a truer reading of Fleming too, for in the novels, Bond openly regards M as a father figure whom he not only respects but loves. At the close of *On Her Majesty's Secret Service*, Bond's faux family is out in force for his wedding – you will note, no real family members here.

Bond is not only an orphan; he is an only child to boot. We have 'father' M and 'grumpy uncle' Q. Moneypenny is allowed one more burst of romantic unrequited love, as she cries and Bond throws her his hat as a bouquet. But Moneypenny is family too.

And no matter how rude Cubby Broccoli and others were about Lazenby afterwards, Maxwell remained touchingly loyal to him. She insisted, for instance, that he was much nicer than the publicity would have it: 'I asked George to come and run the raffle at a charity event for nurses,' she said. 'And he accepted at once. I think he's a nice fellow.'[3]

There was almost a glitch with *Diamonds Are Forever*, for Moneypenny did not appear in that book at all. But then, as Maxwell recalled, 'Harry Saltzman rang me and said they couldn't have a Bond film without me. So they wrote a part in.'[4] Indeed they did. Moneypenny on this occasion was an undercover passport officer at Dover Hoverport.

The arrival of Roger Moore in 1973 brought another small gear shift in Lois Maxwell's performance. This was in part inevitable because they had both been in the same year at drama school in 1944. On top of this, Maxwell had guest starred in the Moore TV vehicles *The Saint* and *The Persuaders!*. Now both Moneypenny and Bond were amused middle-aged flirts, dallying with bunches of flowers and arch banter as Moneypenny sent this more waggish figure on his way with reprovingly arched eyebrows.

But there was more genuine warmth there too; you could see that this Bond and Moneypenny, while they could never be lovers, could be seriously good friends. In *For Your Eyes Only*, Bond is extravagantly complimentary as Moneypenny applies her lipstick in a secret filing-cabinet mirror. In *Octopussy*, Bond's waggishness extends to giving Moneypenny a single red rose, while bestowing the rest of the bunch on her young assistant Penelope Smallbone. Moneypenny's response to this gag is an indulgent smile, although Maxwell did confess that the introduction of the younger woman had rather thrown her off her stride; it caused her on one take to refer to 'Miss Penelope Smallbush', which brought the entire studio to a standstill.

Maxwell's attitude to this extraordinarily strange job – turning up for one or two days on the Pinewood lot, once every two years, while still remaining one of the most recognisable women on the planet – grew a little spikier in the early 1980s. 'I think the Bond films have got progressively worse,' she declared in 1981. 'Now the gimmicks and special effects are more important than the plot or the players. I don't go to the premieres any more.'[5] Come, come, my dear – the gimmicks were *always* more important.

By Moore's final film, both veterans were clearly mature in years. But we knew that anyone who took over the role of Moneypenny could never give it exactly the same kind of life that Lois Maxwell did.

'I'm not complaining,' she said in 1986, as news of her defenestration – together with the casting of Timothy Dalton as the new 007 – came through. 'I'd look silly making goo-goo eyes at a man half my age.'[6]

Maxwell had had roles in other things too, including, as mentioned, TV series such as *The Saint*. She appeared in one episode apparently set in Venice; an artful illusion created by means of back-projection and spliced-in stock footage. In reality, she got no further than Elstree Studios. For many years, Maxwell wrote a column called 'Moneypenny' for a Canadian newspaper. But we might see how the role was a curse as well as a blessing, for it made Maxwell one of the most identifiable – and by extension, typecast – people on the planet. She had survived three Bonds and two Ms.

One wonders, however, how easy it was after her retirement from the role. Maxwell moved around a bit; she went to live in Somerset at one point. But then she moved out to Australia and was there at the time of her death in 2007. One senses that Bond had not made life any easier in financial terms. In 1962, she was paid £100 and told to provide her own costume. By the 1980s, things had obviously improved, but she was still on a day rate.

In 1987, we saw the debut of the woman we must now term 'the forgotten Moneypenny' because, through no fault of her own, the character's impact was dulled for the debut of super-serious Timothy Dalton as 007. Caroline Bliss was the actress concerned, the daughter of a famous composer, young, blonde, very attractive and lacking in Maxwell's more motherly approach.

In her debut in *The Living Daylights*, she was fatally taken out of her proper context; instead of seeing her sitting at Moneypenny's desk, by that familiar green leather door, the producers instead had her talking to Bond in Q's laboratory. So you see the immediate problem for Bliss: how could she be Moneypenny if she wasn't watching Bond throw his hat at the stand, having him present her with a rose and then telling him to 'go in. He's very impatient today'? Setting is all.

Perhaps the producers felt that they couldn't upset the audience with an imposter so soon after Maxwell's departure. Never stopped them with Bond though.

The relationship between Dalton and Bliss is presented as mildly flirtatious, yet still comes across as more brother-and-sisterly, with Dalton's Bond as the rather straight older brother. The other problem for Bliss is that she bore a certain resemblance to that film's leading lady, Maryam D'Abo, and so was unable even to distinguish herself in that way.

Things got even worse in 1989's *Licence to Kill* where, because of the nature of the plot – Bond resigning from the secret service to go on a revenge mission against a South American drug lord – the role of Moneypenny was reduced to a tiny cameo. Perhaps just as well, for in the changing social climate, the idea of a subservient, lovelorn secretary was not tremendously fashionable any more.

After a hiatus of six years caused by legal battles (a gap we shall presently hear more about), the return of Bond in 1995's *GoldenEye* demanded not only a new style of M, in the form of Judi Dench, but a new style of Moneypenny to boot. In came acclaimed Shakespearean actress Samantha Bond – for of course, by the mid-1990s, the idea of 007 films was fashionable once more, and therefore attractive to a whole range of high-calibre actors who might not have been so keen ten years previously.

Acting opposite Pierce Brosnan's smarmy insinuator, Samantha Bond's Moneypenny is a much more sceptical, un-lovelorn figure, batting off Bond's advances and engaged in a constant low-level conspiracy against him with Dench's M. She is also no longer the perpetual singleton. In *GoldenEye*, she reveals that she has been called into the office from a date. Added to this, the Bond family was reimagined as a matriarchy, with Bond as the wayward, though amusing, elder son being ganged up on by cleverer women. In 1999's *The World Is Not Enough*, Moneypenny is on the case when 007 has a quick fling with the wonderfully named MI6 doctor Molly Warmflash (Serena Scott Thomas), both disapproving of him and yet saving him from M's more searching questions.

For *Die Another Day* in 2002, the self-consciously celebratory twentieth film in the series, producers Michael G. Wilson and Barbara Broccoli decided at last to shoot the scene that we all thought we would never see: Bond triumphant at the end of the film, sharing a passionate embrace with Moneypenny. I recall an actual gasp in the cinema as Bond and Moneypenny began their unexpected grapple in her office. Two seconds later and the truth of the scene is revealed: Moneypenny is actually alone, and wearing one of Q's inventions – a holographic virtual reality simulation helmet. It was a very funny moment, and yet it carried a tiny spark of that poignancy I recalled feeling as a child.

It was also a wonderful indicator that no matter how many 007s come and go, the character of Moneypenny – loyal, constant, sighing with unrequited love – is a crucial element of the mix. In 2006, Daniel Craig's debut *Casino Royale* was all the harsher in the complete absence of the character. It seems that we will also be deprived of her comforting presence in 2008's *Quantum of Solace*.

And yet, wonderful job of updating and reinventing that Samantha Bond did, it is Lois Maxwell who will be for ever Moneypenny whenever we think of the character. She was there across fourteen films spanning twenty-three years, an achievement I think (together with Q's reign) unique in cinematic history. She was only ever on screen for two or three minutes per film – yet her wry, amusing and occasionally poignant portrayal of the woman forever left behind made an absolutely indelible mark. To this day, hers remains one of the most recognisable faces on the planet. Moneypenny might not have perhaps been the most rewarding role, financially or artistically – Maxwell once remarked that she 'pretty well said the same thing backwards, forwards, sideways and upside down for a period of twenty-three years' – but it conferred upon Maxwell a rare form of immortality.

In 1987, Bond was about to change again, but for the producers and indeed for MGM/UA who were bankrolling the films, the relatively poor US box office returns for *A View to a Kill* struck a note of worrying mortality. Could the character keep pace with what seemed to be fast-changing times?

CHAPTER TWENTY-ONE ONE FOR THE LADIES

'Thing about Timothy Dalton,' says a female war correspondent and novelist of my acquaintance who covered Bosnia in the early 1990s, 'is that he is the only Bond who looks as though he could actually kill someone. I've seen that look. And Dalton really conveys it. Not like Roger Moore. You can't see him killing anyone.'

My war correspondent friend knows of what she is talking, not least because she was a close family friend of the late Fitzroy MacLean, diplomat, war hero and author of the vivid memoir *Eastern Approaches*, who is often cited as being one of Ian Fleming's real-life inspirations for Bond. Actually, there have been so many of these bloody 'real-life inspirations' that one hesitates before adding yet one more to the list. Yet MacLean ticked all the boxes and was one of the more likely candidates.

MacLean was a diplomat in Russia in the 1930s, during the time of the worst Stalinist purges; his journeys to the remoter regions of that country to find the truth of what was happening led to him being monitored and pursued by the NKVD, the earlier version of the KGB.

Then came the war; while Commander Fleming was deskbound in intelligence, MacLean was out there, notably in the Middle East in the very first days of the SAS. Later, he was instrumental in convincing Churchill to back Tito rather than the royalists in Yugoslavia.

Anyway, back to those physical qualities of Dalton, and the look of a killer. Certainly, the actor was uncompromising and extremely assertive in his professional dealings. Back in 1974, as a young man, Dalton had taken the impossibly famous screenwriter Robert Bolt to court to sue him for lost earnings after a discussed role in a film about Lady Caroline Lamb failed to materialise.

Even before this, Dalton was comically bullish. Cast as Heathcliff in a 1970 remake of *Wuthering Heights*, young Master Dalton airily announced that he had not seen the landmark 1939 Laurence Olivier version: 'I believe, in fact, the film's not very good,' he said.[1]

Dalton was consistently in demand both on stage and in film. We have seen how he was sounded out for Bond after *On Her Majesty's Secret Service*; he was also approached back in 1980, though he sensed on that occasion that he was part of an elaborate casting game designed to keep Roger Moore's wages and eyebrows under control. In 1982, Dalton worked with the legendary (though at that time shunned) film director Michael Powell on a mooted Russian production of *Pavlova*; the Soviet authorities would raise the finance, the Englishmen would shoot and star in it. But then Dalton got an offer to play Hotspur in a Trevor Nunn production of *Henry VI*, to open London's new Barbican Centre.

Dalton also had a nifty line in TV advertisement voiceovers. For a while, he was the 'voice' of Brain's Faggots, a brand of northern meatball.

Woe betide any journalist who sought to learn a little of his personal arrangements. He loved to fish — that's about all they would get. But what about his long relationship with actress Vanessa Redgrave, scion of the Workers' Revolutionary Party? Dalton could have hacks expelled from the interview room before they had even finished enunciating her name. Given the global attention that Bond always attracted, many of Fleet Street's finest rubbed their hands at the prospect of Dalton running the gauntlet of this particular publicity machine.

Possibly, physically, Dalton is the closest actor to Ian Fleming's original conception: dark hair, steely eyes. He even looks a tiny bit like Hoagy Carmichael.

But of all the periods in Bond, it is the Dalton era that now looks the strangest. Here we had an actor — a seriously good actor — suddenly changing all the rules of the game that we had come to know and love for the last twenty-five years. Dalton's first act upon being cast was to go back and read all the Fleming novels very closely, something that he wasted no time telling interviewers about.

He steeped himself in Fleming's Bond, with all the character's bouts of depression, frustration and melancholia. And Dalton impressed this on executive producer and screenwriter Michael G. Wilson; no eyebrows were to be raised archly, no entendres were to be doubled. James Bond was a serious grown-up who, through all manner of bitter experience, knew that his job was lonely and hard.

Everyone seems to have been in agreement that the change of tone was a good thing, that Dalton's Bond had to be substantially different to Moore's. Heavens, this new Bond was even allowed the odd moment in his first screenplay of what seemed like genuine human emotion. 'He was a hard-edged actor who deserved a different kind of script,' said director John Glen. 'It was written to cope with Dalton's acting ability.'[2] Hoy! Rudeness! What about Moore's acting ability? But Dalton's 007 also faced a few fresh social obstacles.

This was the late 1980s and the foundations of Bond's world were beginning to sway in a social earthquake. 'AIDS – don't die of ignorance' warned the posters with pictures of tombstones on them. The warning was even repeated on the postmarks of letters, as if one wanted to be reminded of sexually transmitted diseases when opening the gas bill. The phrase 'casual sex' entered the language as a thing to be denounced.

But in the meantime, this was also a more violent world, where the cinematic heroes – now predominantly Schwarzenegger and Stallone – fired machine guns and were bloodied and would not have touched a tuxedo in a thousand years. This was the era of *Top Gun* (1986) – a noisy period of yobbish right-wing American swaggering, which came just at the point when Soviet leader Mikhail Gorbachev and his glamorous fur-clad wife Raisa (the first ever glamorous wife of a Soviet leader) were charming the Western world with their talk of peace and reform.

In pop-cultural terms, this seemed to result in a period of manic, gloating overconfidence, the American screen filled with heroes who damned well got out there and shot their enemies down at maximum volume. John Rambo even managed to claim some sort of victory in Vietnam. In other words, it was a ghastly period in which to be left-wing; everywhere you looked, there was howling triumphalism, combined with Bonnie Tyler screaming 'I need a hero!' and Madonna tinnily expounding her Material Girl philosophy.

So perhaps the age did demand a tougher, less promiscuous James Bond. But in fact Dalton's arrival in the role came about as the result of a rather convoluted process. According to one source, he was always first choice; Cubby Broccoli had had his eye on Dalton ever since his role in *The Lion in Winter*. But in early 1986, when casting began, Dalton – now the perfect age of forty – was tied up with a film called *Brenda Starr* and a Royal Shakespeare Company production of *The Taming of the Shrew*.

So the next choice was Pierce Brosnan, now a huge success with the American TV comedy-thriller *Remington Steele* and also finally deemed sufficiently old to play an agent who has been around a bit. On top of this,

Steele had reached the end of its run. Brosnan was only too keen. Can you imagine anyone not being so? But his American employers blew it all for him.

The irony was that Broccoli's interest in casting Brosnan led to a sudden resurgence of interest in *Remington Steele*; NBC decided to produce more episodes and Brosnan was held to his contract. He must have spent *days* throwing furniture around in howling frustration. Indeed, he could not resist chewing the sourest of grapes as he made his way to the set of spy thriller *The Fourth Protocol* (1986): 'It is not going to happen,' he said. 'I was offered the role but fate played a part. Certain things in life are meant to happen. This obviously wasn't one of them.'[3]

NBC – or fate, whichever you will – would not budge on that contract; and Brosnan had to be passed over. It is only now, with hindsight, that we can see that he had a lucky escape: if his Bond had kicked off with the chewy and almost indecipherable *The Living Daylights*, Brosnan may not have had the immediate record-breaking impact that he was to have later.

New Zealand actor Sam Neill was another strong runner, and footage from his camera tests still exists; he looks convincing in that tux. At that stage, he was still best known for having played the adult Damien in the third of the *Omen* horror films. Only later would he find greater fame in *Reilly: Ace of Spies* (1990) and *Jurassic Park* (1993). In the screen tests, he went down very well with Michael G. Wilson and Cubby's daughter Barbara; but Cubby himself reserved judgement.

Financial backers MGM had their own idea: what about this Australian chap called Mel Gibson? Up until that point, Gibson had been best known as the eponymous hero of the *Mad Max* dystopian sci-fi films. Broccoli was having absolutely none of it, although I wonder whether Gibson might not have been an inspired choice. Certainly his starring role as a mildly unhinged LA cop in the following year's action comedy-thriller *Lethal Weapon* proved that he could combine doing the rough stuff with being a fine actor. We will say nothing of his recent drunken escapades.

Anyway, the answer was no. And in fact, there was so much faffing about – shooting on *The Living Daylights* had to be postponed expensively by several weeks – that Timothy Dalton completed his work on *The Taming of the Shrew* and became available again.

And so it was in the summer of 1986 that Dalton was unveiled to the world's press as the new Bond. As well as the general response, 'Who?', there was intrigue at this apparently art-house actor stepping up to the plate, and at his repeated assertions that he would take the character 'back to the spirit of Fleming'.

Dalton managed to jump the first hurdle: he got the backing of emeritus Bond Sean Connery. 'I think they have made a very good choice,' Connery proclaimed from on high. 'I haven't worked with Tim but I know him and I think he will be good.'[4]

Once the casting was confirmed, Michael Wilson retooled the script towards Dalton, removing much of the glib humour that had come to be associated with Bond. The launching point was an atmospheric Fleming short story, in which Bond is sent to West Berlin to assassinate a sniper across the Berlin Wall; when it becomes apparent that the sniper is a beautiful young female musician, Bond deliberately messes up the shot. It is a story that came close to the oppressiveness and ambiguity of John le Carré, particularly in its rich detailing of Bond's shabby vantage point and his increasing tension.

Out of this, Wilson and Maibaum formulated a complex story of double-cross and deception which would take Bond from Bratislava to Afghanistan. We open on the Rock of Gibraltar – one of the few remaining outposts of Empire and a rather dreary location – where for the pre-credits, Bond has to hang on to the roof of an escaping jeep hurtling downhill while in pursuit of a spy killer. After this burst of rather humourless excitement – already the new realism of Dalton has seeped in – Bond is sent to protect a defecting Russian called Koskov (Jeroen Krabbe). Koskov is shot at by a beautiful young cellist (Maryam D'Abo) but some instinct tells Bond not to kill her. Back in Britain, Koskov is snatched from his safe house by nordic killer Necros. And that's when it starts to get really complicated.

It's to do with an arms dealer called Brad Whitaker (Joe Don Baker) who lives in North Africa; and it's to do with smuggled drugs as well. And Bond somehow is swept from Vienna to Tangier to Soviet-occupied Afghanistan (those were the days!) in order to break this drugs/arms axis. It is all but impossible to follow. All we need know is that Whitaker is the chief bad guy, Koskov is the sneaky comical second-string bad guy, Necros is the gay-ish Aryan henchman, and Kara Milvoy is the Girl.

Before we get on to how Dalton set his seal, we must acknowledge why it is that Maryam D'Abo's performance as Kara happens to be the hub of the film, and at the heart of why it continues to be such a favourite among women today. At the time, the actress seemed to capture the imaginations of the posher *Tatler*-reading classes – indeed, production on this film made a *Tatler* cover story in 1987. And D'Abo's partnership with Timothy Dalton is fondly remembered as a sort of romantic high point.

Kara Milvoy is a classical cello player who appears to be moonlighting as a KGB sniper. One always hears that musicians' wages are very low. As General Koskov escapes from the opera house to make his defection, Kara is up in a high window, fixing her sights on him. But Bond in turn has his sights on her. As in the short story, some instinct tells 007 not to kill the girl, and he instead fires at her gun, scaring her.

Bond is intrigued. 'She didn't know one end of a rifle from another' as he tells his outraged colleague Saunders. It is also an opportunity to crowbar in a line about 'scaring the living daylights out of her' in order to justify the title. Although a well-known English phrase, it must have seemed utterly cryptic to American audiences.

After Koskov is kidnapped from his English safe house in what appears to be a KGB counter-snatch – it isn't, though, and I hope you're keeping up – Bond sets off to investigate Kara. She is arrested on a tram by the KGB and Bond meets her on her release the next day, when she finds that her apartment has been ransacked. She is known to be Koskov's lover, hence the official interest. Bond offers his help and the two take off, with her cello, in his Aston Martin. In the chase sequence that follows, the Aston deploys some silly missiles and laser beams and eventually, Bond and Kara are forced to escape down a snowy mountain using her cello case as an impromptu toboggan, with her Stradivarius as a rudder.

That is the scene that everyone seems to remember, and again it seems, anecdotally at least, to be unusually popular among women. That cello case sequence is the *Sex and the City* moment of Bond films. There are several factors going on here that I think made it stick out. First of all, Kara is a new and unusual sort of Bond girl, in that she appears from the start to have a well-defined character – normally the female characters kick off as either overly antagonistic or overly soppy and they are always defined by how they react against Bond. Kara doesn't even seem to pay all that much attention to 007 in their first scene. Nor is she presented as the overly obvious sex symbol that most of the previous women had been. No floral bikinis for Maryam!

The second factor – swiftly noted by the press – is that Kara is Bond's only woman throughout the film. The old 'three girl' rule appeared to have been jettisoned as part of the 'safe sex' craze.

'I'd be lying if I said the AIDS business hadn't affected our thinking on this film,' said director John Glen just before the film opened. 'We didn't just sit down at the beginning and say "The bed-hopping has to stop because of AIDS."' But it was a happy coincidence that *The Living Daylights'* storyline only called for one relationship. 'If people want to suggest that James Bond is setting a good example in these times of AIDS troubles,' Glen added amiably, 'then I am happy about that. I am sure the old-style sexual freedom associated with 007 is no longer a realistic reflection of the way people are.'[5]

Wonderfully sweet notion, by the way — as if Bond was *ever* a realistic reflection of the way people are. There it is though.

And in fact the producers were doing something shrewder. Their new Bond had to be distanced from Roger Moore's old eyebrow-raising roué, with all the young female audience alienation that could have resulted. And serious Timothy Dalton was allowed to get equally serious about his heroine.

The producers and Dalton could argue with some justification that this was exactly the spirit of Fleming; go back to the Bond novels and you don't find Bond leaping in and out of bed with everyone. Quite the reverse. He appears instead on several occasions to turn into a bit of a soppy date. Never mind Bond's minor psychodrama with Vesper Lynd in the first book, *Casino Royale*; he also gets saucer-eyed about policewoman Gala Brand in *Moonraker*, and indeed suffers an unhappy ending in that one when it transpires that Gala is already answered for. And look at his relationship with Tiffany Case in the novel *Diamonds Are Forever* — so smitten is he with her at the end that he installs her in his Chelsea flat, with his treasured housekeeper May under instructions to look after her.

Of course, when the books were written in the 1950s, the shocking thing was not promiscuity, which was barely acknowledged in any public sense, but the very notion of sex outside marriage. Bond the eternal bachelor could not bear commitment, either professionally or emotionally; but the relationships in the novels are none the less serious. And this seems to be what we get a taste of in *The Living Daylights*.

In the early stages, Bond is simply there as a guardian and protector, since Kara is supposedly still the squeeze of Koskov. On arrival in Vienna, Bond even surprises the knowing receptionist at the Hotel Splendide with a request for two rooms. But a red-blooded man can only endure so many Viennese horse-drawn buggies, waltzing displays, vile boutiques and fairground dodgem cars, and so Bond makes his romantic pounce on Kara on exactly the same ferris wheel, curiously, that Harry Lime looked down from in *The Third Man*.

So come on, ladies, what is it about this film that so appeals to the romcom sense? Is it Bond quietly going to watch Kara perform at the Bratislava Opera House? Is it that scene where Kara wanders into the Vienna hotel's boutique and Bond buys her that perfectly hideous blue outfit that she takes a shine to? Is it perhaps the scenes in the Tora Bora mountains where Bond is dressed up as a mujahadeen? Or is it the cello case chase and the extraordinarily soppy final scene where Bond and Kara get their first real, proper snog?

It is certainly not the Tangier portion of the film. Nice location filming aside, this is Bond at his very naffest. Bond is there to have it out with General Pushkin (John Rhys-Davies) in a breathtakingly hideous hotel. Will he kill Pushkin? Is Pushkin a baddie? Will anyone please tell us what is going on? And as if all this were not confusing and aesthetically displeasing enough, Bond is also lured aboard a ghastly yacht upon which lurks some long-haired young American twonk wearing leisure slacks and claiming to be Felix Leiter. Oh, and here is Kara, holed up in another hideous hotel, that cello between her knees, having confusingly gone to the trouble of spiking Bond's vodka martini. It is with a sense of head-scratching relief that the film then moves us to Afghanistan (shot in North Africa, since the real location would obviously have been rather fraught).

Incidentally, the final part of the film might in one sense be regarded as the moment when that famous Broccoli sense of staying ahead of geopolitics finally deserted the old boy. By this stage, we are aware that General Koskov and mercenary gunrunner Brad Whitaker are in cahoots. Koskov goes to Afghanistan for some reason that I didn't quite get. But the point is that he takes Bond and Kara. At this stage, in 1987, Afghanistan was still occupied by the Soviet Army, and this is the backdrop against which the climax is played out.

And this is where we might now think that the film has dated horribly; for why demonise the Soviets for occupying a country that Western forces have spent the last six years attempting to control? Koskov's plot appears to involve smuggled diamonds traded for heroin supplied by the mujahadeen.

But Bond gets in with one such character, Kamran Shah, portrayed by Art Malik, and finds himself suddenly in alliance with an Afghan warlord. There would be pretty short shrift if Bond did that today.

It has been incorrectly assumed by some that the Kamran Shah character was based on the young Osama Bin Laden (who, back in the 1980s, was emphatically not the demonic figure that he is now). But in fact, it seems more likely that Shah's real-life equivalent would have been several key Afghan rebels, who were secretly helped by the British in their campaign of resistance against the occupying Soviet forces.

Indeed, it has only recently emerged that during this period, MI6 was actively looking to supply covert assistance to the tribesmen in order to fatally undermine the invasion, and identified well-educated figures to whom they could target aid. Assistance came in the form of hi-tech weaponry and superior intelligence and proved a powerful thorn in the Soviet side.

Malik's Shah is that old, somewhat racist standby, the exotic foreigner with a posh English accent and an Oxford education. Whip away the headscarf and the robes and you expect to see cricketing whites. Naturally the tribesmen around him are leering primitives, gurning furiously at Maryam D'Abo prior to firing their guns in the air. But Kara's chance for a quick canoodle with Bond in Shah's desert apartments, with all the silks and satins that usually go with this style of 'Turkish Delight' fantasy, might have won back the laydeez. The desert setting, after all, is fairly standard Mills and Boon stuff.

Talking of the importance of laydeez, D'Abo's casting was the responsibility of Cubby's daughter Barbara, who stepped up to the plate as executive producer for this film. 'Barbara is a strong lady,' said D'Abo. 'She has a great sense of humour and loves actors so they always feel very safe with her. I was stunned to get the part. I thought of Ursula Andress. But I felt part of a family, and this was especially because of Barbara Broccoli.'[6]

In all the bickering, misunderstandings and making-up that comprise the Kara/Bond relationship, there was also a new, more feminine touch in that this was the most realistic romance that we had seen so far in the series. And yes, that includes George Lazenby and Diana Rigg. Dalton and D'Abo played it absolutely straight down the line – not an entendre to be heard from either of them.

But this plot won't get itself resolved, so it's off on horseback to the Soviet base where Bond plants a bomb on a plane filled with heroin, then taxis down the runway, then lowers the back doors to let Kara on board, then gets into an aerial fight with Necros, thousands of feet up, as the bomb countdown ticks away and Kara struggles to control the plane. In other words, too many things going on at the same time. The fight is tremendous – two stuntmen hanging off some netting trailing out of the back door of this bomber, as the plane swoops upwards and downwards. Once again, this is the sort of thing that computer effects simply can't do as believably. Necros is kicked off and the bomb defused, a crucial bridge is bombed and the heroin disposed of, and Kara narrowly escapes piloting the plane straight into a mountain. Hooray!

There are two postscripts. First is a rather wan sequence where Bond confronts Brad Whitaker in his hi-tech Tangier fastness – all battle simulation noises, toy cannons with real explosives, and flashing strobe lights. Whitaker is crushed by a statue of Napoleon and Koskov is grabbed by Pushkin.

And thence to the one scene that probably hasn't dated quite so well. This is where Kara gives a command cello performance in the Bratislava Opera House and is met backstage not only by our dear old friend General Gogol, but also by M, and indeed also by a troupe of leering, gurning Afghan tribesmen. The geopolitical scenario this paints is dizzying: Russians, British and Afghans, all united in their adoration of a girl with a cello between her knees.

First, Kara is worried by Gogol – but he grants her permission to defect on the spot. Then Kara is upset; where is Bond? It turns out that he has been hiding in her dressing room behind some screens like the Phantom of the Opera; and as they snog, sensitively, the end titles roll.

Two other elements make this a strange Bond film. One is the score from John Barry, which I think is one of his very few off-days. Coincidentally, it also turned out to be his last Bond work.

The oddness in the score is caused by synthesisers, which were the curse of almost every film score in that period. 'I wanted to put in these tracks and they really cut through,' Barry said. 'We've used them on about eight pieces and when we got them mixed in with the orchestra it sounded really terrific with a lot of energy and impact – a slight freshness and a more up to date sound.'[7]

But it is the sound that is now most dated. In place of his characteristic wonderfully off-kilter military marches, there is instead a tinny drum machine with its unwavering yet feeble 'handclap' beat, a flat sound that seems more suited to an unconvincing car chase in a naff TV cop show. It really is lethal – it drains the most exciting set-pieces of all vitality: the blistering fight in the safe-house kitchen, where Necros and a British agent go at each other with electric carving knives and frying pans; the Aston Martin scene, where Bond and Kara plough through road-blocks with missiles and end up skidding around on a frozen lake; and of course that climactic battle in the air. When action is arranged around a hollow little electric beat, you lose any sense of urgency and indeed the ability to suspend disbelief.

On top of this, the title song, performed by the inexplicably popular Norwegian band A-ha, is awful, filled with yet more of those wispy synths and a main lyric that goes: 'Aaah-oh-wah-oh – the living daylights!' What? I mean, what? Naturally, it reached number five in the UK charts, one of the most successful songs of the lot, so what do I know, eh?

But in fairness to Barry, the other odd thing about the film is that the second-string songs – 'Where Has Everybody Gone' and 'If There Was a Man' – are two of the best ever heard in the series. Both are performed by the Pretenders, fronted by Chrissie Hynde, and both are hair-raisingly good. 'Where Has Everybody Gone' is a harsh, bleak composition that Necros always listens to prior to a murder spree. Conversely, 'If There Was a Man' is a liltingly romantic and shamelessly old-fashioned number that also happens to form the core of John Barry's love themes for this film.

Chrissie Hynde has a superb Bond voice and with these songs, we can see that old-hand composer and young popsters were operating in complete harmony. In other words, The Pretenders clearly worshipped John Barry, as well they might.

A sense of harmony was missing, however, from his collaboration with A-ha. Perhaps the band were in some way riled by director John Glen going to see one of their concerts in Croydon and thereafter describing them as one of the hottest acts 'in the hit parade', making him sound like David Jacobs. Perhaps the insolent pups didn't quite realise that Barry is one of the greatest composers of his age. But the song itself was subject to a huge amount of fraught to-ing and fro-ing. Barry was later to describe the band as 'a pain in the arse'.

Interestingly, when Barry sets aside his exciting new drum machine, we hear flashes of him at the top of his game, not just in Kara's beautiful love theme, but also in the brief few minutes of lush, romantic scoring for the Afghan scenes, which have forward echoes of his Oscar-winning work for *Out of Africa* (1989). Shame we couldn't have had more of that.

The other strange element of this film is its handling of humour. Jeroen Krabbe's Koskov — a snivelling, greedy, deceitful specimen — is a nice creation and a tremendous acting job but he is never allowed to fly and really go for the comedy. Similarly, flashes of Bondian comedy, such as the escape in the cello case, are hugely welcome when they come, but very suddenly the tone changes back to pure seriousness — high spirits are swiftly extinguished in favour of Dalton's slightly moist-eyed sincerity.

It is only when it all comes to an end that you put your finger on what you were missing. The traditional Bond mix has been shaken up much more thoroughly than before. Now, it might be said that there weren't a great many laughs in *On Her Majesty's Secret Service* either, but that at least had the distraction of the inadvertently amusing George Lazenby. Here we have an actor trying for the first time ever to make Bond a rounded, functioning human being, and it all sits very oddly with the Aston Martin and the death-defying fights.

Humour was never the strong point of the novels. Very often as a reader, you will find yourself laughing at some absurdity, like Dr Shatterhand's molten enema chamber, and then you stop laughing when you realise that Fleming was being perfectly serious. Indeed, for all of their fairy-tale villains and insanely exotic women and brilliantly inventive ways of killing people, such as the poisoned stilettos, you come to suspect that secretly, Ian Fleming didn't have any sense of humour at all, and that he meant for all of this to be read perfectly straight.

And this seems to be what happens in *The Living Daylights*; little chinks of humour, such as Julie T. Wallace's massive oil-pipe worker smothering her boss to her chest so that he does not notice the flashing lights of Koskov's escape, are overwhelmed by Dalton not acknowledging the joke at all. It is not that his Bond can't laugh — he can, and there is a wonderful touch in his scene with the new Moneypenny when she takes off her glasses and he gently puts them back on again at a skew-whiffy angle — but this Bond is chuckling at something real, and not one of the absurdities that the 007 universe used to throw up with such regularity. He can smile, too, this Bond, and he does so with a sort of dewy-eyed affection at Kara often, but it is not quite the same as the punning quipster that we had hitherto been used to.

If there might have been a trace of new-fangled post-feminism about Kara, it certainly was not reflected in the posters for the film, which were criticised heavily by feminists. The main image is of Bond in that gun-barrel view, facing a blonde in a diaphanous white dress, standing with her back to us, who appears not to be wearing knickers, and whose bust measurements are not quite the same as Kara's.

Such things have been known before: the poster for *For Your Eyes Only* featured Bond framed between the bare legs of a bikini-clad woman holding a crossbow, who was clearly meant to be Carole Bouquet but who equally obviously wasn't. Even in super-equality-conscious 1999, art-house actress Sophie Marceau was surprised to see that posters featuring her image for *The World Is Not Enough* had enhanced her breast dimensions to an almost science-fictional degree.

Well, there it is. These things happen. Something even stranger can happen on Bond posters though, and you see it especially in the promotional painting for *Octopussy*. For some reason, Bond's and Octopussy's legs are disproportionately – almost nightmarishly – long. Their bodies are painted at normal length but at the waist, something happens and the legs end up twice the length they should be. Grace Jones also appears to have weird long legs on the posters for *View to a Kill*, as does Sean Connery on those for *You Only Live Twice*.

Never mind. Here, posters promised us 'the new James Bond – living on the edge!' Living on the edge was something that many of us younger people aspired to do in the 1980s, as we sought to avoid 'selling out'. The film – and Dalton in particular – picked up a few cautiously enthusiastic reviews but ominously, a couple of underwhelmed notices, one from that old friend of the series Alexander Walker of the *Evening Standard*. 'Since he hasn't Connery's sexy cruelty or Roger Moore's flippant sexiness, Dalton elects to play it straight,' Walker wrote. 'And a straight Bond is like a half dozen other heroes of Spy-Land . . . he looks as if he takes it all for real and dislikes much of it.' Walker went on to add: 'Cubby Broccoli should start the think-tank going for the film after this and decide what kind of Bond they want, for at the moment, they haven't got one.'

In the *Guardian*, Derek Malcolm acknowledged what a fine actor Dalton was. 'But the caveat is that a good actor has to have lines,' he said.

A fascinating sign of those times came from elsewhere: Russia. By the early 1980s, and with the spread of home video, Bond adventures were picking up an illicit, underground appeal as forbidden copies circulated throughout the Eastern bloc. Come 1987, and the Gorbachev era of glasnost and perestroika, even the Russian press finally had to concede defeat and acknowledge that these films had penetrated beyond the Iron Curtain. But for one Russian critic, Dalton's ascension to the role was a source of deep, heavy regret.

'The writer reminds readers that Timothy Dalton is known to Russian TV audiences for his role as Rochester in *Jane Eyre*', he wrote. 'He wonders how such a talented actor, a Shakespearean to boot, could find himself in such a cheap cliché as a Bond film. He finds with a shake of the head that Dalton did it for big money.'

When one looks at today's Russia, one quietly marvels that only two decades ago, big money was regarded as a capitalist evil. Happy days!

In 1987, Eon Productions may at least have drawn comfort from the fact that they appeared to be opening up a new market. For elsewhere, there were two looming problems. First, *The Living Daylights* really didn't do very well in the States. Second, Eon had run out of Ian Fleming. That was it. All the stories – the usable ones – had been done.

And the same went for the titles. Unless they decided to make a go of 'The Hildebrand Rarity' or 'Quantum of Solace' (oh, I do beg your pardon – *Quantum of Solace* is of course the controversial titular choice for Daniel Craig's second Bond outing). In one sense, the films had parted company with the source material some way beforehand, from as early as *You Only Live Twice*. But there was still the nagging sense that any film from this point onwards would not quite be authentic Fleming; and if there is one thing we know, Bond enthusiasts are keen on their authenticity.

Since 1982, thriller writer John Gardner had been licensed to produce new Bond novels, and this he did with various degrees of success – *Licence Renewed* and *Nobody Lives Forever* were felt by critics to be fine but the others received more mixed responses. And in any case, they just weren't the same. Very much not the same in fact. They were certainly not material for films. And so for the next production, Cubby Broccoli, with his new co-producer Michael G. Wilson, prepared to take something of a leap in the dark. Audiences were surprised at just how dark this leap was.

CHAPTER TWENTY-TWO NIGHT OF THE IGUANA

Sometimes it can be a shock when one looks back to a year one thought was fun and suddenly sees just how very ugly it was. And 1989 was such a year. After the Thatcher/Reagan axis had popularised – and crucially, made respectable – the notion of turbo-capitalism, we were all made aware of a new species in the City. In London, the so-called Big Bang of 1986, which loosened up a lot of Square Mile regulation, came to revolutionise Britain's financial sector.

And the men and women who inhabited this weird, esoteric world were conspicuous consumers. City bars, once the provenance of dusty port drinkers, suddenly flooded with expensive champagnes. Women wore shoulder-pads and discussed 'power dressing'; men wore boxy double-breasted suits and bright braces and started shouting into the black monoliths that were the original mobile telephones.

This wasn't just the City; among the professional classes, a vulgar celebration of excess was also in fashion. Not for nothing in the late 1980s did the estate agent rise to prominence as an especially disliked figure, concerned only with the acquisition of as much profit as possible.

But as the middle classes suddenly saw no reason to be reticent about their increasing wealth, this era saw fresh neuroses starting to set in. While Communism teetered on the brink of collapse – though in fact practically no one predicted how fast the Berlin Wall would come down later in the year – a new anxiety rose up in the United States to take the place of the Cold War: drug-related crime and the decaying inner cities going up in flames. Narcotics were flooding in from Central America; disaffected youth were becoming addicted not merely to heroin, but to a whole succession of new variations, such as 'crack'. The drug panic tapped into a generalised middle-class fear of the black urban poor which, as we can see on both sides of the Atlantic, has never entirely gone away.

It was around this time that the pernicious term 'underclass' was coined to describe people who were struggling on the urban breadline; pernicious because the term quietly implied a species of subhumanity, a teeming swarm of metaphorical Morlocks that was beyond saving. It was this imagery that provided the trigger for Tom Wolfe's *The Bonfire of the Vanities* (1987), when 'master of the universe' New York city trader Sherman McCoy takes a wrong turn on those dark urban streets and through his own cupidity plunges into a middle-class nightmare. The other end of the social scale was perceived in ugly terms too; not for nothing was Oliver Stone's *Wall Street* (1988), featuring Michael Douglas as the reptilian city dealer Gordon Gekko, such a huge hit. Between the imagery of squalid crack-houses and insanely opulent duplexes, we had a brand new form of Manichaeism to replace the old good-versus-evil certainties of the Cold War.

Action thrillers needed a new twist to reflect this more comfortless world. In 1987, Richard Donner's phenomenally successful *Lethal Weapon* had just that. Teaming Bond-possible Mel Gibson with Danny Glover, this LA buddy-cop picture refreshed the police genre, spawning many sequels that ran well into the 1990s. The Unique Selling Point was that while Danny Glover's cop was old and wise, the Mel Gibson character was hovering on the edge of self-destructive psychosis; his utter suicidal disdain for his own life was what made him a lethal weapon.

Super-heroes were toughening up everywhere. In 1988 came the inauguration of the hugely popular *Die Hard* series where Bruce Willis plays the good guy in a vest, up against a bunch of ruthless madmen led by Alan Rickman in an office block. The blend of humour, suspense and spectacular pyrotechnic violence obviously owed a terrific debt to Bond. What didn't? But by 1989, the truth was that Bond himself appeared to be an anachronistic, unfashionable, marginalised figure. He might still be doing the business in Britain and Europe but super-confident America had her own heroes now.

It was felt within Eon that *The Living Daylights* had clearly pointed the way forward, and that Timothy Dalton's darker, more dangerous Bond should be taken into more suitably murky territory. Although there were no more novels to draw inspiration from, the emotional trigger of the new film *Licence to Kill* came from an unused aspect of Fleming's novel *Live and Let Die* — that is, a ruthless, sickening attack on Bond's American buddy Felix Leiter. This was meshed in with a story about Bond turning rogue in order to make a mission personal — revenge against the Central American drug baron Sanchez, responsible for maiming Leiter and having his new wife murdered.

Even from that very short précis, you can tell that we were in unusual territory for Bond. It is simply impossible to imagine Connery's or Moore's Bond defying M and renouncing his 007 number to pursue a personal vendetta of this sort. Even though Bond did pursue such a vendetta against Blofeld with M's tacit approval. But also quite different was the film's unexotic backdrop: a fictional Central American country providing a base for a cocaine-laundering operation.

The advance publicity material sent out by Eon to the press summed it up: 'A story torn straight from the headlines of today's newspapers.'

We can tell from the lengthy pre-credits sequence that things have got nastier. Villain Sanchez (Robert Davi) bursts in on his lover, Lupe Lamore (Talisa Soto), who is in bed with another man. The miscreant is pulled away, with orders from Sanchez that his heart be cut out. Then Sanchez puts Lupe over his knee and begins to whip her with what is apparently a stingray tail – a detail drawn from the Fleming short story 'The Hildebrand Rarity'. Meanwhile, Bond is in full morning dress, on his way to Felix Leiter's wedding as best man. The pair of them are diverted by the Drugs Enforcement Agency, who plan to trap Sanchez.

Naturally, the drugs boys fail and Felix and Bond – his top hat shot at – succeed. Bond cleverly secures a winch around the tail of Sanchez's getaway plane and pulls him in. But it all feels a little *Miami Vice* – a hugely influential American TV series that started in 1984 and was still popular around this time. What is Bond doing with these Drug Enforcement Agency people who unforgivably run in slow motion? Why does it feel as though he has blundered into an American blockbuster?

The American feel is amplified at the end of this sequence, as Bond and Felix arrive at Leiter's wedding in time. Bond is shown as part of a very American community – and also shown to have a social life of sorts. This has never been the case in any of the previous films. Indeed, Ian Fleming in one interview noted that he never allowed the character any ordinary friends. It looks and feels strange, but that's touchy-feely Americans for you.

Things get no better after the titles – Maurice Binder's last, and the least inspired of the lot, featuring a walloping great bit of product placement for Olympus cameras – for this bloody drug lord story just goes on. Sanchez escapes from custody by means of a guard being hit bloodily with a rifle butt. Then he sends his sinister henchman Dario (a remarkable Benicio del Toro) on a revenge mission against Felix Leiter; this involves the rape and murder of Leiter's new wife Della, while Leiter himself is lowered feet first into a shark tank.

Over Leiter's hideously maimed body, Bond swears vengeance. M demands that he jolly well stop it, Bond defies him and suddenly we are in an altogether new genre for 007; that of the sweaty hombre drugs thriller.

There are small elements we can see in use from Fleming; Sanchez, for instance, is faintly sexually ambiguous – he is forever stroking the face of his young henchman and what is more, he has a pet iguana, around the neck of which he has placed a diamond necklace. In Bond terms, a pet with a diamond necklace can only mean one thing. But the ambiguity is an echo of the novel *The Man with the Golden Gun*, in which Scaramanga seems to develop a slight pash for Bond. Then there are other fragments from the novel *Live and Let Die*; after Leiter is fed to the sharks, his wounded, barely conscious body is left with a note attached: 'He disagreed with something that ate him.'

Also a lift from the novel is the marine store, with its tanks of electric eels and maggots; as in the novel, Bond gets into a scrap in this warehouse, much to the detriment of the exotic fish. The name of the store's slimy owner, Milton Krest, was plucked from the short story 'The Hildebrand Rarity'.

After that, though, we are pretty much in new territory. After fishing around on Leiter's computer, Bond meets up with a contact, Pam Bouvier (Cary Lowell), who turns out to be a CIA agent with a flair for handling shotguns. There is a fine brawl scene in a dockside bar as Dario menaces the pair of them and a vast plastic swordfish is deployed against Bond.

From then on, all is confusion. Bond and Pam (Pam – it's just not a Bond name) fly down to a made-up South American region called Isthmus City, where Sanchez tells the puppet president what to do and funds for his criminal empire are brought in via a fraudulent TV evangelist. We are allowed a couple more moments of familiarity as Bond engages in an underwater scene beneath Sanchez's yacht and yes! his oxygen line gets cut with a knife. There is also a fleeting moment of humour as Bond waterskis barefoot behind Sanchez's drugs-money plane and takes control of it.

But the taste of it is so very wrong. Bond infiltrates Sanchez's operation with the greatest of ease by pretending to ask for a job; Sanchez is all over him like a cheap suit. Bond tries to assassinate Sanchez from a nearby building but is ambushed by some mystery Hong Kong people who turn out to be drugs police; Sanchez has them killed and Bond is taken back to his house, where 007 is given a remarkably tacky boudoir.

But here comes faithful Q! Even though Bond has been abandoned by M, Q can't bear to see him in the field on his own. This marks Desmond Llewelyn's biggest role in any of the Bonds and heavens, it's a relief to see him. He's even brought some gadgets with him. 'Everything for the man on holiday!' he declares as Pam examines a laser-beam-shooting camera.

Then it's off to some form of HQ in the hills – part tacky religious retreat, part cocaine processing plant. Dario spots Bond and blows the whistle on his treachery, Bond is nearly crushed in a cocaine grinder and a convoy of trucks makes off into the hills with the cocaine. Bond and Pam contrive, after about twenty minutes of relentless truck action, to sabotage this convoy, Sanchez confronts Bond and Bond sets fire to him with Felix Leiter's lighter.

There are many American fans of this film who feel that it is a work of high seriousness and the closest thing to Ian Fleming since *On Her Majesty's Secret Service*. I remember seeing it at the cinema in 1989 with the same friends as ever; the pub discussion afterwards centred on how unpleasant and violent and so very tired the whole thing seemed.

For that's the thing – these days, we can see the film on DVD bookended by waggish Roger Moore and saucy Pierce Brosnan and praise it as a one-off experiment. But at the time, it really seemed to many that it was the end of the road for Bond.

The film was plagued with difficulties from the start. The original idea was to set it in China. This idea was abandoned, quite fortuitously, given the worldwide repercussions of the massacre in Tiananmen Square in 1989. Then, when the notion of South America was mooted instead, it was felt that to save production costs, it would be more effective to move the entire crew from Pinewood out to Mexico City. This in turn led to the British press turning a little sour; one of the crucial points about Bond was that this was a series of British films made in Britain with British expertise. The Duchess of York, Sarah Ferguson, made a public intervention pleading with Broccoli and Eon to stay.[1] Imagine not heeding that! The move to cheaper South America looked a little shabby to many journalists.

This was unfair to Cubby Broccoli; throughout the 1980s, the British film industry received fewer and fewer favours from a consistently cost-cutting government and the result was that by 1989, the expense of such a major production would apparently have been prohibitive. Matters were not helped by the fact that Britain was in that year plunging into recession.

Interesting, though, how Eon learned the PR lesson after that; the subsequent Pierce Brosnan films returned to British shores.

But that was also because of practicalities and unforeseen problems on *Kill*'s production. One of these was a side effect of working in Mexico City — the crew felt some discomfort caused by the relative lack of oxygen. Indeed, Cubby Broccoli was hit rather hard at one point and had to be flown out, attached to a ventilator, for medical attention.

Then there was the debacle over the title — a flap that might demonstrate that backers MGM/UA were not feeling madly confident about this attempt to reinvent the whole notion of Bond. The film's original title had been *Licence Revoked*; indeed, that had been the title right up until the point when publicity and marketing material was drawn up. *Licence Revoked* was straightforward and to the point. It was also — and let's be quite honest here — awful. It leaves one feeling utterly inert — two dull words joined to make a dull, unevocative phrase. There were objections on the grounds that American audiences would not understand the word 'revoked'. There were also suggestions that, for foreign audiences, the word 'kill' was easier to translate than 'revoked'. Possibly so, but the real point surely was that the title was simply dreary.

It was also a nod to the post-Ian Fleming Bond novels, a sequence that had begun in 1982 with John Gardner's *Licence Renewed*. As Fleming's agent Peter Janson-Smith told me (before, it must be said, publication of Sebastian Faulks's *Devil May Care*, which he had yet to see), it is an extraordinarily difficult thing to capture that authentic Fleming tone. Kingsley Amis, according to Janson-Smith, was among the very few who completely pulled it off: 'Amis could reproduce the Fleming style without making it look like parody and very few could do that.' But it was the opinion of many reviewers that Gardner was close enough as to make no odds. We see very little of these books now.

So *Licence Revoked* had to go. In its place came the slightly more dynamic, though rather unimaginative *Licence to Kill*. This all goes to illustrate what a fantastic headache the business of a Bond title was to become. Rather like Fleming's literary style, the author's flair for baroque titles was not easily replicated. Try it at home: give yourself a little while to think of a good Bond title. I've done this a few times with colleagues and all we can ever come up with are parody titles — *Forever Dies Tomorrow* and so forth. Serious ones are all but impossible. It is a fine art that has been acknowledged by producer Michael G. Wilson as something requiring a lot of thought and input.

For instance, in 1995, the name of Fleming's house in Jamaica provided an absolute godsend with *GoldenEye*, because it could also plausibly be the name of a sinister satellite system. It had also been the title of a 1991 TV biopic of Ian Fleming with Charles Dance in the lead role, and filmed on location at Goldeneye itself.

You could see the title struggle all over again with 1997's *Tomorrow Never Dies*, which made no sense. This had originally been *Tomorrow Never Lies* and referred to the newspaper *Tomorrow* owned by media magnate villain Elliot Carver. The new title came about, so the film's publicity office claimed, as the result of a serendipitous typo on an internal memorandum. In other words, it was adopted chiefly because it sounded good.

For my money, the best of the non-Fleming titles came with 1999's *The World Is Not Enough*. In fact, it was pretty damned perfect – exciting, evocative, blackly humorous – and it came from a line in the novel *On Her Majesty's Secret Service* where it is revealed to be Bond's family motto. On this occasion, it was a perfect fit for a complex story of oil pipelines, stolen nuclear weaponry and patricide.

But the titles appeared to come off the rails again with 2002's *Die Another Day*. One critic suggested that it was the result of the screenwriters randomly selecting words from other titles and slotting them together. But then it emerged that the title was slightly more literary than the sneering critics might have thought; in fact it came from A.E. Housman's poem cycle *A Shropshire Lad*, although its original meaning became a little skewed. The verse went:

> But since the man that runs away
> Lives to die another day
> And cowards' funerals, when they come,
> Are not wept so well at home,
>
> Therefore though the best is bad
> Stand and do the best, my lad;
> Stand and fight and see your slain
> And take the bullet in your brain.

Imagine if Madonna, performer of the title song, had sung that instead of her own silly lyrics!

For 2006, and the dynamic reinvention of the entire series with new Bond Daniel Craig, it was at last deemed safe for Eon to buy up the rights to the one Fleming novel that had thus far eluded them, together with the title that was once a byword for naffness: *Casino Royale*. Given that these are still two of the tackiest words in the English language, regardless of the earlier 1960s film, it was brave of Eon to flaunt them in this manner. It worked. And they are clearly hoping the same will go for the enigmatic mouthful that is *Quantum of Solace*.

All of which digression has pulled us away from the curious aesthetics and script judgements of *Licence to Kill*. As mentioned before, director John Glen – back for his fifth Bond film in a row – felt that an increase in violence was necessary to keep the character contemporary. We might try and justify this decision by pointing to the biggest family film of 1989 – Tim Burton's wild gothic reimagining of *Batman* – and noting that that production too had an undertow of unpleasant violence, including scenes of acid attacks.

But the sourness and seaminess of this Bond really does take one aback. For instance, Sanchez's right-hand man Milton Krest, as portrayed by the old American character actor Anthony Zerbe. No steel teeth, no razor-edged bowler hat – he simply oozes sleaze. Whether leching around Lupe Lamore or looking shifty when Bond escapes his clutches, it is a fine piece of acting but he is a rather lowering character.

Even his demise is repugnant; suspecting him of having stolen all his money, Sanchez traps Krest in a decompression chamber and reverses the controls, so Krest's head expands grotesquely and explodes. It is a scene that makes you want to retch. And that, by and large, is not something you want from a Bond film.

Then there is the chilliness of the entire premise; that is, Bond exiling himself from his faux family in order to pursue a vendetta. There is little question that no matter how harshly Robert Brown portrays M, the character is still very much a father figure to Bond. This is most apparent when Bond is ordered to hand over his gun and instead vaults over the edge of (what happens to be Ernest Hemingway's) verandah. Fellow agents fire at him – but M knocks the arm of one of these men to the side, with the claim that the bullets might hit a passer-by.

Nor are the Bond girls much help this time around. Lupe (whose name is distractingly pronounced 'Loopy') barely fills one dimension – villain's girlfriend with victim status. She makes *Thunderball*'s Domino look like Anna

Karenina. Then there is Pam (Pam! Once again, it is *so* not a Bond name), who is not much more than a hard-eyed video game character. This is a unique Bond also in the sense that you couldn't really care less if Bond declined to snog either of these two women.

All of which is a shame because Robert Davi as villain Sanchez – apparently loosely based on the US government's *bête noire* General Noriega – is more than creditable. He is jolly good, flitting with ease between light menace and creepy psychopathic intensity. If he had been in a different screenplay – one a little more ambitious than merely smuggling liquid cocaine in petrol – he might just have been one of the best bad guys. I recall seeing the actor interviewed on the BBC's Terry Wogan chat show upon the opening of the film; he looked so proud to have joined the pantheon of Bond villains, and quite happily told his host about the iguana wearing the diamond necklace.

And twenty-two-year-old Benicio del Toro made a superbly unsettling villain's sidekick, giving the role of Dario an intensity that was of course later to become the actor's trademark. He too paid ample tribute to the simple honour of having appeared in a Bond film.

The truck convoy sequence at the end was all the demonstration we needed that the series was at this point creatively exhausted. Bond hangs off trucks, villain fires machine guns, trucks drive along dusty desert roads, trucks roll down hills – it is all flat and uninspired and leaden. And also fundamentally un-escapist. As the old joke goes: I can get all that at home.

But consider the extraordinary production line that was Bond. Apart from the enforced year's break in 1976, Eon had been trotting out these films initially at the rate of one a year and throughout the 1970s and 80s at one every two years. Each adventure took five or six months to film and much longer to plan; so, as one film was in production, the next one along was already in pre-production.

In other words, the whole thing was a vast and awesome undertaking and it is easy to see how, in an uncertain cinematic climate, the films temporarily lost their way. To take a more recent – and much more short-lived – sequence of films made in a similar way, the second and third films in the *Pirates of the Caribbean* series were made back-to-back; but the third was universally trounced by the critics as uninspired. See how easily it can happen?

Licence to Kill made money, for sure, stacks of it. But in the accustomed Bond stratospheric stakes, it tanked. It did badly in Britain and lethally, it did worse in the States.

Novelist Hilary Mantel was among those who found herself holding her nose, in *The Spectator*: 'It is a very noisy film,' she said. 'There is a weary and repetitive note to the frenzy . . . the sex is low key and off-screen but there is a smirking perverse undertow which makes the film more disagreeable than a slasher movie.' Meanwhile, *The Times*'s critic noted that 'Robert Davi could be a drug runner from any thriller.' And the *Mail on Sunday*'s Tom Hutchinson observed that Dalton was 'as glum as a le Carré character . . . his performance tries to make sense of what is nonsense in the first place'.

In Britain, the film was hit by the censors giving it a 15 certificate, the first time this had ever happened to Bond. Even violent *Batman* managed to get away with a 12. I am with the censor on this one. The cartoon violence of *Batman* is in a different league to the realistic horrors conjured by *Kill*.

Dalton was having none of it, however, when news of the certification came through. 'That's stupid,' he said. 'I watched a preview at a packed cinema and kids aged 12 and 13 were lapping it up. They loved it. They don't get upset by bloodshed.' We will simply have to agree to disagree on that one. But he had more to say: 'Should parents want to take their daughter to *The Accused*, because it is of social significance, they can't.'[2] *The Accused* was a hard-hitting, critically acclaimed drama about a bar-room rape in which the victim, played by Jodie Foster, subsequently finds herself up against a hostile legal process that tries to prove she somehow provoked the attack. I still think Dalton had an odd idea of what constituted the perfect family night out.

As it happened, it was poor old Dalton who took much of the blame in the press for the perceived shortcomings of the long-running series; but actually his Bond was an intriguing experiment in trying to give flesh to Fleming's dream. We can see how Daniel Craig is now following a similar approach.

'Dalton was the actor most steeped in Fleming's novels,' says Peter Janson-Smith. 'He knew them inside out and he is a very good actor too but somehow he didn't quite . . . he never really looked the part and I think the reason is that he looks too kind, it was too difficult to imagine him really beating anyone up.'

Quite a different view to that of my female war correspondent friend, rehearsed in the previous chapter – that Dalton was the only Bond who looked as though he could kill – but in a curious way, both opinions are quite valid. Dalton's Bond was a man who knew that he was employed as a blunt instrument; but he could not help his humanity getting in the way.

His stricken reaction to the murder of Leiter's wife is one such moment. And rather than simply killing Sanchez in the end, he has to show the man why he is being killed; Bond opens his hand to reveal the engraved lighter that Felix gave him. It is only as Sanchez suddenly realises that Bond sets him on fire.

But in the midst of this darkness, Dalton also lightens things a little. His redemptively comic exasperation with Q is a terrific relief – especially nice is the scene in the South American hotel where Pam stomps off into her room and Bond realises he is going to be sharing a room with the elderly quartermaster. In another scene, Bond is rather sharp with Pam; it is Q who takes her to one side and says 'Don't judge him too harshly, my dear.'

In other words, Dalton made 007 a believable man; unfortunately, without the benefit of a third film, we can't really see how he would have settled further into the role, and to what degree he might have lightened it from this point. It would have been interesting to see him in a rather more escapist and amusing plot.

And all right, although *Kill* in general is awful, what did for Bond at this stage was a set of cultural circumstances that the production team could have done nothing about. For by 1989, the very notion of Bond seemed naff and outmoded and to some, rather offensive. The sense that fashion and contemporary thought had left Bond behind had been creeping up throughout the 1980s. Now that feeling seemed to reach its peak.

We were in the age of post-feminism, but the role of Bond girl was still irredeemable; in social terms, it was arguably an increasingly meritocratic age, and the idea of a dinner-jacketed hero with a Received Pronunciation accent now felt odd. The thawing of the Cold War caused other uncertainties – even though screen Bond had never fought the Soviets, the popular misconception was that this was the character's *raison d'être*. Where would he find fresh super-villains to fight?

And truth be told, we were all a little Bonded out. When in 1989 the BBC TV comedians French and Saunders produced a parody of Bond title sequences, making their full-figured selves the dancing silhouettes, the audience bayed with laughter. Now we were looking at these films as the stuff of kitsch memories, there to be scorned along with flared trousers and driving gloves. They weren't even such big events on television any more. Familiarity and repetition had dulled enthusiasm.

The title song of *Licence to Kill* tells us all we really need to know. Starting with a virtual repetition of the opening bars of *Goldfinger*, it proceeds into a hearty yet wholly unmemorable soul rendering by Gladys Knight which sounds like about six thousand other songs recorded in that year. It was very straight, and clearly pitched directly at American tastes. As was the entire film, with its slow-motion DEA men and jokes about fraudulent television evangelists.

It was coincidental that following *Kill*, the Bond series was forced into its longest hiatus; a matter of a grinding, gruelling Jarndyce v. Jarndyce legal case involving MGM's new owner and screening rights. But when Bond failed to return in 1991, there was not much of an outcry. This was the gravest crisis that the whole enterprise faced. Was it possible that Bond might finally be killed off by indifference?

No press calls for the world's journalists. No publicity shots of the latest Bond girl perched on the latest Bond car. No head-scratching over the announcement of somewhat obscure titles. The period between 1989 and 1995 was a very strange, rather echoing time not just for diehard Bond fans but also for those millions of us who were used to the bi-annual appearance of these films, and the ritual troop to the cinema to see them. Where were we to find the shooty-bang heroics now?

It was incorrectly assumed by many that *Licence to Kill* had been so very bad that it had succeeded in killing off the entire series. This was not so. In fact, the backer MGM needed Bond; 007 was a rare banker in an uncertain cinematic world. The problem came when MGM was bought up by an Italian financial concern and Eon suddenly found that the rights to TV screenings of Bond were being sold for below-market rates. This was worse than any bothersome case brought by Kevin McClory wanting to remake *Thunderball* all over again. In a new video age, it was a direct challenge to Eon's ability to continue making money out of the considerable 007 archive.

Cubby Broccoli was advised that any legal challenge he mounted would be dicey, and that if he lost the case, he could say goodbye to millions. He decided to press on none the less. He was no longer a young man – indeed, he was in his early eighties. But it seems reasonably clear that this was an issue of legacy; that he was determined that Eon should live on through his stepson Michael G. Wilson and daughter Barbara, and that the company should not be hindered in any way.

As is usual with any financial suit, the case proceeded to drag on for year after wearisome year. It must have been the source of much corrosive anxiety, for at the time it seemed to many onlookers that the longer Bond was off the screen, the more difficult it might be to reintroduce the world to this kind of hero.

Wispy rumours occasionally emerged in the early 1990s; such as that Timothy Dalton had been signed up for his third Bond epic and that a script was in development. There was also the rather startling manifestation of a kids' cartoon series called *James Bond Junior*. In 1991, the cartoon surfaced in America: the Bond of the title was James's nephew, the setting was Warfield boarding school for young spies and the hero faced familiar adversaries such as Jaws, along with new menaces such as Goldfinger's daughter Goldie Finger. And of course it was aimed squarely at young children.

Although back then it seemed very odd for the 'franchise' to be extended in this way – this cartoon series was approved and overseen by the Bond office – Eon and Glidrose had a much smarter idea along the same lines a few years ago. They engaged the writer, television comedian and sometime hit pop musician Charlie Higson to write a series of Young James Bond novels, kicking off with *Silverfin* (published in 2005). These novels, set during 007's schooldays, depict the hair-raising adventures of his adolescence (minus the galumphing double entendres).

Higson is a wonderful writer; but what he and his publishers are (unconsciously?) doing is herding a whole new generation of youngsters towards the secret agent's film exploits. Friends of mine recently had a nine-year-old girl and her parents to stay; the girl's first request was whether my friends had any DVDs of old Bonds.

But the absence of Bond in the early 1990s also created moments of what seemed pure eccentricity. In 1992, when I was a feature writer for the *Mail on Sunday*, I was sent down to Portsmouth to interview a sixteen-year-old lad who was shooting his own, home-made Bond movie called *No-one Lives Forever*. He had hired a tuxedo, enlisted his girlfriend to be the Bond girl and also got some help from an old chap who developed hovercraft, and who was willing to supply hardware for this local amateur production.

But the teenager's plans came stuttering to a halt when Eon Productions got in touch with him. They demanded – rather to his astonishment – that he desist, and in not especially friendly terms. Bond was theirs and theirs alone. So he desisted, but not before letting his feelings be known to the press. Much was made of Eon's oversensitivity. In general terms, though, they did have to be rather careful, for damage of any kind to Bond's image during his enforced sabbatical was likely to be long-lasting.

The early 1990s threw up their summer blockbusters. *Batman Returns* (1992) brought more of Tim Burton's gothic sensibility to what was perhaps a lighter entry than the first. Bruce Willis was back Dying Harder, in an airport, and then on the streets of New York. Harrison Ford provided American secret service thrills as CIA man Jack Ryan in Tom Clancy's *Patriot*

Games (1992). The more austere Kevin Costner put his back into reinventing an old genre with *Robin Hood: Prince of Thieves* (1991), with Alan Rickman's insanely camp Sheriff of Nottingham stealing the film from under Costner's nose. Also in 1991, Arnie was back in *Terminator 2: Judgment Day*. And all the while, special effects and subject matter appeared to be moving on from secret agents in tuxedos.

If things weren't about stylised sci-fi effects, then they were about 'grunge', the term affixed to the early 1990s youth craze for behaving like every other young person in history and slobbing out. In 1992 came the release of Mike Myers's immensely cheering slacker comedy *Wayne's World*, featuring as its leads two dim metalheads. Two other immensely dim and popular figures were Bill and Ted, who reached their heights of comic genius in *Bill and Ted's Bogus Journey* (1992). We must always bear in mind that in Bond terms, this was precisely the sort of audience that the films had to grab every time – and still do for that matter, for it is the American eighteen- to twenty-five-year-olds who stampede into cinemas in greater multitudes than anyone else on the planet.

In 1994, James Cameron (later the Oscar-winning director of 1997's *Titanic*) unwittingly refreshed the entire Bondian genre with a comedy thriller called *True Lies*. In this picture, Arnold Schwarzenegger plays a secret agent who from necessity keeps his profession hidden from his wife and family. But as he gets caught up in wilder and wilder adventures, from a horseback chase through an LA office block to the detonation of a nuclear bomb – with Art Malik as the bad guy – wife Jamie Lee Curtis begins to suspect that her husband is not the nine-to-five man he claims.

The film was a riproaring success and the critics adored it. But what some of the critics said must have proved a worry for Eon: the view was that *True Lies* knocked Bond on the head for good; that it was smart, knowing and funny in a way that the last few Bond films had not been. How could any new 007 production compete against this?

Interestingly, the critics missed the real point: that Cameron's film had made fantastical secret agenting a viable genre once more. The outrageous stunts and over-the-top nuclear threat pointed a way forward for Bond in these post-Cold War years. Spies still had their uses.

That said, a great many were writing off both the fictional and real-life sort. Ever since the autumn of 1989, when first Czechoslovakia broke free of Soviet control and then the Berlin Wall came down in Germany, it seemed to some, to quote Francis Fukuyama's famous phrase, that 'the end of history' had arrived. Liberal democracy had apparently triumphed. The Cold War was over. And so with it was apparently an entire era of espionage and counter-espionage.

Many former certainties began to crack. Astonishment over the collapse of the Berlin Wall – watched by billions worldwide, mouths open with wonder, as West and East Germans took chunks out of the concrete – was followed a year later when F.W. de Klerk, leader of the oppressive apartheid regime in South Africa, suddenly released the world's most famous political prisoner, Nelson Mandela, paving the way for the swift dismantling of the entire apartheid apparatus. These things would never have seemed possible either in the 1970s or the 1980s.

In the summer of 1990, Iraq's dictator Saddam Hussein invaded the neighbouring country of Kuwait. America, under President Bush, and its European allies, decided to respond with force. This was the first real geopolitical crisis faced without the West also having to measure Soviet response.

The early 1990s also presented a hostile social and cultural environment for Bond, and for any other male action hero like him. For so long a preserve of the left, the feminist movement had by now transmogrified into post-feminism; women were finally not only breaking through corporate glass ceilings, but also not behaving like ball-breakers to do so. Exaggerated shoulder pads were deemed grotesquely unnecessary. There was no reason why a woman could not be CEO without compromising her essential femininity.

But equally, in fictional terms, the world no longer had any use for the passive heroine, there simply to be an adornment on the arm of the macho hero. As a footnote in Bond terms, the notion in the early 1990s of having a title sequence involving naked silhouettes writhing and dancing about would have been laughed scornfully out of the room.

Also at this point, Britain, Europe and the US were in recession. Whereas in the 1970s and 1980s, such economic cyclones hit the poorest hardest, this one hit the middle classes too. For the first time, we became aware of people who had defaulted on their mortgages, of homes being repossessed. Some optimists endeavoured to turn the tight circumstances round into a positive new social movement – 'downsizing'.

The glitzy materialism of the 1980s, on both sides of the Atlantic, was gladly forsaken in favour of a more frugal, homespun approach to life. It is no coincidence that the glossy American TV soaps *Dynasty* and *Dallas* came to an end and were superseded by slower, more thoughtful serials such as *Thirtysomething* and *Twin Peaks*. But what this also meant by implication was that a conspicuously consuming spy, clad in tailored tuxedo, gobbling Beluga caviar and necking Bollinger, would not have hit quite the correct note.

So however much grief the MGM court case caused the Broccoli clan, we might argue that Bond's enforced period in exile was a stroke of tremendously good luck. Any further outing for 007 in 1991 or 1992 might have finished him for ever – a spy out of time and out of place. But gradually, as economies recovered, and as the world adjusted to the notion of America being the sole superpower, things started to look a little favourable once more. Plus the enforced break gave Eon much-needed time to recharge, to sit back and have a considered look at what the Bond series needed next to see it thrive once more.

I don't suppose we will ever know exactly what made Timothy Dalton suddenly decide to hang up the Walther PPK holster in 1994. With a new Bond in pre-production, he elected to bow out with a hugely graceful resignation letter, pointing out what good friends, as well as colleagues, the Broccoli clan were, but how he had been identified with the role of Bond for quite long enough. Eon's response was equally graceful and Dalton did indeed remain a firm family friend. But it set the press off into a foam of excitement, and one might be tempted to wonder if this resignation didn't also come as a godsend to Eon. For it allowed them once more the worldwide publicity that the search for a new Bond always brought.

Who would get the shoulder-holster this time? Hugh Grant, newly famous for *Four Weddings and a Funeral* (1994)? Brooding Clive Owen, star of many a small-scale Brit-movie? Mel Gibson again? It was interesting that Hugh Grant was being mentioned by the press at all. His screen persona of hesitant, archly witty fop would, in previous years, have been seen as most un-Bond-like. But the enormous surprise success of *Four Weddings* – particularly in America – had taken everyone aback.

Here was a comedy about some amusing upper-middle-class people going to each other's weddings, and about foppish Hugh falling for the blank American Andie MacDowell. It was cleverly constructed and played with great warmth but still, how could this have been enough to make it such a toweringly iconic English film? It was down to Grant, portraying a form of English manhood that had never before been sympathetically projected. He became the acceptable face of the previously unacceptable classes. To the critic of *Time* magazine, he was a perfect hero for a feminist age.

For my money, Grant would have been better cast as the umbrella-twiddling John Steed in the ill-fated 1998 film remake of *The Avengers* instead of Ralph Fiennes. Come to think of it, Grant's then girlfriend Elizabeth Hurley would have made an extremely fine Mrs Peel. A little more on that film later.

In the mid-1990s, British film was enjoying one of its spluttering moments of renewed success. Young director Danny Boyle was swiftly rising to great prominence, first with the nail-chewing Edinburgh thriller *Shallow Grave* (1994), starring Ewan MacGregor, and subsequently with the jaunty heroin-based black comedy *Trainspotting* (1996), also with MacGregor. This, again, was a huge and unexpected hit in America, and portrayed a pleasingly grimy mirror image to the Britain portrayed in *Four Weddings*. A few years later, Ewan MacGregor was to be regularly touted as a potential new Bond.

So no, not Grant. Nor Clive Owen. For Eon went back to the man they thought might have done the trick in 1986. In 1994, a bearded Pierce Brosnan was unveiled to the world's press as the new 007.

CHAPTER TWENTY-FOUR WE KNEW THE NAME, WE KNEW THE NUMBER

Chris Donald, creator of the adult comic publishing sensation *Viz*, coined exactly the right phrase for the phenomenon: 'retro chauvinism'. He was referring to that period in the mid to late 1990s when, in an apparent fightback against the ubiquity of feminism, the image of 'the lad' apparently found new legitimacy.

The lad was there to be heard in the burgeoning pop movement of Britpop: in the songs of Blur, and of Pulp. 'Grass is something you smoke, birds are something you shag', sang Jarvis Cocker in 'I-Spy', itself a back-handed homage to the rich espionage melodies of John Barry. The figure of the lad was there in elaborate Guinness advertisements. He was there in the stadium terraces, cheering on the resurgent popularity of football.

In 1994, a brash new magazine aimed at young men, called *Loaded*, hit the news-stands; it had little patience with the old feminist arguments that female pin-ups 'objectified' women. It was amusingly and unashamedly sexist and crucially, the enterprise worked because the very idea of it – scantily clad women coupled with features about mad extreme sports – was at that time shockingly incorrect.

The rise of the lad came at a time when the British economy was finally emerging from the gloom of recession and when, in terms of arts and culture, there seemed to be a new feeling of energy and optimism. In 1994, following the premature death of Labour leader John Smith, the young Tony Blair was elected by the party to be his successor. And it was reasonably clear almost immediately that he was poised to take over from a badly stumbling and exhausted Conservative government led by John Major.

This was a while before the coining of the phrase 'Cool Britannia', but as 1995 came around the sense in London was that we were seeing almost a rerun of the 1960s; in terms of fashion, art, pop and film, the British once more seemed to be the main innovators. London itself, now poised to take over as one of the world's great financial centres, was becoming awash with money and, for the first time since the 1980s, the results could be seen in the amazing amount of construction work (chiefly around the former docks of Canary Wharf) and the explosion in the number of obscenely expensive restaurants.

While all of this was going on, the seventeenth Bond film was in production after a break of six years. The screenplay, from a story by Michael France, was by Jeffrey Caine and Bruce Feirstein. Feirstein was an American who, as mentioned earlier, had written the humorous book *Real Men Don't Eat Quiche*. He was a highly prolific journalist who had worked for, among others, *Vanity Fair*, *Spy*, the *Washington Post* and the *New York Times*. The ebullient director was Martin Campbell, who years back had directed episodes of a British comedy-drama series called *Minder* as well as a superbly unsettling anti-nuclear thriller called *Edge of Darkness*.

The new Bond film was to be called *Goldeneye*. The fact that there had already been such a production – a biopic of Ian Fleming – a few years back scarcely mattered. 'Goldeneye' of course was the name of Fleming's Jamaican home. In fact, Fleming had originally got the name from a secret Second World War naval operation, presumably, in its turn, named for that particular species of wildfowl. Whatever, it struck exactly the right note.

But throughout 1994 and 1995, there had been rumours in the film industry that all was not well with this new Bond production; that Eon had been rattled by the exuberant success of James Cameron's *True Lies* and that a number of changes to the screenplay had been made. '*True Lies* does give us a challenge,' Barbara Broccoli was reported as saying. 'Let me assure you, the new Bond film won't be anything like the old Bond films.'[1]

Happily, this was a whopping great fib. Martin Campbell was happy to step in with another colossal fib in 1994. 'The bimbo aspect of the previous films,' he said with a straight face, 'is probably slightly offensive now.'[2] This while he was simultaneously filming scenes in a sauna with a character called Xenia Onatopp.

The British press was largely rather unhelpful to Eon as the film's production wore on. Baz Bamigboye, the *Daily Mail*'s highly respected showbiz editor, was a regular Cassandra, reporting on script panics and tepid secret preview screenings at the Wimbledon Odeon where it was claimed that the audience didn't get all the jokes.

Respected cinema historian David Gritten caused further pain in 1995 with a piece that questioned the entire point of the exercise:

You start to wonder if the world needs another film with such a predictable outcome, and before long you're pondering the need for any more 007 – ever. In the past decade, Bond films are widely believed to have run out of steam . . . Bond is an anachronism, a character who only made sense in the 1960s. His role in British intelligence as an agent with a licence to kill, was primarily to combat Soviet Communism, but in the six years since the last Bond movie, the Berlin Wall has been dismantled . . . The Bosnian crisis is a daily reminder that goodies and baddies don't present themselves so clearly . . .[3]

This despite the fact that, strictly speaking, cinema Bond had never fought the Russians. But Gritten was not alone in this damaging misconception.

None the less, in 1995, in true Bond fashion, filming took place in Switzerland, Monte Carlo and the Caribbean. And in a truly wonderful Bond first – unthinkable even ten years previously – location filming also took place on the streets of St Petersburg.

For the first time, the producers conspicuously looked to young British talent to fill the role of the villain: this time Sean Bean playing Bond's former 00 colleague Alec Trevelyan, aided by an equally young and upcoming Alan Cumming as sneaky computer programmer Boris Grishenko. Meanwhile, Robbie Coltrane was drafted in as Russian mafia boss Valentin Zukovsky.

The girls this time – although in press interviews they rather crossly asked to be referred to as 'Bond women' instead – were Izabella Scorupco as Natalya and Famke Janssen as the divertingly sinister assassin Xenia Onatopp, who squeezes men to death between her thighs.

The story appeared complex but actually was reasonably simple. In 1986, on a joint mission inside Soviet Russia, Bond and Trevelyan are ambushed; Bond escapes, Trevelyan is apparently shot. In 1995, a satellite tracking base in the snowy wastes of Russia is destroyed and its GoldenEye satellite operating device goes missing. Young computer expert Natalya escapes from the base but back in St Petersburg soon finds she is being targeted by shadowy forces. Bond is set on the trail of GoldenEye and discovers that Trevelyan is still alive and now the head of the Janus crime syndicate. He has long been plotting revenge on the British government for the deaths of his parents, who were White Russians betrayed in the war.

In a sequence of cliffhanging action scenes, Bond and Natalya alternately escape devilish traps and set off in pursuit of Trevelyan to Cuba. There they find – hooray! – that he has a lair underneath an artificial lake, and a plan to send out an electromagnetic pulse from the GoldenEye satellite that will knock out every electronic device in Britain and enable him to rob the Bank of England. What could be more pleasingly Bondian?

But from the pre-credits scene onward, what marked this Bond film out was an entirely new quality of self-awareness, of knowingness. Since the late 1980s, the notion of post-modernism – broadly, the idea that every fictional construct is ultimately self-referential – had been seeping into popular culture. In most cases, it was a supreme irritant. Somehow not in this case.

We open on a breathtaking shot of a vast concrete dam, somewhere deep within Russia. A figure is running along the top of the dam. He is photographed from above, so we do not see his face. But we are perfectly well aware of who he is. Especially when he clips something to his ankles, spreads his arms out wide, and leaps off the edge out into empty space. It's Bond – bungee-jumping! This activity (I've done it myself, leaping from a 250ft disused railway bridge in New Zealand – don't ask me why, just seemed like a good idea) was invented by the Kiwis in the late 1980s and by the time of *GoldenEye* was becoming quite a popular form of scarifying entertainment.

So anyway. At the base of the dam, Bond is upside down. In a nice echo, the next time we see him – surprising a Russian guard in a loo cubicle – he is also upside down. In our first proper glimpse of our new hero Pierce his face is half-lit in a dark corridor, looking tough, but already with an unmistakable twinkle of humour in the eyes. This initial hint of comedy comes as a vast relief after the last few films.

Bond seems to be here, with colleague Alec Trevelyan, on a sabotage mission, although we all know that it hardly matters one way or the other. 'For England, James,' says Trevelyan, and in the cinema where I watched the film in 1995, the audience laughed. It wasn't an ironic laugh, not entirely anyway. There was a tingle of genuine pleasure that a modern hero could say something so unashamedly, and absurdly, patriotic.

Here comes the Russian army; Trevelyan is shot. Bond, crouching behind a trolley with a squeaky wheel, laden with canisters of deadly chemicals, gets out of the building. The sequence that was to follow confirmed to audiences worldwide that not only was Bond back, but also that we had badly missed nonsense like this. Bond sees a small plane about to take off from this mountaintop plateau. Clearly it is his only means of escape. He yanks out the pilot, but fails to board the craft himself. It is now trundling down the runway, pilotless. Shaking off soldiers and grabbing a motorbike, Bond gives chase. At the end of the runway is a cliff; the plane simply tumbles over. And Bond drives the motorbike over the edge as well. What in blue blazes is he up to?

Well, of course he is sky-diving after the plane as it plummets down that seemingly bottomless ravine. And he manages to get into it. And then, sweating, with fists on shaking joystick . . . a few moments' pause. Then we see the plane climbing triumphantly out of that trench and over the now exploding Russian base. It was the best pre-credits sequence since the ski stunt off the mountaintop in *Spy*. And, certainly in the cinema I was in, it had a similar effect. As one, the audience rose for an ovation, as though Her Majesty the Queen had wandered in front of the screen.

If the entire thing seemed a little self-reflexive, well – everything was back in 1995. Literature was filled with novels-as-novels and unreliable narrators. Composers such as Michael Nyman were in their element offering up reinterpretations of Purcell and Mozart. There was an unprecedented amount of enthusiasm for retro-entertainment, such as the craze for 'easy listening' which hit the nation's nightclubs in 1995. Easy listening music took all the Hammond organ tunes used in 1960s lifts and in 1960s television programmes and offered them up as legitimate dance music. Everything was ironic. Even the newly revived decorative lava lamps were ironic. It was too much to expect Bond not to be ironic too.

Yet that was not the only tone that *GoldenEye* offered; if it had been, we might not have seen another James Bond film afterwards. No, the title sequence tells us that a quite new dimension is being brought to the entertainment; and that is the film answering all those newspaper columnists who wrote that Bond had no place in the modern world.

Resident titles guru Maurice Binder had died in 1991. He was succeeded, brilliantly, by Daniel Kleinman, and the *GoldenEye* titles still stand as a hugely amusing work of art in their own right. In recognition, perhaps, of lad culture, and of the idea that if you are going to do Bond then you have to do it wholeheartedly, the titles are full of semi-naked women, against various backgrounds of burnished gold – so much for Martin Campbell's claim that the 'bimbo aspect' was out. But the twist is this: against this cloudy gold backdrop, the women are wielding sledgehammers. And they are smashing up the old icons of Communism: giant sculpted heads of Stalin and Lenin;

the hammer and sickle. The half-naked women are also seen pulling down a statue of Lenin.

It is cheeky, funny, surreal and utterly arresting. This, combined with the pre-titles, was also a tremendous relief. For in that first ten minutes or so, Michael G. Wilson and Barbara Broccoli convinced audiences and critics alike that Bond was not only in safe hands, he was on better form than he had been for over a decade.

Also terrifically important was the title song. In 1992, EMI had released a compilation album of all the James Bond songs and it had become, in its own curious, slightly nerdish way, the secret CD at the back of everyone's collection. It was an acknowledgement of the cult status that these shrieking ditties now had. The question of what Bond song was the best became a subject for pub debate. Louis Armstrong singing 'We Have All the Time in the World'? Nancy Sinatra's rendering of 'You Only Live Twice'? (This was certainly deemed good enough for a sample to be used in Robbie Williams's 1998 hit 'Millennium'.) For Bond's return, it was clear that the song would have to have punch, as well as paying tribute to all of its predecessors.

The result, composed by Bono and The Edge of U2 fame, was sung with tremendous gusto by Tina Turner and in its twisty, turny, faintly 1960s melody offered a wry homage to the entire spy genre. However, one significant person did not like it. At the London premiere of the film, Shirley Bassey, the senior Bond chanteuse, complained that the song lacked structure. In the film, it certainly did – for the song had had to be cut in length to fit the title sequence. The full version as heard on the soundtrack album is much more pleasing.

Director Martin Campbell was quite clear how he should approach the entire enterprise, and about the importance of humour. '[The plane stunt was] slightly ludicrous,' he said. 'Everyone laughed at it. There had been a lot of negative press before the film was released, journalists asking "Is Bond washed up?" But when people saw scenes like Bond's first meeting with M, they saw it had changed.'[4]

Indeed, that first meeting with M is the film's other stroke of genius, even though the dialogue is amazingly ker-plunking. Bond has been in the South of France, being 'evaluated' by strait-laced Foreign Office official Belinda (Serena Gordon); this takes the form of a car-chasing duel with Xenia Onatopp, involving a long line of cyclists who all fall over as the cars pass at high speed. Any 'new man' tics given to Bond by Timothy Dalton have been erased by Pierce Brosnan. He smirks, he ogles – he even wears a 1970s cravat. And beneath his gear stick is a chilled bottle of Bollinger.

Once again, the principle was that if you are going to reintroduce Bond, you might as well make him the real unreconstructed deal and make a comic virtue of it.

So Bond is summoned to see M; instead of a crusty old man, she now takes the form of Dame Judi Dench. She is every bit as stern as her predecessors and famously accuses Bond of being a 'sexist misogynist dinosaur, a relic of the Cold War'. In other words, Bond's boss is also openly questioning whether 007 still has any place in this bright new world.

This was a question, by 1995, that the British security services were apparently asking themselves. Following the fall of the Berlin Wall, the operatives of MI5 – the identities of whom used to be fiercely guarded with D-notices – were shyly emerging blinking into the national spotlight. The most prominent figure to do so was the woman upon whom this new M was based – Dame Stella Rimington, the Director General of MI5. The first we the public ever saw of her was a blurred shot taken in the street and published, after a tussle, by newspapers. Thereafter she became more and more prominent. In 1995, the year of *GoldenEye*'s release, she made this speech in the Guildhall:

> The clarity which the Cold War brought has gone. As is all too evident, the collapse of centralised controls in parts of the former Soviet Union as well as in the Balkans has provoked regional instability. From that may come new sources of terrorism and heightened risks from the spread of chemical, nuclear and biological weapons. New types and new sources of terrorist violence have emerged. They work in relatively unstructured groups, make no claim for their attacks, and appear to have as their aim the creation of maximum alarm and insecurity.

Her prescience makes fascinating reading now. And in the altogether sillier world of film, she was providing the blueprint for all future Bond scenarios.

The set design of M's office also tells us that the world has moved on; it anticipated by two years PM Tony Blair's apparent impatience with the trappings of history. Instead of the wood-panelled walls, and the leather-covered door, and the bookcases and the antique desk and the fire and the naval paintings, this new M's office is ultra-modern and sleek, with glass surfaces and neutral colours.

And instead of being in Whitehall, as previously represented by the shot of the red double-decker and the brass nameplate 'Universal Exports', MI6 is finally – and for the first time – explicitly named as Bond's employer. We even have an establishing shot of MI6's new headquarters by the Thames at Vauxhall. It seems odd that it took seventeen films for this aspect of Bond to be made explicit, but then it wasn't until the mid-1990s that the security services had drawn so much attention to themselves.

There is also a new axis between M, Moneypenny and Bond; for both women, he now represents an incorrigible man who must be kept in check. Moneypenny even insinuates that she has a romantic life far away from him. In this first outing, as mentioned, the dialogue is clonking, especially M's speech about bean-counting and sending men to their deaths. But we, the audiences, were in a very forgiving mood.

The other notable thing about *GoldenEye* is the amount of time it takes for the film to get going: the entire sequence of the destruction of the Sevrenaya satellite station, though suspenseful and necessary, means that we have about half an hour before Bond gets to do anything at all. Here we are introduced to computer programmers Natalya Simonova (Izabella Scorupco) and Boris Grushensky (Alan Cumming), and unusually for Bond there is some deft characterisation. In previous Bonds, the action has always centred solely on 007; here Natalya's plight as the sole survivor of the GoldenEye magnetic pulse – and of Xenia Onatopp's murderous machine-gun attack – is pushed centre stage.

So Bond is sent off to investigate the mystery of the GoldenEye electro-magnetic pulse and arrives in St Petersburg. Back in 1995, this was extremely thrilling new territory. The very idea of Bond in Russia was somehow taboo. And even though by this time it was ruled by President Yeltsin, with fast progression to apparent democracy while the oligarchs made themselves extremely rich, the entire landscape still felt uncertain. In the wake of the collapse of the old system, there was a vertiginous rise in criminal empires, and the resulting violent turf wars. One had the sense that anything might happen to Bond here.

And indeed it does. From a meeting with Valentin Zukovsky (Robbie Coltrane), who fills us in on Britain's behaviour towards Lienz Cossacks after the war, to a night-time meeting with the scarred Alec Trevelyan in an eerie scrapyard filled with abandoned statues of Lenin and Stalin, to a rousing tank chase through the streets of St Petersburg, we all knew that 007 was finally back on track. Indeed, the shot where 007's tank crashes through a lorry carrying Perrier bottles also marked a return to the days of outrageous product placement.

This sequence, involving countless cars piling up and splashing into the waters of the canal, was an exercise in real ingenuity. At the time, I marvelled that the St Petersburg authorities had allowed so much mayhem to take place. In fact, only a few shots were taken there; the rest was an artful montage of set design and tight editing filmed on a specially built St Petersburg street on the banks of the Grand Union Canal in Hertfordshire, near Watford.

Thence to a sequence where Bond, still in his stolen tank, chases Alec Trevelyan's special private train – all filmed on a disused length of track near Peterborough, Cambridgeshire. The film's interior scenes were shot not at Pinewood – it was all booked up for Tom Cruise's *Mission: Impossible* – but at a specially constructed studio at Leavesden, Hertfordshire. After the Mexico debacle of *Licence to Kill*, there was something oddly reassuring about the very idea of Bond being back on his home turf.

It is always interesting to watch an actor in his first outing as 007 – let us not forget how awkward and unsure Connery seemed back in *Dr. No*. Brosnan seems to step into the shoes rather faster than most. But of course he was the first actor to have been steeped in decades of screen Bond, as opposed to simply reading the books. Brosnan always said in interviews that it was seeing *Goldfinger* in London as a fifteen-year-old lad that changed the course of his life and showed him what film could do.

In the 1970s, Brosnan, who was then, as he said, very 'Sarf London', first went to art college and then enrolled at the Drama Centre, where he studied for three years. Small roles followed in the TV series *The Professionals* and as a sinister silent Irish assassin in the seminal docklands thriller *The Long Good Friday* (1980). Brosnan was young enough to be of the generation where Bond automatically meant the man on the screen as opposed to the man on the page. Thus it is that we can see elements of both Connery and Moore deliberately incorporated in this first performance; the toughness and insane insouciance combined not merely with wry comebacks but also a taste for clomping double entendre.

Each previous new Bond had his 'family' – M, Moneypenny – to remind us all that this, after all, was still the same man. This time around, the only link with the past was the indefatigable Desmond Llewelyn as Q. It might perhaps be imagination but in the scene in Q's laboratory, where he is peevishly guiding this new 007 through his gadgets, Llewelyn appears to be looking not at Brosnan, but at prompt cards. Be fair to the man. He was in his early eighties. And happily, he was able to do two more Bonds after this one, and seemed on better form on these other occasions; the relationship between Q and Brosnan's 007 was the warmest and most affectionate of the lot.

So, other than the Aston Martin (hooray!) and the watch with the laser beam (a slightly post-modernist hooray, since it is there to remind us of the similarly outrageous watch-with-saw in *Live and Let Die*), we also had a most ingenious gizmo: a bomb disguised as an ordinary ballpoint pen with a clicking top. It is armed and ticking with two clicks, defused with three. The simplest idea, but one that made for a brilliantly sweaty moment of suspense near the end, where enraged Boris (Alan Cumming) has taken the pen from Bond and is twiddling and clicking it manically, having no idea what it could do. This was the sort of wheeze at which producer Michael G. Wilson was – and indeed is – absolutely brilliant.

By means of new-fangled computer, Natalya and Bond track Trevelyan to Cuba, and she and Bond pitch up at an obscure little resort called Guantánamo. Seven years before the arrival of the barbed wire and orange jumpsuits, it looks rather pleasant, and affords the scriptwriter and director the opportunity to give Bond a moment of humanity. Pierce Brosnan was, from the start, very keen that he be allowed to demonstrate that the character had layers. Indeed, in his introductory press conference, he announced that 'We want to peel back some layers of his character and see what demons might be there'.[5] Unfortunately, the result here is a wince-inducing scene by the sea.

First, it is filmed like an advert for some ghastly brand of rum, all coloured filters over the sunshine. Secondly, it features Bond sitting on a beach in naff white trousers, squinting at the waves. I know he is on a beach in the novel *On Her Majesty's Secret Service*, thinking about his childhood, but it is excruciating to actually watch. Then there is the dialogue between Bond and Natalya – all about survival and why Bond always ends up alone – which makes one draw one's knees up to one's forehead in an effort to block it out. You can see what they are trying to do – and by the time we get to *Casino Royale* in 2006 it works terrifically well – but until this point in *GoldenEye*, we have simply been enjoying the comical excitement. Happily, after this clonking effort at characterisation is over, we get back to the business in hand.

Where is Trevelyan's secret lair? Bond and Natalya circle the area in a plane but all they can see is an unnaturally blue lake. Of course, we were all leaping up in the cinema and shouting: 'It's not a real lake, it's not a real lake,' for this was a further self-referential treat (harking back to *You Only Live Twice*) woven into the screenplay.

Beneath the water is a satellite bowl half a mile wide, and beneath that . . . Trevelyan's secret HQ! This is the first proper Bond villain HQ that we have had since the late 1970s. How we have missed it. All those different levels, all those technicians twiddling knobs, all those monitor screens, all those flashing lights. It is almost enough to make one sigh with unadulterated pleasure, except for the fact that in aesthetic terms, this villain's HQ has a touch of the out-of-town shopping mall about it, a flavour of Thurrock Lakeside, with its brass railings and curved staircases. But never mind, this is mere churlishness; for in a further self-referential twist, Trevelyan is honouring several of his villainous predecessors by pointing his lethal satellite in space at Earth, and threatening to wipe out all of Britain's electronics in one magnetic pulse.

Unusually, though, for a Bond movie, the climax involves a terrific and utterly suspenseful hand-to-hand fight between Bond and Trevelyan, atop the vertiginous height of the satellite dish. And it is all rather more believable than before – noses being bloodied, hands gripping desperately to rungs prior to being stamped on – and expertly choreographed. We hadn't seen such an involving tussle since the train compartment battle of 1963's *From Russia with Love*.

At the time, some reviewers felt that Sean Bean was a little young for Nehru-jacket duties. In fact it is greatly to the film's advantage that this new, rebooted Bond has a much more active and vital adversary than before. And Trevelyan's story and motivation makes a tremendous change; the use of a still controversial wartime episode when the British forces handed over the Lienz Cossacks to the Soviets is eyebrow-raising. 'Not our finest hour,' murmurs Bond as Zukovsky fills him in on the back story of how Trevelyan's parents were among those Cossacks, ultimately slaughtered by the Russians.

What made this element doubly surprising is that it came on the back of an enormous libel trial on the same subject. Lord Aldington sued historian Count Nikolai Tolstoy for claims concerning the episode, and he won a colossal sum in damages. When *GoldenEye* came out, a journalist shrewdly rang Lord Aldington for his views on Bond's 'finest hour' line. 'It is said without studying the facts,' said Lord Aldington. 'America and Russia agreed. They had been fighting with the Germans and it was necessary to get our people back.'[6]

For the rest of us, it was not so much a question of historical accuracy as plausibility. Given that Trevelyan's parents were Lienz Cossacks 'betrayed' by Britain, and that the boy, sent to an English school, was obviously traumatised by the whole thing, you do wonder how he managed to get through MI6 vetting and eventually gain promotion to 006. Och well, one can be too picky.

Overall, though, these new acknowledgements of reality were the crucial element that gave the film its overall sense of Bond authenticity. Robbie Coltrane's Valentin Zukovsky was a terrific idea for a character: a shady Russian criminal working within the chaos of the post-Communist years to transform himself into the sort of legitimate businessman that the oligarchs were seeking to portray themselves as. So good was Coltrane – previously best known for the harrowing TV crime drama *Cracker* – that the character returned in *The World Is Not Enough* in a rather more substantial role. Another cheering figure was a returning Joe Don Baker, this time playing the CIA operative Jack Wild. Unlike the hapless Felix Leiter, Baker's droll figure pops up at unexpected moments simply to give Bond a helping prod.

With Bond, this sense that it is the real deal is utterly crucial. As we saw with *Never Say Never Again*, audiences knew immediately when they were being sold counterfeit goods. By the end of *GoldenEye*, any audience apprehension that the Broccoli clan had lost the knack, or that James Bond was ready for the scrapyard, was wonderfully forgotten. Trevelyan is vanquished, finally impaled by his own satellite guidance system, and before Bond and Natalya get the customary end-of-film snog, they are surprised by a party of camouflaged marines. It was all very nicely judged: light-hearted, creepy where appropriate, laughs following the tightly edited action.

And the general critical response? The weeks between the end of shooting and the opening of the film were clearly a time of terrific suspense at Eon. As mentioned, there had been press rumours throughout production that the film was 'troubled'; and before its release, plenty of newspaper columnists openly questioned whether anyone would ever want to go and see this style of film again. For the first time in six years, the Bond publicity machine started cranking into action. Happily, this time, they had a rather clever and cheering tag-line: 'You know the name. You know the number.'

And the first reviews after that Leicester Square premiere were almost universally adulatory. This time, the red-top tabloids and the snootier broadsheets seemed to be in accord – that this was a teasingly top-notch return to Bond form, reminding everyone of exactly what had been missing.

'Big, bold, and Bond at its best,' said the *Daily Mail*'s normally acerbic Christopher Tookey. 'All present and politically incorrect . . . one of the very best Bond movies.'

Veteran critic Alexander Walker went further. 'It is everything we hoped for and nothing we feared,' he wrote. '*GoldenEye* is the best adventure for many a year. It is the Bond film with everything. Pierce Brosnan is the best Bond since Sean Connery . . . he fires from his hip and his lip with equal accuracy.'

Word on a hit travels fast around the world. And very swiftly, *GoldenEye* broke Bond records, making more money than *Moonraker*. So, then, this Pierce Brosnan? Why was he regarded as being so much better than Roger and Timothy and George put together?

The curious thing about him now, when one watches the films, is that he is almost a composite Bond, in looks, and in manner and speech too. The accent contrives to be English, Irish and American, sometimes within the space of one sentence. Though obviously a very good-looking chap, Brosnan's face in the role of Bond seems almost to be a computer-generated generic idea of what a Bond face should look like. The hair, the flinty eyes are almost ticked off a list. The clothes – Bond, it seems, has not lost his taste for hideous Euro-tailored blazers and action slacks – recall Roger's lounge lizard excesses. But this did not – and indeed does not – stop women fancying him. I was recently in the manager's office of some firm in Perth, Scotland. This manager still had on display on her walls publicity shots of Brosnan from *GoldenEye*.

Brosnan's Bond is presented as being 'unreconstructed' while at the same time being something of a new man. In his scenes with Famke Janssen, the actor has a most insistent way of emphasising the sledgehammer double entendres. Also he assumes a hugely off-putting facial expression when eyeing up various other female characters – an expression that involves pursing the lips, slightly tilting the head, and slowly moving the jaw. The most terrible outbreak of this physical tic comes in *The World Is Not Enough*, when Bond wanders through a casino wearing X-ray specs.

The wandering Brosnan accent was arguably a strong reason for his greater success in America than his predecessor Dalton. For the first time, it was possible for Stateside audiences to imagine that Bond might be one of theirs. Indeed, as the huge US takings for Brosnan's subsequent adventures demonstrate, he might just be the Bond that Americans took most closely to their hearts.

The triumphant return of Bond also brought fresh competition from a newly revived spy genre: one blockbuster film that surprised no one with its success; and one low-budget comedy that paradoxically proved to be one of the biggest headaches that Bond in his new incarnation was going to face.

They tried Derek Flint. And Matt Helm. And Napoleon Solo. But somehow the Americans could never quite find a Bond replicant who would do better business across the world than 007. In 1996, actor Tom Cruise stepped up to the plate with his lavish remake of the 1960s spy show *Mission: Impossible*. In this, he was to take the central heroic role of agent Ethan Hunt.

This Hunt could do everything our man could do. He could cause chaos in exotic foreign locations – shootings, explosions, chases, you name it. He could wear tailored suits. He could deploy unlikely gadgetry to aid his daring espionage sorties. He could face heavies in unarmed combat. He could even deploy one-liners if the occasion strictly demanded it.

The idea of the original show was that it was all down to ingenious teamwork. Cruise appeared to do away with this notion in the first five minutes of the film as the exceptionally starry team (among whom were Emilio Estevez and Kristin Scott Thomas) were dispatched during the course of some nonsense in a Prague embassy. Thereafter it was agent Ethan Hunt doing his Bond thing: getting together with French actress Emmanuelle Béart, raiding the CIA headquarters while dangling on a sort of human spider web (director Brian de Palma was always good at these Hitchcockian suspense contrivances), sparring with villain Vanessa Redgrave and clinging to the front of a speeding Eurostar train during the film's kinetic climax in the Channel Tunnel.

In other words: set-pieces, locations, sex and spying. A more direct challenge could not have been issued. Only one slight let-down in this effort: the plot ultimately hinged on that old heart-sinker – wait for it – the traitor in the organisation. No spoilers here, so I shan't tell you who. But it is a plot device that always somehow manages to tangle a narrative up and make one lose one's concentration.

The two sequels we have had so far did not repeat this mistake. And they made Ethan Hunt even more of a Bondian lone wolf than before. Possibly the best of the lot was 2006's *MI3*, directed by J.J. Abrams and featuring quite brilliant villainy from Philip Seymour Hoffman, as well as two humdinger set-pieces – one involving helicopters flying through a wind farm, and the other involving a raid in the Vatican – that were every bit the equal of Bond. We might well see further episodes of this series – as I write, there are speculative newspaper reports of a fourth instalment being mooted. I always worry that films like this will one day run out of gravitas-loaded actors to be the villains.

Eon have always been keenly aware of competition. But in 1997, as production got under way on the troubled eighteenth Bond film *Tomorrow Never Dies*, potential upset came from the most unlikely source. While a phenomenon such as *Mission: Impossible* could be accommodated and indeed arguably increase the public appetite for spying drama, comedy was harder to fight. At the time, no one could have known that Mike Myers's *Austin Powers: International Man of Mystery* would have any impact at the cinema at all. When it opened in the summer of 1997, it received appreciative reviews and performed reasonably well, but not spectacularly. Its effect, however, on the entire business of cinema spying was terrific.

The first *Austin Powers* was not a direct send-up of Bond. The character of this 1960s agent, unfrozen and brought back to life in 1997, was a composite of various figures, including David Hemmings's photographer in *Blow Up* and jackanapes dandy Jason King, all topped off with an absurd Michael Caine accent. His 1960s leather-catsuited partner Mrs Kensington (Mimi Rogers) is obviously Mrs Peel. Playing the M figure – the wonderfully named Basil Exposition – is Michael York.

But the villain, Dr Evil (Myers again) – well, with this portrayal, Myers sounded the death knell for the traditionalist Bond super-villain. Bald, scarred, Nehru-jacketed Dr Evil operates from what he himself terms his 'underground lair'; he has a sidekick, Number Two (Robert Wagner), with an X-ray eye patch; he dreams of owning a shark with a laser beam in its nose; he uses killer robot women called 'Fem-bots'; he has a cat; and he plans, via the hijack of a nuclear missile, to hold the world to ransom for 'one meeeeellion dollars!' In other words, it is blissfully funny, but in that first film, Myers also absurdly gave Dr Evil a dimension of pathos, in his complete failure to bond with his son Scott. As the teenager recoils from him, Dr Evil wails: 'But who will try to take over the world when I'm dead?' The scene where they attend a group counselling session, and Dr Evil is forced to describe his own strange Belgian father who claimed to have invented the question mark, is perhaps the funniest in the film.

Having done reasonably well at the cinema, the film went on to video, and that is when it achieved its stratospheric success. Word of mouth spread and it sold millions. At first glance, you might think that Eon Productions would be flattered by such an ultimately affectionate spoof. But, lethally, Myers had homed in on the Bondian element of larger-than-life villainy with such accuracy as to make it all but impossible for such a figure ever to feature in the real films again.

Myers shrewdly gave Dr Evil even more screen time in his sequel, *The Spy Who Shagged Me* (1999), and the whole thing was more identifiably an attack on Bond, with Dr Evil's stylised base on the moon. This was, according to reports at the time, the first of Eon's skirmishes with Powers. The company objected to the title but Myers cheerfully went ahead anyway and the film was a monstrous box-office success. The cult of Powers was now reaching a worldwide audience not entirely dissimilar to 007's. Even stronger objections from Eon were raised when it was announced that the third Austin Powers film would be called *Goldmember*. Eon tried to argue that this really was too close to their franchise. New Line Pictures hit back with an unattractive proposal. Instead of that title, they suggested, they could instead call the film *You Only Shag Thrice*. Eon backed down and *Goldmember* opened in 2002, breaking box-office records for comedy.

By this stage, the films had become so much their own thing – a blend of *Carry On* double entendre and scatological slapstick – that they had ceased to offer a consistent send-up of Bond. Indeed, the appearance in the third film of Michael Caine as Powers's father re-emphasised the central joke of the ghastliness of Britain in the 1960s. Beyoncé Knowles's winning turn as Foxxy Cleopatra, meanwhile, was an elaborate bow to 1970s blaxploitation.

But it was Myers's exquisitely camp performance as Dr Evil which once again dominated the film. The joy of it was that under the exultant malevolence, there was still a note of genuine vulnerability; Evil's inability to hold even a faux family structure together with his clone Mini-Me and furious son Scott mirrored Powers's failure to bond with his own father. With this new slant on super-villainy, Myers was implicitly pointing to an emotional vacuum at the core of most Bond films, in which heroes and villains both had to construct fake families around them in order to compensate for the lack of any true connection in their lives. For a comedy series so reliant on sex and bodily function gags, Myers's Dr Evil was still a much more layered creation than Ernst Stavro Blofeld.

A little later on, Barbara Broccoli gamely denied that the *Austin Powers* films had presented any form of challenge to the Bonds; indeed, she averred that they served a fantastically beneficial purpose.

'*Austin Powers* is an outright comedy and ours is an action adventure with a bit of tongue-in-cheek,' she said. 'Both films are very far apart. We have to be careful to not fall into "*Austin Powers* land" when we are writing a scene . . . Since *Austin Powers* is such a great spoof of the old Bond films, I think it just helps people enjoy going to the movies and seeing this sort of genre. It's all a win-win situation.'[1]

As it happened, the tone of the villainy was a talking point during production of *Tomorrow Never Dies*. In fact, there were a great many talking points, it seems, including what the villain's scheme should actually involve this time around. The man in the black hat this time is international media tycoon Elliot Carver, played by the highly respected British actor Jonathan Pryce. And his scheme of starting a new world war sparked by conflict between Britain and China was based on Britain's 1997 handover of Hong Kong to China.

One might see how such a starting point had the lure of topicality; but it really wasn't at all practical, or even especially tasteful, to hinge a film around this event. So screenwriter Bruce Feirstein had to think again. Incidentally, early press rumours about the film stated that the working title had been *Avatar*, that one of the locations would be Australia and that Sir Anthony Hopkins was up for playing the villain. At least they got the villain's nationality right.

According to many reports, the screenplay for *Tomorrow* went through a number of revisions, right up until the days when certain scenes were due to be shot, and the actors were being handed last-minute dialogue changes just before going in front of the cameras. On the other hand, actors such as Brosnan and Pryce seem to recall no such thing. Perhaps they were simply being polite. That's show business.

But back to the question of villainy: Elliot Carver's final scheme is still to provoke war between Britain and China, but with the aim not of global domination or extortion but simply to improve the ratings and sales of his TV current affairs shows and newspapers.

On the face of it, a nice Bondian idea: in a new modern age of internet, satellite TV and global news coverage, what better man to have as villain than a chap who wishes to manipulate reality and then to relay this reality back to eager audiences? Jean Baudrillard would approve. In an age when even events such as the 1991 Gulf War were being described as 'media wars', such a scenario would have a pleasingly dark, satirical tone to it, a sort of *Dr Strangelove* for the 24/7 media age.

Where it goes wrong, however, is the curious naïvety of the script; it is as though Bond and satire really cannot mix at all. An intelligent villain such as Carver would surely have been utterly alive to the ironies and paradoxes thrown up by his diabolical scheme. This man, however, seems disappointingly linear about it all. He sinks British naval ships, blames the Chinese, tension rises, he hopes newspaper sales will go up and he will get a monopoly on the Chinese media market. That is that. No subtle sense of usurping the very principles of democracy – just galumphing lines about blackmailing the President with an indiscreet picture of a cheerleader – or even especial relish in composing the optical illusion that will lead to war. And why is Carver so sure that when hostilities break out, people will choose to hear all about it from *his* newspapers and TV channels? What if they favour his competitors?

In any case, in what sort of world would the Americans stand back blithely as Britain and China prepared to go to war?

The other enormous problem with the narrative of *Tomorrow Never Dies* is that MI6 is on to Carver from the very start; after all, it is from his space satellite that the false navigational positions for the British naval ship have been beamed. So from Carver's very first scene, we not only know exactly who the bad guy is, but also exactly what he is up to and how he is achieving this end. So the screenplay can only go in one possible direction, which is a series of increasingly repetitious skirmishes between him and Bond.

And this is one of the problems that actor Jonathan Pryce faces. His initial instinct appeared to have been to camp Carver up. When interviewed, he was eloquent on the delight of having been cast as a Bond villain, which he viewed as one of the great iconic roles of cinema. 'I have always wanted to say, "Good evening Mr Bond,"' said Pryce. And you can see in the finished film that this glint of delight is always struggling to break through.

Indeed, there is one moment when it does so, after Carver has captured Bond's colleague Wai Lin (Michelle Yeoh) and advances on her while making bizarre karate moves. The problem, it seems, was that British director Roger Spottiswoode (who, among many other things, had previously helmed the 1990 thriller *Air America*) apparently wanted Carver played absolutely straight down the line. This clash of approaches is a niggling fault that runs all the way through the film. Is Carver a grave threat to all that Western democracy holds dear, or is he a mwa-ha-ha-ing panto dame?

It's a tougher deal than it looks, being a Bond villain. If one plays the role as a psychopathic boiled egg (Donald Pleasance), one gets criticised for sailing over the top. But take a more subtle approach – Louis Jourdan, or more recently, Mads Mikkelsen in *Casino Royale* – and the film reviewers complain of wanness. So which way does one jump? In 2002's *Die Another Day*, Toby Stephens as Gustav Graves opted for a permanent sneer that had a number of reviewers sneering themselves; in 1999's *The World Is Not Enough*, Robert Carlyle gave his Renard an almost Boris Karloff edge of pathos. But still the carpers carped.

Of course, Bond is only as good as his enemies; in *Tomorrow Never Dies*, what we were watching was an attempt to update the villainy and make it relevant to a modern world. But Jonathan Pryce perhaps saw the role as part of a longer tradition than that and could not resist ramping it up a notch. And is it just imagination, or did make-up actually give him a pair of unobtrusive fangs? Anyway, hats off. Pryce certainly enjoyed himself enough to drop in on the set of the following Bond, *The World Is Not Enough*, to catch up with the crew.

None of these points are to say that the film is unentertaining; quite the reverse. It is a very watchable film indeed. Spottiswoode directs with great visual flair; this is the first time since the glory days of Ken Adam that a Bond film has been so aesthetically pleasing. From the pre-credits crisis involving a nuclear missile heading for a secret arms bazaar in the Hindu Kush, to another eye-poppingly glorious opening title sequence from Daniel Kleinman, this time using X-ray and fibre-optic imagery as a backdrop for the dancing girls, to the pervasive electric blue that characterises Carver's scenes, this is the film where the director and the producers really sought to haul Bond into the modern age.

At one point, the cool, bright architectural lines of Norman Foster take centre stage as Bond and Wai Lin get into trouble in one of Carver's printing plants. As we know from London's Canary Wharf tube station, Foster is an admirer of Sir Ken Adam, so it is pleasing that he himself should have been behind a Bond set.

While checking Carver out at a launch party in Hamburg, Bond runs into Carver's wife Paris (played by Teri Hatcher, now a Desperate Housewife), who happens to be an old flame. Naturally Bond and Paris must canoodle; this is one scene where the pleasing aesthetics are replaced momentarily with something from an Ann Summers catalogue, with Bond unzipping Paris's frock and the frock falling to reveal Paris's saucy knickers and suspenders. In the cinema where I saw this film, this shot got a huge laugh – a laugh that I suspect Spottiswoode was not looking for.

Prior to this knicker unveiling, moreover, Bond appears to have made his way through half a bottle of vodka. I like a drink as much as the next man but I can understand the MGM executives who apparently commented on the amount of liquor consumed over the course of this entry.

Naturally Elliot Carver can't take this betrayal lying down and Paris is murdered by the splendidly deadpan marksman and torturer Dr Kaufman (played by Vincent Schiavelli). Bond escapes, links up with Chinese agent and kung fu expert Wai Lin, and the action thence moves to Vietnam, where Carver is up to no good with a rogue Chinese general.

The next hour is simply filled with noise. Bond and Wai Lin are ambushed in her secret HQ and have a very long fight with various kickboxers; Bond and Wai Lin are handcuffed together and try to make a getaway on a motorbike across the roofs and through the streets of Saigon; Bond and Wai Lin locate and infiltrate Carver's stealth ship, from which, with a giant drill, he is sinking British ships in the waters of the South China Sea.

The broad explanation for the almost ceaseless action/gunfire/explosions was that the genre as a whole had moved on significantly, and that younger audiences would have less time for more reflective scenes. This was the sophisticated computer-game generation, who were used to linear narratives taking them from one burst of violent action to the next. However, for those of us in the audience who didn't regularly stay up until 3 a.m. playing *Resident Bloodlust 4: The Howling*, it was an extremely tiring piece of cinema.

None the less, World War Three looms and Carver is writing the headlines for tomorrow's papers. A missile fired from his stealth ship at Beijing – a missile made to look like it was from a British naval ship – and his great conflict will begin. In the meantime, Wai Lin is drowning underwater in chains and Bond is desperately fighting the obligatory gayish Aryan henchman, this time by the name of Mr Stamper.

Of course, Bond gets there in the end, but only by firing endless rounds from machine guns, which personally I find as depressing as Roger Moore once did. This was simply not the territory of a family film, even though it was certified 12. And the underlying message was rather depressing: that the good guys could only prevail by means of superior firepower. But clearly I was — and still am — in the wrong, for the film hauled in over $300 million, slightly more than the sum earned by *GoldenEye*.

There is still something slightly unsettled about the film though, and it is to do with the producers continuing to justify Bond's existence, as though we the audience were not yet convinced.

Pierce Brosnan, as one would expect, is rather more at home in this second outing; the scene where M and Moneypenny both brief and tease him while being driven at breakneck speed through the streets of London made a pleasant change from the usual static office scene. His relationship with Michelle Yeoh also made a nice change; although Bond girls right from the start have claimed that they are independent and able to look after themselves, Wai Lin genuinely is on Bond's level. The scene when he watches her casually walking down the wall on a cable in Carver's German printing press made for a nice laugh. Unfortunately, other than the fighting and the independence and the resourcefulness, there is not a great deal more to her character, but one can't ask for everything.

Q is present in order to provide product placement for Avis car rental, it seems; decked out in scarlet corporate blazer, Desmond Llewelyn takes Bond through the workings of his remote-control product-placement BMW. (The spectacular and funny scene in which Bond is chased while guiding the car from the back seat was filmed in the car park of north London's Brent Cross shopping centre — a day in the sunshine for one of Britain's least exotic locations.)

But the motivation for the entire escapade is the one thing that never rings true, and as such, it is throughout like an itch that you can't scratch. To put it baldly, even in the unlikely event that a world war would cause newspaper sales to rise, surely it would simply have been easier and cheaper for Carver to lure new readers in with giveaway DVDs and CDs? And even if he is sufficiently demented to believe that what he is doing makes sense, surely everyone working for him would find a way to have a little word in his shell-like? Curiously, in many other Bond movies, the impossible leaps of villainous logic don't jar quite so badly. The problem here is the near-realism of the film's overall style. Carver doesn't seem to fit even into his own world.

We are not here to carp though. Oh, hold on, we are, just for a few moments longer. For in the later part of the film, the only scene that provides any respite from the noise of the gunfire is – yes! An underwater scene! Involving Bond and Wai Lin exploring the submerged wreck of the HMS *Devonshire*. Except this time around, we are missing the air-pipes getting cut and a shark appearing unexpectedly in a hatch doorway.

There were many other reasons to be cheerful, principal among them the debut of new composer David Arnold. It was clear, even from his score for the pre-credits sequence, that Arnold had been brought up on a ceaseless diet of John Barry (who had bowed out of the films after 1987's *The Living Daylights*), and had absorbed all of his lessons, while finding a way to subtly update the whole thing. After the low-key, subdued nature of the *Licence to Kill* score provided by Michael Kamen, and the compelling though not truly Bondian industrial clangs and chants of *GoldenEye* composed by Eric Serra, it was lovely to hear such a direct tribute to the composer who had been partly responsible for the initial success of the series.

Arnold did not hide his fan credentials: 1997 brought his tribute album *Shaken Not Stirred*, which featured cover versions of James Bond songs by contemporary artists. Especially good were Iggy Pop's surprisingly moving interpretation of 'We Have All the Time in the World', Chrissie Hynde's raw reading of 'Live and Let Die' and Pulp's breathy, saucy approach to 'All Time High'. And so Arnold's score for *Tomorrow Never Dies* features, among other things, swift references to the staccato opening bars of *From Russia with Love*. The title song, performed by Sheryl Crow, is a teasing 1960s throwback, featuring the exquisitely unfeminist lyric: 'Darling I'm killed – I'm in a puddle on the floor, waiting for you to return.'

It seems that Arnold had originally intended a different song to kick off with, although one that still involved the refrain 'tomorrow never dies'. In the end, 'Surrender', sung by K.D. Lang, ran over the closing credits instead. 'She was terrific, my first choice for the opening titles,' said Arnold. 'There aren't many singers around who can carry it off like her, we don't have any contemporary Shirley Bassey figures who have that rum sense of wry humour to sing Bond convincingly. K.D. Lang took a lot of trouble,' he added. 'She asked me what Tomorrow Never Dies means so she could get into character. I didn't have the slightest idea.'[2]

Arnold's score also featured an extraordinary number of references to the original Monty Norman theme; it was dotted all over the film, styled in a slightly retro fashion, just in case we needed reminding that it was Bond we were watching.

And happily, Barbara Broccoli and Michael Wilson felt that they had found their resident composer. Arnold has continued to this day and at the time of writing is working on *Quantum of Solace*. On his debut, he managed to bestow a sense of coherence to a film that often couldn't quite cover its prodigious narrative leaps.

Another problem for Broccoli and Wilson must have been the tendency on the part of the press – especially in the wake of Austin Powers – to view Bond as a somewhat camp, purely post-modernist entertainment. They can't have been terrifically pleased when one of the film's costume designers confided to the *Telegraph*'s diary column that in the film, Bond 'was to face a fate worse than death – the villain makes him change into an utterly ghastly cheap blue shirt'. As it happens, the villain did indeed do that, after Bond was hauled from the water after the deep sea scene – but it is not exactly central to the action.

How could Eon toughen Bond up further and drag him away from the retro-imagery of the 1960s and 70s?

What helped was the cementing of the new Bond 'family'; Judi Dench settles completely into the role of M – she and Samantha Bond's Moneypenny are now a rather smart double-act, wise and indulgent women trying to keep the wayward tearaway Bond in check.

Incidentally, what is the lure for Dame Judi, who will also be present in *Quantum of Solace*? After all, she is every bit as much a classical actor as Dame Diana Rigg. But interviewed recently, Dame Judi said that as well as being great fun, the films might also serve a greater purpose.

'I'll tell you, quite seriously, the reason why I keep playing in Bond films . . .' she told the interviewer in May 2008. 'I'm passionate about the theatre, but through Bond I now have an incredible fan base of young men between my grandson's age and about 15 years. And the thing is, if these boys think it's so cool to be in a Bond movie, then find out that I am also a theatre actress, then they might go to the theatre as well.'[3] You wish, Dame Judi!

This MI6 ensemble also features Michael Kitchen as Bill Tanner, a figure always mentioned in the novels as Bond's best friend in the service; and Colin Salmon as Charles Robinson. Unlike the 1980s Bonds, where M and Moneypenny were there purely as introductory exposition or as gag suppliers, this MI6 line-up is eager to grab more of the screen time.

M this time has to pit herself not merely against Carver, but also the mulishness of the Admiralty and the politicians who listen to it. This is an extremely welcome extra dimension that does much to anchor the new interpretation of Bond in the modern world.

There is a theory among Bond fans that it is always the third Bond film in any sequence – be it Connery's third or Moore's third – that tends to have extra punch and confidence and consequent success. This was about to be true of the Brosnan era. In *GoldenEye* and *Tomorrow Never Dies*, we see the whole series in the process of readjustment. By 1999, Eon had the formula absolutely, brilliantly right once more.

CHAPTER TWENTY-SIX ART AND CRAFT

According to producer Michael G. Wilson, at the very start of pre-production on any Bond, when story ideas are being thrown around, he always asks himself: 'What is the main worry in the world right now?' In this respect, the diabolical villain's scheme featured in 1999's *The World Is Not Enough* was rather ahead of its time.

The premise of this, the nineteenth Bond film, was that Europe and the Western world were intensely vulnerable to terrorist attacks on oil pipelines running through former Soviet states; and more, that the West was economically vulnerable to the plutocrats in those former Soviet states who now owned the lines and the land through which they ran. One can almost see Russian president-to-be Vladimir Putin linking his fingers and narrowing his eyes as, a few years later, he used the supply of gas through Russian pipelines as a weapon against the smaller states that wished to escape his power.

More than this – if we can ever look at the Bond films as a weather-vane of universal anxiety – the very region in which this film was set, the Caucasus, was, following the bloody and violent break-up of the old Yugoslavia throughout the 1990s, a new locus for fears about geopolitical stability. By the mid-1990s, Baku, in Azerbaijan, was acquiring a name among Western businessmen eager to get into a new Eastern market, as a modern-day lawless frontier town. The unleashing of raw capitalism through these former Communist states created repercussions that we are still feeling today.

Then there was the chief worry following the disintegration of the Soviet Union: what would become of all those nuclear weapons and atomic fissile materials that were now in the hands of semi-independent states? Wasn't there every possibility that enterprising terrorists could buy themselves some weapons-grade plutonium?

If these sound rather heavy ingredients for a Bond, this time the cocktail was shaken up with more comedy. And the return of Bond to his position as the stylish turn in which serious actors wanted to appear was confirmed by the cast attracted for this one, including scary Robert Carlyle, fresh from his triumph in *The Full Monty* (1997), the bittersweet Sheffield-based film comedy in which he portrayed a former steel worker who gets together with redundant colleagues to form a male strip act.

Here, things were scarcely less intense as he essayed the role of living-dead terrorist Renard. Then there was the return of Robbie Coltrane in a beefed-up reappearance of Valentin Zukovsky; and French art-house sensation Sophie Marceau as the pivotal character of Elektra King. The character's unusual Christian name provided the clue as to her real role in the drama. The other Bond girl role was filled by pneumatic American Denise Richards, rather brilliantly playing an atomic scientist called Dr Christmas Jones. For those of us in the audience having trouble following the complex plot, her line, 'Could you put that into English for those of us who *don't* speak spy?' was especially welcome.

And it was a fiendishly complicated affair, starting with M's old friend, an oil pipeline tycoon called Sir Robert King, being assassinated within the walls of MI6. Some years ago, Sir Robert's daughter Elektra had been kidnapped by terrorist Renard. Under advice from MI6, Sir Robert refused to pay the ransom. Elektra escaped, but only by shooting her way out, and was severely traumatised by the experience. Now, after the murder of Sir Robert, it seems that Renard is back. Bond is sent out to Baku in Azerbaijan to offer personal protection for Elektra but gradually finds that all is not quite as it seems. And following the theft of some weapons-grade plutonium from a former Soviet base in Kazakhstan, it becomes apparent that one of the King pipelines is going to be used to destroy Istanbul in a nuclear blast.

Or something like that. There's an out-of-commission nuclear submarine in the nail-biting climax as well. But unlike its immediate predecessor, what this Bond film got exactly right was tone: even though there are terrific moments of both excitement and comedy, it is rather darker and also rather more romantic than before.

Two young new screenwriters were brought in: Neal Purvis and Robert Wade, whose biggest previous credit had been the pop video-esque British highwayman romp *Plunkett and MacCleane* (1999), also starring Robert Carlyle. Rather like the new house musician David Arnold, one sensed from their script that they had been bottle-fed on Bond, and indeed they returned for *Die Another Day* and *Casino Royale*. Meanwhile, script polishing services were provided by Bruce Feirstein.

Taking the helm as director was Michael Apted, curiously best known not only for *Gorillas in the Mist* (1987) and the thriller *Gorky Park* (1984) but also for the ground-breaking 1960s British TV documentary series *Seven Up*, which took a cross-section of schoolchildren, with the intention of returning to them every seven years to see what had happened and how their lives had turned out.

Apted outlined his directorial duties: 'You have to deliver icons,' he said in an interview. 'Girls, gadgets, action and exotic locations. Hence Bilbao and the Guggenheim building. When the Bond films started, exotic locations meant palms and beaches, which aren't exotic any more. We had locations where you might not want to take your vacation but had an unusual side to them.'[1]

This was certainly the case in the unusually long pre-credits of *World*. We open in the aforementioned Bilbao, where Bond is in an armed stand-off in the office of a sinister Swiss banker; in the chaos that follows, Bond is forced to launch himself out of a window, a rope attached to his trouser belt, the other end of the rope attached to an unconscious heavy who doesn't realise he is about to be slammed against the window frame. Back in London, Bond meets M and Robert King. King is blown up; the assassin – a beautiful woman last seen in the office of the Swiss banker – is in a speedboat in the middle of the Thames. Bond grabs Q's rocket-powered boat and gives chase.

Perhaps the ensuing locations looked exotic to ninety-nine per cent of the audience. But my Docklands-based friends and I, plus all the people in the Docklands cinema at which we saw the film, were wildly excited for a different reason. For this chase took the Cigar Girl (as the assassin was called in the credits) and Bond down to London's East End; into the silvery docks of the Isle of Dogs, through the creek of Jacob's Island in Bermondsey; out to the newly built Millennium Dome; and through the relatively new ersatz canal system that runs through the back of Wapping. In other words: Bond was in our neighbourhood! Having a chase though waterways that we lived around! The honour! At one point I leapt up in the auditorium, pointing, and shouted: 'My flat!' Several other people in the audience did the same. Well, it *was* very exciting.

Rather more exciting, in fact, than the chase itself, which was as ponderous as all boat chases are, no matter how many 360-degree boat jumps, ersatz canals and faked-up fish restaurants are packed in.

More fascinating were the behind-the-scenes arrangements in order to secure permission to film on the Thames right outside Parliament. Naturally, to do such a thing – in other words, to commandeer the river in the very centre of London – was an extraordinarily big deal, and one which eventually went slightly higher than the remit of the Port of London Authority. Initially, MI6 refused permission for filming outside its riverside Vauxhall HQ. Bafflingly so, since this HQ is – thanks to its tremendous post-modern ugliness – one of London's most visible and prominent landmarks.

Craftily, producer Michael G. Wilson made an appeal to the Department of Culture, Media and Sport, and specifically to arts minister Janet Anderson, who had been calling for more films to be made on British soil. Anderson in turn contacted the Foreign Office, which has ultimate control over MI6. The real-life M was overruled. There was a short sequence in which Cigar Girl aims a rifle at the HQ and a mocked-up Westminster Pier is destroyed by a jet-boat-created tsunami. Robin Cook, then Foreign Secretary, remarked through a press secretary that 'After all Bond has done for Britain, it was the least that Britain could do for Bond.'

It was a telling genuflection, for Bond was not only a 'British success story' but also very much something that the government wanted to co-opt into its vision of 'Cool Britannia', this notional nation of innovative, cutting-edge culture and fashion. How very dated such an idea seems now.

But Eon paid the government back handsomely for the use of the Thames. The sequence comes to an end at the Millennium Dome, where Cigar Girl improbably hijacks a hot-air balloon, Bond clutching on to the end of a guy-rope. That Dome! In 1999, it was still in the process of construction, with the aim of opening on the millennium New Year's Eve. And it was the hottest of political potatoes.

The Dome had cost a majestic £750 million to build (one still wonders quite how), and the government was under almost daily attack about the sort of exhibits that it would feature; critics raged that the whole thing was a fuzzy, unfocused, politically correct festival of nonsense. As it eventually turned out, they weren't far wrong. But to feature in a Bond film, even for two minutes (Bond lets go of the guy-rope as the balloon explodes and he tumbles down the side of the Dome, finally getting caught up in one of its cable supports), was an invaluable endorsement. If it was good enough for Bond, wasn't it good enough for everyone?

'The stakes couldn't be higher,' reported the excitable *Sunday Times* in

August 1998. 'Insiders at the Dome could salvage the project in real life by harnessing the global box office appeal of the Bond films.'

And by 2007, Eon's faith in what had previously been regarded as the mother of all white elephants finally paid off as the structure became the O_2 entertainment centre – suddenly one of the most popular spots in London.

The few minutes set in Bilbao showed us, incidentally, that the Spanish still regarded Bond as some sort of showbiz god. For the very short sequence where Brosnan walks along a street on his way to the Swiss banker, and the shot where a stunt double leaps out of the office window, an excitable crowd of thousands of people turned up for filming. 'It's like Beatlemania,' said Brosnan, being ushered through the throng. This was a rather sweet echo of the excitement in 1963 in the streets of Istanbul when the *From Russia with Love* crew turned up.

In Bilbao, as the stuntman jumped out of the window, the crowd 'oooohed' and 'aaahed' appreciatively as if this were a live show staged primarily for their benefit. But as we Docklanders also knew, there is something terribly exciting about the world of Bond coming to one's own ordinary neighbourhood.

Anyway, with MI6 temporarily evacuated to a very familar Scottish castle (used in countless other films and television programmes, including *The Avengers*), we were also given what now looks like an intensely moving farewell scene. For this proved to be Desmond Llewelyn's final appearance as querulous quartermaster Q.

Bear in mind that this was an association stretching back over thirty-six years – what other actor could have claimed such longevity in any film series? And by 1999, the actor had become famous behind the scenes for two particular reasons. First, he loathed being made to wear shorts for filming (ever since sporting them in *Thunderball* and *You Only Live Twice*) and with each fresh Bond, the crew would try to trick him into thinking that shorts were necessary once more. Second, the man knew next to nothing about technology. One could see, even as he was being interviewed by an American presenter on the set of *The World Is Not Enough*, that the workings of Bond's latest gadgets were still pretty much a mystery to him.

But that mattered not a jot. It was the relationship between Bond and Q that counted. In this one, Q appears to be preparing for retirement, grooming R (played unsubtly by John Cleese) as his replacement. Q gives Bond two pieces of advice. 'Never let them see you bleed,' he says. 'And always have an escape plan.' With this, the old gentleman presses a button and glides down through the floor.

A few weeks after the film opened, Llewelyn was involved in a fatal car accident. He died aged eighty-five. The Bond film now looked like the sweetest and warmest of send-offs. Not least because the relationship between Llewelyn and Brosnan – elderly uncle and mischievous nephew – had a note of genuine affection.

So it's time to track down the terrorist Renard, who has a fascinating gimmick: Bond shot him some time ago. The bullet, we are informed via 3D presentation given by the brilliantly named Dr Molly Wildflash (Serena Scott Thomas), lodged in his brain and at some point will surely kill him. Until then, however, Renard has lost all feeling and thus is becoming a superman, stronger and able to withstand any kind of pain. What might seem authorial tricksiness soon becomes something rather more resonant.

Bond is sent off to Baku to shadow the traumatised Elektra King. He arrives as she is facing down a religious protest, giving assurances to an Orthodox priest that her proposed pipeline will not destroy a sacred cave. But when Bond and Elektra helicopter up to the mountains and inspect the pipeline on skis, they are attacked by rather nifty para-hawks – like parachutes with jet-skis attached. When they are caught in an avalanche, Bond's handy gadget anorak expands into a protective sphere, saving the day. But poor Elektra has the heebie-jeebies.

What you see instantly with Sophie Marceau's performance is that she has found the perfect midway line between being wholly straight and camping it up. The whole thing is very slightly exaggerated but in a way that feels utterly natural within the slightly exaggerated context of the film. In an interview, she said: 'It is Bond and you have to remember that it is fantasy.' But the level of injured realism, a blend of vulnerability and malice, that she brings to the part elevates her far above the common run of Bond girls.

According to director Michael Apted, 'they fought hard to get her', and it paid off. Even though all the pre-publicity cheerfully gave away the fact that she was the villain, the scene when she finally turns on M and reveals that she had her own father murdered still carried an unusual weight of emotional shock for Bond. By the way, that name Elektra: in the Greek tragedy by Euripides, it is Electra who exacts bloody revenge after the murder of her father Agamemnon. Biding her time for some years, she and her brother Orestes eventually lure their unfaithful mother Clytemnestra to a farmhouse and run her through with a sword. Matricide, patricide – all adds up to the same thing.

A more traditional Bond girl, provided perhaps to reassure us that some things never change, is Denise Richards as the nuclear weapons expert Dr Christmas Jones, who first appears on screen in a crop top and hot pants, standard garb for nuclear weapons experts. Richards was previously best known for her role starring opposite Matt Dillon in a steamy caper called *Wild Things* (1998). She admitted in interviews that she had never really seen any Bond films previously, and was thus largely unaware of the iconic status of her role. She brings a sceptical charm to the whole thing, batting off Bond's unsubtle romantic intentions until the film's perfectly horrid final line, of which more a little later.

We catch our first glimpse of Eastern European villain Renard in an eerie night-time scene outside a cave in Azerbaijan, around which strange perpetual fires burn. He can pick up searing coals without feeling a thing (more than can be said for his hapless sidekick, who is made to hold one as punishment for some footling misjudgement). The bald head and facial scars are a little suggestive of a previous Blofeld; but the performance is instantly arresting. No other actor has made the villain such an unknow-able yet somehow creepily sympathetic psychopath. In an interview, Carlyle said: 'It is the best fun to be the bad guy,' and acknowledged the competitive nature of such a role – 'You always want to be the very worst bad guy.' But this macabre revenant, deprived of the senses of taste and touch, is a notch above. Early on, M reveals that Renard has also been operating in the Balkans and Chechnya. Which makes him a prescient forward echo of the world's wider preoccupation with terrorism.

Also a notch above are the action sequences, in which we see the return of our dear old friend the countdown. There is a shooty-bang confrontation in the cavernous subterranean halls of the weapons plant in which Renard has planted a ticking LED device – a satisfying reimagining of the Bondian Big Set – and there is a terrific episode inside Elektra's oil pipeline as Bond and Christmas, shooting at seventy kilometres per hour through the tunnel in a rigging pod, must intercept a plutonium bomb which has been sent zinging down that same pipe, and which is fast gaining on their pod. In a change from the previous film, we are not overwhelmed with ceaseless machine-gun fire. 'Gunfire can get noisy and tedious,' said Michael Apted.[2] Well said, man! The relief is great.

'Pierce said: "Give me more stuff to do," ' Apted also said. 'He wanted depth and complexity which meant the same had to go for the other characters.'[3] This, of course, is quite a big thing to ask in a Bond film since the very nature of the form means that the character must stay broadly the same from film to film. But here, Bond's relationship with Elektra is given an extra dimension or two, as first they have the inevitable tumble, and then it gradually dawns on Bond that she has betrayed him. More striking yet though is the painful love scene between Elektra and Renard; that bullet lodged in his head has deprived him of his sense of touch, but not of his desire. And so, impotent, he is forced to watch as Elektra caresses herself with ice cubes. 'Remember . . . pleasure,' she breathes, rather heartlessly. That is why it was so vital to hire a European art-house icon. No one else could have got away with a line like that.

The mere idea of the film, however, appeared to cause some difficulties in Marceau's personal life. It was reported that she split with Polish director Andrzej Zulawski because of his 'constant criticism' of her choice of film roles.[4]

There's humour in the screenplay too, provided by the welcome return of Robbie Coltrane as Zukovsky, with rap artist Goldie playing his preposterous golden-toothed sidekick. Zukovsky has embraced the new capitalism of the East, trading in huge vats of sticky black caviar and running a casino. He is here as Bond's unlikely ally and is present for another ingenious action sequence, featuring helicopters with rotating chainsaws dangling beneath.

Better yet is the depiction of his casino. In previous Bonds, such places were portrayed as sophisticated international spots, filled with tuxedos and cocktail dresses and impossibly rich Euro-folk and tinkling lounge music. This one is the same, except the ingredients are shown to be irredeemably vulgar. And thanks to Bond's X-ray specs, we can also see that it is a Wild West sort of casino where men and women alike are carrying huge amounts of concealed weapons beneath their shiny finery. Zukovsky's own glittering tuxedo is a synecdoche for this entire Bondian subgenre. Of course, a few years down the line, we were invited once more to regard casinos as a little classier than this.

Towards the end of the film, Elektra tricks M into coming out to Baku and kidnaps her just as Bond is trying to defuse the pipeline nuclear bomb. For the first time ever, we see Bond's superior in a situation of direct peril, held prisoner in a lighthouse just off the coast of Istanbul. Renard informs her she is to die the next day and his thunderously impassioned speech about what M did to Elektra, 'leaving her to the mercy of a man like me', is rather stirring because we see that he does have a point. Incidentally, on seeing that Judi Dench was going to be held in the villain's HQ, her husband Michael Williams said to her: 'My God, darling, is it up to you to save the world? We're all done for.'

Well, the world-saving duties are divided between M, Bond and Christmas Jones, still wearing less than the average atomic scientist. Bond and Christmas get into the hijacked nuclear submarine from which Renard is going to incinerate Istanbul; the climax, involving the craft turning on its end, Bond almost drowning in a small airlock and a fight to the death, involving a nuclear device that looks like a giant fountain pen refill, is an absolute nailbiter.

Prior to this, Bond has been tortured by Elektra in a quaint-looking antique garotting chair; upon being freed by Zukovsky after near-strangulation, Bond shoots Elektra dead. He then spends a distastefully long time over her corpse as M looks on, hand over mouth, as well she might. But the point was that this time round, the Bond producers road-tested a little emotional resonance. And the ceiling didn't fall in on them.

The reviews were almost universally enthusiastic as well. Papers in both Britain and the US responded very favourably to the new Bond tactic of giving the thing a bit of heart. In some ways, Broccoli and Wilson were responding to a general trend in popular culture. This was very much the time of Bridget Jones, the rise of the so-called rom-com and of a renaissance in American television that featured a lot of what producers tend to call 'big emotion'. Even globally successful sitcoms such as *Friends* would often feature, among the farces, scenes of a poignant nature. Another 1999 release, *Notting Hill*, a comedy written by Richard Curtis, and starring Hugh Grant and Julia Roberts as the bookshop bumbler and the Hollywood movie star who fall in love, honed this blend of broad, daft comedy and unashamed soppiness to perfection.

And the Bond producers were always very aware of the need to continue to appeal to their female audience. One might say that the previous film's predominance of machine guns and punching and zero emotional spark made it tremendously off-putting. From the very start, in the romance of its locations and its soft-lit aesthetics, *The World Is Not Enough* saw an attempt not only to give Bond a grown-up relationship, but also to do the same for the villain.

We also had a tremendously fine score from David Arnold; settling down into the post-Barry era, it was by turns lush and punchy, featuring an unusually slow and melancholic title song sung by Shirley Manson of the deeply fashionable band Garbage.

Interestingly, the film's depiction of MI6 constituted another shift; we had come a long way from the gentle clubland fantasy of M's log-fire-lit office, with M answering to the genial defence minister Freddie Gray (always played by Geoffrey Keen). This version of MI6 was intended as more realistic – but it somehow also fitted more closely with how Americans might imagine the British secret service operated.

'We do not negotiate with terrorists,' announces M near the film's start. As it happened, in real life, this public position was well known not to have been the case – after all, the security services had been involved in the early 1990s in Prime Minister John Major's discussions with the Provisional IRA. The result, in 1998, was the Good Friday Agreement, which began to bring hard-won stability to Northern Ireland after decades of terrorism and sectarianism and bitterness.

The MI6 of Bond was a curious beast. On the one hand, it appeared formidable in intellect and technology; yet on the other hand, it was howlingly clod-hopping. What other security organisation on Earth would first allow its headquarters to be blown up, and then its boss to be kidnapped and held hostage on a Turkish lighthouse?

But this was Bond once more surrounded by a faux family. As well as Q and M and perpetually amused Moneypenny, there was Chief of Staff Bill Tanner (Michael Kitchen, looking perpetually harassed) and cool-as-a-cucumber Charles Robinson (Colin Salmon). In any American film, these figures would play a much more active part in the story; here, they are there in essence to cheer on Bond, and to grudgingly admit that his instincts and hunches are right whereas theirs are always wrong.

Compare this cosiness with the chillier depiction of security services given throughout the mid to late 1990s in the smash-hit American TV series and film spin-off *The X-Files*. Mulder and Scully, both CIA agents, investigate the paranormal and other-worldly; and in the course of various scarifying adventures involving aliens, monsters and UFOs, it slowly becomes apparent that their own services are conspiring in dreadful secrets, exceptionally harmful to humanity. For Mulder and Scully, not even their own colleagues can be wholly trusted.

This cynicism about the guardians of the interests of the state was something that could never be reproduced in Bond. For an international audience, MI6 essentially translated as 'Queen and country' – an almost feudal idea.

Brosnan was already proving exceptionally popular with American audiences, and this film cemented his appeal to a transatlantic female audience. By this stage, his Bond accent was wandering all over the place. In one scene, he announces to Denise Richards that his name is 'Buhnd. James Buhnd.' At other times he is Irish; occasionally, most startlingly, he is straightforwardly English. On the plus side, Brosnan had been working on his stern stare and his scenes with Sophie Marceau, during which said stare was deployed heavily, generated a certain spark.

One of the only real off-putting elements was his handling of the seemingly obligatory double entendres, which he tended to murder with a sledgehammer (or perhaps it is simply that the lines were so awful that any approach would have seemed unacceptable – actually, I think this more likely, since in other circumstances Brosnan is a terrifically gifted light comic actor). The final line, famously, is the expected clinch between Bond and Christmas, where Bond declares 'I've always wanted to have Christmas in Turkey'; but it appears that almost everyone else in the entire world loved this gag, so I must be wrong.

Also profoundly off-putting is the gurning lech-face that Brosnan puts on while wandering through Zukovsky's casino in his X-ray specs – all puckering lips and corrugated eyebrows. No one has pulled faces like that since the 1970s, and even then, they tended to be pulled by milkmen greeted at the door by Diana Dors lookalikes in baby-doll nighties.

No matter. Brosnan seemed to be enjoying himself and that was the main thing, although the actor played it cool in interviews. 'It's fun and I'm more relaxed,' he said in one.

The third Brosnan film was a rip-roaring triumph. It now seemed funny to think that just ten years previously, the series was widely regarded as being dead in the water. So it was natural that the next entry in the series would again feature Pierce Brosnan at the helm. And because the film would be marking an anniversary of sorts, it was going to be rather more self-referential than usual.

CHAPTER TWENTY-SEVEN BIRTHDAY BOY

As literary critic Umberto Eco pointed out in the 1960s, a Bond story is essentially a rigidly structuralist thing, composed of binary opposites – that is, hero/villain, hero/girl, and so forth – and it works by means of constant repetition.[1] In 2002, the deliberately self-referential entry *Die Another Day* had more of these binary opposites than most.

For this, Brosnan's fourth Bond film, one of the ideas was to acknowledge that this was cinema Bond's fortieth anniversary – *Dr. No* had opened in 1962. So the new film would contain a number of throwaway references to previous Bond epics, which would be a treat for the fans. And since, by 2002, everyone in the audience was by definition a Bond fan, then the jokes would be lost on no one.

By this stage, the Bond archive had found new life, through sales first of videotapes and then of much more detailed DVDs. For the first time, Bond enthusiasts could watch their favourite old films while listening to producers and directors giving a running commentary. The result, it seems, is that for anyone other than a casual viewer, the Bond universe – the girls, the gadgets, the cars – is one in which it's possible for most to pass muster in pub quiz questions on the subject. In Britain, for example, in the BBC's popular soap *EastEnders*, there is a character called Bradley Branning who takes his Bond fannishness to the lengths of having Bond Fact contests with his friends, and who also embarrassingly impersonates Sean Connery.

Writers Neal Purvis and Robert Wade fit, it seems fair to say, into this category of fan-boy. Barbara Broccoli said fondly of them: 'They were extremely inventive writers, big Bond fans and they pitched great ideas.'[2]

And so the story they came up with was itself an echo of a previous tale – the novel of *Moonraker*. In *Die Another Day*, Bond comes up against a rich and malevolent businessman calling himself Gustav Graves. Graves would appear to be the darling of the Establishment, receiving honours from Buckingham Palace, with friends in high political circles, and what is more, a member of the gentlemen's club Blades. The scene where Graves and Bond engage in a fencing match that gets ferociously out of hand, practically destroying this club, was filmed at the Athenaeum in Pall Mall. This venerable club also played host to the 1998 film of *The Avengers*. On both occasions, extras dressed as old buffers were required to lower newspapers in shock.

It is only Bond who smells a rat about this Graves and his ambitious Project Icarus, a giant space mirror intended to bring artificial sunlight to corners of the Earth having trouble with crops. It is not merely that Graves appears to be trading in conflict diamonds; something about the man himself screams out 'wrong'un'.

And indeed he is. Graves is in fact a lunatic North Korean general called Moon, missing presumed dead. He has gone and got himself a DNA transplant and is now planning to use Project Icarus – in essence, a giant laser beam from outer space – to destroy the minefield-studded border between North and South Korea, and to sizzle Japan.

In other words, in essence, Graves is the Hugo Drax of Ian Fleming's original novel: a ginger-haired cad with an astounding secret identity.

The space laser was a cause for celebration among those who felt it was time for the series to return to the quasi-science fiction escapism seen throughout the Roger Moore years. The idea for a giant mirror to bring light to the Earth sprung from a story featured in the *Sunday Times*, a newspaper once famed for the inventiveness of some of its scoops. Those of us who follow such things recall fondly that paper's assertions that armies would soon be fighting with invisible tanks and state-of-the-art robots. Anyhow, the *Sunday Times*, around the turn of the millennium, predicted with poker face that scientists were looking into ways of reflecting sunlight from space in such a way as to make icy northern tundras lush and fertile. Talk about tampering with the forces of creation! And as such, an idea much better left to the confines of a gleefully traditionalist Bond movie.

Also tremendous this time around were the actresses taking on the now proud mantle of Bond girls. Young English actress Rosamund Pike essayed the role of Miranda Frost, PA to Graves but also an agent for M; and the Oscar-winning Halle Berry took on the role of Bond's ally and CIA agent Jinx.

Another piece of tremendous casting came with the English actor Toby Stephens playing the perpetually sneering villain Gustav Graves. And stepping up to the directorial plate was the surprisingly radical choice of Lee Tamahori, the New Zealander who had been responsible for *Once Were*

Warriors (1994). The story was intended to move from North Korea, to Cuba, to Iceland, and then back again. So far, so pleasingly traditional. But then producers and director thought of shaking things up a little in the pre-credits.

Bond surfs into North Korea, as one so frequently does; takes on the identity of a diamond smuggler; gets found out; gets into hovercraft chase across minefield with psychopathic Colonel Moon. Then, as Moon tumbles over a waterfall, Bond is captured, taken to a dank prison and tortured. Opening titles.

All very wrong-footing, especially as Danny Kleinman's consistently superb titles now show us a stylised version of that torture. As the credits roll, there are scorpions, electric shocks, Bond dunked in ice, Bond being beaten up – while around him, those dancing female silhouettes, composed this time of fire and ice, take on a demonic aspect, seemingly caressing him. One senses that Fleming would have approved of this sadomasochism.

And over all this plays Madonna's – ahem – *different* approach to a Bond song. It is all extremely disorientating. What about the stunt escape, the glib getaway line? We have never seen Bond being treated so badly before. As the film gets under way, we learn that he has been in this hell-hole for fourteen months. Brosnan, sitting in a dark corner in tattered rags, has a straggly beard to prove it. For us Bond aficionados, this is perilously close to documentary realism.

Just as abruptly, Bond is removed from Korean jail, driven to a misty shoreline and told to walk along a jetty into the fog. Bond is convinced he is about to be shot in the back. But he isn't. He walks on into that fog. Although in no way spectacular, it is one of the series' most striking and resonant shots; that of our broken hero walking into uncertain, blank oblivion.

Well, we can dispense with any metaphysical ideas: Bond is being prisoner-swapped with a Korean bad guy called Xao who, thanks to Bond's tinkering with explosives and diamonds, now has diamonds embedded in his face. If you are going to give your henchman a camp characteristic, it doesn't come camper than this. Back at a US base, Bond is under sedation and under suspicion of having leaked secrets under torture. M – by now, Judi Dench has made the part completely her own – is horridly pointing out to him that he is of no further use to her as a secret agent.

In other words, for the film's first half-hour, the producers have tried to stretch the Bond formula in quite a new way, taking the character to the extreme of shutting himself down and inducing a self-inflicted heart attack. We are meant to feel for Bond now it becomes apparent that not even M loves him any more. Actually what happens is that Brosnan's acting style is so naturally light that we feel very little of the sort. We know that our slick-haired quipster will be back. But as an experiment, you could see that Wilson and Broccoli were thinking ahead in terms of testing Bond's limits.

This being Brosnan – and we being the daft, escapism-seeking audiences that we are – the scene in which straggly Bond escapes, books into a luxury Hong Kong hotel, then has a simple wash and brush-up before donning a suit and tie, is the point at which this particular film takes off. Beards and torture are all very well, but come on! Give us the smoothie!

And as the action moves to Cuba (filmed in fact in Cadiz), that is exactly what they do. Bond, at a beachfront bar, watches dumbstruck as Halle Berry's Jinx rises from the sea in exact imitation of Ursula Andress forty years ago. The bikini was not the same, obviously, but costume designer Lindy Hemmings went to the trouble of providing Jinx with a waistband knife of exactly the same design. It is a terrific scene, somehow bringing us full circle on those forty years while acknowledging the changes that have taken place. While Jinx's Venus act makes her as much the subject of 'the male gaze' as any of the Benny Hill girls, the character's subsequent engagement with Bond – she is much more sexually direct than him, and indeed he becomes the subject of her appraising gaze – tells us that perhaps genuinely for the first time, Bond has met his equal.

Incidentally, top marks to Halle Berry for her 'this ocean is lovely and warm' acting. In fact, the conditions in Cadiz were both atrocious and freezing and the sea was incredibly cold. A later scene involving Jinx running up a hill in a summer dress, while firing at a helicopter, and then removing that summer dress to reveal another bikini was every bit as freezing. 'It's what you sign up for,' said Berry with admirable stoicism, neglecting to add that in fact, very few Oscar winners have signed up for this sort of thing before.[3] Indeed, it now seems rather wonderful that an Oscar winner would wish to rise from the sea at all. But Halle Berry did go on to make some rather eccentric career choices after *Monster's Ball* (2001).

The purpose of the Cuban escapade is to infiltrate a sinister clinic in which, both our hero and heroine learn separately, rich folk are being offered DNA transplants, presumably being provided with raw material by poorer folk. To be utterly honest, I am still having some trouble getting my head around this notion. I mean, I know it's fantasy, but really! Xao is interrupted by Bond halfway through the course of having the basis of his humanity replaced, and thus is stuck with a bald head and glittering cheeks. Worse things could happen. And Jinx blows up the clinic. It is all rather good – if baffling – fun. And in the revolving mirrors of the clinic corridor, we spot an oblique and brilliantly pointless reference to Scaramanga's fun house in *The Man with the Golden Gun*.

The fun has to stop for a moment though. This, after all, was just over a year since the terrorist attacks of September 11. 'Things changed while you were away,' M tells Bond in a disused tube station. Well, yes, they did, but do we really want M telling us this in the middle of a daft escapist fantasy? Sam Raimi's *Spider-Man* (2002) understandably had to have certain scenes reshot in order not to include the Twin Towers. But here one is jabbed by the sheer wrongness of the reference. Certainly to those of us in that 2002 audience – some fifteen months after we had absorbed the events of that day, no matter how historically resonant (or unresonant) they were – this reference to a recent real-life atrocity was both immediately jarring and somehow lacked perspective.

It was understandable that Broccoli and Wilson should want to acknowledge it, I suppose, since the media in America and Britain and indeed across the world were utterly mesmerised by the attack for months afterwards. And if President Bush was to be listened to, the world had a new enemy; and Bush was the sheriff whose job it was to round them up. 'They're bad people,' was his response to complaints that prisoners in Guantánamo Bay were held in barbaric conditions with no suggestion of a trial or hearing.

Quite by chance, North Korea was named in 2002, along with Iraq and Syria, as belonging to Dubya's famous 'Axis of Evil'. Neat timing once more on the part of Michael Wilson and Barbara Broccoli. North Korea's ruler Kim Jong Il is known, among his many eccentricities, to be a terrific film buff. *Die Another Day* can't have been much to his taste – indeed, as soon as the film was released, so too was a ringing North Korean denunciation.

Posted from the Secretariat of the Committee for the Peaceful Reunification of the Fatherland, it read more disapprovingly than a Nina Hibbin review: '*Die Another Day* is a dirty and cursed burlesque aimed to slander North Korea.' Fair cop, guv. Do go on. 'It clearly proves that the US is the root cause of all disasters and misfortunes of the Korean nation and is an empire of evil. The US is the HQ that spreads abnormality, degeneration, violence and fin de siècle corrupt sex culture.' Nothing much we can disagree with there. Eon should have slapped that communiqué on the posters.

So anyway. We're one year on in the plot – do keep up – and in the midst of what is shaping up to be a magnificently frivolous James Bond film, M has to go and say that the world has changed. Pleasingly, Bond tells her: 'Not for me, it hasn't.' And then he sets about his proper business, which is paying a visit to the new Q (John Cleese) for a nostalgia-soaked session in the gadget lab.

We are reacquainted with Rosa Klebb's lethal shoes (which for some reason Bond sniffs); the alligator submersible from *Octopussy* (how sweet that the world's least-loved gadget should get a look in); the jet-pack from *Thunderball* (still not madly convincing after all these years). It is an affectionate and rather shrewd scene that draws our attention away from the fact that it is not Desmond Llewelyn providing the irascible comments. Instead, Cleese steps into his shoes, making the new Q slightly more querulous and barbed. New gadgets this time include an ultrasonic ring that can shatter glass. Oh, and an invisible car.

With Bond, the amount that the production team can get away with is normally dictated by context. For example, if Hugo Drax in *Moonraker* has an entire orbiting space station, then he and NASA can have fully functioning laser guns too. Here, though, fans winced in distress. The special effects concerned in making the car disappear were all very fine and the pseudo-scientific explanation for it – the car's outer body covered with a zillion tiny screens reflecting back what a zillion tiny cameras see, or something – holds water at least for the amount of time that Q is speaking the line, though no more.

But really, it won't do. Apart from anything else, it doesn't seem necessary in the end; the cliffhangers that invisibility is called upon to solve – largely being rammed by another car – could have easily been negotiated by Bond in different ways. It seems odd, having set out at the start of the film to make Bond so vulnerable, that in the second half, they give him the armoury of a super-hero.

This is because the film itself is heading into the realms of the comic-book adaptation. The advance in computer-generated effects made this kind of thing inevitable, for what genre better showcases the eye-popping effects that can now be achieved while sitting at computer screens? Sam Raimi scored an enormous hit in 2002 with that first *Spider-Man* film, in which the webbed wonder was seen to swing from tower block to tower block via his jets of sticky thread. *The Mummy Returns* (2001) similarly relied on filling the entire screen with wonders and horrors conjured directly from a computer program.

For Bond, the cartoon outlandishness begins as the action moves to Iceland, where Gustav Graves has built an opulent ice palace, complete with bedrooms and cocktail bars, purely for the purpose of attracting the world's press to his latest publicity stunt. Here, under cover of darkness, Graves unveils his apparent scheme, demonstrating how his mirror in space can bring sudden sunlight pouring down at any time. The sneer on his face, however, would be sufficient to tell even the most naïve of us that this isn't quite all there is to it.

Back in his private HQ, Graves has a psychedelically lit face-mask, under which he lies at strategic moments. He is discovered thus by Xao, who looks like a cowled bling version of Bergman's Death. What is this set-up for? The gene therapy, we are told, has rendered Graves unable to sleep, ever. Thus, to avoid insanity, he must spend an hour or so each day under his dream simulator. It's a rather nice, creepy idea but there is precious little time to dwell upon it, for Jinx is captured, attached to some industrial machine, and threatened with death by industrial laser. Then Bond is captured and Gustav Graves at last reveals his true identity.

Graves claims that he modelled his new 'disgusting' incarnation on Bond – the show-offy parachute jumps, the insane self-confidence. This is an old Bond trope, the villain secretly envying Bond's style and swagger and seeking to acquire some of that savoir-faire for himself. If you can call it savoir-faire. Personally, I have never felt tempted to wander into a casino in a tuxedo, or to give a barman an almost autistically precise list of ingredients for a bloody cocktail. But then I am a fan of Roger Moore's reversible safari suit, so what do I know about style?

It is at this point that Rosamund Pike steps forward to reveal that her character Miranda Frost is in fact a bad girl; and a bad girl with real icy gusto. Later Pike starred in a new stage play called *Hitchcock Blonde*, and here she recalls the phrase perfectly in that curious mix of ice and malice. It is simply inconceivable that an actress of her standing would, back in 1983, have touched Bond with a barge-pole, even with rubber gloves on.

And thence to the film's only regrettable section; given the setting, it would have been daft not to have a car chase on the ice, and Xao and Bond do. Fair enough, especially when juiced up with the super-fast/suddenly super-slow editing. But then Graves deploys his sun laser and everything turns a bit CGI.

The golden beam that pursues Bond ineluctably across the ice is well done; the effect, however, when Bond's vehicle topples over the edge on an ice cliff, and the subsequent effect involving Bond, an improvised parachute and a tidal wave, make one involuntarily bury one's head deep in one's hands. Previously, all Bond films had prided themselves on 'doing it for real'; as far as possible, the stunts you saw were the stunts that were actually filmed. Here, Bond became a bad cartoon. No matter how much hard work the effects department put in – and obviously they did – it entirely failed to convince.

We are back to the simplest reason: camera angles that ring entirely untrue. There is simply no point in costly computer simulation if we are looking at the faux event from a completely unfeasible angle, such as the shot where we are some way above Brosnan clinging to the edge of the ice cliff. And as for surfing the tidal wave . . .

Be fair. It's only two or three minutes of screen time. And it was a trap that practically all film-makers were falling into. Director Lee Tamahori considered that this sort of thing would form a large part of the future of Bond. In 2006, Martin Campbell was to prove him spectacularly wrong.

In contrast, the car chase on the ice was staged for real and proved a production nightmare: for a start, it seemed, when the crew were just about to fly out to the location, that the ice was insufficiently thick. They faced the unpleasant prospect of stuntmen and expensive cars disappearing down holes. When shooting began, the ice was tested every day and was deemed just – just – thick enough. However, to be completely on the safe side, members of the crew and their equipment had to be positioned some distance from each other so that they would not place excessive strain upon the ice. Now that's what we call proper Bond!

And then, as the car chase returns to the ice palace, we are back in the exaggerated reality that Bond does best – a big studio set disintegrating, this time gushing with millions of gallons of water, as 007 races to dispose of irritant Xao and rescue Jinx from the ice bedroom in which she is ingeniously drowning. This was the biggest set that production designer Peter Lamont had been asked to create in years, and all for just a few minutes of screen time. In other words, yah boo sucks to Tamahori's incorrect predictions. In Pinewood, engineers had to create special drainage gullies for those flooding scenes that also involved a car flying through the air and falling into the water.

The idea of the ice palace sprang from a newspaper feature that Barbara Broccoli read about an ice hotel in Sweden. This hotel was small — structure is, of course, rather difficult, when you are working with nothing but frozen water — but none the less a thing of beauty and a photographer's dream. I am surprised Barbara Broccoli only read the one piece. I seem to have seen that same feature at least four times every year since about 1990, with each visiting journalist claiming to be among the first. But that's not to detract from the attractiveness of the idea here: and the film did wonders for tourism in Iceland.

Previously, the country and its capital Reykjavik had been best known for the eccentric pop singer Björk and previous to that, a pivotal East–West summit in 1986 between Reagan and Gorbachev. *Die Another Day* did much to show off the eerie beauty of the green-blue glaciers, though other scenes involving boiling geysers never quite made out of the cutting room.

A little more unlikely on the location front was the use of south Cornwall to double for both Iceland and North Korea. In fact, some shots of Graves's Icelandic geodesic domes, filled with tropical flora, were filmed at Cornwall's Eden Project, while the film's final scene — Bond and Jinx canoodling in an oriental shack on the Korean coast — was filmed just a few miles away.

For some tourist authorities, getting a Bond is almost the same as getting the Olympics. These are films with a worldwide audience and each country is always showcased strikingly. The sight of Roger Moore raising his eyebrow at the Pyramids did the previously unattainably exotic (and to some, rather intimidating) Egypt a power of good — particularly among British tourists, who by that stage would have just about forgotten Suez. Thailand and Sardinia received similar lifts in the 1970s.

Sometimes the exotic locations don't need such a boost. Possibly Venice could have rubbed along quite happily without the extra publicity of either *Moonraker* or *Casino Royale*. And in *Die Another Day*, one location shot, on the south side of Westminster Bridge in London, has caused tourists frustration. We see Bond walk across the bridge, run down the steps in front of the old GLC building, turn, and open an old wooden door with a large key. The door in the film leads to the disused and secret tube station Vauxhall Cross. In real life, the door leads to a store cupboard. This hasn't stopped countless curious tourists tugging at it. Bloody fools.

Until the film's final climactic half-hour, this whiz-bang self-homage has contained too many good ideas, with not enough time to dwell on each. We love Toby Stephens's inability to sleep, for instance, but there is not a moment to hear more. And utterly science-fictional though the notion of DNA transplantation is, it would have been good to hear a bit more about real-life DNA research that might have sparked the notion. And a bit more on the intriguing relationship between Graves and Miranda Frost. And a bit more about how Graves came to model his new incarnation on Bond. Ultimately, though, why grumble? All this is better than a film such as *The Man with the Golden Gun*, operating on barely half an idea.

And the lead-in to the climax offers up yet one more tantalising morsel, in the abrasive relationship between Judi Dench's M and her American counterpart, played by Michael Madsen. Both are in a secret HQ in South Korea as Graves's doomsday beam draws ever closer to that minefield on the 38th Parallel. What the scene seems to be saying in subtext is: America is not in charge of plucky old Britain. M can more than hold her own against these brash Yankee bullies and emphatically does not have to follow the commands of her ghastly counterpart. In real life, things appeared somewhat different.

The following year, in 2003, Prime Minister Tony Blair stood shoulder to shoulder with George W. Bush in making a case for effecting regime change in Iraq. The contents of the dossier presented to Parliament, allegedly 'sexed up' with claims of Saddam's weapons of mass destruction, led to a widespread view that Britain – and Blair – had become America's poodle. No doubt until we hear the real reasons for the 2003 invasion of Iraq, at some point in the distant future, the arguments will go on. But Bond's MI6 seems a rather more sturdily independent organisation than perhaps its real-life counterpart has been.

And what relationship could be more special than that between Bond and Jinx, equal allies in defeating Graves at the end? I say equal: for all her firepower and wit, Jinx has already had to be rescued twice by Bond, first from the industrial laser, and then from drowning – two cliffhangers that would not seem amiss in *The Perils of Pauline*, were it ever to be remade. Never mind, for our heroes now have to get on board Graves's private jumbo jet the *Antonov*, just as it is taxiing down the runway, a little beyond the 'final boarding' call. Somehow, after some excellent impersonations of running from both actors, Bond and Jinx clamber on to the accelerating beast via the undercarriage, a superb top tip should you ever find you have missed the gate for your own flight.

Up in the air, as the golden beam of death sizzles across the land (I am reminded of Bulldog Drummond's Carl Peterson, and his 1920s Dirigible of Doom), Graves, wearing lethal body armour that can electrocute his foes, is getting ready to reveal his new identity to his old general dad. Dad is not having any of it. We sympathise a little with Dad, for of course his boy has scrambled and swapped all his Korean DNA for that of a sneering ginger with a passing resemblance to Maggie Smith (Stephens's mother). We sense correctly that Dad's disapproval is not going to go down well with his psycho son. None the less, it is an impressively written and played scene unusual for Bond: a son wanting nothing more than the approval and praise of his distant, cold father.

And as soon as son murders father with an electrified embrace, those old forces of tragedy kick in, with Bond's arrival on the flight deck. Equal partner Jinx has set the plane's autopilot straight for the solar death ray and so we have our climax. Bond and Graves bitterly slug it out as the craft disintegrates around them, while the lightly clad Jinx and Miranda Frost fight rather fetchingly with sabres. Graves, eventually, is sucked into one of the plane's engines – a not especially poetic comeuppance – but Miranda is skewered with a dagger, a book called *The Art of War* affixed to her chest. Much more fitting. Bond and Jinx make their absurd escape from the plummeting plane, via one of the helicopters in the hold, and we have the final traditional canoodle, Jinx's navel sporting a conflict diamond. All good harmless fun.

Certainly the critics and audiences thought so. The film reviewers had once more reached the stage where they felt it would be pointless to apply the normal rules of judgement to what had again become a pop-cultural juggernaut. '*Die Another Day* is an impressive production,' said *Standard* critic Alexander Walker. 'He who is tired of Bond is tired of life.'

Some were impressed by Brosnan's beard ordeal in the first part of the film. But Peter Bradshaw of the *Guardian* was peevish about the comic-book aspects. 'The digitised stunts are an unconvincing cheat,' he wrote, 'and Bond also has the naffest gadget in Bond history: an invisible car. Why? What, at this high level of gadgetry sophistication, is the point of an invisible car? It must cause more problems than it solves. Hmm . . . where did I park the – oww!'

Perhaps we all felt this. But that did not stop us piling in to see it in our millions – in financial terms, *Die Another Day* smashed all Bond records with a haul of $450 million.

Even Madonna's idiosyncratic title song did rather well in the UK and US charts, for some reason. Look, I'll be frank, it's all too blippy and bleepy and Madonna's electronically modulated voice sounds like Minnie Mouse and there isn't much of a tune and the lyric 'I think I'll die another day' lacks the grand melodrama that we have come to expect from the genre. Perhaps the electronic bleeps were supposed to be reminiscent of that weird bit of musique concrète that kicked off *Dr. No*. And the whole thing might now be filed under 'What was she thinking of?'

Madonna's enthusiastic participation, however, was the further seal, certainly for American audiences, of the cool/kitsch status of the films. She also earned a cameo appearance in a basque arrangement as a fencing instructor called Verity, who appears to operate out of gentlemen's club Blades. Madonna and Pierce Brosnan have a moment of double-entendre exchange, involving him 'rising to the occasion' and her 'getting the point', which demonstrated that Madonna could not begin to comprehend the subtlety of the tradition of English sauce. You would think that her geezer film director husband Guy Ritchie might have coached her with a few *Carry On* DVDs.

That ferocious fencing fight in Blades, incidentally, does much to remind us what good shape Brosnan was in for a fifty-two-year-old. Apart from his strange running style, which appears to be based on a piston-driven steam engine, you never have difficulty envisaging his Bond performing all those extraordinary feats of athleticism. But the filming proved wearing.

While shooting in Pinewood (doubling for North Korea), the actor in one shot was called to run for an armoured vehicle and leap aboard, and damaged his knee in the process. The injury kept Brosnan out of action for a few sweaty days, as everyone tried to work out whether he would be back in action at all. A film of this size and scale, like a supertanker, takes an awful lot of time to change direction and recasting the lead would have cost gazillions in production hold-ups. Of course, as we observe, Mr Brosnan was Mummy's brave soldier and returned to filming very quickly. But, as Barbara Broccoli pointed out, a production like Bond required ever increasing amounts of physical stamina from its leading man. Perhaps this was a small factor in the decision that was to follow a couple of years on.

Given that the film is a celebration, we now sit back and wonder quite what Ian Fleming would have made of it were he still with us. On the one hand, we might imagine him frowning at something seemingly made to appeal chiefly to teenage boys in American multiplexes. We might picture his eyes narrowing as Pierce Brosnan's accent takes one of its whimsical journeys back and forth across the Atlantic. The laser beams, the geodesic domes, the giant mirrors in space . . . and yet, and yet. In spirit, none of this is *remotely* different to the film that kicked it all off in 1962.

For lasers from space, read rocket-toppling; for scary oriental Dr No, read scary oriental Colonel Moon; for tarantulas, read scorpions; for Honey Rider and Miss Taro, read Jinx and Miranda Frost; for occasionally disorientating editing in *No*, read ditto for *Day*; and for Britain holding its own against a much more powerful US in the Caribbean – well, read exactly the same in Iceland.

The central romantic relationship would not have detained Fleming for long; in his fiction, most of Bond's sexual involvements have a twist of poignancy somewhere along the line. But from the start, the films were tonally different from the novels. And as to the multiplex-pleasing accusation: if Saltzman and Broccoli, back in 1962, could have got their baby on to coast-to-coast screens, they would have considered their job extremely well done. In other words, for all that we might think that the gloss and the futurism and the pace and the style of *Die Another Day* was a world away from the black cars and back-projections and cross-fades of *Dr. No*, the two films are in fact almost twins. Facile, frivolous, logic-defying nonsense – and none the worse for that.

But Eon also knew from experience – they had known since the sci-fi excesses of *Moonraker* in fact – that they could not continue down that path. Each new Bond movie has to pull off the difficult trick of presenting a contrast with the one that came before, while remaining in essence the same. Broccoli and Wilson had no cause for concern in the wake of *Day* – its takings not merely from cinemas but also from DVD sales and rentals, plus all the other associated Bond merchandise, ensured that their hero had a healthy future.

But the two of them were, as always, alert to fresh competition, and both were expert at sniffing the air and detecting changes in cinematic fashion. Come 2003, they decided on the most surprisingly radical plan of all: that is, to finally buy the rights to Fleming's first Bond novel, *Casino Royale*; and then to adapt it as faithfully as possible, and in so doing fundamentally to reinvent the entire idea of Bond.

O f all the authors idolised by Ian Fleming, the one who made him almost
boyishly happy prior to publication of *Casino Royale* was W. Somerset
Maugham, the celebrated, though now half-forgotten, writer of literary
fiction who had himself also written a spy novel featuring the protagonist
Ashenden. Fleming had speculatively sent the old author a proof of *Royale*.
Maugham wrote a kind letter back to Fleming, telling him that the book
had kept him from his sleep in his anxiety to finish it, and that the card-table
battles between Bond and the villain Le Chiffre hit a note of 'perfect
tension'. Fleming could not contain his happiness, replying with a note of
self-deprecation that he was delighted Maugham had enjoyed his 'cosh
boys-own story'.[1]

He then gauchely asked for permission to use Maugham's comments on
the novel's dust jacket. While one can imagine this sort of thing from a first-
time author in his twenties, it sits less naturally with a hardened newspaper
man in his mid-forties. Perhaps it is this very boyishness that also gave
Fleming the priceless capacity for heroic daydreaming that formed the
obvious psychic core of all the Bond novels.

Later in his own career, Fleming himself was compared by one critic to
Maugham with his short story 'Quantum of Solace', which focused not on
guns and exploding suitcases but on the destructive breakdown of a
marriage, the story related to Bond by a colonial governor. Had Fleming
lived longer, we might have seen more of this. It was reasonably clear that
he yearned to be regarded as a proper literary figure, as opposed to a
purveyor of superior B-movie thrills.

These days, critics and authors alike are almost agreed that such
distinctions are false; that a brilliant, many-layered detective novel such as
P.D. James's *Devices and Desires* has just as much legitimacy as *Bleak House*. Back
in the 1950s and 60s, the rigidity of academics such as F.R. Leavis (with his
self-proclaimed 'canon' of great English literature, in which D.H. Lawrence
featured largely) held general sway. Then in the 1970s and 80s came the
critical movement of deconstruction, and with it the great sweep of

'cultural studies', in which university lecturers fell over themselves trying to ensure that no work was considered superior to any other, and that 'value judgments' were not attached to 'texts'. A TV serial like *Crossroads* was equally deserving of study as *Crime and Punishment*.

Now things appeared to have settled a little again. When, in 2004, Penguin Books began reissuing the James Bond novels as prestigious silver-jacketed Penguin Modern Classics, it appeared that Fleming's work had found a new level, one which would have made the man himself swell with pride. Regardless of aphorisms concerning books and covers, it is quite remarkable what the status of Penguin Modern Classic can do. It can genuinely change your view of a novel that you might once have regarded as simply a bit of throwaway nonsense.

This is assuredly the case with *Casino Royale*. In an old 1970s cover, with girl in cocktail dress posing by a giant gun, you are inclined to whip through it in the space of about thirty-nine minutes, and then vaguely wonder what all the fuss was about. By contrast, the smart silver-jacketed incarnation invites you to ponder a little further the complexities and meanings of Fleming's yarn, as well as admire his muscular prose style.

'Bond is Fleming's dream of a self that might have been,' his biographer John Pearson once wrote. 'A tougher, stronger, more effective, duller, far less admirable character than the real Fleming . . . *Casino Royale* is an experiment in the autobiography of dreams.'[2]

Certainly the novel starts in a faintly dreamlike way with Fleming's evocation of a casino at 3 a.m. The story that pacily unfolds (the book only runs to about 60,000 words) involves 007 being told to target SMERSH agent Le Chiffre at the gaming tables of Royale-Les-Eaux and to beat him at chemin de fer. Le Chiffre has been expansionist in his criminal dealings, investing heavily in a chain of brothels which were closed down by the French police. And now he owes rather a lot of money to his Soviet paymasters – fifty million francs, in fact, money that he can only obtain at the table. Bond, to his horror, is sent female help, in the shape of Vesper Lynd; he is also aided by French bureau chief René Matthis. Into the mix are thrown a pair of prototype Bulgarian suicide bombers (the suicide is inadvertent) and an infamous torture scene in which a naked Bond is tied to a wickerwork chair with the seat cut out, and Le Chiffre repeatedly hits his testicles with a carpet beater.

Although this is the scene everyone remembers, it is in the book's chilling climax, long after the dispatch of Le Chiffre, that you can really see Fleming's nascent talent for the form. Bond and Vesper take off down the coast; Bond is in love with her, but Vesper is behaving mysteriously. They stay at hotels, row furiously, make love with equal force, and all the time we sense that something terrible is closing in on them both. Who is the man wearing the black eyepatch in the black sedan that they see repeatedly?

The book ends tragically – Vesper takes her own life with an overdose before she can be unmasked as a double agent in the pay of the Soviets; she was doing it to help save her incarcerated Polish husband. 'The bitch is dead,' says Bond, trying to give the impression that he can shake this off. But it is clear that the humanity he tries to keep submerged is horribly bruised.

So far, so good. But when Michael G. Wilson and Barbara Broccoli announced that this would be the next film, few imagined that they would try to remain faithful to the novel. After all, tense though it is, it is also very small-scale – a couple of suspense scenes in the casino, a passage where Bond checks his room for bugs, and a long, doomy denouement in an almost empty landscape. Surely, like the dreadful 1967 film of the same name, Eon would find a way of smuggling a red LED countdown in there?

It also seemed apparent, by 2003, that Pierce Brosnan might not get to make his fifth Bond film. First, in interviews, he appeared to be havering over the idea of donning the tuxedo again. This gave way to what sounded like a note of genuine hurt when it became apparent that Eon were looking for a new, markedly younger Bond. Poor old Brosnan. He now advertises L'Oréal anti-wrinkle cream for men on television, with the tagline that he doesn't mind getting older 'but I don't want to let myself go'.

But his post-Bond career has been pleasingly rich and varied. He won plaudits for his self-parodying turn as a ruthless assassin in the comedy The Matador (2004). And in the summer of 2008, his deft comic skills won over vast audiences in the surprise hit film adaptation of the Abba stage musical Mamma Mia, in which he starred alongside Meryl Streep and Julie Walters and proved himself winningly unable to hold a tune.

With the prospect of fresh casting for Bond, the showbiz correspondents were set off on their favourite goose chase. Who was it to be this time? Ewan MacGregor? Liam Neeson? Dougray Scott? Gay actor Rupert Everett put himself in the frame, partly to illustrate the hypocrisy of Hollywood casting – by doing so, he illustrated the fact that only a very unusual producer would contemplate casting a gay man as über-heterosexual Bond, whereas straight actors frequently portrayed gays. Everett maintains that he would be a very good Bond, and one does wonder.

At one stage, there was the suggestion that young – very young – New Zealand actor Eric Bana, then twenty-six, could be in the frame for the role. There were ripples of disquiet; surely 007 could not be a callow youth? Actually, though, watch Bana's performance in Steven Spielberg's *Munich* (2005), in which he portrays one of the Israeli agents sent out to assassinate the terrorists who murdered Israeli athletes. He combines vulnerability with steeliness and it was clear that Broccoli and Wilson were also after those exact qualities.

Bear in mind that even the most garish comic-book films were starting to look for the humanity in their heroes. Tobey Maguire was much praised for his awkward and occasionally touching performances as Peter Parker/ Spider-Man in the Sam Raimi films. The *Batman* franchise was given an extraordinary sense of depth by the casting of intense Christian Bale as broody Bruce Wayne. Mere CGI spectacle was no longer enough. Heroes now had to have equally vivid emotional lives.

Barbara Broccoli said in an interview that as soon as they knew they were doing *Casino Royale*, they also knew they would need a new type of lead. For this would be the story that showed how Bond got started on his 007 career. It would be left to the audience to puzzle out how this adventure could also be set in the present day. The broader idea was that this was the genesis of Bond, the mission that made him into a toughened secret agent. This Bond was to be more impetuous, with rougher edges, prone to errors of judgement. Also a man prone, against every fibre of his training, to falling in love. In other words, it needed an actor with some range and depth.

It was Barbara Broccoli who first saw the potential in blond Cheshire-born thirty-eight-year-old Daniel Craig, and who mentioned him to the casting woman Debbie McWilliams. Craig had starred alongside Bana in *Munich*; he also had the lead roles in the Matthew Vaughan gangster thriller *Layer Cake* (2005) and in the creepy adaptation of Ian McEwan's *Enduring Love* (2004). Previously he had been best known to British audiences for his roles in *Love Is the Devil* (1998), playing the lover of artist Francis Bacon, and as George 'Geordie' Peacock, pulled into a seedy world of pornography in the seminal BBC TV drama *Our Friends in the North*.

Unlike Brosnan or Moore, Craig did not have that smoothie background in light comedy adventure. Every part he took seemed to have some density.

None the less, when he was finally revealed to the world's press as the new Bond in 2005, countless eyebrows shot up in the manner of Roger Moore.

That press launch in London didn't help; as a stunt, the actor was conveyed to the Thameside conference by means of a naval speedboat, swivelling and swerving all over the river. Fine, apart from the limp orange lifejacket that poor Craig was made to wear, draped over the shoulders of his Bondian suit. The effect was instantly to make him look like a wuss. 'It might have been better,' the actor said later, 'if I had worn a pair of little orange inflatable arm-bands.'[3]

This was only the start of some magnificently unhelpful, and inaccurate, press reporting. There was a story that in rehearsals for a fight scene, Craig had several teeth knocked out; another claimed that he couldn't drive. When the first publicity shots of Craig's Bond in florid holiday shirt and chinos were issued, style columnists threw their hands up in horror at this deviation from Bond's usual savoir-faire. A website, CraigIsNotBond.com, started up and soon was making news itself as fans piled in to register their dismay at the casting of a blond Bond. They complained that he looked wrong, and that you couldn't have a Liverpudlian playing 007. The howls – as they so frequently do on the internet – became progressively louder and more wounding. The British tabloid press was absolutely tickled.

In a mix of anger, despair and exasperation, Michael G. Wilson rang an old journalist friend of his on one of the tabloids and asked: 'Why are the press being like this? What's setting them off?' The journalist, a veteran hand, said he had no idea, and went off to tell his editor just how hurt the folks at Eon were. Curiously, this small intervention seemed to do some good on that particular paper – normally, nothing can deter a tabloid in full cry.

Craig had little choice but to put up with it but it was clear that he was, to put it mildly, taken aback. 'I'd be lying to you if I said I ignored it all,' he told one interviewer. 'And it's that horrible thing with the internet, it's like the drug we've got in the front room. It's playground stuff and it's like "f*** off, I've got more important things to think about." And I've got two choices. I can either buckle under it or knuckle down – and hopefully the latter has happened.'[4]

Production this time around was moved to studios just outside Prague in the Czech Republic. Funny to think that just twenty years previously, such a thing would have been impossible thanks to the Iron Curtain. In 2005, it occurred to no one to make such a connection. The reason, as ever, was that it helped to keep costs down, though Eon also promised that the next film would see the crew returning to Pinewood. They have remained true to their word.

Signed up as director once more, after his triumph with *GoldenEye*, was Martin Campbell. It appeared that Eon were once more looking to him to reinvent the entire series.

And indeed, so he did. Although the finished film, at two hours and twenty-five minutes, is much too long, this was the first time in decades that everyone – from the most highbrow critics to the spottiest US adolescent – appeared to be in agreement that in Bond terms, the thing was an absolute revelation.

To begin with, Campbell throws out those white circles dotting across the screen. Instead, for our pre-credits, we are in black and white. Yes, black and white. It all kicks off at the Prague station of MI6, where Bond is confronting the double-dealing station chief. This scene is intercut with a brutal, grainily shot fight in a bare public washroom, with Bond seeming to drown his opponent by holding his head down in a basin. Back in that office, the treacherous chief observes that Bond needs two kills in order to attain 007 status; that the first kill is difficult but the second is much . . . At this, Bond pulls the trigger and says, 'Yes. Considerably.' Back to the washroom, where the apparently drowned man, revived, picks up his gun – and Bond whirls and shoots, right down the gun-barrel.

That was it. No special effects, no gimmicks, no stunts and no colour. I was in the press preview audience at the Odeon Leicester Square for one of the first screenings in November 2006 and I recall how restive this made not only me, but those around me. What were they doing messing around with our favourite film formula?

One of the answers, it seems, is that Eon were answering the tremendous popularity of the *Bourne* spy films, starring Matt Damon. These tales of an amnesiac American agent and his amazing way of constructing gizmos and gimmicks out of ordinary household items had started with *The Bourne Identity* in 2002 and spawned two sequels. It was the huge success of the second film, *The Bourne Supremacy*, helmed by British director Paul Greengrass, that especially made Eon sit up and take note.

These films were almost designed, like Len Deighton's Harry Palmer, to be the opposite of Bond; here we had a plainly dressed agent who, even though he zigzags across the world on a quest to uncover his true self and vanquish the mysterious enemies that lurk in the shadows, is the reverse of Bond's conspicuous consumer. Moreover, the edgy editing of these films is where we see the true skill come in. In isolation, the plots are simply variations of Hitchcock's perennial innocent man on the run; but the action sequences are so dazzlingly fast and crisp that one is left with the erroneous impression that events of some significance are going on. No big sets; no fruity villains (save for the presence of Albert Finney in the third instalment); and no laser beams from space.

Our own Mr Bond is due this change of style, it seems, but thankfully before we can get down to it, Daniel Kleinman's brilliantly stylish titles – this time featuring silhouettes not of dancing ladies, but of Bond fighting various heavies, against a richly textured series of playing-card backdrops – are there to reassure us that we are indeed at a Bond film. Over this is the most energetic opening song they have had for years, belted out by someone popular with young people called Chris Cornell. The song, with its loud scrunchy guitars and much more insistent rhythm, calls attention to the fact that altogether, this is going to be a much more masculine Bond film than usual. It will also be, as we shall see, the first Bond adventure in which 007 himself, as opposed to the laydeez, is 'objectified'.

After the credits, we are thrown off guard again by a scene in Uganda that introduces us to the reptilian Le Chiffre (played by Danish actor Mads Mikkelsen). A local warlord is entrusting him with a very large sum of money for investment purposes in order to secure fresh arms. From here, we move swiftly to Madagascar, where young master Bond – he has, remember, only just attained his licence to kill – is monitoring a terrorist suspect, while at a public gathering to watch a cobra fight a mongoose.

Said suspect – played by spectacular free runner Sébastien Foucan – makes a bolt for it and escapes to a building site where he and Bond climb and leap up and down scaffolding and lift shafts before slugging it out atop a vertiginously high crane. As if this weren't enough, Foucan escapes into the grounds of an embassy, Bond follows him, and what follows is simply five minutes of shooty-bang violence as practically the entire embassy is destroyed.

Like the titles, serious masculinity is foregrounded in these opening scenes; indeed, until M makes her first appearance some twenty minutes into the narrative, no other woman has featured on screen at all, which is almost unthinkable for a Bond film. It has all been entirely sweaty, glowering men. None more glowering than Craig, whose face in repose is like that of an Easter Island statue. And these first few minutes must see some sort of record for the sheer number of punches being exchanged.

But this is all to re-establish Bond as a 'blunt instrument', to use Fleming's phrase. Indeed, M specifically refers to him as such. One key scene takes place in M's Docklands penthouse (Bond has cunningly broken in). As M castigates him for killing a terrorist in plain view of the world's media, Bond comments tersely that she clearly wants him to be 'half monk, half hitman'; the tension in this formerly familiar relationship is intriguingly ramped up by the intensity of Craig's performance. For the first time, you sense that M is talking not to a debonair man-about-town, but to a ruthless, and possibly unstable, paid assassin.

Mads Mikkelsen as Le Chiffre, villainously bobbing about on his naff luxury yacht in Nassau, restores the old balance a little with a terrific post-modern gag. A gambling colleague stares as blood begins to ooze from the side of Le Chiffre's eye. Le Chiffre notices, and dabs at it with a handkerchief. 'A fault in the tear-duct,' he says by means of explanation, adding darkly: 'Nothing sinister.'

It's a lovely visual touch that recalls Christopher Lee weeping tears of blood in the denouement of *Dracula Has Risen from the Grave* (1968). In the novel *Casino Royale*, Fleming had given Le Chiffre uncannily prominent whites of the eyes, occasionally lending the man's face a blank, 'doll-like' appearance. He is not alone. In the novel *On Her Majesty's Secret Service*, Bond notes that when the sun shines on to Irma Bunt's ski visors, her eyes are suddenly as glassy and lifeless as a doll's. Auric Goldfinger, too, seems to have this curiously dead, empty stare. Meanwhile, Rosa Klebb's mouth 'opens and shuts like a trap, as though operated with wires under the jaw'.

In his book *The Violent Effigy*, a study of the works of Charles Dickens, Professor John Carey wrote of the abiding fear that can be triggered by the idea of inanimate objects suddenly acquiring a life of their own, and how this was a recurring leitmotif in the author's work. What Fleming does is to reverse this: he takes seemingly living people and turns them into creepy, unknowable effigies, creating a tremendous sense of the *unheimlich* about them.

In the film, Mads Mikkelsen's right eye fills with blood in moments of stress; but this baroque touch is offset by his continual use of an asthma inhaler, rooting this villain very much in our world, and not in some dreamlike Fleming twilight.

Bond, meanwhile, by means of tracing mobile records on a computer, links Le Chiffre back to the terrorist he killed in those embassy grounds. This scene makes spying look terribly simple. We could all do it these days. All you need is a phone and access to Google Earth and off you go. As seems semi-traditional, M wants Bond to take some time off; Bond ignores her and jets off to Nassau where, forty years previously, he was saving the world from Largo's hijacked nuclear missile. The old place seems to have changed a little since then. Certainly it is much less dull.

For a start, the hotel is not quite so objectionable as its black-tiles-on-the-bathroom-wall 1960s counterpart. In fact, in the scheme of things it's quite neutral. In one nice gag, Bond, dressed in a strange shirt with epaulettes, is mistaken for a car-parking attendant. We shall turn shortly to the question of this new Bond and class because, unconsciously, it is right at the centre of the film.

For the moment, though, we note approvingly his materialisation at a gaming table, at which he wins an Aston Martin from a bad-tempered second-string heavy. We also note the appearance of said heavy's girlfriend, Solange (Caterina Murino), who we know right from the very start is going to canoodle with Bond, then pay the fatal price.

Hey: these were the rules set out in the 1960s, as famously given to *You Only Live Twice* screenwriter Roald Dahl; he was firmly instructed by Saltzman and Broccoli that there must be three girls, one of whom is bad, one of whom is good but must get bumped off in an inventive way, and one of whom is also good, and is there for snogging purposes in the final reel.[5] Now on this occasion there are only two girls. In a nice reversal, it is Solange who first witnesses Bond rising from the waves, à la Ursula Andress.

For this occasion Bond has chosen to wear a pair of figure-hugging powder-blue bathers that the actor understandably seems to be regretting now. One's mind, for a moment, is reluctantly yanked back to Connery's inexplicable powder-blue shorty towelling poolside outfit in *Goldfinger*.

Craig has insisted that he will not be wearing similarly slinky items in his second Bond outing. But what will the laydeez do? In the wake of *Casino*'s release, Britain's army of 'Glendas' – that is, the female columnists of all the national newspapers, so named after *Private Eye*'s generic satire 'Glenda Slagg' – spent about a month drooling over Craig's scanty swimmers. The noise these writers made drowned out the reviews of the film. And the picture of Craig walking out of the sea has been reproduced more than any other single Bond image, save the Ursula Andress original.

We don't see Solange actually being bumped off, we simply see her body the next morning, which somehow makes it worse, because it is all left to our imaginations. Something John Glen and the producers should have borne in mind when making *Licence to Kill*. None the less, the consistency is appreciated.

And before we see poor dead Solange, we witness the event that leads to her death; Bond outwitting a dead-eyed terrorist on the runways of Miami airport. The terrorist is aiming to destroy a prototype Super-Jumbo, all for the purposes of a massive Le Chiffre financial scam involving airline share prices. But after a blistering fight aboard a fuel truck – in real life, just one of the hundreds of punches thrown would have knocked me out for a month – Bond foils the plot by a matter of centimetres, and the terrorist goes up with a bang. As a result, Le Chiffre loses the Ugandan warlord's millions on the Stock Exchange and poor old Solange ends up being the scapegoat, being dangled sightlessly in a hammock by the blue waters of the ocean.

By the way, in the midst of all this, we cannot help but notice that M appears to have ditched Miss Moneypenny in favour of a male secretary whose name I haven't been able to catch. A nervy fellow he seems too; joining M at Nassau, the secretary retches at the sight of dead Solange in the hammock. Brave would be the Bond screenwriter who suggested some sexy byplay between this new operative and Bond.

M's Nassau jaunt, incidentally, gives actress Judi Dench a nice few days on location which, if Julian Glover's account still applies, adds up to a jolly lavish trip at Eon's expense. Since we are being reminded that this is all at the very start of Bond's 00 career, M is being sharper with her charge than on previous occasions, and he seems to be more insolent in return. Interestingly, though, the whole idea behind the relationship – that M and Bond both do extremely worthwhile and good jobs in a hostile and unstable world – is one that doesn't change. 'Christ, I miss the Cold War,' exclaims M at the start, but in fact, in Eon's vision of MI6, the secret service hasn't changed at all. It always acts for the common good and it is beyond corruption. There are very rarely any traitors in *this* organisation. The narrative tensions are still being triggered by foreign outsiders.

So, Le Chiffre has to win his money back and aims to do so at Casino

Royale in Montenegro, part of the former Yugoslavia and an unusual Balkan destination for Bond. 007 is being sent to join his big winner-takes-all card game. In other words, he is fulfilling yet another male fantasy, which is that of being paid to play cards. On the way there, we have the scene – other than that of Bond rising from the ocean – that, according to anecdotal evidence, made the biggest impression on the female audience. It is where, aboard some sort of trans-Europe express, Bond first meets Vesper (Eva Green), the Treasury official who is going along to sort out the finances of his epic game.

Their exchange in the train restaurant car – a setting deliberately reminiscent of the same scenario in Hitchcock's *North by Northwest* – crackles with, for Bond, an unusual amount of character insight. In the space of a few lines, Bond and Vesper home in on what they see as each other's vulnerable points: in Bond's case, Vesper deduces that because he wears his suit with disdain, his entire upbringing and schooling was bought by the grace of another, and the fact that he received this charity made him a target for his fellows. It is the first time in the films that we learn that Bond is an orphan.

Bond's filleting of Vesper's character is equally sharp and humorous and it turns out that they are both orphans. Unlike Cary Grant and Eva Marie Saint in that earlier dining car, sex is not on the agenda tonight here; but from the off, we see our Bond more obviously taken with Vesper than he seems to have been with anyone for a while.

Actress Eva Green was previously best known for her starring role in Bernardo Bertolucci's saucy Paris-in-1968 drama *The Dreamers* (2003); what makes her so captivating from the off here is that they have somehow made her look like a silent movie heroine, with dark clothes and vast expressive eyes. But the curious thing is that we are not supposed to be looking only at her. It becomes clear in this scene that the entire film is inviting us to examine Bond, mentally and physically.

Vesper makes a reference, somewhat startlingly, to Bond's 'perfectly formed arse'; she also comments that she has 'sized him up'. Later, stripped naked and tied to a chair, Bond is admired by Le Chiffre – 'You have looked after your body, Mr Bond.' But it is not just the characters cooing over his rippling pecs. The camera is doing it the whole time too. Not only in the (repeated) shots of Bond rising from the sea, but also in those following a machete fight on the emergency stairs of the Hotel Splendide. Bond returns to his room, rips open his shirt to examine his wounds, and then stands there by the mirror, staring into his own eyes. For a moment, we are destabilised – what is this silent man thinking? In fact, it is the very first time any such thing has happened in a Bond film. But the camera returns to that bare chest and six-pack.

In fairness to Daniel Craig, he has clearly been working out a great deal more thoroughly than his predecessors. But the extent to which Bond's body is almost fetishised by Campbell's camera is intriguing. They would never have got away with doing this to a Bond girl. Or to Roger Moore. Something similar seems to be the case with the footballer David Beckham who, in the early months of 2008, was to be seen on posters on the sides of London buses, wearing nothing but Armani underpants, in reclining poses that you would not automatically associate with a thirty-three-year-old father of three.

The term 'metrosexual' doesn't cover it, and in any case, one can hardly accuse Craig's gruff Bond of metrosexuality. All right, girls, yes, I know – these men are jolly handsome. And any man who has ever attended a gym will at some point have wanted to acquire a similar physique. What is so interesting is the balance shift, and in the case of Bond, a shameless appeal to pull in the female audience; a female audience that might have lost a little patience with death lasers from space.

So, Bond faces Le Chiffre across the exclusive gaming table of the Hotel Splendide. Not just for one game, but for many. And not just any old game, but possibly the most complicated card game ever depicted in a Bond film, where twos and fives seem to be flush, but then someone else can suddenly win with a jack. Those of us who, in real life, struggle to remember the rules of blackjack, are always going to be defeated by scenes like this. On TV, comedians the League of Gentlemen frequently addressed the inability to follow cards with the invention of a surrealistically complex card game called 'Go Johnny, Go, Go, Go, Go'. This is how I feel here.

Is this a game of poker? Whatever it is, Bond and Le Chiffre are playing for millions and the camera roves very much in its own time around the table. There is even a leisurely dissolve to another card hand. Given the apparently non-existent attention span of the average American teenage viewer, this was a spectacular act of courage and chutzpah on the part of the producers. As I recall, not even in the novel does the card match go on quite so long.

And the players are allowed breaks, too. This gives them opportunities to get into machete fights with peeved Ugandan warlords, and to drink poisoned cocktails, and for Bond to resort to a glove-compartment heart resuscitator to fight off lethal digitalis. It also gives Bond a chance to come to the end of his tether with Le Chiffre, and to pursue him across a crowded gambling floor holding a steak knife. Bond is only stopped from killing him by the appearance of our old (and yet completely new) friend Felix Leiter (portrayed by Jeffrey Wright). It's another interesting scene: that Bond has a licence to kill is something we know very well – but how well can he contain his killing instinct?

Craig throughout is terrifically good at suggesting this troubling instability. We have come a very long way from the smooth insouciance of Connery. In one scene, Vesper has had a dinner suit made for Bond, to his annoyance. But when he tries it on, he sees that she was right; and as he admires himself in the mirror (again), we deduce that this is a man to whom style and class do not after all come naturally.

This is also suggested in Craig's accent. When you first hear this Bond speak, you assume that for the first time in many years, the character has the traditional middle-class accent of southern England. But as the film progresses, you also hear the glottal stops, the slight lengthening of certain vowels. Someone else used to do that: former Prime Minister Tony Blair. On one occasion in the 1990s, when being interviewed by Des O'Connor on ITV, the premier didn't enunciate a single 't'. The clearly intended effect was to project classlessness; that he might somehow belong to any one of a number of British social tribes.

It's not quite as extreme as that for Bond, but you are left wondering – does Craig's accent have this classless quality for the benefit of American viewers who are now accustomed to full-on Received Pronunciation being used only by villains? It is also presumably employed to tone down any suggestion of privilege on Bond's part. In other words, not so very different from Connery's original Scottish brogue in the role.

Anyway, Bond eventually wins the card game and this is where the plot goes haywire. Vesper is kidnapped, Bond is captured and tortured by means of a knotted rope being whacked around his nether regions. But then Le Chiffre is shot by someone, Bond wakes up in a clinic, he convalesces, he and Vesper go to Venice, he discovers Vesper has rerouted the millions from the gambling table to a mystery organisation – and thence to the climax set in a crumbling Venetian palazzo sinking fast into the Grand Canal.

To be honest, I don't know many people who were able to follow this part of the film, but it didn't seem to matter to anyone. Because by now the focus was fully on Bond himself, and the forces that motivate the man. Earlier, while recovering from the nether-whacking in a wheelchair, blanket over his knees, this vulnerable Bond declares to Vesper that he is in love with her. Considering their relationship thus far has been so spiky, she reciprocates with surprising ease. Indeed, Bond is so mad for her that he sends an e-mail of resignation to M. His plan is that he and Vesper can just travel the world and get bog-standard jobs when they need to. 'Though that'll probably have to be you,' he tells her.

As in the novel, we can feel that this is going to end in tears; Vesper's glimpse of a mysterious man with one darkened spectacle lens on the Venice quayside is the portent of doom.

Another portent of doom is the red dress that Vesper wears when she makes that trip to the bank to divert Bond's winnings. Bond is alerted to the missing money by M and pursues Vesper through Venice, catching brief glimpses of the scarlet dress in the distance. In other words, it is a cheeky homage to the 1973 Nicolas Roeg horror film *Don't Look Now*, where Donald Sutherland is tormented by what he thinks is the vision of his dead daughter in a bright red raincoat.

There is a watery climax inside the ruined palazzo; Bond shoots out the building's flotation balloons and the house begins to crumble and sink. Bad guys whom we have not seen before have shut Vesper in one of those old-fashioned gate lifts. Bond eventually kills the baddies but the lift plunges under the water. And Vesper – startlingly – locks the gate, preventing Bond from rescuing her. She brushes her cheek against his hand – then breathes in the water. Eva Green is quite extraordinary in this sequence. The silent movie heroine aspect of her character is brought to the fore, her wide, tragic eyes fixed on Bond's.

He eventually surfaces with her limp body and mouth-to-mouth fails. Back on his boat, M is on the line from London to fill him in. It is the most powerful scene yet seen between Bond and his boss. She asks if he wants to take time off. 'Why should I need time?' says Bond sharply. 'The bitch is dead now.' But M pulls him up, in a way that it is quite impossible to imagine dear old Bernard Lee doing. As in the novel, Vesper was being blackmailed to ensure the safety of her lover, which is why she was in cahoots with the mystery bad guys. But M tells Bond that Vesper also obviously ensured that said bad guys did not kill Bond. In the end, Vesper saved him. The reaction shot on Bond's face is intriguing. Are those really tears in his eyes? We are not quite close enough to see.

There is a brief coda; Vesper has sent Bond a text message with the details of a 'Mr White', who seems to have been the man behind Le Chiffre, and the film closes with Bond shooting him in the leg and then introducing himself. With the phrase 'The name's Bond, James Bond,' Monty Norman's old theme suddenly blares out. In the preview screening I attended, there was a huge wave of applause.

And critically, this is possibly the most successful Bond film of the lot. Everyone from the most downmarket tabloids to the most highbrow arts journals raved about its qualities. 'The best Bond film in decades,' declared the *Daily Telegraph*'s normally austere Sukhdev Sandhu. Exultant reviewers took note of the sharpness of the dialogue, the intensity of the relationship between Craig and Green, and Craig's against-the-grain performance.

'*Casino Royale* has pulled it off on all counts,' declared Deborah Ross in the highbrow *Spectator*, adding feverishly:

> It delivers the basic goods — the chases, the fireball explosions, the lavish glamour, the Aston Martins — yet it is also intelligent, moving, involving and sexy. You will be shaken, stirred, left to settle, then shaken and stirred all over again. I'm still shaking and stirring as I write. Why? Daniel Craig. He is stunning; a serious actor who not only takes the part seriously, but does so with astonishing presence, an athlete's grace and an almost animalistic power that he manages so skilfully to temper with a softer soulfulness. When he is on screen you cannot look at anything else.

Steady on, madam.

Also terrifically impressed was the normally cynical Peter Bradshaw of the *Guardian*: 'Craig was inspired casting,' he wrote:

> He has effortless presence and lethal danger; he brings a serious actor's ability to a fundamentally unserious part; he brings out the playfulness and the absurdity, yet never sends it up. He's easily the best Bond since Sean Connery and perhaps even — well, let's not get carried

away . . . the key to his X Factor is that Craig looks as though he would be equally at home playing a Bond villain.

There was controversy too. In Britain, the film was given a 12A certificate; none the less, families piled into the cinemas with children much younger than that. And they were disconcerted to be confronted with much more graphic violence than before. One father was overheard during the torture sequence telling his puzzled young son that the villain was 'hitting James Bond's bottom'. In other scenes, there was frequently blood on show, something highly unusual in Bond.

But unlike the moribund violence of *Licence to Kill*, all of this was very much there to serve a greater purpose. For the first time – remarkable, this, in a series that is forty-five years old – we were shown Bond's vulnerability. At the end of the cliffhanger at Miami airport, Bond has cuts and bruises all over. After the machete fight at the Hotel Splendide, his shirt is shockingly covered with blood. But the coda to that scene shows us that violence now does have consequences.

A traumatised Vesper, who has witnessed Bond strangling his attacker to death, sits silently beneath a dripping shower in her cocktail gown. Bond gently sits down beside her. Vesper whispers that she can't get the blood off her hands. Slowly and softly, Bond takes hold of her hand, then starts sucking her fingers. We have never before seen such tenderness in Bond. It is little wonder that the critics went mad for it.

And it has broken further Bond records, having raked in somewhere in the region of $500 million in cinema ticket and DVD sales. What a risk, though! Because there have been so many Bonds across so many years, there is a general assumption that production must have a trace of the autopilot about it; another year, another super-villain trying to conquer the world.

Casino Royale demonstrates just how much thought and care is poured into the nurturing of this series. Regular writers Neal Purvis and Robert Wade were joined this time by another hand, Paul Haggis, specifically brought in to sharpen up the relationship between Bond and Vesper, and to remove Bond's traditional quipping style. At one point, Vesper tells Bond that he has 'put his armour on again', referring to the way that he masks his feelings. To which Bond replies that he has 'no armour left', and that he feels that what 'little soul' he has left should be preserved by him getting out of the secret service and devoting himself to life with her. You can't see dear old Roger doing that, can you?

At one point in the film, prior to Bond and Vesper tipping up at the Hotel Splendide, there is one tiny, throwaway, but very funny gag referring to the old style of the films. Bond has received an envelope containing their false passports and cover stories. With an absolutely deadpan face, he tells Vesper that she is to be known as 'Miss Stephanie Broadchest'. Vesper cries out in indignation. The rest of us laugh – well, at ourselves really, for having been amused by such stuff in the first place.

But it is interesting too; at the time of writing this, *Quantum of Solace* is still in production. Michael Wilson and Barbara Broccoli have promised that in terms of style, they are going to follow the same template. But what this means is that we can't really go back to the old ways. The elephantine double entendres are gone. We can no longer have girls called Pussy or Plenty; we can no longer have villains who live in volcanoes and stroke cats; and I suspect it will be rather a long time before we see another death laser from space. But that is not to say that Bond is finished. Completely the reverse. On the evidence of this film, I'd guess that the character will prove even more enduring than Sherlock Holmes. The future looks utterly intriguing.

CHAPTER TWENTY-NINE YOU CAN NEVER KISS DEATH GOODBYE

In 1903, in an early Edwin S. Porter film called *The Great Train Robbery*, a character called Barnes, the leader of the outlaws, takes a gun, aims, and fires 'point-blank at the audience', as the script direction notes. The effect upon audiences was apparently electrifying, with people imagining that they had genuinely been shot. At the very dawn of this new medium, it was a moment of cinema at its very purest.

In 1962, a man in a pork pie hat striding purposefully to the left of the screen turned and fired upon us again. In 2002, the twentieth time he had done this, we actually saw a bullet zing towards us.

As I say: it is cinema at its very purest. As indeed is the entire Bond phenomenon.

It makes no difference that he was born on the printed page. For the vast majority of people, Bond is a figure that they associate with any one of six actors who have played the role. And a 'Bond film' is an extraordinarily distinctive and shrewdly calculated thing that utilises the medium to its utmost. Art-house enthusiasts might yelp that Bond can hardly be placed in the same bracket as *Throne of Blood* or *Wild Strawberries* as a work with any aesthetic depth. They might go on to argue that you cannot even distinguish between the different directors of the films. But that is not really the point. Bond exists as the purest expression of the entertainment possibilities of the big screen.

It's odd, but the entire attraction of these films appears to be the fact that we all know exactly what we are going to get. We queue for our tickets for each fresh Bond happy in the knowledge that whatever the tone, whatever the style, there will be certain key ingredients and the hero will win the day. At the time of writing, press reports have been covering the casting of *Quantum of Solace*; we know that up-and-coming British actress Gemma Arterton will portray Agent Fields, an attractive ally of Bond's with perhaps a slightly comic dimension.

We know that there will be a sequence involving the *Palio*, the spectacular annual Siena horse race. We know that the action will move to South America. And we know that Mathieu Amalric will play the 'ecologist' villain Dominic Greene and that he will seek to convey his evil by putting a 'manic Blair twinkle' into his eyes. And we know that Alicia Keys and Jack White have been granted the honour of performing the film's main theme with a song called 'Another Way to Die'. The first time, incidentally, that a Bond song has been a duet.

We are fed these titbits via the press by means of reassurance; they tell us not only that a new Bond film is coming, but also that it will have babes and fights and stunts and top-drawer villainy. It won't be two hours of Bond sitting alone in a room, looking tearfully out of the window and slowly emptying a bottle of whisky as he watches the rain trickle down the pane.

If Bond were a television series, then a form of scenario like the one above would be possible; short small-scale episodes encourage more intimate drama. But that is exactly the point. Bond is cinema, and what is more, he is über-cinema. He brings with him bangs and flashes and sex and kinetic energy. He brings bright colour and arresting images thrown up by intriguing locations.

And because we all know him so well, Bond also brings with him a sense of cinematic community. When we all troop along to see the new Bond, we know that every single person sitting in that darkened auditorium with us is in on the joke. We are all primed, not merely to laugh at the more outrageous stunts, but also to thrill, with big grins on our faces, as the denouement draws close. A work of art-house cinema can evoke multiple responses from the smallest audience; Bond, on the other hand, is absolutely relentless in giving you no choice in the matter of enjoyment.

I sense that this is really what lay behind Nina Hibbin's deep dislike of the films. It wasn't so much the ideology she was objecting to; it was the sense of being bludgeoned into following a crowd response. It sounds as if, to her, the spontaneous laughter that greeted Bond's callous post-kill quips was oppressive, rather like lads in a pub raucously encouraging some yobbish nitwit in his 'banter'.

Conversely, though, I think this is the real secret behind the success of the character. It is difficult to think of any other series of films in which that sense of sly complicity between audience and producers is so very strong.

Think about this for a second: put to one side all of Ian Fleming's novels and concentrate instead on Bond the character as drawn by the films.

Fleming we know gave Bond his own tics and neuroses; the screenwriters for the most part eliminated them. So, the man on the screen, the man we have seen doing his stuff twenty-one times over? Who exactly is he?

For all the raving about Connery and the way that he established the character, the fact is that there wasn't a whole heap there. Connery's Bond was dark, he was sexy, he moved like a panther through the dark, and as the films went on, he got porky and his hair became plasticised, like that of a *Thunderbirds* puppet. By *From Russia with Love*, we learned that Bond had a cool sense of humour – as displayed by his insouciance throughout the Russian embassy bombing – although he seemed willing to share the joke only with us in the audience and never with his fellow characters.

He was capable of being shocked – witness the look on his face as he beholds the gold-painted Shirley Eaton in *Goldfinger*. But other than the burning of his comrade Quarrel in *Dr. No*, violent death seems not to arouse any sense of pity in him. Poor old poisoned Aki in *You Only Live Twice* barely gets a backward glance.

If George Lazenby brought anything at all to the party, other than a dubbed voice and a neat trick of turning his trouser pockets into gloves for the thrilling cable-car escape sequence, then it was a sense of an idiot whose heart was still open to love.

Roger Moore's Bond occasionally referred to his former wife Tracy, though very reluctantly. In *The Spy Who Loved Me*, agent Anya does the prodding. Bond responds as though she is asking him about his piles. What we learn about Bond from Moore is that he is an amusing – and amused – cynic, happily nestling in the bosom of the Establishment. But already, halfway through the run of the series, we still have no clue at all to Bond's hinterland. We don't know what music he likes, we don't know what books he reads, we have absolutely no idea how he might spend a quiet Sunday afternoon off. Does he even have any friends to hang out with? Unlike Fleming's Bond, screen Bond literally has no life outside those two hours of adventure.

Timothy Dalton's Bond comes along to try to put that right. It is just about possible to imagine this Bond lying awake at night, glittering eyes staring at the ceiling, either agonising over something or being boilingly cross about something else. But then we have to ask: why would we *want* to imagine such a thing? Doesn't really lift the spirits, does it?

Pierce Brosnan comes along and pulls off the very difficult trick of appearing to have even less hinterland than the Roger Moore version. In his first outing, Bond's face is a portmanteau of frowns, squints and sexually inspired gurning. We are invited to consider that this Bond has moments of regret but we don't believe it for a moment. What we do believe, however, is that this Bond is occasionally a little more delinquent than he has been before. In all the car chases and shoot-outs, there seems to be a dogged determination to defy HQ; Connery's Bond was anti-Establishment too but his unquestioning devotion to M was much stronger.

We're still no closer to discovering what this man does in his leisure hours though. Even Fleming's Bond managed the odd round of golf or the occasional walk in Regent's Park to smell the newly mown grass. Daniel Craig has, to an extent, changed that. We know now at least that the character does have the odd moment of quiet, horrified reflection.

But forty-five years is an awfully long time to spend getting to know even a little about such a character. Is Bond even intelligent? Over the years, we have seen him get out of innumerable scrapes and foil countless plots; but he never seems to have used any native ingenuity. Rather, his is repeatedly a triumph of physicality and superior technology. From jet-packs to laser beam watches, the old spirit of heroic improvisation is missing. Which is presumably why the makers of the *Bourne* films made their main character such a dab hand at turning household implements into lethal weapons.

In terms of actual spying, James Bond in fact appears to be rather bad at what he does; not only, as Sir Roger Moore has pointed out, is the man recognised by every barman and hotel receptionist the world over; he is also forever being ambushed and caught by his enemies.

In *The Spy Who Loved Me*, Bond's attempted disguise as marine biologist James Stirling is marked by his ability to memorise different types of tropical fish. But a good memory is not by itself an indicator of intellect. And anyway, the very instant that Bond leaves Stromberg's aquarium, the villain orders that he should be killed. So that didn't go very well. In *Moonraker* and *A View to a Kill*, Bond employs futuristic gizmos for the purposes of safe-cracking. On both occasions, the villains know fine well what he has been up to. It is astonishing that the man has survived so long.

But this was the genius of Saltzman and Broccoli. They knew that they couldn't make the character off-puttingly clever, for where then would be any sense of danger? They also knew – and this, I think, is the most brilliant calculation of all – that they were aiming for the broadest reach of the audience, the widest common denominator, and they had to make films that seemed smart but were in fact utterly dumb.

It is eerie brilliance because at no stage in a Bond film do you ever get the sense that you are being talked down to. Rather, there is just enough plot-twisting going on, enough loud bangs and crashes, to convince you that you are following a proper and involved narrative. When in fact you are doing absolutely nothing of the sort. Saltzman and Broccoli must have known this, just as they must have known that the smarter people in the audience would be laughing at it all, and the less smart laughing with it.

And I take my hat off to them, for that is the absolute core of top entertainment. No one feels cheated, no one feels left out, everyone leaves the cinema with a smile on their face, feeling that they have had a terrific night out. Even after *You Only Live Twice*. If there is a film out there more stupid than *You Only Live Twice*, I'd like to see it; but at no point during *Twice* do you ever spot how utterly galumphing it is. The production consistently draws the attention away, by means of Ken Adam's astonishing designs and John Barry's wonderful music and the pace of Peter Hunt's innovative editing. This is why I have seen it at least twenty-three times with no diminution of pleasure.

Peter Hunt must step forward to take a bow. For he was the man who established the rhythm of Bond. When we think of Bonds, we very rarely think of the films' individual directors, which is odd. You would imagine that each man (no women, not yet) — from Terence Young to John Glen — would have brought a distinctive style. But the secret of Bond as cinema — at least, until *Casino Royale* — is not in the composition of the frame, or the emphasis on different actors exploring different line readings. It is the way that the scenes are cut. One visual flourish that we always recall from the early Bonds is the sudden speeding of the film during action sequences, be it Bond dropping on a guard's head in the pre-credits of *Goldfinger* or fighting with a cross-dressing SPECTRE man in a chateau in *Thunderball* or scrapping with Largo at that film's climax.

To an extent, *Casino Royale* changed that. Martin Campbell gave the film a distinct, carefully lit visual style and even, for the first time, leitmotifs (such as the repeated use of mirrors during or after scenes of violence). Interesting, though, that once again, there was a lot of emphasis on cutting-edge editing, especially in the pre-credits fight sequence.

This is perhaps why a Hitchcock Bond film might not have been any good. Remember that Universal executives sounded him out about the possibility in the early 1960s. But a Hitchcock film is about the building of character before then subjecting that character to various ordeals. And suspense is not created by lightning-fast edits. Quite the reverse. Very often, the cutting pace was kept cunningly slow. Hitchcock would have homed in on Bond's intriguing flaws – look at how he brought out an innate cruelty, as well as heroism, in Connery in *Marnie* – and he would not have had much truck with the barely single dimension of Dr. No. He would have had to invest this monster with an intriguing sliver of humanity.

But we are not at a Bond film for explorations of the darker corners of the human heart. We are here for something more akin to a carnival. A carnival filled with countless wonders and distractions. Look at the ritual of Q's laboratory. Did any of us ever stop to think just how astonishingly and comically useless most of those prototype gadgets were? In *For Your Eyes Only*, Q is testing out an umbrella with spikes at the end of its spokes that are activated by moisture. Why? If this is an instrument of assassination, it relies first of all upon the target not only carrying it, but also opening it up. But what if it isn't raining?

Take the fake Indian rope trick featured in *Octopussy*. The rope is genuinely stiff to allow getaway. But, but, but . . . Or what about the razor-edged tea-tray demonstrated in *The Spy Who Loved Me*? Hovering in mid-air, it flies along the path of an electro-magnetic coil and decapitates its target. So where, Q, do you plan to use this device? A Lyons Corner House?

But it's interesting, isn't it, that we demand that this is all somehow 'done for real' and not computer-generated? In *The Lord of the Rings* or *King Kong*, we would find it very odd if these were accomplished without recourse to the snazziest special effects. But for Bond, it is almost as if we want to see it live. Recall the real-life crowds in Bilbao watching the filming of *The World Is Not Enough*, how they literally 'ooohed' as the stuntman jumped out of the office block window. This is how we all watch Bond. When the character tumbles out of a plane or falls off a cliff, we know very well that we are not watching Sean or Roger. Equally, though, we know that we are watching a man who really is falling through the sky. There is the thrill, and then the payoff laugh as he executes a cheeky manoeuvre to get out of danger.

The sex is also involved in the payoff laugh. Not merely through the use of insane names for women or even through the weird lines that both Bond and the women seem to find seductive; but also through the filming of the sex scenes themselves. Because these are, by and large, family films, the bed scenes are about as erotic as a damp dog's blanket.

And on top of this, they are dazzlingly naff. I refer you to George Lazenby's purple-hued tryst with Angela Scoular in *On Her Majesty's Secret Service*; to Sean Connery and Jill St John reclining on what appears to be a circular glass aquarium in *Diamonds Are Forever*; to Roger Moore and Britt Ekland in Christopher Lee's chocolate-brown bedroom at the end of *The Man with the Golden Gun*. Let's just remind ourselves of the dialogue in this scene. M calls up on Scaramanga's elevating phone ('Something's come up,' says Bond); then, as M asks to speak to Goodnight, Bond announces that she is 'just coming'.

Incidentally, the sex is just as naff in the novels; the difference is that Bond's hands spend more time straying towards the heroines' 'behinds', as Fleming often puts it. On one occasion, he places his hands upon the heroine's 'swelling buttocks'. Imagine how that might have translated to film. And in terms of sex, the other difference is that Fleming is taking it seriously. Broccoli knew, however, that for the films, it had to be played light, and it had to be played naff.

The payoff laugh is the thing that will keep Bond going as all other franchises wither away. This, again, was the genius of Saltzman and Broccoli. They made Bond satire-proof by making the audiences laugh along with the films. Remember: for all its brilliant deconstruction of Bond villainy, *Austin Powers* could not send up the figure of Bond himself. The screen character somehow defies this sort of take-off.

And in the humour of the Bonds, we find one of the keys to his longevity: the character's meta-existence. It is possible in the future that cinema will be a 3D affair, that we will sit in circular amphitheatres watching holographic images; the mooted Steven Spielberg adaptations of Hergé's Tintin will, it is suggested, be part computer-generated. Whatever form he comes in, I think it's a reasonable bet to say that even in a hundred years, Bond will be there. One reason is that the idea of the films as cinematic event is greater than the sum of the films themselves.

When we queue to see a Bond, we are not queuing to see a thriller. Oh, we know there will be excitement, but it is meta-excitement. We are in fact queuing to see our favourite tropes and leitmotifs being run through in a way that is at once familiar yet new. Like our favourite daydreams, the films must have certain, almost archetypal elements in order to work properly.

As a church service must have its structure and its responses, so Bond must go through the Jungian progressive stages from 'fantasy' to 'nightmare' to 'catharsis'.

If the films weren't so big, so universally popular, they would fall perfectly into the category of 'cult'; that is, not only in the sense of appealing to fannish enthusiasts, but also in the sense that they are built up of single discrete elements that are just as important as the prevailing narrative. An example: no matter how harrowing the adventure, the audience knows that when it hears the line 'Oh, James' moaned by the leading lady, the film's payoff canoodling scene is ending, and the closing credits are about to crash in.

Oh, James . . . it is most often said about this cinematic chimera that men want to be him and women want to sleep with him. I am not sure that always applies. For instance, chaps, how many of us actually wanted to be Roger Moore? Ladies, how many of you had to fight a near uncontrollable passion for Timothy Dalton?

But after all these years, we can see now what he and the films really are: the Bond adventures are a curiously flattering distorting mirror through which we watch not only our sexual and consumerist fantasies, but also a gaudy reflection of the world that we all live in. 007 is not merely guaranteed entertainment (though that is quite a feat in itself); he is in some ways a strange means for us all to check up on the state of the nation, and of the world.

We return to the notion of authenticity — the immediate sense that this fantastical secret agent, moving through his fantastical exotic world of trollops, countdowns and cats, is the real deal. It's those little white circles, moving left across the black screen at the very start. Those circles are the hallmark; what they signify is that you are about to see a unique sort of film that no one else can replicate satisfactorily. And the chief purveyor of this sense of authenticity is not actually author Ian Fleming — but the Broccoli family.

In the 1970s, on those rare occasions when we nippers picked up a reissued Ian Fleming novel — in those days, the covers featured sultry 1970s ladies wearing bright yellow cocktail gowns and posing next to giant guns — we had the sense when reading that there was something amiss, especially in *You Only Live Twice*. To us children of the 1970s, not even Fleming seemed authentic — these books were just so different from the films. Where were the space capsules? The monorails? Why did Bond keep saying 'To hell with you'? Who exactly was this Loelia Ponsonby?

In 1977 and 1979, it was acknowledged by the publishers that the gap in narrative content between the novels of *The Spy Who Loved Me* and *Moonraker* and their respective film versions was too vast. Something had to be done. So screenwriter Christopher Wood 'novelised' his own scripts, resulting in new books, *James Bond IN The Spy Who Loved Me* and *James Bond IN Moonraker*, both books featuring poster images of Roger Moore on the covers. It was a neat, structuralist pirouette. And for my generation of pre-teens, *these* books were proper, real James Bond. Heresy, I know, but it can't be helped. I believe literary critic Terry Eagleton terms it 'reader reception theory'; that is, the author or auteur can intend anything they jolly well like, but the only interpretation that matters is that of the reader or audience.

These days, there are a number of septuagenarians for whom Sean Connery is the only real Bond. I know of some younger folk who believe, sweetly, that Pierce Brosnan is the real deal.

For all of us, though, there is the sense that as long as Eon Productions stays in business and keeps turning out these silly, thrilling films, with whatever actor they deem best reflects the prevailing social climate, they will 'keep it real'. Bond will never send himself up, or disappear up his own fundament. It is a highly particular form of story-telling that frequently seems to break all sorts of structural rules. But we really wouldn't have it any other way.

This is why four of the most cheering words in the English language are: James Bond Will Return.

NOTES

1 Authenticity

1 Saltzman quoted in Alexander Walker, *Hollywood England* (Harrap, 1974)

2 Ibid.

3 Ibid.

4 Ibid.

5 Andrew Lycett, *Ian Fleming* (Weidenfeld, 1995)

2 You've Had Your Six

1 Andrew Lycett, *Ian Fleming* (Weidenfeld, 1995)

2 Albert R. Broccoli with Donald Zec, *When the Snow Melts* (Boxtree, 1998)

3 Quoted in Tony Bennett and Janet Woollacott, *Bond and Beyond* (Macmillan, 1987)

4 Lycett, *Ian Fleming*

5 John Pearson, *The Life of Ian Fleming* (Jonathan Cape, 1966)

6 Mark Amory (ed.), *The Letters of Ann Fleming* (Collins, 1985)

7 Connery interviewed in *Rolling Stone*, 1983

8 Quoted in Bennett and Woollacott, *Bond and Beyond*

3 Europe by Train

1 From the British Film Institute Screen-Online Len Deighton entry

2 Andrew Lycett, *Ian Fleming* (Weidenfeld, 1995)

4 The Glittering Prize

1 Benjamin Woolley, *The Queen's Conjuror* (Flamingo, 2001)

2 Nigel West (ed.), *The Faber Book of Espionage* (Faber, 1993)

3 Shirley Eaton interviewed on American television

4 Francis Wheen, *Tom Driberg – His Life and Indiscretions* (Chatto & Windus, 1990)

5 Honor Blackman interviewed on the documentary *Avenging the Avengers* (Channel 4, 1993)

6 The ad in question can be seen as an extra feature of the *Goldfinger* DVD

5 Raincoats, Walls and Betrayals

1 Andrew Lycett, *Ian Fleming* (Weidenfeld, 1995)

2 Ibid.

3 John le Carré, *The Spy Who Came in from the Cold* (1963)

6 Great Balls of Thunder

1 Connery interviewed in *Sunday Express*, February 1965

2 Broccoli interviewed in *Sunday Express*, 1980

3 Auger interviewed in *Daily Mail*, 1965

7 Spies in Our Eyes

1 Alexander Walker, *Hollywood England* (Harrap, 1974)

2 Susan Sontag, 'Notes on Camp', an essay in *Against Interpretation* (1963)

8 This Dream Is for You

1 Connery interviewed in *Daily Mail*, July 1966

2 Connery interviewed in *Daily Mail*, May 1965

3 The clip features as an extra on the DVD of *You Only Live Twice*

4 Connery interviewed in *Daily Mail*, 1967

9 The Other Fella

1 Dame Diana Rigg, television interview

2 Andrew Lycett, *Ian Fleming* (Weidenfeld, 1995)

3 Albert R. Broccoli, interviewed in *Sunday Times*, December 1969

4 Albert R. Broccoli with Donald Zec, *When the Snow Melts* (Boxtree, 1998)

5 Peter Haining, *James Bond: A Celebration* (W.H. Allen, 1987)

10 A Little More Cheek

1 Albert R. Broccoli with Donald Zec, *When the Snow Melts* (Boxtree, 1998)

2 Connery interviewed in *Guardian*, December 1971

3 Quoted in Donald McCormick, *The Life of Ian Fleming* (Peter Owen, 1993)

4 Broccoli with Zec, *When the Snow Melts*

5 Guy Hamilton interviewed for DVD release of *Diamonds Are Forever*

6 Jill St John interviewed in *Empire* magazine, November 2002

7 Connery interviewed in *Sunday Express*, September 1973

11 Dark Unconfident World

1 Howard Sounes, *Seventies* (Simon & Schuster, 2006)

2 Broccoli interviewed by Jean Rook, *Daily Express*, 1974

12 Man at Austin Reed

1 Quoted in Roger Moore, *Roger Moore as James Bond: Roger Moore's Own Account of Live and Let Die* (Pan Books, 1973)

2 Moore interviewed in *Evening Standard*, 1972

3 As quoted in *Daily Express*, 1973

4 Kotto interviewed for the DVD release of *Live and Let Die*

5 Quoted in Roger Moore, *Roger Moore as James Bond*

6 Moore interviewed in *Sunday Express*, April 1973

13 Will He Bang? We Shall See

1 Quoted in *Empire* magazine, 2002

2 Guy Hamilton interviewed for DVD release of *The Man with the Golden Gun*

3 Britt Ekland interviewed in *Daily Mail*, 2008

4 Alexander Walker, *National Heroes: British Cinema in the 70s and 80s* (Orion, 1985)

14 England Needs Me

1 Quoted in Andrew Lycett, *Ian Fleming* (Weidenfeld, 1995)

2 Quoted in Tony Bennett and Janet Woollacott, *Bond and Beyond* (Macmillan, 1987)

3 Michael Smith, *The Spying Game* (Methuen, 2003)

15 Once More Round the World

1 Moore interviewed by Victor Davis, *Daily Express*, 1979

2 Moore interviewed by Clive Hirschhorn, *Sunday Express*, 1978

3 Quoted in Andrew Lycett, *Ian Fleming* (Weidenfeld, 1995)

4 *Daily Express*, 1979

16 The Smack of Firm Espionage

1 *Daily Mirror*, May 1981

2 Bouquet quoted in *Daily Mail*, 1980

3 Lynn-Holly Johnson interviewed for DVD release of *For Your Eyes Only*

4 Michael G. Wilson interviewed for DVD release of *For Your Eyes Only*

5 John Glen, *For My Eyes Only* (Batsford, 1998)

6 Broccoli interviewed by Roderick Mann, *Sunday Express*, 1980

7 Moore interviewed by Roderick Mann, *Sunday Express*, 1980

17 You Can Never Say Never Twice

1 Moore interviewed in *Sunday Express*, 1982

18 Most Disarming

1 George MacDonald Fraser, *The Light's on at Signpost* (HarperCollins, 2002)

2 Moore interviewed in *Daily Express*, 1983

3 Dunaway interviewed in *Sunday Express*, 1982

4 MacDonald Fraser, *The Light's on at Signpost*

5 Ibid.

6 Moore interviewed for DVD release of *Octopussy*

7 Ibid.

19 Microchips with Everything

1 Albert R. Broccoli with Donald Zec, *When the Snow Melts* (Boxtree, 1998)

2 Maxwell interviewed in *Mail on Sunday*, 1985

3 Berry quoted in *The Times*, 2002

4 Quoted in Martin Sterling and Gary Morecambe, *Martinis, Girls and Guns* (Robson Books, 2003)

5 John Glen, *For My Eyes Only* (Batsford, 1998)

20 Darling Moneypenny

1 Maxwell interviewed in *Daily Sketch*, 1951

2 Fleming interviewed in *Daily Mail*, 1963

3 Maxwell interviewed in *Daily Mail*, 1970

4 Maxwell interviewed in *Daily Mail*, 1972

5 Maxwell interviewed in *Daily Mail*, 1981

6 Maxwell interviewed in *Mail on Sunday*, 1986

21 One for the Ladies

1 Dalton quoted in *Evening Standard*, 1970

2 John Glen, *For My Eyes Only* (Batsford, 1998)

3 Brosnan quoted in *Daily Mail*, 1986

4 Connery quoted in *Daily Express*, 1986

5 Glen quoted in *Sun*, 1987

6 D'Abo interviewed for American TV documentary, 2002

7 John Barry, from the sleeve notes of original CD score, *The Living Daylights*

22 Night of the Iguana

1 Duchess of York quoted in *Mail on Sunday*, 1988

2 Dalton quoted in *Daily Mirror*, 1989

24 We Knew the Name, We Knew the Number

1 Barbara Broccoli quoted in *Daily Mail*, 1994

2 Campbell quoted in *Guardian*, 1994

3 David Gritten, *Daily Telegraph*, 1994

4 Campbell interviewed for American TV documentary

5 Brosnan quoted in *Guardian*, 1994

6 *Sunday Telegraph*, 1995

25 We're in a Puddle on the Floor

1 Barbara Broccoli interviewed in Steven Priggé, *Movie Moguls Speak* (MacFarland and Co., 2003)

2 David Arnold interviewed in *Evening Standard*, 1997

3 Dench interviewed in *Daily Mail*, 2008

26 Art and Craft

1 Apted interviewed for American TV documentary, 1999

2 Ibid.

3 Ibid.

4 As reported in *Daily Telegraph*

27 Birthday Boy

1 Umberto Eco et al., *The Bond Affair* (MacDonald, 1966)

2 Barbara Broccoli interviewed in Steven Priggé, *Movie Moguls Speak* (MacFarland and Co., 2003)

3 Berry interviewed for American TV documentary, 2002

28 The Autobiography of Dreams

1 John Pearson, *The Life of Ian Fleming* (Jonathan Cape, 1966)

2 Ibid.

3 Craig quoted in American TV documentary

4 Craig interviewed in *The Times* magazine, 2006

5 Roald Dahl, *Playboy*, 1967

RELATED READING

Ambler, E. *The Mask of Dimitrios* (Hodder & Stoughton, 1939)

Ambler, E. *Here Lies* (Weidenfeld & Nicolson, 1985)

Amis, K. *The James Bond Dossier* (Pan, 1965)

Amis, K. (writing as Bill Tanner) *The Book of Bond* (Pan, 1965)

Amory, M. (ed) *The Letters of Ann Fleming* (Collins Harvill, 1985)

Bennett, T. & Woollacott, J. *Bond and Beyond* (Macmillan, 1987)

Booker, C. *The Seventies* (Allen Lane, 1980)

Broccoli, A.R. with Zec D. *When the Snow Melts* (Boxtree, 1998)

Deighton, L. *The Ipcress File* (Hodder & Stoughton, 1962)

Eco, U. *The Bond Affair* (MacDonald, 1966)

Glen, J. *For My Eyes Only* (Batsford, 2001)

Honan, P. *Christopher Marlowe: Poet and Spy* (Viking, 2005)

Housman, A.E. *Poems* selected by Alan Hollinghurst (Faber & Faber, 2005)

Levin, B. *The Pendulum Years – Britain and the Sixties* (Cape, 1970)

Lycett, A. *Ian Fleming* (Weidenfeld, 1995)

MacDonald Fraser, G. *The Light's on at Signpost* (Harper Collins, 2002)

McCormick, D. *The Life of Ian Fleming* (Peter Owen 1993)

Moore, R. *Roger Moore as James Bond: Roger Moore's Own Account of Making Live and Let Die* (Pan, 1973)

Pearson, J. *The Life of Ian Fleming* (Jonathan Cape, 1966)

Pincher, C. *Their Trade Is Treachery* (Sidgwick & Jackson, 1979)

Priggé, S. *Movie Moguls Speak* (Macfarland & Co., 2003)

Sandbrook, D. *White Heat* (Little, Brown, 2007)

Smith, M. *The Spying Game: The Secret History of British Espionage* (Methuen 2003)

Sontag, S. *Against Interpretation* (Eyre & Spottiswoode, 1967)

Walker, A. *Hollywood, England* (Harrap 1974)

Walker, A. *National Heroes* (Orion 1985)

West, N. *The Faber Book of Espionage* (Faber, 1993)

INDEX

A-ha 272
d'Abo, Maryam 266, 267, 270
Ackroyd, Peter 241
Adam, Sir Ken 13, 14–15, 18, 23, 24, 44, 64, 77, 78, 84, 100, 102, 103, 104, 138, 142, 165, 184, 190, 191, 192, 199, 203, 205, 206, 365
Adams, Maud 168, 171, 172, 233, 236, 237
Allen, Woody 95
Ambler, Eric 3, 35
Amis, Kingsley 21, 281
Andress, Ursula 21, 28, 29, 95
Andrews, Julie 70
Andropov, Yuri 229, 245
Apted, Michael 321, 324, 325, 326
Armendáriz, Pedro 38
Arnold, David 316, 320, 328
Atkinson, Rowan 225
Auger, Claudine 79, 82, 83
Austin Powers 78, 309, 311
Avengers, The 32, 60, 91, 92, 127, 247, 250, 331

Bach, Barbara 185
Baker, Joe Don 266, 305
Baker, Stanley 10
Barry, John 37, 44, 54, 56, 64, 76, 77, 86, 102, 106, 127, 204, 237, 251, 271, 272, 273, 365
Bart, Lionel 37
Basinger, Kim 223, 225, 226
Bassey, Shirley 54, 204, 316
Bean, Sean 296
Beatles, The 32, 45, 63
Bedlam 56
Berkoff, Steven 233, 240
Berry, Halle 192, 248–249, 331, 333
Betjeman, John 46
Bianchi, Daniela 38, 45, 46, 47
Billion Dollar Brain 72
Binder, Maurice 54, 55–56, 77, 209, 248, 278, 298
Blackman, Honor 59, 60, 91, 92
Blair, Tony 300, 339, 356
Bliss, Caroline 260
Blofeld, Tom 167
Blondie 163

Bogarde, Dirk 4, 89, 134
Bond, Samantha 260, 261, 317
Bouquet, Carole 212, 213, 216
Brandauer, Klaus Maria 223, 225, 227
Brezhnev, Leonid 229
Broccoli, Albert R 6–7, 8–13, 14, 19, 24, 25–26, 28, 29, 31, 32, 36, 43, 48, 76, 77, 81, 83, 84, 85, 100, 103, 111, 112, 115, 116, 117, 118, 124, 125, 127, 128, 129, 130, 131, 132, 136, 142, 148, 152, 166, 179, 182, 183, 185, 194, 197, 205, 220, 221, 222, 231, 244, 265, 275, 280, 281, 288
Broccoli, Barbara 261, 265, 270, 288, 295, 299, 311, 317, 327, 330, 334, 342, 346, 347, 360
Broccoli, Dana 9, 213
Brolin, James 230
Brosnan, Pierce 231, 260, 264, 265, 293, 297, 299, 300, 302, 303, 306, 307, 311, 315, 323, 324, 326, 329, 333, 340, 341, 342, 346, 363
Brown, Robert 283
Browning, Ricou 79
Brownjohn, Robert 54
Buchan, John 52
Bulldog Drummond 11, 12, 340
Burgess, Anthony 181, 182
Burgess, Guy 40
Burton, Peter 17
Burton, Richard 6, 72, 81, 195

Cain, Syd 119
Caine, Michael 71, 72, 94, 310
Callaghan, James 126, 180
Cameron, James 295
Campbell, Martin 295, 299, 349
Carlyle, Robert 320, 325
Carrera, Barbara 224, 227
Casino Royale:
    novel 1, 3, 268, 344, 345
    TV play: 4
    1967 film: 94–96, 200
    2006 film: 5, 84, 141, 178, 344–360, 365
Cats, Persian 108–109
Celi, Adolfo 78, 83
Chandler, Raymond 62

Charteris, Leslie 150
Chernenko, Konstantin 245
Childers, Erskine 52
Chiles, Lois 199
Christie, Julie 82, 83, 86
Cilento, Diane 80, 111
Cleese, John 323, 335
Coburn, James 88, 89
Cocker, Jarvis 163, 237, 294, 316
Cockleshell Heroes 7
Coltrane, Robbie 296, 301, 305, 320, 326
Connery, Sean 7–11, 19, 27, 28, 30, 31, 32, 33,
    37, 41, 42, 45, 46, 48, 53, 54, 56, 57, 59, 63,
    65, 66, 67, 77, 79, 80, 81, 82, 98, 105, 111,
    112, 116, 118, 130, 131, 139, 144, 222, 223,
    224, 226, 227, 266, 363
Connolly, Cyril 31
Conti, Bill 210
Coward, Noël 28
Craig, Daniel 111, 200, 347, 348, 351, 352, 353,
    355, 356, 358
Cumming, Alan 296, 301
Cumming, Sir Mansfield 51, 52
Curtis, Tony 150

Dahl, Roald 100, 352
Dalton, Timothy 259, 260, 262–264, 265, 266,
    267, 268, 274, 275, 277, 285, 292, 363
Damon, Matt 349
Darby O'Gill and the Little People 9
Darling 86
Davi, Robert 278, 284
Dawson, Anthony 18
Dee, Doctor 50
Dehn, Paul 61
Deighton, Len 37, 43, 49, 70, 71
Del Toro, Benicio 278, 284
Dench, Dame Judi 260, 300, 317, 327, 332, 339,
    353
Diamonds Are Forever
    novel: 129, 134, 268
    film: 109, 110, 129–144
Die Another Day 192, 200, 248, 261, 282, 330-343
Die Hard 277
Dr. No
    novel: 11, 20, 23, 26
    film: 1, 13, 14–33, 177, 342, 363
Dr Zhivago 83, 106
Dor, Karin 104
Dunaway, Faye 83, 236

Duran Duran 251

Eaton, Shirley 56, 67
Easton, Sheena 209, 210, 221
Eco, Umberto 330
Ekland, Britt 171, 172, 173
The Entertainer 6

Feirstein, Bruce 295, 311
Feldman, Charles 94, 95
Ferguson, Sarah 280
Fleming, Ann 17, 21, 30, 31
Fleming, Ian 1–13, 17, 21, 23, 25–26, 30, 31, 32,
    34, 36, 43, 46, 47, 67, 70, 71, 73, 76, 77, 82,
    98, 99, 121, 134, 152, 153, 166, 182, 196,
    200, 278, 295, 342, 363
For Your Eyes Only
    story: 215
    film: 79, 109, 197, 207–221, 274, 366
France, Michael 295
Fraser, Antonia 51
Fröbe, Gert 54, 57, 59, 60
From a View to a Kill 246
From Russia with Love
    novel: 12, 34, 35, 134
    film: 34–49, 363
Fu Manchu 12, 29
Fullerton, Fiona 251
Funeral in Berlin 72

Gaitskell, Hugh 30, 40
Gardner, John 275, 281
Gavin, John 130
Gayson, Eunice 16, 27, 37
Get Carter 140
Gielgud, John 3
Gilbert, Lewis 87, 103, 106, 108, 184, 185, 197
Glen, John 121, 216, 219, 247, 253, 264, 268
Glover, Bruce 133
Glover, Julian 151, 152, 213, 214, 216
GoldenEye
    TV film: 282, 295
    film: 260, 294–307
Goldfinger
    book: 47, 53, 109, 351
    film: 47–67, 178, 352, 363
Goldmember 310
Gorbachev, Mikhail 246
Gotell, Walter 189, 233, 252
Grant, Cary 7, 13, 69

Grant, Hugh 292, 293
Gray, Charles 109, 133, 138
Green, Eva 200, 354
Greene, Graham 36
Greer, Germaine 136

Haggis, Paul 359
Hama, Mie 110
Hamilton, Guy 27, 53, 58, 64, 66, 131, 136, 157, 158, 160, 167, 168, 170
Hamlisch, Marvin 186
Harris, Cassandra 215
Harty, Russell 247
Hatcher, Teri 313
Heath, Edward 145, 146
Hedison, David 156
Hendry, Gloria 157
Hibbin, Nina 49, 64, 65, 105, 362
Hildebrand Rarity, The 275, 278
Hitchcock, Alfred 3,5, 13, 36, 65, 68–70
Holder, Geoffrey 157
Holness, Bob 5
Holly-Johnson, Lynn 214
Howard, Trevor 7, 9
Hughes, Howard 138, 142
Hunt, Peter 17, 19, 42, 44, 77, 118, 119, 121, 124, 365
Hynde, Chrissie 272

In Like Flint 88
Indiana Jones and the Temple of Doom 235
Ipcress File, The 37, 70–72, 94

James Bond Jr 289
James, Clifton 159
Janson-Smith, Peter 31, 93, 148, 165, 281, 285, 286
Janssen, Famke 296, 306
Johnson, Lyndon B 85
Johnson, Paul 30
Johnson, Richard 7
Jones, Grace 247, 249
Jourdan, Louis 233, 240
Jurgens, Curt 185

Kennedy, John F 25, 36
Kerr, Deborah 95, 96
Kershner, Irvin 223
Kiel, Richard 187, 202
Kitchen, Michael 317, 328

Kitzmiller, John 22
Kleinman, Daniel 54, 55, 298, 313, 332, 350
Korda, Alexander 3
Kotto, Yaphet 153, 161
Krabbe, Jeroen 266, 273
Krushchev, Nikita 25
Kubrick, Stanley 15, 184, 191

Lady Vanishes, The 36
Lamont, Peter 233, 338
Landau, Martin 13, 93
Last Year at Marienbad 34
Lawrence of Arabia 27, 48
Lazenby, George 113, 114, 116, 117, 118, 119, 120, 121, 122, 124, 125, 126, 127, 128, 131, 258
Le Carré, John 43, 49, 52, 72, 73
Le Queux, William 51, 52
Lean, David 4, 27, 48, 235
Lee, Bernard 16, 105, 133, 220
Lee, Christopher 20, 169, 175, 177
Legrand, Michael 225
Lenya, Lotte 37, 38
Licence to Kill 87, 141, 253, 260, 276–287
Live and Let Die
    novel: 3, 4, 13, 152, 216, 277
    film: 150–164
Living Daylights, The
    short story: 266
    film: 260, 262–275
Llewelyn, Desmond 43, 44, 57, 66, 220, 280, 303, 315, 323, 324
Lonsdale, Michael 198, 203
Look Back in Anger 6
Lord, Jack 17
Lorre, Peter 4, 68
Losey, Joseph 89
Lowell, Cary 279
Lumley, Joanna 113, 194

McCartney, Paul 162
McClory, Kevin 5, 9, 76, 77, 183, 221, 222
McCowen, Alec 223, 225
MacDonald Fraser, George 231–232, 235, 239
McGoohan, Patrick 7, 90, 91
Maclean, Donald 40
Macmillan, Harold 25, 33, 84
Macnee, Patrick 91, 247, 250
Madonna 246, 332, 341
Maibaum, Richard 26, 61, 131, 207, 247, 266

Malik, Art 270
Man from U.N.C.L.E., The 93
Man Who Knew Too Much 68, 69
Man with the Golden Gun, The
    novel: 166, 279
    film: 43, 165–179
Mankiewicz, Tom 131, 160, 167, 168
Mantel, Hilary 285
Marceau, Sophie 320, 324, 326, 329
Marlowe, Christopher 51
Marnie 65
Martin, George 162
Mason, James 7, 13
Maxwell, Lois 16–17, 77, 150, 202, 247, 256, 257–259, 261
Mikkelsen, Mads 29, 350, 351
Mission: Impossible
    TV series: 93, 308
    film: 94, 308, 309
Modesty Blaise 89
Moonraker
    novel: 4, 196, 268, 330
    film: 87, 195–206, 335, 364
Moore, Roger 7, 94, 117, 150–151, 152, 153, 155, 156, 157, 158, 160, 161, 162, 163, 164, 169, 170, 175, 176, 177, 185, 193, 194, 195–196, 198, 203, 204, 205, 213, 219, 220, 224, 231, 236, 239, 241, 244, 252, 253, 255, 258, 363
Munro, Caterina 352
Myers, Mike 309, 310

Nelson, Barry 4
Never Say Never Again 222–228
New Avengers, The 78
Newman, Paul 70
Niven, David 8, 95, 96
Nixon, Richard 126, 146, 176
Norman, Monty 17, 19
North by Northwest 13, 354
North Sea Hijack 195
Notorious 69

Octopussy
    short story: 231
    film: 43, 74, 223, 229–243, 274
Olivier, Laurence 6
Offence, The 131
On Her Majesty's Secret Service
    novel: 32, 58, 82, 113, 303, 351

    film: 113–128
O'Rahilly, Ronan 126
Osborne, John 6

Paluzzi, Luciana 80
Persuaders, The 150, 164
Philby, Kim 40
Picker, David 130
Pike, Rosamund 331, 336
Pleasence, Donald 108
Powell, Michael 263
Prisoner, The 90, 91
Profumo, Jack 39
Pryce, Jonathan 311, 312, 313
Purvis, Neal 320, 330, 359

Quantum of Solace
    short story: 344
    film: 283, 360, 361
Quatermass 196
Quennell, Peter 21

Raiders of the Lost Ark 34, 234
Raven, Simon 114
Reagan, Ronald 74, 212, 217, 229, 242, 245
Red Beret, The 7
Reed, Carol 4
Remington Steele 264, 265
Rhys-Davies, John 269
Richards, Denise 320, 325, 329
Rigg, Diana 92, 114, 117, 118, 119, 120, 122, 123, 125
Rimington, Dame Stella 300
Roberts, Tanya 247
Rohmer, Sax 12

Saint, The 94, 259
St John, Jill 136, 367
Saboteur 68
Sakata, Harold 66
Salmon, Colin 317, 328
Saltzman, Harry 6–7, 8–13, 14, 24, 29, 32, 36, 43, 48, 71, 76, 77, 81, 84, 85, 94, 100, 103, 111, 112, 115, 116, 117, 128, 129, 130, 131, 148, 152, 162, 165–166, 179, 258
Saturday Night and Sunday Morning 6
Savalas, Telly 114, 118, 122, 125
Scorupco, Izabella 296, 301
Scoular, Angela 113, 150, 367
Sellers, Peter 73, 95, 96

Semple Jr, Lorenzo 223
Seymour, Jane 152
Shaw, Robert 37, 42
Simon, Carly 186
Smith, Putter 133
Somerset Maugham, W 3, 52, 68, 344
Soto, Talisa 278
Spender, Stephen 21
Spillane, Mickey 2
Spottiswoode, Roger 312, 313
Spy Who Came in from the Cold 72, 73, 74
Spy Who Loved Me, The
  novel: 182–183
  film: 180–194, 363, 364
Stamp, Terence 89
Star Wars 196
Stephens, Toby 313, 331
Sydow, Max von 223, 225

Tamahori, Lee 331, 337
Thatcher, Margaret 74, 207, 208, 209, 210, 211,
  212, 217, 218, 229, 245, 246
Thunderball
  novel: 5, 77
  film: 76–87
Tomorrow Never Dies 79, 282, 311–318
Topol 215, 216
Torn Curtain 70
Trevelyan, John 30
Trials of Oscar Wilde, The 7
True Lies 290, 295
Turner, Tina 299

Van der Zyl, Monica 28
View to a Kill, A 244–255, 364
Villechaize, Herve 168
Villiers, James 220
Vitti, Monica 89

Wade, Robert 320, 330, 359
Walken, Christopher 246, 247
Walsingham, Sir Francis 50–51
Warwick, Dionne 76
Waugh, Evelyn 17, 31
Welles, Orson 95
Wild Geese, The 195
Willis, Bruce 277
Wilson, Harold 40, 84, 126, 176, 180
Wilson, Michael G 206, 217, 247, 263, 265, 266,
  275, 281, 288, 299, 317, 319, 322, 327, 334,
  346, 360
Wiseman, Joseph 28–29
Wood, Christopher 184, 193, 197
Wood, Lana 137
World Is Not Enough, The 121, 282, 307, 319–329,
  366

Yeoh, Michelle 312, 315
You Only Live Twice
  novel: 98, 99, 100
  film: 98–112, 257, 363, 365
Young, Freddie 106
Young, Terence 7, 10, 16, 18, 19, 21, 27, 32, 42,
  45, 77, 87

Zerbe, Anthony 283